A TRAILS BOOKS GUIDE

PADDLING NORTHERN MINNESOTA

86 GREAT TRIPS BY CANOE AND KAYAK

LYNNE SMITH DIEBEL

trails books

AN IMPRINT OF BOWER HOUSE

DENVER

BowerHouseBooks.com

Editor: Stan Stoga
Photos: Robert Diebel
Maps: Magellan Mapping Company
Design: Emily Culp
Cover Photo: Richard Hamilton Smith

Printed in Canada

Library of Congress Control Number: 2004116028
ISBN 978-1-931599-51-1

10 9 8 7 6 5 4 3 2

Disclaimer: Many of the activities described in this book can be dangerous, especially when weather is adverse or unpredictable, and when unforeseen events or conditions create a hazardous situation. The author has done his best to provide the reader with accurate information about water travel, as well as to point out some of its potential hazards. It is the responsibility of the users of this guide to learn the necessary skills for safe water travel, and to exercise caution in potentially hazardous areas. The author and publisher disclaim any liability for injury or other damage caused by water travel or performing any other activity described in this book.

CONTENTS

ACKNOWLEDGMENTS

This book is dedicated to my husband, friend, and favorite paddler, Bob.

My husband, Bob, and I paddled every mile of every river and every lake in this guide (1,148 miles, plus about 150 miles that I chose not to include), and it was a real joy to explore so many beautiful waterways; to learn so much of the history of these very waters; to see that there is so much wildness remaining in Minnesota; and to meet the generous and welcoming people of northern Minnesota, many of whom went out of their way to help us.

Of all the people I need to thank, the one who deserves thanks the very most is Bob. Not only did he paddle every mile of every trip, rain or shine, warm or cold, with me, but he also took all the photographs and drew all the preliminary maps. This is his book as well as mine. I'm more grateful to him than I can possibly express in this acknowledgment.

Our children helped as well. Our son Matthew, who is a doctoral candidate in limnology at the University of Wisconsin–Madison and works for the U.S. Geological Survey in hydrology, calculated all the gradients and reviewed the manuscript for water flow accuracy. Matt, along with Rebecca Gass, introduced us to whitewater paddling. Our son Gregory cheerfully solved every vexing computer problem I had while preparing the manuscript. Greg, Matt, and our other son, James, as well as Rebecca and our friend Steve Tupper, joined us on the kayaking trips in Voyageurs National Park. Our daughter, Anne, gave needed feedback and encouragement. I am grateful to them all. I am grateful too to my mother, Mary Smith, who, with my father, Lucian, taught me how to paddle a canoe on Cedar Lake when I was a little girl. I also thank my sister, Virginia Smith, and our friend Noam Wiggs, who joined us on a great BWCAW trip.

Thanks to Mike Chicanowski, Rich Enochs, and We-no-nah Canoe for our superb canoe, the Royalex Spirit II, which now has about 1,400 miles on it. You were right, Mike—it was just what we needed. So many Minnesotans helped me gather all the facts and information I needed. I will try to list them all and beg forgiveness of those I omit. Thanks especially to Fran and Al Prussner of Hubbard; Jolie and Brian Ensign in Ely; Randy Carlson of the University of Minnesota–Duluth's Kayak and Canoe Institute; Steve Mueller of the Minnesota DNR's Trails and Waterways Division; and Chris Soper and Bill Gorden in Big Falls.

Thanks also to Kevin Gross and Don Gregerson in Bigfork; Sam Johnson of the DNR; Willard Larson in Isanti; Terry Larson of Northern Adventures; Mary Rea and Carroll Kukowski of the Aitkin County Historical Society; Barry and Linda Babcock of Hackensack; Jerry Dorff of Wild River Outfitters in Grantsburg, Wisconsin; Marty Severson in Merrifield; John Crandall in Wadena; Brenda Davis in Floodwood; Dick Brumwell and Chuck Healy and Arlen Schalekamp in Red Lake Falls; Hank Wells and Bill Krueger in Roseville; Carol Brewton and Sue O'Brien in Winona; Mark and Vicki Swedeen in Northfield; Len Crowley and Sally Arnold in Minneapolis; Karen Terry at the DNR office in Fergus Falls; Jeff Olson of Otter Tail Power Company in Fergus Falls, Gordon Hydukovich of Fergus Falls; Eric Hudspith of Albert Lea; Darwin Markgraf of Grand Rapids; Peter Hark of the DNR; and Greg Mitton of the USGS.

I am most appreciative of the work of Mike Svob, who wrote *Paddling Northern Wisconsin*, *Paddling Southern Wisconsin*, and *Paddling Illinois* for Trails Books and whose format for those books has been the model for this guide. I also thank my editor, Stan Stoga, whose expertise and cheerful guidance were always welcome, and Candy Parrell, Erika Reise, and Anita Matcha of Trails Media Group. In addition, thanks to Marily and Doug Crews-Nelson of Magellan Mapping Company for their fine work of computer-rendering the maps.

Northern Minnesota's lakes, especially the lakes of the Boundary Waters Canoe Area Wilderness (BWCAW), are legendary. Devoted lake paddlers could probably be content with a lifetime of just paddling the BWCAW. The woods of northern Minnesota are also laced with wild, beautiful rivers, many with great stretches of exciting whitewater and others offering quiet, scenic floats. To the east of the BWCAW lies Lake Superior, vast and spectacular; to the west of the Boundary Waters are the big lakes of Voyageurs National Park. Both are great destinations for experienced sea kayakers.

This book is a collection of paddling trips that will take you to these wonderful places. Many of the trips are good for beginning paddlers; others require more advanced or expert skills. An appendix in the back of the book categorizes trips by skill level. The trips can be divided into three groups: river trips for canoe or kayak, sea kayaking trips, and Boundary Waters trips. Several of the Boundary Waters trips are also designed for kayakers: the portages are short and some allow wheels, and the lakes are big, which both minimizes portaging and takes advantage of the sea kayak's exceptional seaworthiness.

The river trips are through beautiful country and are fun to paddle. Much of the land you will paddle through on these trips is relatively (and sometimes completely) undeveloped. Many of the rivers have stretches of lively water, ranging from gentle riffles to the Class III–IV whitewater of the Vermilion and the Lower Saint Louis, but numerous quieter rivers are included as well. Rivers like the Crow Wing, the Big Fork, the Cloquet, the Mississippi, the Upper Saint Louis, and the Vermilion invite multiday canoe-camping trips.

MINNESOTA'S WATERY TREASURES

Paddling opportunities abound in Minnesota. Perhaps no state in the Union can equal the number, variety, and sheer beauty of its rivers, streams, and lakes. To get the most out of your paddling adventures, you should know a few things about Minnesota and the rich and unique character of its endless string of waterways.

Three Watersheds

One of Minnesota's many natural attributes is its being the site of no fewer than three major watersheds. The first involves the Mississippi, North America's most famous river. "The Father of Waters" originates in Lake Itasca in the northern part of the state, gathering water from the many tributaries in its watershed as it begins its 2,500-mile journey south to the Gulf of Mexico.

The two other watersheds are created by the Laurentian Divide, a line of low, rugged hills that wanders across northern Minnesota. North of the line, rivers such as the Big Fork and the Red River of the North flow northward to the Rainy River and then all the way into Canada's Hudson Bay. South of the line but north of the Mississippi watershed, water flows from the huge Saint Louis River basin north and west of Duluth, and from all along the north shore of Lake Superior, into the big lake, where it heads for the Atlantic far to the east. On mining land near Hibbing is a height of land that the Ojibwe called Hill of Three Waters, where the tribes once held council meetings. Here, these watersheds intersect in a triple divide: rain that falls here flows into all three watersheds.

Some of the other places where these watersheds meet are where the predecessors of modern paddlers—Native Americans, voyageurs, and early explorers—used portages to make these northern rivers into river highway systems long before there were any roads or railroads in Minnesota.

River Highways

If you were an eighteenth-century voyageur who needed to travel from Duluth Harbor to the Mississippi, you would first portage for seven miles around the great falls and rapids that are in today's Jay Cooke State Park near Duluth. Then you would paddle up the Saint Louis (no small feat with its strong current) to the mouth of the East Savanna River, which is at today's town of Floodwood. After paddling up the gentle Savanna, you would cross the dreaded Savanna Portage (another state park), a long and miserable hike through a mosquito-infested swamp to the West Savanna River. You would then paddle down the West Savanna; through Big Sandy Lake; and finally into the Mississippi River, which then offered you a new route south.

Another route took early travelers farther up the Saint Louis to the Embarrass River. From a point on the Embarrass that is north of today's town of Biwabik, they hiked across the Laurentian Divide to the Pike River. They followed the Pike, which used to be called the Little Vermilion, north into the Hudson Bay watershed and the fur trading posts on Lake of the Woods along the Canadian border.

Homemade waterslide on Little Fork.

Typical river level gauge on a bridge pier.

The most famous early river highway extended from the mouth of the Pigeon River at today's town of Grand Portage through a series of portages, lakes, rivers, and more portages to Lake of the Woods. This "customary route" of the voyageurs was so well traveled that it was chosen as our boundary with Canada at the Treaty of Paris in 1783. Much of this route now lies within the BWCAW and Voyageurs National Park.

THE RIVERS IN THIS GUIDE

Of the many rivers in northern Minnesota that I examined when setting out to do this book, I narrowed my search down to the 20 that seemed to have the qualities I think make a great paddling trip. By the way, I defined northern Minnesota as that part of the state north of a line running along the lower edge of Mille Lacs Lake (the Kettle River begins north of the line, so it is included). Along the length of these 20 rivers (one of which is really a chain of lakes connected by streams), I chose between one and nine segments that seemed to me to provide the best paddling.

Offering a mixture of rivers that differ in size and shape was also an important consideration in my choices. The rivers selected range from narrow and intimate, like the Upper Kettle, to wide and majestic, like the Lower Saint Louis. To make the paddling experience as enjoyable as possible, I also chose rivers for their aesthetic appeal, a task that was both easy and challenging. Easy because these northern rivers are scenic (some spectacularly so) and often wild and undeveloped; challenging because there were so many gorgeous possibilities to choose from. I tried to avoid rivers that were in developed areas heavily lined with cabins and houses. If there is some development along a river, this fact is mentioned in the narrative.

As should be the case, safety played a major role in the decision as to which rivers to include, and an awareness of water levels is crucial in preventing unpleasant consequences on the river. Although water levels are fairly predictable, several dry years render "predictable" a relative term. If you're planning a trip when the precipitation has been quite low, be sure to check the water levels carefully. Most of the rivers in this guide can be paddled through at least June. If a river is usually better run in the spring months, this is indicated in the trip description. The access points indicated in the guide are reasonably convenient and safe, ranging from bridge crossings on quiet country roads to established DNR accesses with signs, parking areas, and sand or concrete ramps.

The whitewater sections of the rivers are primarily Class I–II. Several Class II–IV runs, like the Saint Louis between Scanlon and Thomson and the Upper Cloquet, are also included. Some rivers, like the Vermilion and the Little Fork, have rapids that must be portaged as well as runnable rapids. I did not include rivers that primarily rate Class IV or above, like the north shore streams, or rivers that are too remote and run too briefly to make reasonable planning possible, like the north shore streams or the 3.5 miles of Class II–III on the Sturgeon.

For the most part, I have avoided rivers with human-made dams to portage, and only a few have any of those pesky beaver dams to scramble over. I also avoided sections of river noted for logjams, like portions of the Sturgeon, opting instead for segments that are more reliably free-flowing.

Most of the routes do not include long lake crossings, although some, like the Crow Wing, the Otter Tail, the Vermilion, and the Pine, cross small lakes. The trips also avoid areas with heavy motorboat traffic; we encountered surprisingly few motorboats on all the rivers we paddled.

THE BWCAW

Choosing just 17 days of paddling in the Boundary Waters Canoe Area Wilderness was challenging, as this vast wilderness has so many wonderful possibilities for routes. This guide does not presume to be a comprehensive description of paddling in the BWCAW. Instead, it's a sampler. The trips described in this book range from an easy one-day trip with a quarter-mile portage to a six-day trip with many portages, one a mile long. I focused on trips that offer a good scenery-to-portage ratio, but often lots of portaging is the only way to see the beauty of the Boundary Waters. It's also part of the journey and the mystique.

Five of those days of paddling were chosen for their easy portages, making them as well suited to kayaking as to canoeing. The introduction to the section on the BWCAW later in the book covers issues specific to this area.

THE SEA-KAYAKING LAKES

To try to capture the grand variety of paddling experiences available in Minnesota, I've included several trips designed for sea kayaking. Four of these follow the Lake Superior Water Trail, an ambitious three-state, two-country project that will eventually extend all the way around the big lake. With the addition in 2004 of 25 more miles to the trail, kayakers will find access points and camping along a 106-mile stretch of Superior's North Shore, from Duluth to Grand Marais. In those 106 miles, however, several long stretches are without access points. The four trips described in this guide all have reasonably short distances between access points, set along a stretch of shoreline that is truly spectacular, especially when viewed from the water. Also included here is a trip that involves an open crossing to the Susie Islands, a lovely uninhabited archipelago offshore of Pigeon Point near Grand Portage.

I've also included in the guide two trips geared toward kayaking within the confines of Voyageurs National Park; they involve paddling along Kabetogama, Rainy, Namakan, and Sand Point Lakes—big, windswept bodies of water open to motorboats. Because there are lots of "back channels" created by the numerous islands on these lakes where a paddler can avoid the motorboat traffic, they are great for paddling as well. These two trips, as well as the circuit of the Kabetogama Peninsula mentioned in the sidebar to the Voyageurs 1 trip, are also canoeable, but sea kayakers will find these big waters especially well suited to their boats.

Lake Superior and the lakes of Voyageurs National Park are great waters for experienced sea kayakers, but these are not lakes for beginners. Paddlers who are new to sea kayaking should first have instruction and practice on less-challenging water before attempting these trips. See also the introduction to the "Sea Kayaking Trips" chapter later in the book for more information on dealing with open-water conditions.

USING THIS BOOK

River Trips

All of the trip descriptions in this guide include the same elements in the same order, making it easy to find the essential information for a safe and successful trip. Each trip is intended to take one day of paddling, but some days will be much longer than others. Paddling rates also vary widely. Paddling skill, type of boat, weather, current speed, and dawdling time all influence the rate at which a trip will be run, but most paddlers can plan roughly on a speed of two to three miles per hour. Many of the trips can be shortened by using alternate accesses or combined with other trips on the same river for a multiday trip.

Each narrative begins with a description of the river's character, a mention of what skills are needed to paddle the river safely, the wildlife you might see, any fishing opportunities, and special highlights of the trip. Additional information, like biking or hiking trails, is also included here. The essential information needed to plan a trip comes next. The remainder of the trip description takes the reader down the river, from put-in to takeout, mentioning topography and landmarks, describing riffles and rapids, and pointing out riverside rest stops and campsites.

River Maps

Each trip description is accompanied by a map on the facing page. The maps have been purposely kept as simple and concise as possible for easy readability and reference; nonessential details are not included. What is included: roads needed to get to the access, shuttle route roads, access points, the paddling route with mile markers, railroads, rapids, cities and towns, campsites and campgrounds, state parkland, and bicycle routes. A key on each map identifies the symbols used for these elements.

Also included are easily identified features such as tributaries, large islands, bridges, and electrical power lines that can be used to determine your location on the map. You may also want to carry a compass for checking the direction of the river's flow at a given point; this can be useful in helping to find your location when comparing the compass reading to the direction of the river on the map.

Paddlers cast their shadows in the Boundary Waters.

An important note on names and numbers of roads and highways: in recent years, Minnesota has been renaming and renumbering roads to conform to the needs of the 911 system. While we have made every effort to ensure that the maps have the most up-to-date and accurate road designations, the state is continuing its renaming and renumbering process, with the result that occasional discrepancies may exist between our maps and the new road names and numbers.

The mile markers for each river segment have been calculated as accurately as possible and can be confidently used to estimate the length of a trip and the time you would expect to spend on the water. But because every paddler takes a slightly different route down a river, mileages can vary slightly as a result.

Rapids are marked with hash marks. For an explanation of rapids classifications, see the "Paddling Safety" section later in this introduction.

If you want additional maps, consider buying a Minnesota Atlas and Gazetteer, published by DeLorme Mapping Company (www.delorme.com/atlasgaz), a book of 76 detailed maps that is especially helpful in navigating back roads and finding campgrounds and state parks. This is a map you'll want to keep in your vehicle at all times.

Topographical maps, especially the 7.5-minute series, offer a fascinating perspective on the land through which you'll be paddling; they even indicate individual buildings along a river. Information on ordering maps is available from USGS Information Services, Box 25286, Denver, CO 80225 (888-275-8747; www.geography.usgs.gov/esic/to_order.html).

To help you decide whether you're paddling past private land or public land, knowledge that is especially helpful when you need to stop unexpectedly or to determine alternate access points before paddling, you can use Minnesota DNR maps for a selected number of canoe routes; the maps have shading that differentiates public and private land. These maps do not cover all the rivers in this book. The list of routes and digital versions of the maps are available online at www.dnr.state.mn.us/

canoeing/routes. To order free paper versions of the maps, call the DNR Information Center at 888-646-6367. The DNR also publishes Public Recreation Information Maps (PRIM), which divide the state into 51 areas. These maps, which identify public and private land and show all public-water access points, are available at state parks or online at www.dnr.mn.us/maps/prim.html at a cost of $4.95 per map.

Biking Trails

Because paddlers often like to combine canoeing or kayaking with bicycling, the maps include biking trails, which can also be useful if you're doing a bicycle shuttle, even if only part of the route is on a trail.

The Minnesota DNR Web site (www.dnr.state.mn.us/state_trails/list.html) describes in detail the Heartland, Paul Bunyan, Taconite, and Willard Munger Trails, the state trails designated for biking (among other activities), and has online maps in both PDF and GIF formats. The Paul Bunyan Trail also has its own Web site (www.paulbunyantrail.com), as do the Munger Trail (www.munger-trail.com), the Mesabi Trail (www.mesabitrail.com) and the Gitchi-Gami Trail (www.ggta.org/index.php), for which the DNR Web site also provides a map. A useful guidebook, *Bicycle Trails of Minnesota* (Second Edition), published by America Bike Trails, contains maps and descriptions for over 100 trails throughout Minnesota.

Camping

When camping facilities are available, either on the river or within a reasonable distance of either access, these are listed in the narrative and shown on the map. DNR riverside campsites are usually marked along the shore with a canoe camp symbol on a brown and gold sign. These sites almost always include a picnic table, a fire ring, a cleared area for tents, and an open-air latrine.

Many of the rivers in the guide run through state forestland, where camping is allowed without a designated campsite. The DNR canoe route maps (see the "River Maps" section) are useful in finding a place to camp that is indeed on public land.

Several rivers, like the Red Lake River, the Crow

Wing, and the Mississippi, have riverside county or community campgrounds. These sites charge fees that are collected on an honor system. Park officials periodically check for compliance, however, and if a camper has not paid, the fee increases significantly.

If a state park is within approximately 25 miles of a trip segment, it is mentioned in the narrative, along with the phone number of the visitor center. Minnesota has an extensive system of beautiful state parks with excellent campgrounds that include visitor centers, electrical hookups, and convenient shower houses. If you're fond of having many of the comforts of home when you camp, you'll appreciate these facilities. Campsite reservations (866-857-2757; www.stayatmnparks.com) are arranged through a central booking agency and are a good idea on weekends and holidays and anytime at the north shore parks.

Several private campgrounds are also mentioned, particularly exceptional ones, and the contact information for these is provided.

Canoe and Kayak Rental and Shuttle Services

Any outfitters that are located within a reasonable distance of a trip segment are listed. Some outfitters will provide shuttle service for a fee even if you don't rent a boat from them.

Shuttle Routes

Each of the trip narratives contains a brief description of the most "comfortable" shuttle route from the put-in to the takeout, but it's not always the shortest route. That's because I've tried to suggest routes on paved roads rather than on gravel roads, even though the latter may cover fewer miles. Nevertheless, in a few cases, gravel roads were the only sensible choice. Other local roads besides the main shuttle routes are shown on the maps to provide you other viable options for traveling in the area.

If you've never shuttled people, boats, and equipment between the put-in and the takeout and wonder how it works, here are some suggestions. For groups with more than one vehicle, the process is usually simple, but there are several ways to accomplish the task.

The most common is for the whole group to drive to the put-in, or meet there at a designated time, and drop off all canoes and gear, and people to watch the stuff. One driver per vehicle drives to the takeout, where they leave all the vehicles except one. The people in that group then get into the one vehicle and drive back to the put-in. After everyone paddles downriver to the waiting vehicle(s), two people in one vehicle drive back up to the put-in to fetch the vehicle that was left behind, while the others are free to load up and leave.

Another option is to meet at the takeout and leave one vehicle there. Stuff everyone, their canoes, and their equipment into the remaining vehicle(s), drive to the put-in, and paddle down the river. Two (or more, depending on the number of vehicles) people then drive back to the put-in together and pick up the vehicle(s) that were left. This method saves time at the beginning of the trip but may require extra roof rack space to carry the canoe that was on the vehicle left behind. Yet another method, when some paddlers want to take out early, is to

Campsite in the Boundary Waters.

leave their vehicle(s) at an alternate access so they can take out there.

A bike shuttle works well if you have only one vehicle. Just chain the bike to a tree or some other permanent fixture at the takeout, drive to the put-in, leave your vehicle there, and paddle downriver; one person then stays with the canoe and the other rides the bike back to the vehicle at the put-in. The pedaling makes a nice change from the paddling. Some bike shuttlers add a small motorized friction drive to a standard bike to make a long or hilly journey easier. Staton, Inc. (405-605-3765; www.staton-inc.com) and several other companies make an easily installed friction drive kit that will motorize your bike. Another nice thing about the contraption is the gas mileage: about 130 mpg. A bicycle can also be carried in the canoe, eliminating the need to leave it at the takeout and offering the flexibility to choose an alternate takeout.

Gradient

Gradient is the rate of a river's descent, expressed in feet per mile (fpm). The average gradient of a river segment is calculated by dividing the number of feet of elevation that the river drops by the length of the segment in miles. The importance of knowing the gradient of a river you're going to paddle is that riffles and rapids are usually found on rivers with a gradient higher than 3 fpm. On a river with a gradient of 10 fpm or more, you can generally expect challenging whitewater. Gradient is only one factor in predicting what the water will be like, but it should alert you to possible dangerous conditions.

It's important to understand that a river segment with a low gradient may have short but high gradient drops that are balanced by long sections of flat water, like Vermilion 2 and 3. Always find out the gradient of any significant rapids on a river segment as well as the average gradient.

Water Levels

Water level is one of the most important things to know about a river, primarily because you want to have a safe paddle. EVERY RIVER IN THIS BOOK IS DANGEROUS TO PADDLE AT HIGH WATER. Rivers are often high in the spring, when debris from the runoff is racing downstream in ice-cold water. Although paddlers are sometimes tempted by the excitement of high water in the spring, never paddle a river that has this lethal combination of hypothermia-inducing cold, fast water, and obstacles. At the other extreme, a river that's too low is a river that's no fun to paddle. Scraping your way down a shallow rock-strewn river is miserable and hard on the equipment.

For each river trip, you'll find sources of water level information listed, including Web sites that list U.S. Geological Survey (USGS) and U.S. Army Corps of Engineers (USACE) automated gauges and painted bridge gauges that are read and reported by DNR volunteers, then listed on the DNR Web site (www.dnr.state.mn.us/river_levels/index.html) or are available at the DNR Information Center (888-646-6367). Please note that the DNR readings are updated weekly, not daily, and that the data for gauges read by volunteers may not be up-to-date. In addition, the DNR is in the process of converting the data sources for some river routes from volunteer

readings to automated USGS gages. In these cases, the old data interpretation will not apply to the USGS data, and an interpretation of the new data may not be immediately available from the DNR.

Readings are given in two different ways: flow, expressed as discharge in cubic feet per second (cfs), or water level, expressed as gauge height or stage in feet. Some rivers have no gauges and thus no data are available. In this case, local rainfall or readings from a nearby gauged river can be somewhat useful in predicting levels.

The USGS Web site (waterdata.usgs.gov/mn/nwis/rt) lists what's called "real-time data" for 106 gauges in Minnesota, data that are usually less than four hours old. Paddlers should explore all the features of this useful Web site. In addition to "daily streamflow conditions" in both cfs and gage (a USGS standard variant of the word gauge) height, this site gives the recent rainfall for the gage area, historical data, gage location, and other information. The other useful Web site is that of the USACE (www.mvp-wc.usace.army.mil/dcp/), which gives readings in "stages" (height in feet) for some rivers that are not on the USGS site. There is no interpretation of the meaning of the data for paddlers on either Web site, but paddlers can extrapolate information from the historical data.

Included in each trip description in the guide are interpretations of the available data for paddlers, with an emphasis on the moderate water levels that generally mean a good paddle. These interpretations are based on my own experience as well as on reports from other paddlers and from the DNR. The levels I list are suggestions only and not a guarantee of a safe or enjoyable paddle. Many other factors, including the equipment you use and the weight of the load in your canoe or kayak, will determine whether you scrape or float.

Finding accurate information before your arrival at the river can sometimes be confusing and frustrating. Always remember that data reports can be incorrect: the gauge itself can be improperly calibrated or the data inaccurately reported. Note that the final decision on whether to paddle a river is yours alone. Use your judgment: if a river looks too high to paddle, then it almost always is. Pack up and go home, or go for a bike ride. Conversely, if the river looks too low to paddle, do your canoe or kayak a favor and don't paddle. See "Paddling Safety" later in the introduction for some indicators of dangerous water.

Paddlers often call nearby state parks, campgrounds, or outfitters to find out what the level is like on a river. If you're trying to decide whether to drive to a river and are uncertain about data from other sources, the information that local sources provide can be quite useful. If someone in the area tells you that a river is high or low, the information is probably accurate.

Water level is also a partial predictor of how long your paddling time will be. The higher the water, the faster it will flow. If a river flows at one to two miles per hour at low to average levels, which most do, then moderately high water may bump that flow up to three to four mph, significantly changing your paddling time. Low water and low flow may mean that you'll want to shorten your trip by using an alternate access. Water level isn't the only factor; the way you paddle—letting the river do the work or racing downriver, calling hut!—also helps determine your time.

Accesses

Most of the accesses in the guidebook are easy to spot from the river, and those that aren't are noted. If you're concerned that you might paddle right past a takeout, tie a bright ribbon on a tree branch or some other fixed object near the river when you run the shuttle. The accesses that are next to bridge crossings may adjoin private land; be careful to use only the road right-of-way for your parking and access. These are quiet rural roads and parking on the shoulder is common, but do be careful to lock your vehicle.

Trip Descriptions

The remainder of each trip narrative provides a thumbnail description of what paddlers can expect to see along their journey from put-in to takeout, including river conditions, changes in direction, impediments, landmarks, fauna and flora, and other sites worth noting. Reading the narrative before you paddle can help you decide whether you'll enjoy that particular stretch.

Fishing

Fishing on a canoe trip can be great fun, whether or not you catch dinner. Whenever a river is known for especially good fishing opportunities, like the channel catfish on the Saint Louis or the smallmouth bass on the Otter Tail, this fact is mentioned in the trip description. Fish populations that are known to exist in a river on a smaller scale are also noted. If you plan to do any fishing, you will of course need a Minnesota fishing license, available at many gas stations and sporting goods stores.

River Reading and Boat Maneuvers

Many of the rivers described in this guide are primarily quiet water that will provide safe and pleasant excursions for paddlers of all skill levels, even beginners, provided they have some basic knowledge of river reading. So, if you've paddled on lakes but rarely on rivers, you'll need to learn to read a river. All river paddlers should have this ability, and they must learn to maneuver a canoe and handle unexpected situations or difficulties.

Reading the river is an important skill that improves with practice. Instruction with an accredited instructor is the best place to start. Learn to predict what lies in those waves ahead, the appearance of downstream and upstream Vs, what an eddy line does to a boat, the dangers of strainers and other obstacles, the difference between a pillow rock and a standing wave, the dangers of holes, and the intricacies of rock garden navigation. Once you have some instruction, practice on gentle rivers until you feel confident before launching a more challenging expedition. Paddling a river is much more fun when you have the skills to handle the challenges.

PADDLING SAFETY

If you've ever been in a tight situation on a paddling trip, you already know the importance of knowledge, skills, good judgment, and proper equipment in dealing with the problem. In general, the more experienced you are, the more respect you have for the inherent risks a paddler faces and the keener your skills and judgment become.

Before you even plan a trip on a new river, be sure you have the skills to paddle a river safely, the ability to read the water, and knowledge of both the potential risks of paddling and how to deal with the difficulties that may arise. Practice your skills, especially river rescues, on safe and familiar water. Develop the necessary respect for risk that will prevent you from overestimating your skills. Take the right equipment (see the checklist later in this section), including a snug-fitting, comfortable personal flotation device (PFD, or life jacket) for each paddler. ALWAYS WEAR YOUR PFD. Most canoe and kayak fatalities involve paddlers who aren't wearing one. After raising four children to be safe in the water sports that they love, I never go out in a canoe or kayak without my PFD.

As you plan your river adventures, learn as much as you can about the river you want to paddle. Paddle with friends who are experienced or with a group or club that has experienced paddlers. Minnesota has a number of great paddling organizations and schools that plan regular outings on many of the rivers in this book. A list of organizations, schools, and clubs is contained in appendix 4.

The following are some of the hazards you may face while out on the water. The list is intended as an introduction to the subject, certainly not as the last word. The best strategy before attempting whitewater paddling—before any level of paddling, for that matter—is instruction with an accredited teacher.

Broaching

When a canoe is pushed sideways, or broadside, to the current, the force of a strong current may pin it against an exposed rock, bridge pier, or other obstacle. This is known as broaching or pinning. The beginning paddler's instinct is to lean upstream away from the rock and into the onrushing water, allowing the boat to fill with water. A strong enough current will then wrap the boat, with you in it, around the rock or bridge pier. However, if you remain calm and immediately do a hard downstream lean toward the rock, you can prevent this potential catastrophe. Maintain the downstream lean to keep the boat from filling with water and you may be able to wiggle it off the rock. You may also be able to climb onto the rock to lighten and free the boat. If other paddlers are with you, they may be able to help. A rescue from shore may be necessary if the boat is pinned and filled with water.

To avoid a broach, keep your boat parallel to the current, pointed either upstream or downstream, so that it either hits obstacles head-on or slides along the side.

Cold

Springtime paddlers in northern Minnesota face the very real risk of dumping into the ice-cold water of rivers that have only recently thawed. Falling into water this cold often produces hypothermia, a potentially fatal chilling of the body's core that also quickly drains the paddler's strength, as well as his or her ability, and will, to survive. If you paddle when the water is below 55 degrees, or when the water temperature and the air temperatures don't add up to over 120, it's essential to wear a wet suit or a dry suit and carry extra clothes in a dry bag. If you're an inexperienced paddler, wait until warmer weather and water before paddling.

Holes

When fast water flows over a ledge or a rock, it curls back on itself on the downstream side, forming a turbulent depression in the water that's known as a hole, a reversal, or a hydraulic. Small to moderate holes form on the rapids of the Upper Cloquet, the Lower Saint Louis, and some other rivers in this book, but at moderate water levels, most of these can be run or even surfed by experienced paddlers. Some large holes become quite "sticky" and are called stoppers or keepers. These dangerous holes can trap and kill a swimmer and should be avoided, by portaging if necessary. Paddlers who cannot recognize the difference should avoid all but the smallest holes. At moderate to high water levels, two large holes form below Electric Ledge on the Lower Saint Louis. Low head dams almost always form stoppers, but there are very few of those on the rivers in this book.

High Water

In the spring and after heavy and sustained rainfall, many rivers like the Kettle will fill and rise quickly and dangerously. The result is very fast, unpredictable, powerful current; huge waves; and big, sticky holes. In the spring, tree branches and other debris may be washed downstream by the icy-cold water. If you see the water rushing through the shoreline trees or shrubs; if the water is turbulent and muddy, with whirlpools visible; or if you see floating branches or other debris, the water is too high to paddle.

Strainers

When a tree or brush extends into the current, it's called a strainer. The water flows through the strainer, but paddlers and canoes are caught and trapped. Strainers can also be bridge piers or undercut rocks. They may look innocent, but the current can trap both paddlers and their boats in the tangle of branches or under the rock, with potentially fatal results. Stay well clear of strainers.

Ledges and Falls

You'll find ledges on some of the rivers in this book—McCabe's Rapids and Cedar Rapids in Cloquet 3, for example. Falls are more dramatic, with a sudden vertical drop of several feet or more. Little American Falls in Big Fork 4 and Liftover Falls in Vermilion 1 are examples. Ledges and falls are signaled by a horizon line, a clear line across the river where the water drops over, often accompanied by mist and a roar. When approaching a ledge or falls, scout carefully before running it. If in doubt, always portage. The current often increases as you get nearer to a falls or rapids, so don't get too close while boat scouting.

Dams

Several trips in this book take paddlers near dams, like the Friberg Dam in Otter Tail 1 and the huge Thomson Dam in Saint Louis 5. While these hazards are always clearly marked, never underestimate the great danger of getting too close to the edge of a dam. Always take out as far away from the dam as possible to avoid the strong current that builds near the edge. When you put in below a dam, stay away from the recirculating currents that form there.

Wild River Outfitters in the town of Big Falls, along the Big Fork.

Capsizing

The question is not if you will dump; the question is when. Everyone who paddles regularly will, at some time, capsize. Don't panic; hang on to your boat, keeping it downstream of you so that you can't be crushed between the boat and a rock. Your PFD will help protect you from rocks, but only if you're wearing it! If you're headed into dangerous rapids or toward a hazard, however, let go of the boat and swim on your back, with your feet downstream and your toes out of the water. If you're near an eddy, swim that way. Don't attempt to stand in rapids; one of your feet may get trapped between rocks and the fast water will push you under and keep you there. This is a common cause of drowning among paddlers.

If you're paddling in a group, there are other people available who can help you first and your boat later, a situation that brings up two other issues: paddling with at least one other person and learning river rescue techniques. As part of learning to be a better paddler, you should learn and practice rescues; using a throw bag effectively can help a fellow paddler out of a difficult situation.

Rapids

Riffles and rapids are the spice in the relative calm of a river's regular flow. Most of the rivers in this guide have at least a few riffles. Riffles are fast, mostly unobstructed water with small waves, water that is easy, fun, and exciting to paddle. Riffles are great for beginning river paddlers to learn to maneuver on, and they're also enjoyable for experienced paddlers.

Standing waves, also called haystacks, often form in rapids when the river races through a tight spot or a drop into slower water. These wave chains usually mark the deep water and the best route for paddlers to follow, but if the waves are too high, they can swamp an open canoe. Kettle 4 and Red Lake 1 have long chains of big waves when the water is moderate to high.

Successfully running difficult rapids can be quite thrilling. This excitement is a big part of what draws many paddlers to rivers, and yet the excitement comes from the inherent danger of the fast water—danger that

An island campsite on Alpine Lake.

must be thoroughly respected. Inexperienced paddlers often underestimate the risks, with sometimes catastrophic results. An expert paddler knows when rapids are unrunnable and has a profound respect for all safety precautions. However, even experienced paddlers make the mistakes that come from not scouting when they should, underestimating the difficulty of a drop, or paddling when the water is too high. Each paddler has a responsibility to understand the difficulty of a river and its rapids before paddling.

To paraphrase Tolstoy's comment about families, all rapids are alike in certain ways, but each is different in its own way. The International Scale of River Difficulty is a system that was devised to find the ways in which rapids are alike, classifying them into six categories in order to help paddlers become aware of the relative dangers posed by a river. Because each rapid is different, these ratings have a degree of subjectivity and imprecision. However, the scale is widely accepted and is far, far better than nothing at all, and it's used throughout this guide. Remember that whenever the water is high or cold, a run should be rated one class higher.

Class I: A step up from riffles, with fast water and some waves, but not too large; some obstructions, but not too many. These are easily run by beginning whitewater paddlers who have river paddling and maneuvering skills and experience. The dangers are small if you have to swim. The Crow Wing and the Whiteface have numerous stretches of Class I rapids.

Class II: Fast water with big waves, ledges, and more rocks, often close together and awkward to maneuver around. Excellent river-reading skills are needed to weave through the boulder gardens that characterize the Class II rivers in northern Minnesota. Broaching is a definite possibility, and rescue may be difficult. Some Class II rapids, like the Lower Kettle at moderate to high water, can be quite long, with the potential for problems becoming much greater than on a short Class II. Class IIs are also found on the Sturgeon, the Little Fork, and the Upper Cloquet. Class II covers a wide range of difficulty; rapids that are at the upper end of the class, like Cedar Rapids on the Upper Cloquet at moderate to high levels, are noted as Class II+. Class II rapids are appropriate for experienced whitewater paddlers only.

Class III: Very difficult rapids with large, irregular waves that may be difficult to avoid and that can swamp an open canoe; drops of three feet or more; complex maneuvers in strong, pushy current. Scouting is important; holes, strong eddies, and other powerful current effects are found, especially on large-volume rivers. Long swims and injuries while swimming are more likely. Rescue can be quite difficult. Class III rapids are suitable for experienced advanced paddlers only.

Class IV: Intense, powerful, but predictable rapids requiring precise boat handling in turbulent water. May feature large, unavoidable waves; unavoidable holes; and constricted passages demanding fast maneuvers under pressure. Rapids require "must-do" moves under pressure above dangerous hazards. Consequences of capsize may be catastrophic and rescue is quite difficult. These rapids are appropriate only for highly skilled paddlers with extensive experience in difficult whitewater.

Class V: Extremely long, obstructed, or very violent rapids that expose a paddler to added risk. Big drops may contain large, unavoidable waves and keeper holes or steep, congested chutes with complex, demanding routes, and broaching or pinning situations. Rapids may continue for long distances between pools, demanding a high level of fitness. Class V rapids present serious danger to life and little chance of rescue. Class Vs are appropriate only for teams of experts under perfect water level and weather conditions.

Class VI: Extreme and exploratory, these runs have almost never been attempted. The consequences of error are probably fatal and rescue is nearly impossible.

An Important Warning

If you have any uncertainty about the character or difficulty of rapids facing you, get to shore above the rapids and scout it carefully. Scouting is an opportunity to learn more about a river as well as an essential step to protect your own safety. IF IN DOUBT, ALWAYS PORTAGE. Never let pride or pressure from others push you into attempting rapids that are too difficult for your skills and experience. As we get older we think we are immune to peer pressure, but don't bet on it. Sometimes the most "skilled" paddler is the one who portages when others paddle. A good rule is to ask yourself, "Could I run this without mishap 9 out of 10 times?" If the answer is no, portage. Also, always wear your PFD, and don't paddle alone.

A CANOE TRIP CHECKLIST

Beginning paddlers may want to use this basic checklist to make sure that all their gear and equipment for a trip is available and in good working condition. Experienced paddlers can use the list to brush up on the lists that they may have developed. Even people who paddle a lot sometimes forget things that they really need.

- Snug-fitting and comfortable PFD (life jacket) for each paddler
- Extra paddle
- Sunscreen and bug spray
- Hat
- Shoes that protect your feet from rocks
- Rain jacket and pants
- First aid kit
- Food and plenty of water in plastic bottles
- Bailer and sponge
- Keys to shuttle vehicle or bike lock
- Dry bag to hold change of clothes, wallet, camera, and cell phone
- Map and compass
- For whitewater: flotation bag, tie-downs, whitewater helmet, and wet suit (depending on conditions)
- For camping: camping equipment and food packed in dry bags, a bear rope in bear country

PRIVATE-PROPERTY ISSUES

Minnesota's position on paddlers' rights is somewhat ambiguous and more restrictive of paddlers than that of its neighbor, Wisconsin. There are several issues to consider, the first being ownership of the waterways. Much of the land along Minnesota's rivers and lakes is privately owned, but all navigable waters in Minnesota are public waters, where the state of Minnesota owns the streambed below the ordinary low-water level. Navigable waters are defined by Minnesota as those that "are used, or are susceptible of being used, in their natural ordinary condition, as highways for commerce, over which trade or travel are or may be conducted." All the waterways described in this book are navigable and thus public waters.

The public may legally use any public waters, but getting to that water often involves the second issue: riparian rights, or shore land property rights. Where a public road with its right-of-way or a public access abuts a river or lake (navigable or not), the public has riparian rights and may access that water. In places along a public waterway where there is no public access point, the landowner has riparian rights, and members of the public must get verbal or written permission from the landowner to cross that property. Crossing private property to get to a public waterway is trespassing and subject to prosecution.

Once safely on the water, paddlers must still remember the shoreline issues. The legality of using private shoreline is a fuzzy area. Strictly speaking, paddlers may only use the surface of the water or anchor on that water. Landing on private shoreline or wading in the shallow water along private property may be interpreted as trespassing. It's particularly important to observe this rule where "No Trespassing" or "Keep Out" signs are posted. Paddlers who land on a shoreline and are asked by the landowner to leave should do so immediately, without argument. However, the Minnesota attorney general's office says a paddler may briefly stop on private shoreline in the natural course of paddling down the river, to take a short rest, to wade through a shallow area, or to use a well-established but private portage trail around rapids.

Along many of the rivers in this book, the shoreline is primarily state forestland, where camping is allowed whether a campsite has been established or not. According to the DNR, forested areas are open unless posted, but agricultural land doesn't need to be posted for trespassing to be illegal. Paddlers have the final responsibility to determine whether the land is private or public and to obtain any necessary permission to camp on private property.

Property owners do have one responsibility. They may not build fences or dams that interfere with the normal passage of watercraft that are typical to the waterway. On the Otter Tail River, for example, a landowner has strung an electrified wire fence across the river that endangers canoeists at some water levels. Although the fence is marked with a strip of red cloth, the fence is probably illegal because it's considered a danger to the public; the DNR is working on getting it raised or removed. It is, however, also illegal and definitely inadvisable for canoeists to cut fences. Fortunately, a fence like this is a rare occurrence. In over a thousand miles of paddling, we encountered only one. Cooperation and mutual respect should be the goal of both paddlers and landowners in all these issues.

BOAT REGISTRATION

All canoes and kayaks owned by Minnesota residents and used on rivers and lakes in Minnesota must be registered with the state of Minnesota. The dealer from whom you buy the boat will tell you how to do this, or you can contact the state DNR (888-646-6367; www.dnr.state.mn.us/licenses/watercraft/index.html) for more information. If you reside in another state and are using a boat that you own on Minnesota waterways, it must be registered in that state. If your state doesn't require registration, you must purchase a Minnesota registration sticker. One nice thing to remember about boat license fees is that they're used to build and maintain public water accesses.

PADDLING ETIQUETTE

The same rules of courtesy that apply in all human endeavors apply in paddling: treat others as you would wish to be treated, respect private property, take responsibility for your own safety but help others when you can do so without endangering yourself, abstain from alcohol and drugs, don't bring the noise of the modern world into the quiet of a wilderness river, and share the work (and the fun) when you paddle in a group. Finally, in the words of the U.S. Forest Service, LEAVE NO TRACE, so that others will find the same beautiful river that you found.

BIG FORK RIVER 1
County Road 14 to Bigfork (19.3 miles)

The Big Fork is a wonderful camping river, with lots of wilderness stretches, well-spaced DNR campsites, good muskie fishing, plenty of wildlife, and some Class I rapids for spice. For those who like to watch wildlife, this is the place to have a chance of seeing trumpeter swans, mergansers, Canada geese, mallards, kingfishers, bald eagles, various hawks, turkey vultures, river otters, and ermine. The deep pools in the river are muskie territory.

Camping is available at two DNR campsites on the river and at a camping area with drinking water and a shelter at the access in the town of Bigfork. Car camping with hot showers is available at Scenic State Park, 218-743-3362, about 7 miles southeast of the town of Bigfork on County Road 7.

Canoe rental and **shuttle service** are available through Bigfork River Canoe Outfitting, 218-743-3274, in Bigfork.

The 14.5-mile **shuttle route** runs north and then east on County Road 14, north on Highway 6, east on County Road 14 again, and south on Highway 38; after crossing the river, immediately turn right, before the convenience store, to reach the access.

The average **gradient** is 0.9 foot per mile.

Water levels are best in May and June; the free-flowing current is also the quickest then and after a good rain. You'll find a gauge on the Highway 38 bridge in the town of Bigfork. Although the river is runnable at water levels as low as four feet at Bigfork, you'll scrape your way through rapids when it's this low. You'll have a much better run between five and seven feet. Above seven feet, the river is not really safe to paddle. You can get bridge gauge readings from the DNR, (888-646-6367; www.dnr.state .mn.us/river_levels/index.html)

The turnoff for the access is .12 mile north of the County Road 14 bridge, marked with a sign for Harrison Landing. Just past the access ramp is the campground. After you **put in**, remember to duck a little when you slide under County Road 14, a low, creosoted wooden bridge with very little headroom when the water level in Bigfork is five feet or above. If the river is too high, **portage** on river right.

The waters of the Big Fork, dark with tannin, flow through a marshland with a spacious view. The river is about 240 feet wide, its grassy banks forested with white cedar, birch, poplar, and spruce. The Big Fork was a log-driving river a century ago, and you'll probably spot half-submerged logs, left behind when huge rafts of lumber rode the spring runoff downstream to Canadian sawmills. Avoid deadheads, as some call them. Watch for barely submerged boulders as well.

At mile 1.3, the river runs through Robb's Rapids, a short, easy Class I drop. An island splits the channel at a bend in the river; go left and weave your way through 100 yards of boulders. Soon after, a few houses appear on the left, near several grassy islands. After County Road 14 crosses the river again, the houses disappear and the river, deep and dark again, flows through another flat marshland lined with willow and alder thickets.

The river narrows again before Hauck Rapids at mile 4.9; you'll see a warning sign on the right, just past a cluster of houses. These Class I rapids are served up in two parts: first some boulder dodging, and then a chute that curves right a little.

About 2 miles past the rapids, you'll spot a big rock outcrop on the right. This is a heavily wooded area, with lots of floodplain maples and few houses. Little Minnow campsite appears on the left at mile 8.3. At the time this book was researched, the tree that held the campsite sign had been chewed down by pesky beavers. Much more evidence of beavers appears in the next 2 miles.

Hafeman Access (mile 10.3) is across Highway 6 from Hafeman Boat Works, the workshop of a builder of traditional birchbark canoes. Ray and Christie Boessel welcome visitors to Ray's workshop. Christie's grandfather, Bill Hafeman, started building birchbark canoes in 1921. For information about visits, contact Hafeman Boat Works (218-743-3709; 59520 Highway 6, Bigfork, MN 56628). Downstream of the bridge, bluffs wooded with dark spruce and white birch rise above the river, and there are almost no houses. About 4 miles from the city of Bigfork, houses begin to appear again.

As you get into town, a sign warns you of a bend to the left with a boulder field on the right; stay left. You'll pass a long line of cedar posts, evidence of the logging era. **Take out** on river right .4 mile before the County Road 38 bridge.

A calm stretch of the Big Fork.

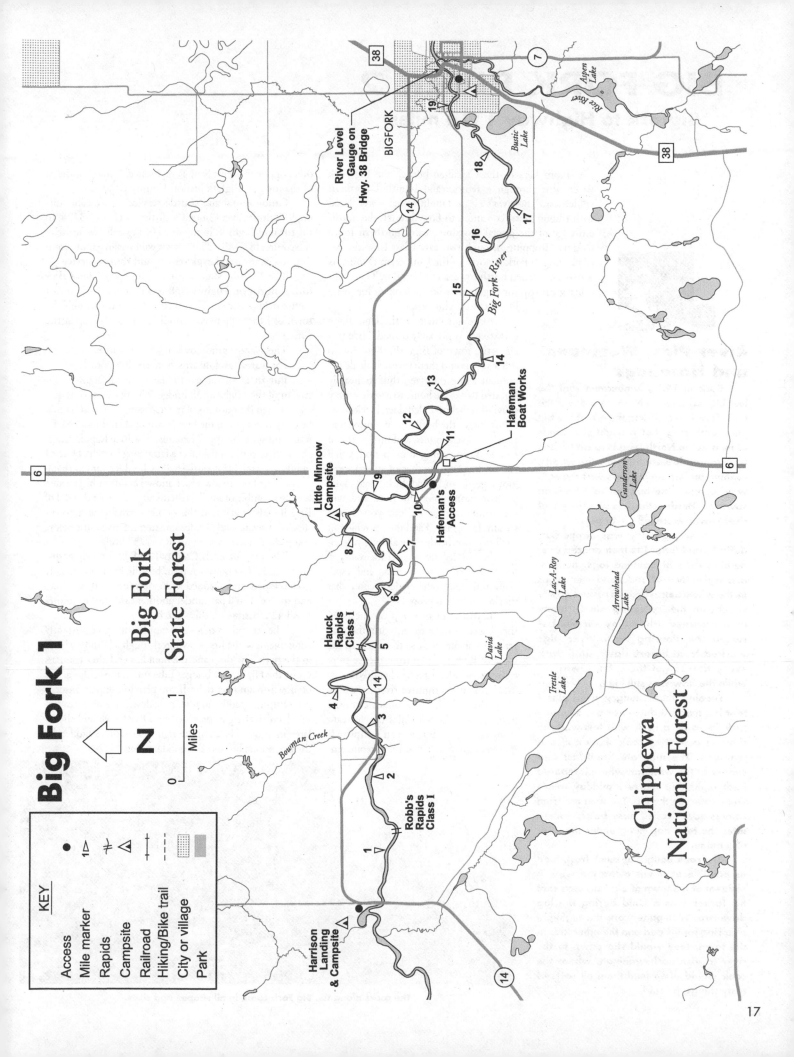

Big Fork 1

N

Miles
0   1

KEY

●	Access
1△	Mile marker
≠	Rapids
△	Campsite
┼	Railroad
----	Hiking/Bike trail
▓	City or village
▒	Park

Big Fork
State Forest

Chippewa
National Forest

BIGFORK

River Level
Gauge on
Hwy. 38 Bridge

Big Fork River

Hafeman
Boat Works

Hafeman's
Access

Little Minnow
Campsite

Hauck
Rapids
Class I

Robb's
Rapids
Class I

Harrison Landing
& Campsite

Bowman Creek

Aspen Lake

Rice River

Bustic Lake

Gunderson Lake

Lac-A-Roy Lake

Arrowhead Lake

Trestle Lake

David Lake

38

7

38

14

6

6

14

14

19

18

17

16

15

14

13

12

11

10

9

8

7

6

5

4

3

2

1

BIG FORK RIVER 2
Bigfork to Highway 1 (14 miles)

River Pigs, Wanigans, and Nosebags

Back in 1937, lumbermen sent the last big log drive in Minnesota down the Little Fork River, ending the era of the big pine lumbering that brought thousands of men to the North Woods to cut timber. Until railroads were built into the woods, running timber down rivers was the only way to move the huge pines to distant sawmills. Herding the logs was the job of river cowboys, called "river pigs."

A river pig's day was dangerous, difficult, and long. The men danced over floating rafts of bobbing logs, pushing and prying them off rocks and over rapids as the whole extravaganza rushed downstream on the icy spring runoff; many men drowned when they slipped between the floating logs. River pigs worked from before dawn until dark every day to get the rafts downriver while the flow was still high.

Feeding these hungry river pigs—four big meals a day—was the daunting task faced by a cook who followed the drive in a floating cook shack called a wanigan. The men ate breakfast and supper at the wanigan where it moored each night, but the two midday meals were eaten on the job. The men ate from canvas sacks called nose bags, named after the feed bag hung under the nose of a horse.

The cook bought as much fresh food as possible at towns along the way. A resident of the town of Big Falls says that his father was a child during the log drive era. Wanigans were the highlight of spring for his dad and the other kids in the town; they would slip down to the river to visit each wanigan, where the cook would often feed them all sorts of tasty things, he said.

From here to the Canadian border, the Big Fork River runs through a remote and beautiful northern wilderness. The river's clean, tannin-tinted water, laced with ribbon grass, continues to flow through the northern edge of the glacial moraine area of northern Itasca County, dropping through two easy Class I rapids. Because the Big Fork is north of the Laurentian Divide, its waters are headed north toward Hudson Bay. This is another great trip for beginners who are looking for just a little taste of whitewater.

Although much of the land along this stretch is privately owned, once you leave the town of Bigfork, there are no other towns and there is very little development along the river; thus its heavily forested banks are home to a wide variety of wildlife: white-tailed deer, black bears (don't forget the bear rope if you plan to camp), beavers, otters, and turtles. If you paddle during a migration period, you'll see an amazing number of mergansers, loons, geese, and wood ducks. Bald eagles are common along the river and will sometimes appear to lead you downstream, flying ahead and then perching in a tall tree, one beady eye watching you approach. The fishing is good for walleyes, northerns, smallmouth bass, and especially muskies. Some anglers report that they've landed sturgeon.

If you want to **camp** on the river, there's a camping area with drinking water and a shelter next to the access in the town of Bigfork and a convenience store right across the street. The DNR also maintains two primitive river campsites along this stretch. Rice Rapids campsite is on river right 3.8 miles downstream from the access. Busticogan campsite is on river right a mile past the takeout. An-

other option is Scenic State Park, located 7 miles southeast of the town of Bigfork just off County Road 7.

Canoe rental and **shuttle service** are available through Bigfork River Canoe Outfitting, 218-743-3274, in the town of Bigfork. In the town of Big Falls, Wild River Adventures (877-481-2569; www.wildriveradventure.com) provides **canoe and kayak rentals and shuttle service.**

The 14-mile shuttle route from the town of Bigfork is north on Highway 38 to Highway 1, then east to the bridge access. The route takes you through the town of Effie, where you should consider a stop at the Effie Café.

The average **gradient** is 1.3 feet per mile.

For **water level** information, see Big Fork 1.

Put in at the access in the town of Bigfork, upstream of the Highway 38 bridge. The Big Fork runs quietly through the outskirts of town, passing scattered houses, before plunging into the heavily wooded land that characterizes most of this trip. Then, just past Rice Rapids campsite on river right, you'll meet a fairly long stretch of Class I rapids—a straightforward, shallow boulder garden that'll scrape your boat in low water and wash out in high water, leaving a tumble of small, crisscrossing waves. At the end of Rice Rapids, you'll find the wooden remains of a homesteader's private cattle bridge crossing the river, just before you paddle under the County Road 237 bridge.

The river parallels County Road 42 for a short distance, and a few houses appear, but the banks are mostly undeveloped and wooded with deciduous trees, cedar, and spruce. You'll pass under another bridge, the County Road 42 crossing, on this stretch.

The second set of Class I rapids—more consistently runnable than the first—swings through a bouldery bend in the river. The drop and the boulders end after you pass under the Highway 1 bridge. **Take out** at the bridge access on downstream river right. If you plan to camp at Busticogan campsite, paddle another mile downstream; the campsite is on river right, preceded by Deer Creek and then a large meadow. The campsite sign is sometimes hidden by the tree leaves, but there's a good landing.

The rocks along the Big Fork come in all shapes and sizes.

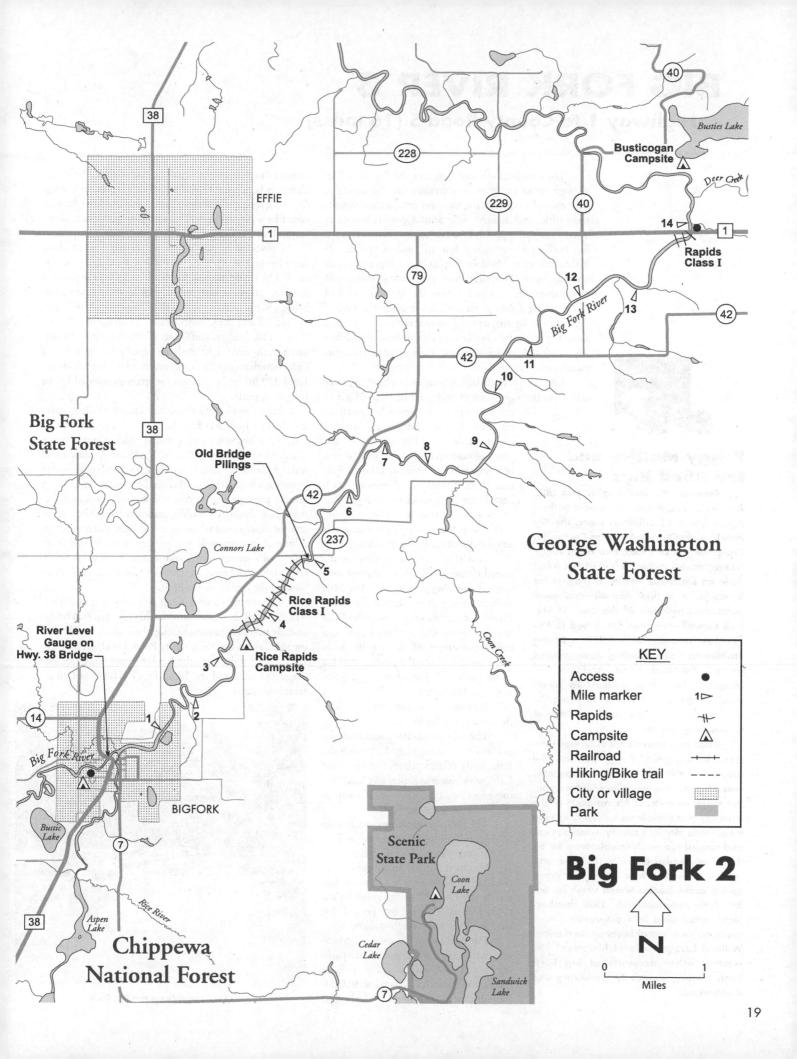

EFFIE

Busticogan Campsite

Busties Lake

Deer Creek

14 Rapids Class I

Big Fork River

12

13

11

10

9

8

7

Old Bridge Pilings

George Washington State Forest

6

5

Rice Rapids Class I

4

Rice Rapids Campsite

3

Connors Lake

Coon Creek

Big Fork State Forest

River Level Gauge on Hwy. 38 Bridge

1

2

Big Fork River

BIGFORK

Bustic Lake

KEY

Access ●

Mile marker 1▷

Rapids

Campsite △

Railroad

Hiking/Bike trail

City or village

Park

Scenic State Park

Coon Lake

Big Fork 2

N

Chippewa National Forest

Aspen Lake

Rice River

Cedar Lake

Sandwick Lake

0 — 1 Miles

BIG FORK RIVER 3
Highway 1 to County Road 5 (16 miles)

Peggy Mattice and the Blind Pigs

Between Muldoon Rapids and Little American Falls, there once was a gathering of about 15 buildings along the Big Fork River that the loggers called Craigville. Craigville doesn't look like much today (in fact, there's nothing left of it), but it has quite an illustrious history. A magnet for lumberjacks on their day off—and some permanent residents of the town of Bigfork as well—the place flourished in the first few decades of the 1900s. During Prohibition years, bootleg liquor flowed freely in the North Woods, and there are alleged to have been at least 26 "blind pigs" (illegal liquor stores) in Craigville and nearby along the southern edge of Koochiching County.

Blind pigs weren't the only entertainment in Craigville. Peggy Mattice, the madam of the last brothel in Craigville, was a legend. She was a beautiful woman, but tough as nails. Older residents of the area say that sometimes lumberjacks who frequented Mattice's rowdy establishment and caused too much trouble were hit on the head, hauled down to the river, and stuffed through a hole in the ice. When spring came, bodies would wash up below Little American Falls. Now, lumberjacks often died in work-related accidents, so no one could ever prove a thing. Willard Larson, a local historian, has written other accounts of Big Fork River history, especially lumbering and the railroads.

The root beer–colored waters of the Big Fork flow through more lovely, remote country on this trip. The river meanders quietly for the most part, although scattered riffles and shallow rocky areas appear at low water levels. This quiet pace is interrupted, however, when the Big Fork races through a fun, half-mile-long Class II stretch known as Muldoon Rapids. The riffles and rapids result as the Big Fork slides from the gentle morainic hills of northern Itasca County into the low, flat land of Koochiching County, land that was once the bed of Glacial Lake Agassiz, a vast, ancient inland sea. Beginners shouldn't have any trouble with the riffles, and paddlers who don't feel comfortable in Class II water can hike the established portage trail.

Like the previous trip, this segment of the Big Fork takes you through miles of undeveloped land. Much of the land is privately owned, but you'll see very few houses. Instead, the wooded banks are home to lots of wildlife, and you'll almost certainly spot bald eagles, beavers, otters, and white-tailed deer. As is true all over northern Minnesota, black bears live in these woods too, so if you plan to camp, bring your bear rope. The Big Fork's clean water also supports an excellent fishery, especially for muskies.

Two river-access campsites, maintained by the DNR, offer the most convenient **camping** on this trip. The first, Busticogan campsite (named for Chief Busticogan, a famous Ojibwe who lived near here more than a century ago), is a mile downstream of the put-in. Muldoon campsite is on the portage trail for Muldoon Rapids. For other camping options, see Big Fork 1.

For **canoe** and **kayak** rental and shuttle service, see Big Fork 2.

The 12-mile **shuttle route** from the put-in is west on Highway 1, through the little town of Effie (home of the Effie Café, with homemade pies and local history) to County Road 5, then north to the bridge over the Big Fork.

The average **gradient**, including Muldoon Rapids, is 2.0 feet per mile.

If you plan to run rather than portage Muldoon Rapids, you'll want a **water level** of between five and seven feet on the Highway 38 bridge gauge in the town of Bigfork. See Big Fork 1 for sources of water level information.

Put in at the public access on downstream river right, where you'll find a parking lot and a well-maintained carry-down access. You'll launch at the end of the Class I rapids that start upstream of the bridge.

In moderate to high water, the mile that follows the bridge alternates between riffle and easy Class I rapids. At low water, you'll scrape. Busticogan campsite is on the right, preceded by a big meadow. The sign may be hidden in the leaves, but there's a good landing.

Groves of beautiful big old cedars appear along these banks, the exposed roots of which are almost sculptural. The shade of these lovely old trees is so dense that nothing grows under them. You'll slide under two bridges in the next few miles, the County Road 40 bridge at mile 2.7 and the County Road 229 bridge at mile 4.6. Between the bridges, you'll pass a beautiful stand of white birches on river right with an equally lovely grove of cedars overhanging the banks on river left. At the County Road 229 bridge, watch out for strainers trapped by the bridge supports.

After the County Road 229 bridge, shallow water and lots of boulders for about 2 miles means lots of scraping at low water and scattered riffles at higher water. Then, at mile 8.5, you'll meet Muldoon Rapids, a half mile of bouldery Class II rapids, with standing waves up to two feet in high water. You can boat scout Muldoon or use the **portage** trail to take a look, but this straightforward drop through a boulder garden shouldn't be a problem for experienced whitewater paddlers. You may scrape a little at low water. If you portage, the 165-rod (half-mile) trail—steep, rocky, and sometimes brushy—is on river right. Muldoon campsite is along the trail, overlooking the rapids from a bluff.

The second County Road 40 bridge is at mile 10.1. The Big Fork meanders considerably between that bridge and the **takeout**, passing through land that's mostly state owned. Take out at the County Road 5 bridge, on downstream river right, near the former site of Craigville (see "Peggy Mattice and the Blind Pigs"). This is not an established access.

Class I rapids on the Big Fork.

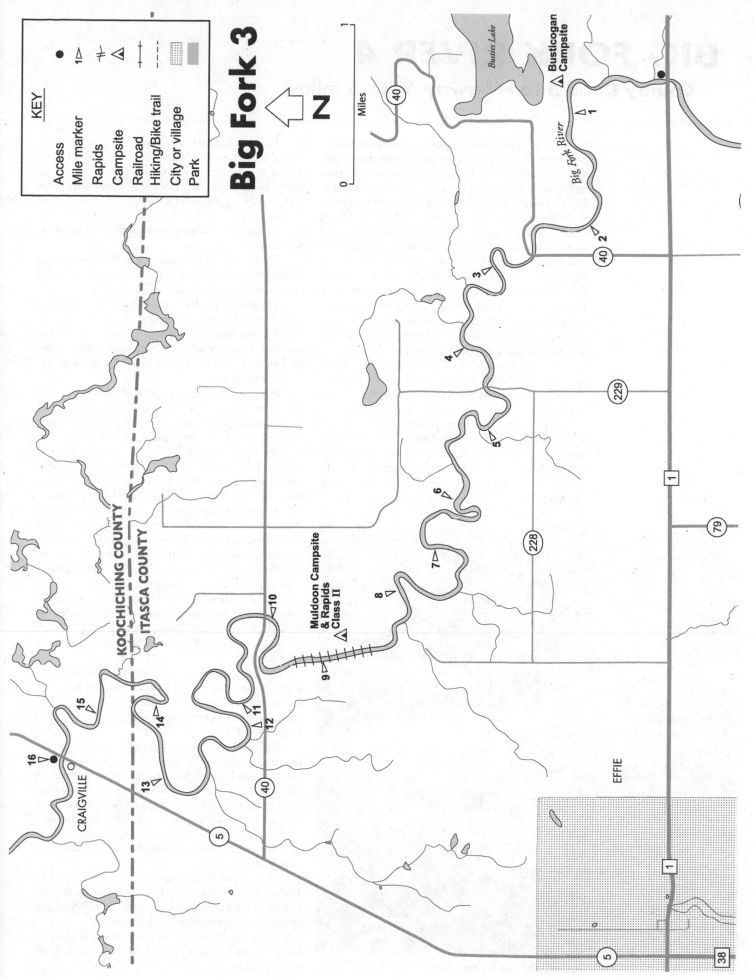

Big Fork 3

N

Miles
0 — 1

KEY

●	Access
1△	Mile marker
≠	Rapids
△	Campsite
┼	Railroad
- - -	Hiking/Bike trail
▦	City or village
▓	Park

Bassies Lake

Busticogan Campsite

Big Fork River

KOOCHICHING COUNTY
ITASCA COUNTY

Muldoon Campsite
& Rapids
Class II

CRAIGVILLE

EFFIE

BIG FORK RIVER 4
County Road 5 to Highway 6 (15.5 miles)

The Big Fork serves up another remote and beautiful trip on this section. The growing river meanders quietly for 2 miles and then suddenly surges over a massive and scenic bedrock outcrop at Little American Falls (Class IV–V). Forcing its way through a 10-foot-wide opening in the bedrock, the Big Fork's coppery waters fall six feet, crashing into a deep pool where the resulting foam and back roller create the look of a huge, noisy root beer float. After the quiet introduction of the first miles, the river's big drop is quite a surprise. A short, established portage trail takes you around the falls, past a campsite, and down to the pool below, where the fishing for walleyes, smallmouth bass, and northerns is excellent. At low water, several isolated pools form in rock bowls around the falls, sometimes trapping groups of hapless fish.

After the drama of the falls, the Big Fork is peaceful again until, 8.5 miles downstream, it dances through a twisting, Class I rapids 5 miles before the takeout at the Highway 6 bridge, known locally as Second Bridge.

If you want to **camp** on the river, the DNR-maintained campsite at Little American Falls is on the portage trail, left of the falls. A Koochiching County campground, Little American Falls Campground, is across the river at the top of a high, steep bluff. A wooden stairway extends partway down the bluff but ends about 10 to 15 feet above the water (depending on the water level), leaving a steep, sandy slope to negotiate. The county campground is also accessible by car from County Road 5 and is often used by anglers who climb down to the river to fish the pools. Another site, Old Hudson Bay Farm Campsite, is easily accessible on river right 2.5 miles before the takeout.

See Big Fork 2 for **canoe and kayak** rental and **shuttle service.**

The 8.3-mile **shuttle route** from the County Road 5 bridge is north on County Road 5 to Highway 6 and then south to Second Bridge.

The average **gradient**, including the six-foot drop at Little American Falls, is 1.9 feet per mile.

A **water level** of between five and seven feet at the town of Bigfork will make your passage through the mild rapids a pleasant one. See Big Fork 1 for more water level information.

Put in on downstream right at the County Road 5 bridge. In the first 2 miles before the falls, the Big Fork runs quietly through a stretch of mostly public land. Great stands of white birch, vivid against the dark of tall spruce and ancient cedars, make a beautiful backdrop for your paddle. Blue herons, kingfishers, and bald eagles are common along here, as is the other wildlife described in previous segments. You may hear a pileated woodpecker.

As you approach Little American Falls at mile 2.0, the increasing noise, the bedrock outcrop, and the clear horizon line will let you know what's ahead. Several danger signs are posted to alert you, just in case. Don't go near the edge of the falls; the 12-rod-long **portage** trail begins on river left, at a takeout tucked into a curve in the rock. A wide expanse of bedrock flanks the falls at low water and you can walk close to the drop, but at higher water these rock flats may be covered. The campsite on the portage has a picnic table, a fire ring, and an open-air privy.

To reach the campground on river right, you must wade (at low water) or paddle across the river below the falls and climb a steep bank to the wooden stairway that leads up to the county campground, a parking lot, and County Road 5.

About 2 miles downstream of the falls, wooden pilings that are the remains of an old logging bridge cross the river. The Big Fork flows quietly and slowly through this stretch until you reach Powell's Rapids, a lovely Class I rapids at mile 10.5 that curves past a farm on river right. This winding boulder garden is marked with a warning sign and the concrete remains of a bridge abutment on river left and is decorated throughout with some handsome rock outcrops.

Watch carefully on river right at mile 13 for the Old Hudson Bay Farm campsite; leaves may conceal the sign, but you'll see a picnic table under a rustic shelter. Just past the campsite is a beautiful big meadow.

Take out on downstream left at the Highway 6 bridge (Second Bridge). A long timber stairway leads up to the parking area.

Little American Falls on the Big Fork.

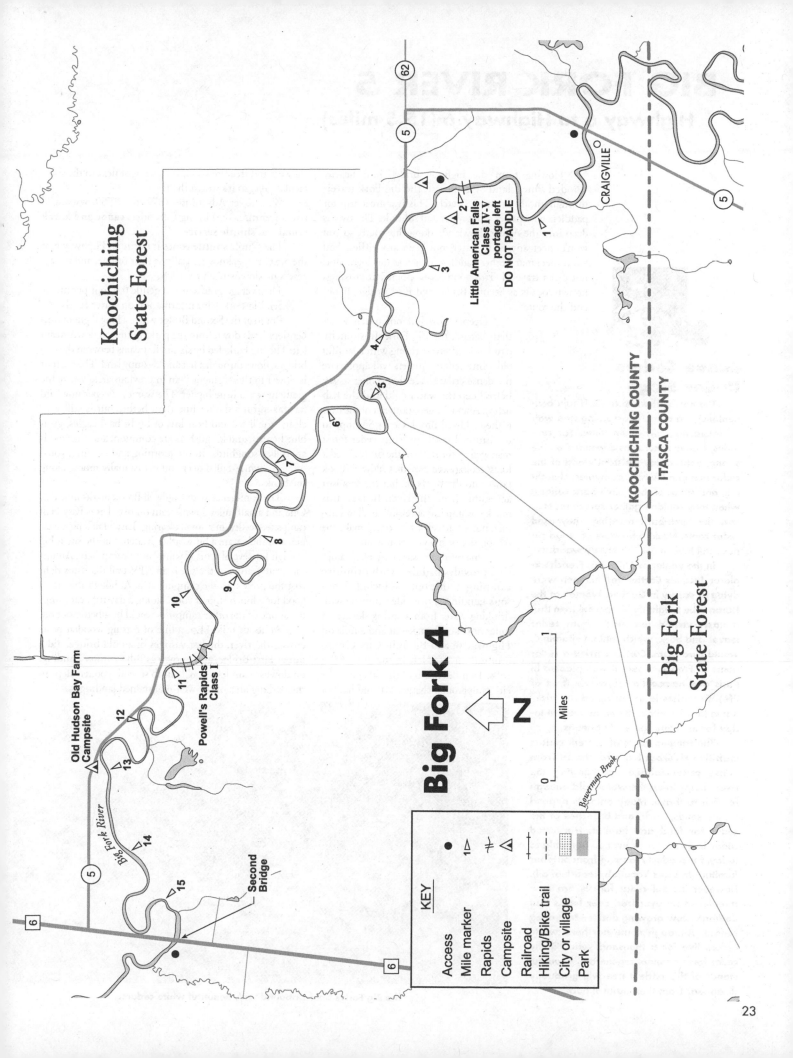

Big Fork 4

N

Miles

0 — 1

KEY

●	Access
1▷	Mile marker
✦	Rapids
△	Campsite
┼┼┼	Railroad
– – –	Hiking/Bike trail
▓	City or village
▓	Park

Koochiching State Forest

Big Fork State Forest

KOOCHICHING COUNTY

ITASCA COUNTY

Bowerman Brook

CRAIGVILLE

Little American Falls
Class IV-V
portage left
DO NOT PADDLE

Old Hudson Bay Farm Campsite

Powell's Rapids Class I

Big Fork River

Second Bridge

BIG FORK RIVER 5
Highway 6 to Highway 6 (15.5 miles)

Flowing from the highway bridge into heavily wooded Pine Island State Forest, the Big Fork travels through another remote stretch. This is a great trip for paddlers who prefer quiet water and solitude. The river is deep into the Agassiz Lowlands along this route, so you won't meet any whitewater, not even any riffles. You won't meet many other paddlers, either, as this segment is not often traveled. Two good access points, at crossings known locally as Second Bridge and First Bridge, bookend the route.

Deeper now but not much wider than before, the Big Fork slips quietly past banks often overhung with beautiful old white cedars. Anglers will appreciate the dense cedar shade that ecologists say helps keep the water cold and the fish happy. About 2 miles southeast of the river is the Caldwell Brook Cedar Swamp, an undisturbed northern white cedar forest managed by the state for the study of cedar forest ecology and growth. Caldwell Brook flows into the Big Fork, but the area isn't accessible from the river. In fact, this mucky swamp isn't accessible at all in summer, but white cedar fans could make the trip on skis or snowshoes in winter.

One river campsite, Easy Half campsite, provides paddlers with primitive **camping**. Other options include Johnson's Landing, a riverside campsite with drinking water from a spring, located 5 miles north of the takeout and a mile off Highway 6; and Big Falls City Campground, on river left in the city of Big Falls, 14 miles north of the takeout. The city campground charges $10 and has hot showers and free firewood. It's also right next to the spectacular falls, so it's worth the fee.

Wild River Adventures (877-481-2569; www.wild riveradventure.com) in Big Falls offers **canoe and kayak rental** and **shuttle service**.

The 5-mile **shuttle route** is north on Highway 6 to the next bridge, known locally as First Bridge, and the access is on downstream river left.

The average **gradient** is a gentle 0.6 foot per mile. See Big Fork 1 for information on **water levels**.

Put in at the Second Bridge where a long flight of timber steps leads down from the parking area on downstream left. The Big Fork, fed by six small streams between the two bridges, flows through a flat and swampy land. The current is slower in this segment than in previous areas where the gradient was a little higher. The water is deeper now and has taken on a darker hue than before but is still very clean. You'll see and hear lots of birds: bald eagles, great blue herons, and kingfishers are common, and the woods are full of songbirds. In the morning and evening, you'll often see white-tailed deer and occasionally moose along the banks.

The confluence with Caldwell Brook marks mile 8.3. One and a half miles downstream on river left is Easy Half campsite, nestled in a small clearing. Easy Half's picnic tables and shelter are a bit weather-beaten, but the site is big enough for several tents if you plan to camp here. An unfortunate feature of the site is an ATV trail that runs right past the privy into the camping area. Although this site is good for a lunch stop, if you're doing a day trip, car camping at one of the other campsites would be a better option.

At about mile 11.5, a line of rotting wooden posts crosses the river, the last vestiges of an old bridge. **Take out** at First Bridge, also known as Bill Counter Landing, on downstream left. You'll climb several wooden steps to the parking area of the well-maintained landing.

Canoe Cedars Under Siege

The northern white cedar (Thuja occidentalis) is a quiet, unassuming tree with an interesting curriculum vitae. For centuries, Native Americans depended on the strong, light, decay-resistant wood of the cedar to make the ribs, gunwales, sheathing, and stems of their birch-bark canoes; when they couldn't gather spruce roots to sew the birch-bark covering, they used cedar roots. Modern builders of wood canoes still love to use this sturdy wood.

In the winter of 1535–36, French explorer Jacques Cartier and his men were dying of scurvy in Quebec. Women of the Huron tribe taught the desperate men that a nasty-tasting tea made from cedar leaves and bark, which contain vitamin C, would cure them. Cartier carried a cedar home to France, where it was planted in Paris and named l'arbre de vie (tree of life). Botanists later Latinized the nickname to arborvitae, the name we use today for its many cultured varieties.

The tangled roots of ancient cedars stabilize riverbanks, and shade from dense cedar foliage overhanging the rivers helps keep the water cold enough for fish to thrive. Many animals depend on the seeds, bark, and branches of the cedar for food and habitat. Harvested cedar is as useful as ever to humankind today, for products ranging from outdoor furniture to Vicks VapoRub (cedarleaf oil). However, boreal cedar forests are now threatened by oversized deer herds that decimate slow-growing and tender young cedars. Although some northern white cedars live for a thousand years, if the cedar forests cannot regenerate, beautiful stands of this ancient tree will gradually disappear from their natural habitat.

The Big Fork's banks abound with beautiful white cedars.

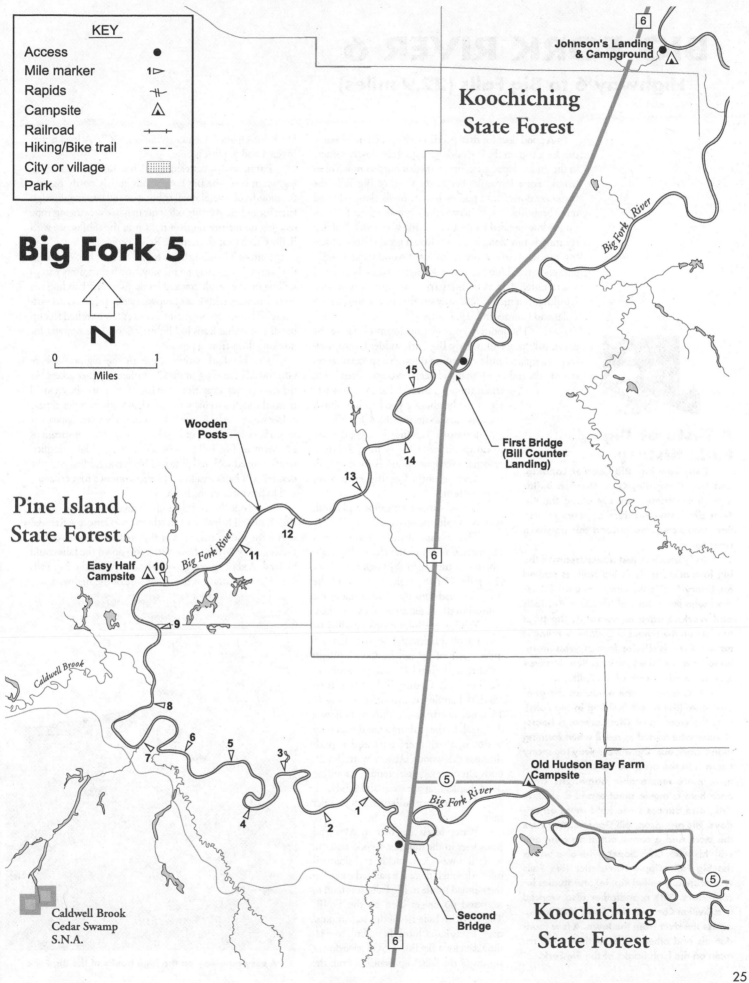

Big Fork 5

KEY

Access	●
Mile marker	1▷
Rapids	⚡
Campsite	△
Railroad	┼┼┼
Hiking/Bike trail	- - -
City or village	▦
Park	▨

N

0   1

Miles

Johnson's Landing & Campground

Koochiching State Forest

Big Fork River

Wooden Posts

15

14

13

First Bridge (Bill Counter Landing)

Pine Island State Forest

12

Big Fork River

11

Easy Half Campsite 10

9

Caldwell Brook

8

6

7   5   3

4   2   1

Old Hudson Bay Farm Campsite

Big Fork River

Caldwell Brook Cedar Swamp S.N.A.

Second Bridge

Koochiching State Forest

BIG FORK RIVER 6
Highway 6 to Big Falls (22.9 miles)

A good float for river paddlers who prefer quiet water, this long trip on the Big Fork River includes lovely scenery in the undeveloped state forestland that borders much of its length. For a few miles before the town of Big Falls, the banks are dotted with houses, but the bluffs along there are quite beautiful. The scenery in this segment ranges from intimate low wooded banks to dramatic high cliffs. Wildlife spotting is fun along here; you have a good chance of seeing moose, beavers, otters, pileated woodpeckers, mergansers, great blue herons, bald eagles, black bears, and white-tailed deer. A two-day trip, camping at Johnson's Landing, is a nice variation; your first day would be 8.5 miles and your second, 14.4 miles.

The journey ends just upstream of where the previously peaceful, steady Big Fork suddenly drops 60 feet in a quarter mile, cascading through a spectacular series of falls and rapids that paddlers should not even think about running. Rated Class IV at low water, at the height of a good spring runoff, the falls rates an unrunnable Class VI.

Johnson's Landing is a good place to **camp**, either by car or from the river. Another excellent option is the Big Falls City Campground (see Big Fork 5 for more information).

For information on **canoe and kayak rentals** and **shuttle service**, see Big Fork 5.

The 16-mile **shuttle route** follows Highway 6 north to the city of Big Falls, where you turn right on Highway 71 for .25 mile. On the right just before the bridge, a road runs for .2 mile under the railroad trestle to the access above the falls.

You can reach Johnson's Landing by turning off Highway 6 at the sign 4.5 miles north of the put-in. Go .7 mile to another sign, turn left, and go .3 mile to the landing. Grumwold's (or Gronwoldt's) Landing is just off Highway 6, 15 miles north of the put-in. Follow a dirt track to the parking area; the landing is down 20 timber steps and a path through the woods. At low water levels, both alternate accesses require climbing down banks that are steep and sandy.

The average **gradient** is 0.8 foot per mile.

Water levels are best in May and June; later in the summer, a good rain can bring the water up quickly and dramatically. Although there is a painted gauge on the railroad trestle in Big Falls, it is hard to read and no longer used by the DNR. The DNR website (www.dnr.state.mn.us/river_levels/index.html) has a link to real-time data for a Big Falls USGS gage downstream of the falls, also available from the DNR Information Center (888-646-6367). A level of between 4 and 5.5 feet is best.

Put in on downstream river left at Bill Counter Landing. From here, the Big Fork winds quietly north, passing the mouths of several small tributaries and curving through large meanders. At mile 6.8, you may see a swinging rope hanging from a tree on river right near the confluence with Reilly Creek (not the same as Reilly Brook.)

Johnson's Landing (mile 8.5) is on river left. Although the campsite sign may be missing, you'll spot timber steps leading up the brush-covered bank. Johnson's Landing is a great campsite, with lots of mown space and an actual outhouse instead of an open-air throne. A few hundred feet up the dirt road that leads to Highway 6, cold springwater for drinking flows from a pipe.

The Big Fork swings close to the highway where Grumwold's Landing (mile 12.4) offers another access. As the river curves away from the highway again, the channel twists through a scenic series of wiggles where riffles appear at low water levels. Another burst of lively water appears at mile 15, near a cluster of buildings. Four miles upstream of the town of Big Falls, you'll see dramatic high stratified bluffs, topped with red pine and birch and riddled with the nest holes of bank swallows. The remains of a root cellar are said to be visible in the bank.

Riverside houses announce that the town of Big Falls is near. The railroad trestle and a "Danger—Rapids" sign warn you to **take out** at the boat ramp on river left. Don't go any farther, however; a trip down the falls could be fatal. A short **portage** road leads toward the Big Falls City Campground on the other side of the highway.

A Taste of Big Falls History

Cody Landing, Bill Counter Landing, Ben Linn Campsite, O. L. Gorden Building: all the names you see along the Big Fork are homesteaders or folks whose lives were centered around this northern river town.

Cody Landing, just downstream of the big falls and rapids in Big Falls, is named for Henry C. (Hank) Cody, an avid fisherman who lived most of his life in Big Falls and worked hard to establish the boat landing on the river. Bill Counter Landing is named for a bachelor farmer who maintained many of the landings. Ben Linn was a homesteader north of Big Falls.

O. L. Gorden, the name on the general store (the oldest building in Big Falls), was the creation of Olaf Larson, a homesteader who turned to retail when farming didn't work out. There were way too many Larsons in the area, so he gave himself a new, more memorable name. His store once held a movie theatre and a skating rink, and dances were held there on Fridays. His grandson, Bill Gorden, now runs the store and a canoe outfitting company with his wife, Chris Soper, who also writes the Big Falls Ripple Newsletter (Big Falls was originally called Ripple) and studies local history. Bill's grandfather also worked in a Civilian Conservation Corps (CCC) camp across the river from the town. A few foundations and other traces of that camp remain on the high banks of the Big Fork.

A cozy getaway on the high banks of the Big Fork.

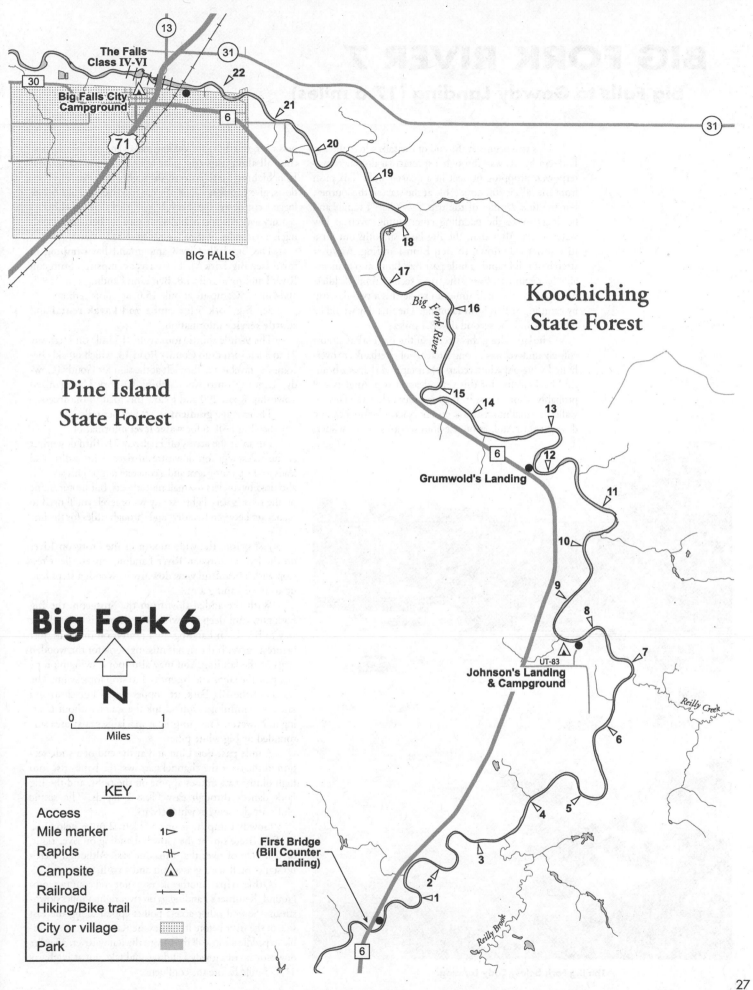

BIG FORK RIVER 7

Big Falls to Sawby Landing (12.6 miles)

The Falls
Class IV-VI

13

31

30

22

Big Falls City
Campground

21

6

71

20

BIG FALLS

19

Koochiching
State Forest

31

18

17

Big Fork River

16

Pine Island
State Forest

15

14

13

6

12

Grumwold's Landing

11

10

9

8

UT-83

7

**Johnson's Landing
& Campground**

Reilly Creek

6

Big Fork 6

↑
N

0 — 1
Miles

4   5

3

First Bridge
(Bill Counter
Landing)

2

1

KEY

Access	●
Mile marker	1▷
Rapids	╫
Campsite	⚠
Railroad	┼┼┼
Hiking/Bike trail	- - -
City or village	▦
Park	▬

6

Reilly Brook

BIG FORK RIVER 7
Big Falls to Gowdy Landing (17.6 miles)

This trip begins at the end of the falls where the Big Fork crashes its way through a spectacular display of waterpower, dropping 60 feet in a quarter mile. The push from the falls is still noticeable at the start of the journey. For the first 2 miles of the trip, easy Class I rapids and boulders make the paddling entertaining, even at low water levels. After that, the Big Fork smooths out for a nice quiet ride down to Ben Linn Landing. Another stretch of mild rapids a mile past Ben Linn, also manageable by beginners, livens the trip a second time. Paddlers who like to take their time can make this a two-day trip by camping at Ben Linn Landing. The first day would be 9.5 miles and the second day, 8.1 miles.

The land along this stretch of the Big Fork is almost entirely undeveloped. Long stretches of riverbank are overhung by big old white cedars, their tapered shapes a beautiful background for this very pleasant trip. Anglers will probably want to cast in the big holes below the falls for walleyes, smallmouth bass, and northerns before heading downstream. And, as on previous sections of this wilderness river, watching for wildlife makes an entertaining pastime all along this trip. The forests of Pine Island and Koochiching State Forests, through which the Big Fork flows, give paddlers a hint of what this river was like before loggers cut down the much bigger trees that stood here a century ago. A stand of big white pines at Ben Linn Landing is a reminder of these forests' grand and stately past.

The Big Falls City Campground has **camping** in town (see Big Fork 5). Three river campsites, Sturgeon River Landing at mile 4.8, Ben Linn Landing at mile 9.5, and Gowdy Campsite at mile 15.6, are more remote.

See Big Fork 5 for **canoe and kayak rental** and **shuttle service** information.

The 9-mile shuttle route runs .15 mile on Highway 71 to a left turn onto County Road 13, which quickly becomes a gravel road. Turn left at the sign for Goudy (Gowdy) Landing onto Koochiching County Unorganized Township Road 290 and follow this road to the access.

The average **gradient** is 2.0 feet per mile.

See Big Fork 6 for **water level** information.

Put in at the access off Highway 71. Turn downriver at the access sign on downstream river right; a dirt road leads to the parking area and a concrete ramp. This access is also used by anglers in small motorboats, but motor traffic on the river is very light. At any water level, you'll need to maneuver between boulders and through riffles for the first 2 miles.

Just before the wide mouth of the Sturgeon River on the left is Sturgeon River Landing, an excellent rest stop with a beautiful view downriver. Wooden steps lead up to the camping area.

With the added flow from the Sturgeon, the Big Fork now runs deep and wide. The current is quiet all the way to Ben Linn Landing. Ben Linn is on the right, just before a curve. If the sign is missing, look for the wooden steps of the landing. You may also spot a swinging rope just past the steps and be enticed to stop for a swim. The waters of the Big Fork are copper tinted but clean and safe for swimming. Don't drink the water without treating it, however. The campsite is in a large grassy area surrounded by big white pines.

A mile past Ben Linn and at the end of a wide section of the river the channel narrows; the banks rise into high bluffs, two houses appear on the right, and the Big Fork dances through easy Class I rapids. The scenic bluffs are dense with white cedars.

Gowdy campsite is on river left, 2 miles before the landing. **Take out** at the Gowdy Landing on river right, on a stretch of river that runs due east. Although there's no sign, you'll see a grassy spit and a path.

Other trips. Another access point and county campground, Keuffner's Landing, is on river right 4 miles downstream. Several other access points appear along the east side of the river before it reaches the Rainy River. It's possible to paddle almost all the way to the Rainy River, 33 miles downstream of Gowdy Landing, and take out at Highway 11, 0.5 mile before the confluence.

The Big Fork below Cody Landing.

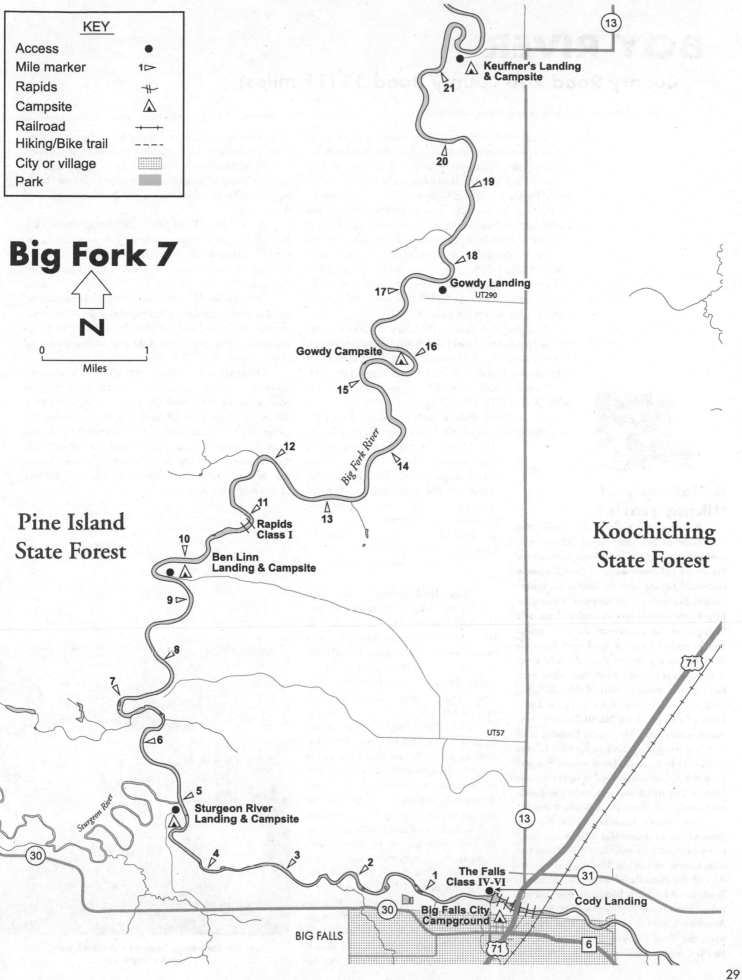

Big Fork 7

KEY

Access	●
Mile marker	1▷
Rapids	─╫─
Campsite	△
Railroad	┼┼┼
Hiking/Bike trail	- - - -
City or village	
Park	

N

0 ———— 1
Miles

Pine Island
State Forest

Koochiching
State Forest

Keuffner's Landing
& Campsite

21

20

19

18

Gowdy Landing
UT290

17

16

Gowdy Campsite

15

Big Fork River

14

12

11

Rapids
Class I

13

10

Ben Linn
Landing & Campsite

9

8

7

6

5

Sturgeon River
Landing & Campsite

Sturgeon River

4

3

2

1

The Falls
Class IV-VI

Cody Landing

Big Falls City
Campground

BIG FALLS

UT57

BOY RIVER
County Road 7 to County Road 53 (11 miles)

Paddlers who enjoy watching wildlife and birds will love this pleasant trip on the Boy. After the river leaves Inguadona Lake, almost no development touches the Boy, and the rolling, morainic land is home to a multitude of animals. You'll see bald eagles, ospreys, herons, mergansers, loons, kingfishers, otters, the ever-present beavers, and lots of turtles. The low banks are wooded, the water is clear, and the sandy bottom is dotted with mussel shells. Rotting wooden posts, all that's left of a historic lumber company splash dam, cross the river at one point. A few riffles appear in the 2 miles before the County Road 53 bridge, but otherwise the paddling is quiet, making this a nice trip for beginning paddlers.

Camping is available at the Chippewa National Forest campground at Mabel Lake, 4 miles from the takeout. Follow County Road 53 east to Forest Road 2104. Turn right and travel south to the campground sign on the right.

Canoe rentals are available from Thompson Rent-All in Walker (218-547-1252).

The 16.5-mile **shuttle route** from Inguadona Lake goes west on County Road 7 to Highway 84 at Longville. Take Highway 84 north to Highway 200. Take Highway 200 east to County Road 53 (Tobique Road). Turn left on this gravel road and head north and then east at the curve; cross the river, and park along the north side of County Road 53, where the shoulder is drier. In a wet spring, this road can be muddy and difficult.

The average **gradient** is 0.7 foot per mile.

Water level readings are not available for the Boy, but the river maintains its water level most of the summer. In late summer, however, when the wild rice is ripe, the river channel nearly disappears in the rice beds. The best time to paddle the Boy is May through July. On a windy day, crossing Inguadona Lake may be difficult.

The County Road 7 bridge over Inguadona Lake Narrows leads to the Anchorage Inn. The inn charges a fee for motorboats to launch there, but if you ask permission to use the launch area, the fee will probably be waived. You can also put in at the County Road 129 bridge over Trelipe Creek and paddle .9 mile to the lake. From the **put-in** or the mouth of the creek .25 mile farther north on the east shore, it's a 2-mile paddle to the north end of the lake. It's hard to see where the channel leaves the lake until you're almost there, but look to the right of the cluster of houses at the end of the lake. The middle of the marshy area is where this segment of the Boy begins,

wide and weedy at first and then more defined, winding first right and then left as the flow gradually forms a river.

Marshy banks and rushes, cattails, lily pads, and river grasses growing in the shallow channel provide a nice hunting ground for great blue herons, which are common along this stretch.

At mile 6.7, the Highway 200 bridge crosses the Boy, offering an alternate access point or a rest stop at the sandy landing on downstream river right. The North Country National Scenic Trail (see sidebar) crosses the Boy at this bridge.

Between the Highway 200 bridge and the takeout, the Boy speeds up a bit. Paddling through two stretches of gentle riffles and dodging some boulders is a nice conclusion to a very pretty trip. **Take out** on upstream right at the County Road 53 bridge.

Other trips: For a longer trip on the Boy, continue downriver to Boy Lake and head north across the east edge of the bay to the outlet for the Boy. Paddle to a takeout on upstream river left at a snowmobile bridge that crosses the river at the end of 24th Avenue NE. The last few miles of the route are through wide beds of wild rice, which become so dense in midsummer that the channel may be only a few feet wide in spots. The total distance of this trip is 8.8 miles.

A Network of Hiking Trails

A wonderful hiking trail crosses the Boy River at the State Road 200 bridge, making it possible for hikers to traverse the entire southern edge of the Chippewa National Forest. Scenic and well maintained, the trail winds westward from the Boy River to the geologically dramatic Shingobee Recreational Area 5 miles southwest of Walker and east through flatter country to the Cass County line. A wilderness route past the lakes and through the forested hills of this glaciated land, this trail is one of the completed sections of the planned North Country National Scenic Trail. The North Country Trail is a big project. When complete, hikers will be able to walk from where it intersects the Appalachian Trail in upstate New York 3,200 miles west to meet the Lewis and Clark Trail in western North Dakota.

The North Country Trail travels through some beautiful wilderness sections of the Chippewa National Forest. It also intersects with a 27-mile paved section of the Heartland State Recreational Trail, used by both bicyclists and hikers, which runs from Walker to Park Rapids. Another blacktop bicycling and hiking trail, the Paul Bunyan Trail, crosses the North Country Trail southeast of Walker.

Cedar pilings from an old splash dam on the Boy River.

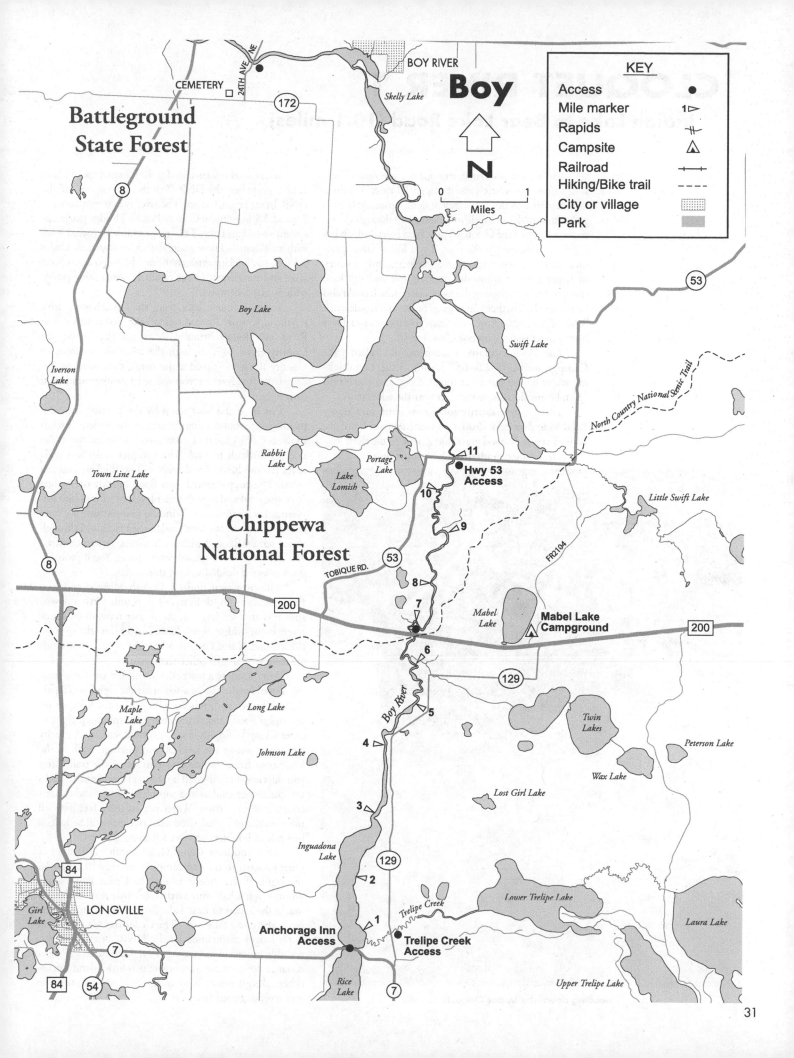

KEY

Access   ●
Mile marker   1▷
Rapids
Campsite   △
Railroad
Hiking/Bike trail
City or village
Park

Boy

↑
N

0   1
Miles

BOY RIVER

Skelly Lake

**Battleground
State Forest**

172

8

53

Boy Lake

Swift Lake

*Iverson
Lake*

Town Line Lake

*Rabbit
Lake*

*Lake
Lomish*

*Portage
Lake*

North Country National Scenic Trail

11
● **Hwy 53
Access**

10

**Chippewa
National Forest**

8

9

53

TOBIQUE RD.

FR2104

Little Swift Lake

200

8

*Mabel
Lake*

7

**Mabel Lake
Campground** △

200

6

129

*Maple
Lake*

Long Lake

Johnson Lake

*Twin
Lakes*

Peterson Lake

5

Boy River

4

Wax Lake

3

Lost Girl Lake

84

*Inguadona
Lake*

129

2

Lower Trelipe Lake

Trelipe Creek

LONGVILLE

1

**Anchorage Inn
Access** ●

● **Trelipe Creek
Access**

Laura Lake

*Girl
Lake*

7

84   54

*Rice
Lake*

7

Upper Trelipe Lake

CEMETERY

24TH AVE. NE

CLOQUET RIVER 1
Indian Lake to Bear Lake Road (10.1 miles)

For a great wilderness trip down a top-notch Class I–III whitewater river, choose the Upper Cloquet. The three trips described in this book may be done separately, but together they make an excellent camping trip through the remote country of the Cloquet Valley State Forest, which has DNR campsites along the river. If you like to cover more miles each day, you could do the whole 33.5-mile journey to Island Lake in a two-day camping trip and still have enough time for scouting the rapids, all of which could also be portaged. Whether you portage or run the rapids, pack lightly if you're camping. This first segment takes you down mostly quiet water, with one Class II rapids.

The DNR operates a campground, Indian Lake **Campground** (218-226-6377), with 25 sites and drinking water by the put-in at Indian Lake, and you'll find several campsites along the river near the takeout.

The 8.6-mile **shuttle route** runs south on County Road 44 to Bear Lake Road, then west (right) on Bear Lake Road, a relatively good gravel forest road, to the river.

The average **gradient** is 2.7 feet per mile.

Heading down the Upper Cloquet.

Water level information for the Cloquet above Island Lake is posted on the DNR Web site, or you can call the DNR Information Center. The river is best run between 3.5 and 5.5 feet on the County Road 44 bridge gauge upstream of Indian Lake. This gauge will be replaced soon with an automated flow gauge farther downstream. Under 3.5 feet, you'll scrape through the rapids; over 6 feet is flood stage and the current in the rapids becomes quite pushy, with 3- to 4-foot waves.

To reach Indian Lake from the Duluth area, drive north on County Road 4 (Rice Lake Road) to County Road 547 (Kelsey Brimson Road, gravel). Go east on County Road 547, through the town of Brimson, to County Road 44 (paved along here), then south to Indian Lake Road, where you will see a campground sign; turn right.

Put in at the boat ramp by the parking area and paddle west around a marshy area to the outlet, which is to the left of a cluster of cabins. At low water, the outlet may be difficult to find. The Cloquet is 40 feet wide here, its low banks lined with willow thickets and red osiers. The copper-tinted river flows quickly over a bed of coarse sand and at high water levels overflows into numerous backwater areas. Winding and narrow, the river runs past high banks with eroded sand faces and through varied terrain forested with birch, aspen, various conifers, and a few noble old-growth white pines. You'll probably meet assorted deadfalls along this stretch.

The river runs under a Duluth Missabe and Iron Range Railway trestle at mile 1.3. A mile farther downstream is another access at the timber remains of a now nonexistent bridge; South Loop Road meets the river on the left and North Loop Road on the right. These roads are rougher than the other access roads.

After running a few riffles in shallow areas and passing a boulder the size of a sedan on the right, you'll pass the confluence with the West Branch of the Cloquet on the right. Soon after that, the river turns sharp right to enter Camp G Rapids, a Class II boulder bed. A nearby landowner mows the level 60-rod **portage trail** on the left. Scout from the top and bottom of the trail. After you skirt another car-sized boulder on river left that kicks the current around at the top of the drop, the clearest course is left of center. Waves two to three feet high fill the rapids, and a good-sized dead tree may still be lodged in a pile of boulders on river left at the bottom.

After you leave Camp G, it's another 3.1 miles of quiet Cloquet to the first campsite, marked by a sign on the right. If that one is taken, the Cedar Bay Campground sign a half mile farther downstream on the left marks the access to Bear Lake Road, which parallels the river where you **take out**. (The Cedar Bay Campground is no longer maintained by the DNR, but camping is possible in several areas along Bear Lake Road.) A short distance downstream, just before two little islands, is another takeout point. Next to the road are an outhouse and several cleared areas.

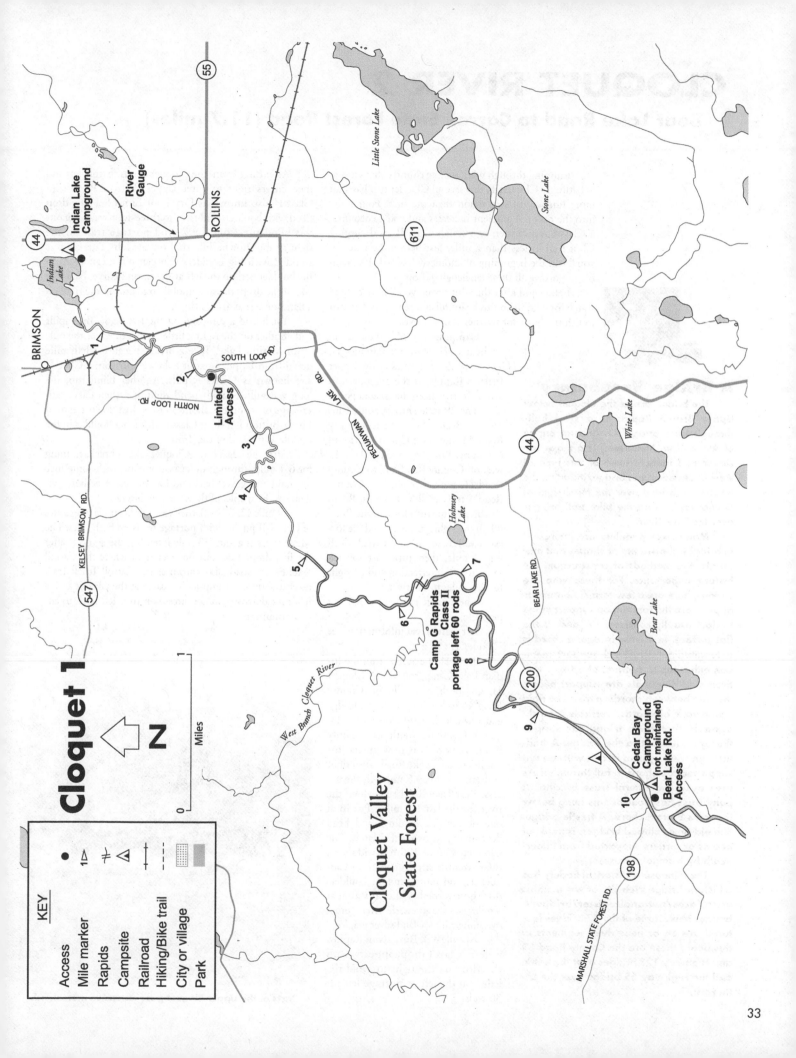

Cloquet 1

N

KEY

- Access ●
- Mile marker 1△
- Rapids ≠
- Campsite △
- Railroad ┼
- Hiking/Bike trail ┄
- City or village ▦
- Park ▨

Miles
0 1

BRIMSON

Indian Lake Campground

River Gauge

ROLLINS

Indian Lake

Little Stone Lake

Stone Lake

611

44

1

SOUTH LOOP RD.

NORTH LOOP RD.

2

Limited Access

3

KELSEY BRIMSON RD.

547

4

PEQUAYWAN LAKE RD.

White Lake

44

Holmsey Lake

5

West Branch Cloquet River

6

Camp G Rapids Class II portage left 60 rods

7

8

BEAR LAKE RD.

Cloquet Valley State Forest

9

200

Bear Lake

Cedar Bay Campground (not maintained)

Bear Lake Rd. Access

10

MARSHALL STATE FOREST RD.

198

CLOQUET RIVER 2
Bear Lake Road to Carroll State Forest Road (11.7 miles)

Running through wild, remote country that's just as beautiful as Cloquet 1, this second Cloquet trip has a lot more fun whitewater action than the first. Four miles into the run, the gradient increases and you'll encounter a Class I rapid, then two tough Class IIs and another Class I all in less than a mile. Just before the takeout, you'll run the beginning of another Class I-II. It's possible to portage all these challenging drops.

Before and after the whitewater, you'll have time to watch for wildlife in this beautiful and remote country or to fish the holes for northerns or walleyes.

Camping is possible at the put-in on Bear Lake Road (see Cloquet 1). There are also campsites below Upper Britton Rapids, at the takeout, and across the river from the takeout point.

The 29-mile **shuttle route** runs east on Bear Lake Road to County Road 44, north on County Road 44 to County Road 547, west and southwest on County Road 547 to County Road 4 (paved), then south on County Road 4 to Carroll State Forest Road. (If you pass the turn for County Road 49 on the right, you've missed the forest road.) Take the forest road south for .8 mile, then turn east for 1.8 miles to a T intersection and go right for 2.6 miles to the river.

The average **gradient** is 3.8 feet per mile.

For **water level** information, see Cloquet 1.

To reach the access from the Indian Lake Campground (see Cloquet 1), go south 1.2 miles on County Road 44 to Rollins. (There's a bridge gauge where the road crosses the Cloquet.) Continue south on County Road 44, which is now gravel, for 4 miles to Bear Lake Road. Turn right and go west for 3.5 miles to the access. Bear Lake Road runs along the river for the last 1.7 miles. **Put in** at one of the dirt landings and head downriver past two little islands. The Cloquet is 80 to 100 feet wide now, the current is stronger than on Cloquet 1, and more random boulders dot the riverbed. Quiet for almost 4 miles past the access, the river is often overhung with lowland silver maples.

At mile 4.3, Buzz Ryan Rapids, a short Class I drop, appears. Run this drop on the right to avoid the ledge on the left or **portage** left for 30 rods.

After Buzz Ryan, the Cloquet bends sharply left and then curves right to enter Upper Britton Rapids (a Class II also known as Dry Foot Brown), a long drop filled with boulders and two- to three-foot waves. Scout this blind run from the 73-rod **portage trail** on the right or the snowmobile trail on the left. This drop is studded with big boulders that can pin a canoe; avoid the boulder bed on the left at the second curve. Near the end of the drop, the snowmobile trail crosses the river on a handsome steel truss bridge.

You'll find a campsite on the left below the rapids and another on the right a little farther down at the outlet of Marion Lake. Take a breath because a half mile down from Upper Britton is Lower Britton, a Class II also known as Dana's Rapids. Another blind run, the long wave-filled rapids bend right and then curve left. **Portage** or scout left, about 36 rods. Just downstream of Lower Britton is a short Class I with a big boulder in the middle at the end of the drop.

After the Class I, the Cloquet takes a break, running for 6.4 miles through quiet bottomland with some nice red sand and gravel bars and lots of beaver activity evident on the trunks of the shoreline birches.

At mile 11.4, Dr. Barney's Rapids begins, a long series of Class I-II pitches with **portage trails** on both sides. The whole series is about .75 mile long, but the access is after the first drop. **Take out** on river right where the Carroll State Forest Road, also known as the Carroll Truck Trail, meets the river. A campsite is located at the takeout and, a half mile downstream, a staircase on river left leads to another campsite.

A Bridge Vocabulary

The bridge across the Cloquet below Upper Britton Rapids is a steel half-through truss bridge. Continental Bridge of Alexandria, Minnesota, is a major designer and manufacturer of this type of steel truss pedestrian bridge, including the pedestrian bridge over the Mississippi at Grand Rapids and the bike trail bridges over the Pine River.

Many river paddlers are interested in bridges: the variety of shapes and materials, the methods of construction, the historic importance. For those who are curious, here are a few terms: Abutments or piers are the foundation support of the bridge, usually concrete. The deck is the flat surface. In a truss bridge, a chord is a longitudinal structural support member, either top or bottom, of a truss; verticals and diagonals are support beams that run between chords; a truss is a rigid framework of chords, verticals, and diagonals that form triangular shapes that give support to the bridge. A half-through truss system is one with an unsupported top chord; a full-through truss uses overhead lateral truss bracing. A pony truss has floor beams hung below the truss bottom chord. A trestle bridge, like old-time railroad bridges, is made of beams or girders supported from underneath by triangular trusses.

The Minnesota Historical Society has a historic bridge Web site at www.mnhs.org/places/nationalregister/bridges/bridges.html. Three of the 27 bridges featured are on or near river segments in this book; these are the County Road 33 and Highway 123 bridges over the Kettle and the Highway 65 bridge over the Little Fork.

Parts of the Upper Cloquet pass extensive marshland.

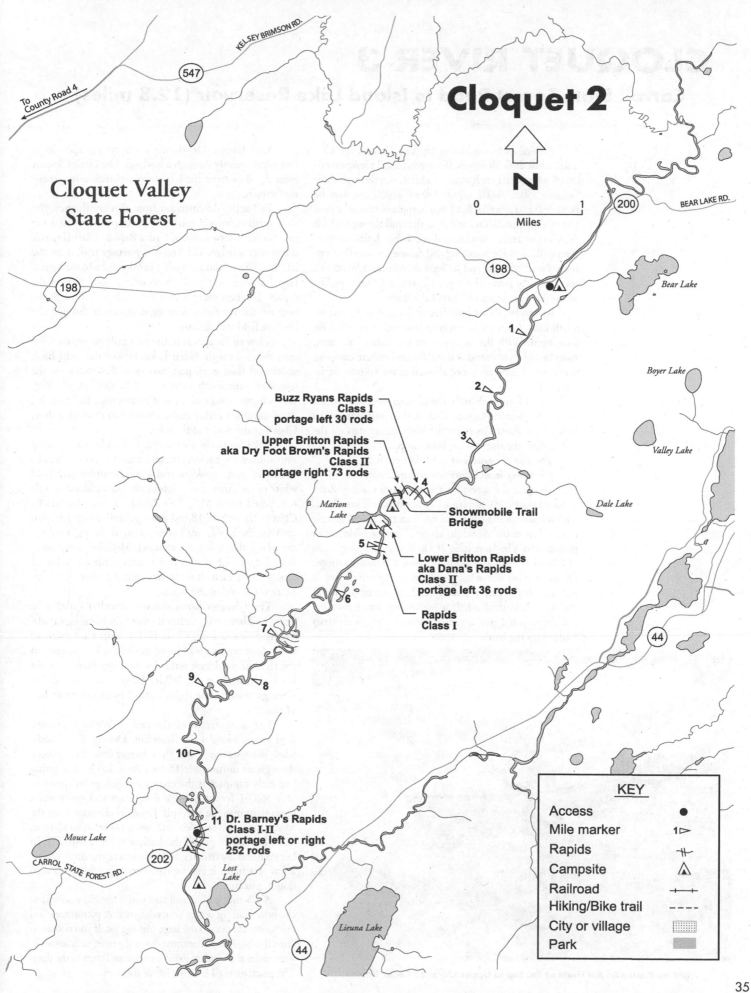

Cloquet 2

N

0   1
Miles

Cloquet Valley State Forest

KEL-SEY BRIMSON RD.

547

To County Road 4

198

200   BEAR LAKE RD.

198

Bear Lake

1

2

Boyer Lake

3

Valley Lake

Buzz Ryans Rapids
Class I
portage left 30 rods

Upper Britton Rapids
aka Dry Foot Brown's Rapids
Class II
portage right 73 rods

4

Dale Lake

Marion Lake

Snowmobile Trail Bridge

5

Lower Britton Rapids
aka Dana's Rapids
Class II
portage left 36 rods

6

Rapids
Class I

7

44

9   8

10

11   **Dr. Barney's Rapids**
Class I-II
portage left or right
252 rods

Mouse Lake

202

CARROL STATE FOREST RD.

Lost Lake

Lieuna Lake

44

KEY

Access	●
Mile marker	1▷
Rapids	╫
Campsite	⛺
Railroad	┼┼┼
Hiking/Bike trail	- - - -
City or village	▦
Park	▓

CLOQUET RIVER 3
Carroll State Forest Road to Island Lake Reservoir (12.8 miles)

A third great wilderness trip that features the Cloquet's most difficult rapids, this segment will please experienced whitewater enthusiasts. Paddlers run through three exciting Class II–III rapids (all of which can also be portaged) and several Class I rapids, some of which cannot. Other than the Alden Lake area, the land through which the Cloquet races is remote and uninhabited, and between the rapids, wildlife watching and fishing are excellent options. Northern pike and walleyes are often caught on this stretch of the river. The trip ends with a 1.5-mile paddle across the open water of Island Lake Reservoir.

Riverside DNR **campsites** are located at the put-in, a half mile downstream on river left, and at mile 7.5 on river right. With the exception of the Alden Lake area, most of the river corridor is public land, where camping is allowed. Camping is not allowed at the takeout on Island Lake.

The 11-mile **shuttle route** runs west on Carroll State Forest Road to County Road 4, then south for 6 miles to the Minnesota Power public water access sign on the left. Follow the signs to the boat ramp.

The average **gradient** is 3.5 feet per mile.

For **water level** information, see Cloquet 1.

To reach the access for this trip from County Road 4 (Rice Lake Road), turn east on Carroll State Forest Road, which leads to the river and two campsites (see shuttle route). **Put in** on river right at one of two possible put-in points. You'll be launching at Dr. Barney's, a long series of Class I-II boulders and waves with five distinct drops. Depending on where you put in, you may run all five or just four. If you prefer, **portage** 252 rods on either side of the river. Less than a half mile downstream, before the last drop, you'll pass a campsite on the left, with stairs leading up the bank.

After leaving Dr. Barney's, the river settles down and winds quietly through a lowland. The Little Cloquet joins the flow from the left along a particularly serpentine stretch.

Two miles downstream from this confluence, the river turns right and you'll see the horizon line and the two- to three-foot waves of Cedar Rapids, Class II+, as it drops over a ledge. The 160-rod **portage trail** is on the left, but scout from the rather brushy right bank; several large boulders next to the bank offer a good view of the rapids. The best route is over the ledge and through the hole on the far right, then right of center through the boulder field that follows.

A few riffles appear in the next mile before the Cloquet flows through Alden Lake. Follow the right bank south and then west, past two areas that widen on the left; then turn south again to paddle through the lake, which features some of the first houses since Indian Lake. After skirting a bed of rushes, you'll run through a short Class I at the outlet of the lake.

The Cloquet is 200 to 300 feet wide now, flowing into numerous backwaters and around several islands. You'll see more conifers and some beautiful stands of white pines. After some high bluffs and an island at mile 8.8, you'll reach McCabe's Rapids, a short but tricky Class II-III with an 18-rod **portage trail** on the left. You can't see the rapids until you're around the right side of the island that splits the channel. McCabe's drops over three ledges with chutes that require some quick lateral moves; enter each chute at an angle. Another island appears at the end of the rapids.

The Cloquet flows through another quiet mile and a half before it reaches its most challenging rapids. White Sides, a long Class II–III drop with two- to three-foot waves and lots of boulders, is best run on the right at moderate water levels. Regardless of water level, definitely scout White Sides from the 50-rod **portage trail** on the right. Lots of boulders mean lots of choices.

Just downstream of the end of White Sides, the river enters Island Lake Reservoir. During dry periods, when the reservoir is low, the Cloquet flows over a ledge through an unrunnable 15-foot drop. In the late spring and early summer, if the reservoir is full, at an elevation of 1,368.61 feet, the ledge disappears and quiet water flows right into the reservoir. For daily elevations, see the Minnesota Power Web site www.shorelandtraditions.com/levels.htm or call the hotline (218-720-2777). In between those extremes, at levels where the drop is only a few feet high, it can be run. Scout carefully and if in doubt, **portage**.

A 1.5-mile paddle will take you across the reservoir to the boat landing where you **take out**. A picnic area and outhouses are next to the large parking lot. If you choose to cross this big lake to continue down the river, paddle southwest under the County Road 4 bridge and then to the dam. The **portage trail** is to the left of the dam.

Right on course on the chute at the top of Upper Cloquet's Cedar Rapids.

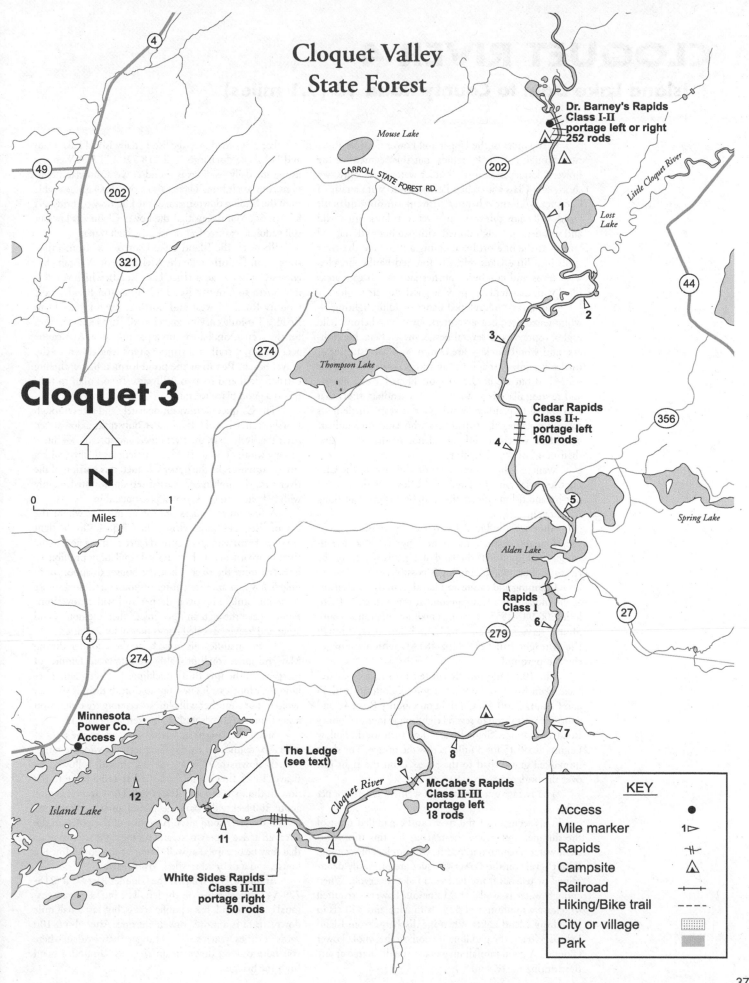

Cloquet Valley
State Forest

Mouse Lake

CARROLL STATE FOREST RD.

Dr. Barney's Rapids
Class I-II
portage left or right
252 rods

Lost
Lake

Little Cloquet River

Cloquet 3

N

0 ———— 1
Miles

Thompson Lake

Cedar Rapids
Class II+
portage left
160 rods

Spring Lake

Alden Lake

Rapids
Class I

Minnesota
Power Co.
Access

The Ledge
(see text)

Cloquet River

McCabe's Rapids
Class II-III
portage left
18 rods

Island Lake

White Sides Rapids
Class II-III
portage right
50 rods

KEY	
Access	●
Mile marker	1▷
Rapids	╫
Campsite	△
Railroad	┼─┼
Hiking/Bike trail	----
City or village	▦
Park	▨

CLOQUET RIVER 4
Island Lake Dam to County Road 15 (9.1 miles)

Many miles of the Upper and Lower Cloquet River run through fast, rocky rapids, but this segment of the Lower Cloquet is almost all quiet water, with only two short, easy Class I stretches. Paddlers who want a taste of Cloquet wilderness beauty without running difficult rapids will enjoy this trip. The river corridor is often wild and wooded, although dotted with patches of developed land—at the one bridge crossing and where the river spills into little lakes. Heavily forested banks threaded with ferns and cranberry bushes and low boggy areas filled with marsh plants provide good wildlife habitat.

Along the undeveloped banks, wildlife sightings—white-tailed deer, beavers, otters, great blue herons, bald eagles, ospreys (and several nests), mergansers, kingfishers, and wood ducks—are common. Three species of turtles—painted, snapping, and wood—also live in the watershed but are harder to spot. Their favored habitat and nesting place is a sandbank or a sandbar, spots that also appeal to paddlers wanting a rest stop. Turtle nests are easily damaged, so paddlers who land on sandbars should be watchful and careful not to disturb turtles, their nests, or their hatchlings.

Walleye fishing is excellent on this part of the Cloquet, especially in the large pool below the dam at the put-in, and fishing for smallmouth bass is good all along this stretch.

Although the DNR has not yet established campsites along this segment, they're working to do that. Meanwhile, more than half the land along this stretch of the river is public, where camping is possible.

Camping and **canoe and kayak rentals** are available at the Indian Point Campground at the west end of Duluth (800-982-2453; www.indianpointcampground.com). Shuttle service for these rentals can be arranged through the Munger Inn (218-624-4814), which manages the campground.

The 10.5-mile **shuttle route** runs south on Island Lake Dam Road to the intersection of County Road 48 and County Road 43. Go right on County Road 48 and continue west through several right-angle jogs to County Road 15 (Munger-Shaw Road), then turn south. Follow County Road 15 for 3 miles across the bridge. The short unmarked gravel road to the access is on the right just over the bridge.

The average **gradient** for this segment is 1.0 foot per mile.

This segment of the river can be paddled most of the summer, but below the takeout for this trip, sufficient water is required to paddle without lots of scraping. **Water levels** on the Lower Cloquet are primarily determined by releases from the Island Lake Reservoir. When enough water is available, Minnesota Power is required to release a minimum of 325 cfs in May and 340 cfs in June from Island Lake. When the discharge from Island Lake is 340 cfs, the paddling is good on the whole Lower Cloquet. A good rainfall may boost the discharge at any time during the season.

For a recorded message listing daily Island Lake Dam and Fish Lake discharges, call 218-720-2777. A Web site listing the daily readings is found at www.shorelandtraditions.com/levels.htm. There's also a river level gauge visible from the landing downstream at the Highway 53 bridge. A level of one foot means that the Lower Cloquet is low but still paddleable; three feet or above is high water.

To reach the Island Lake Dam access from Interstate 35 in Duluth, take the Messaba exit. Messaba becomes County Road 4 (Rice Lake Road), which you follow north to County Road 43 (Emerson Road). Take County Road 43 west and north to Island Lake Dam Road, a 1.4-mile curving gravel road. Turn left at the sign for the recreational area into a parking area. At a canoe access sign, a trail and timber steps lead down to the gravel beach. **Put in** at the pond formed below the big earthen dam and its two spillways. If you plan to fish, this is a good place to start.

The Cloquet narrows immediately and races through two short stretches of Class I water, only riffles at low water. After this lively start, the river quiets and spreads out into a varying width of 80 to 100 feet, sometimes shallow, with a steady current. Like the upper Cloquet, this portion of the river runs through nicely varied terrain, forested mainly with red pine and birch. You'll pass one cabin.

A few more houses appear at mile 1, where the County Road 48 bridge crosses the Cloquet. On the right is a small farm, with an electrified fence running next to the river, in accordance with watershed regulations prohibiting livestock from the river. Then the houses disappear until mile 5.1, when another cluster of houses and docks lines the right bank. The river, deeper and wider now, joins Hunter Lake through an open inlet. Then the houses end again and heavily wooded banks prevail for 2 miles.

If you paddle this stretch of the Cloquet during May and June, you'll probably see numerous families of mergansers, the tiny fluffy ducklings bobbling along behind their mothers. It's best not to disturb them if you can avoid it, but a mother will almost certainly try to lure you away from the babies with a "broken wing" act.

Side Lake, ringed by houses, appears on the right at mile 7.3, connected to the Cloquet by a wide opening. Shortly downstream is a wide marshland, followed by Beaver River, flowing in from the left and adding to the flow (it drains Fish Lake Reservoir). The Cloquet is now about 300 feet wide: dark, deep, and quiet. A power line crosses the river soon after. Atop one of the poles on the left is an active osprey nest, and on the right are two nests that may be occupied as well. Just past the power line is a house, and a railroad trestle is visible ahead.

At mile 8.5, you'll pass the Cloquet River Inn (218-729-5427) boat ramp on the left. The inn, a private seasonal campground, has a public access, but just a half mile downstream is a more convenient one. After about 100 yards of riffles, you'll see the Munger Shaw bridge, where you **take out** on downstream river left around a bend from the bridge.

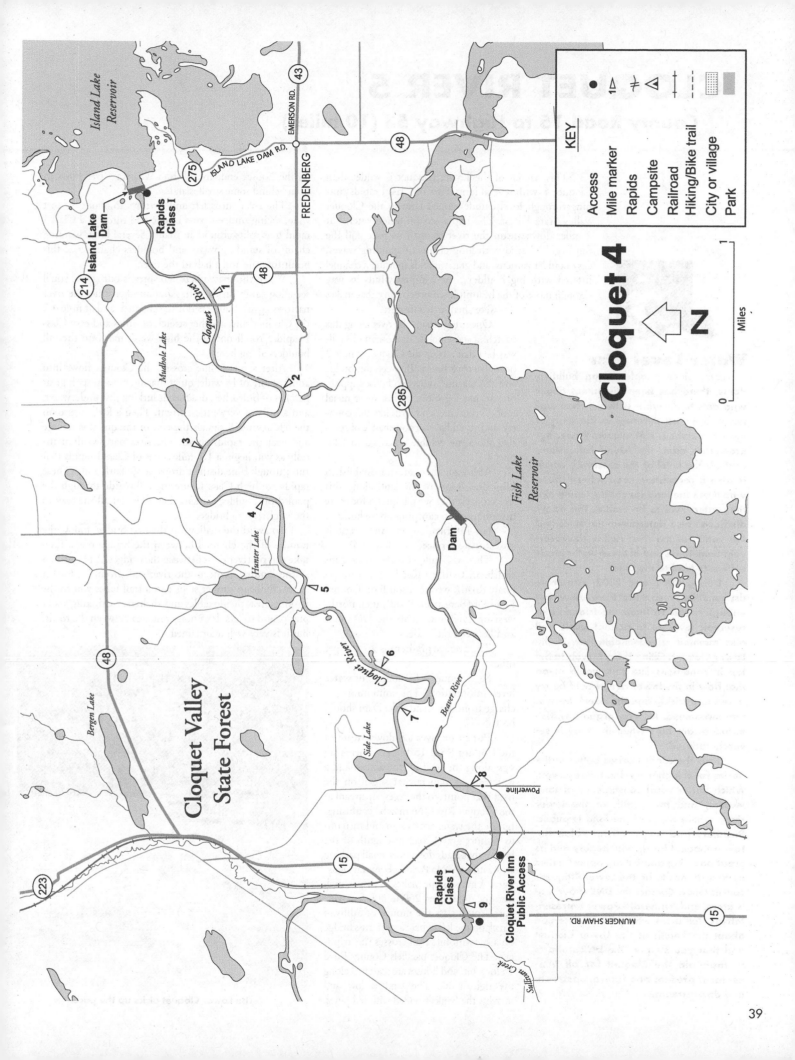

Cloquet Valley State Forest

Cloquet 4

KEY

- Access ●
- Mile marker 1△
- Rapids ≠
- Campsite △
- Railroad ┼┼
- Hiking/Bike trail ┊┊┊
- City or village ▦
- Park ▨

N

Miles
0 1

Island Lake Reservoir

Island Lake Dam

Rapids Class I

Emerson Rd.

Fredenberg

Island Lake Dam Rd.

Mudhole Lake

Cloquet River

Hunter Lake

Fish Lake Reservoir

Dam

Bergen Lake

Side Lake

Cloquet River

Beaver River

Powerline

Rapids Class I

Cloquet River Inn Public Access

Munger Shaw Rd.

Sullivan Creek

CLOQUET RIVER 5
County Road 15 to Highway 53 (10 miles)

Water Level War

Ever since people began building dams, there has been discontent about who gets to do what with the river water, and it's no different in the Cloquet River watershed. A Minnesota Power hydroelectric dam, the Island Lake Dam, controls the level of the reservoir, which is also a recreation area where those who lease the land for cabins would like the water level to be stable. The dam's discharge also determines the level and the health of the river below the reservoir. Sometimes one of these water levels suffers to tend to the other.

During 2002 and 2003, extremely dry conditions meant that there just wasn't enough water to keep the Island Lake reservoir level up to normal levels and also maintain a reasonable flow in the Lower Cloquet. Filling the reservoir to the top in conditions like this would mean that flow in the lower river would be reduced to a trickle and the river's ecosystem threatened. All river organisms, fish included, are hurt when the flow is severely reduced.

Thus the conflict arises between the desire for a higher level in the reservoir, which has a vocal constituency of land leasers, and the health of the lower river, where much of the land is public. Paddlers and anglers who value the Lower Cloquet for its wild beauty and its great paddling and fishing opportunities have a chance to be the Lower Cloquet's constituency. Contact the DNR, your legislators, and Minnesota Power representatives. Tell them why you're concerned about the health of the Lower Cloquet and that you support the DNR's efforts to maintain the Cloquet for all Minnesotans, present and future, upstream and downstream.

This stretch of the Lower Cloquet is wilder than Cloquet 4, with several long series of Class I rapids running through lovely, undeveloped land in the Cloquet Valley State Forest. The trip starts on quiet water, but 2 miles downstream the river changes its pace and the fun begins. Laced with long chains of standing waves, easy boulder gardens, and grassy islands splitting a channel littered with big boulders, the Cloquet winds its way through more of the beautiful, remote country that makes this watershed such a treasure.

One bridge spans the river along this stretch: a snowmobile trail on an old railway bed that crosses the Cloquet at mile 2 on a steel truss bridge. Between this bridge and the takeout, only two houses appear, one an old log cabin with a sheet metal roof. The animals and birds like this country, and you'll have a good chance of spotting the same wildlife described in Cloquet 4.

Although there are no established campsites, most of the land along this stretch is public. See Cloquet 4 for more information on **camping** opportunities.

For information on **canoe rentals and shuttle service**, see Cloquet 4.

The 10.7-mile **shuttle route** runs south on County Road 15 (Munger-Shaw Road), west and south on County Road 94 (Bergstrom Road), then northwest on Highway 53 to the DOT rest area between the bridges.

The average **gradient** is 3.7 feet per mile.

See Cloquet 4 for sources of **water level** information. The minimum discharge from the Island Lake Dam should be 165 cfs.

Put in on river left downstream of the County Road 15 bridge. There's no sign along the road for the access, and a water access sign farther south on the road that points to the access upstream at the Cloquet River Inn may be confusing. Ignore the water access sign and turn onto a short gravel road just south of the bridge that leads down to a small parking area with two "No Parking Between Signs" signs. A grassy slope makes an easy launch into the quiet river, 200 to 300 feet wide here. You'll pass the mouth of Sullivan Creek on the left, where a steel truss bridge on a snowmobile trail crosses this tributary. The Cloquet parallels County Road 15 for a bit, and houses are scattered along the right bank. The land is low and marshy, the banks wooded with red pines.

As the houses end, the Us-Kab-Wan-Ka River flows in from behind some small islands.

The river turns left and narrows to about 80 feet wide, racing under a truss bridge and through a Class I rapid that splits around an island. Several long, winding chains of standing waves and boulders characterize this beautiful mile and a half of the river.

When the river quiets and spreads out again, you'll see a log cabin on the left. After another mile, the river narrows again, boulders dot the channel, and at mile 4.2 the Cloquet runs another stretch of riffles and easy Class I rapids. You'll notice the high-water mark on the tall boulders along here.

After a power line crosses, the Cloquet flows into another one of its wide, quiet marshy moods, with great patches of bulrushes, deadheads lurking just underwater, and a mile of very little current. Then a little house on the left at mile 8 signals the end of the quiet; you'll see and hear the rapids ahead. The river narrows dramatically as you begin a 1.7-mile series of Class I rapids that run through nine distinct drops, some fairly long. These rapids are high Class I, offering a fun ride through the pool-drop boulder gardens that take you all the way to the Highway 53 bridge.

To avoid the shallows at the first bridge, follow the middle of the channel between the bridge piers, then **take out** on river right between the bridges. A plastic mat at the landing protects the riverbank from erosion. A short climb up timber steps and a trail takes you to the parking area, picnic tables and shelters, a drinking water pump, and toilets. It's a noisy rest area between the roads, but it is very well maintained.

The Lower Cloquet picks up the pace.

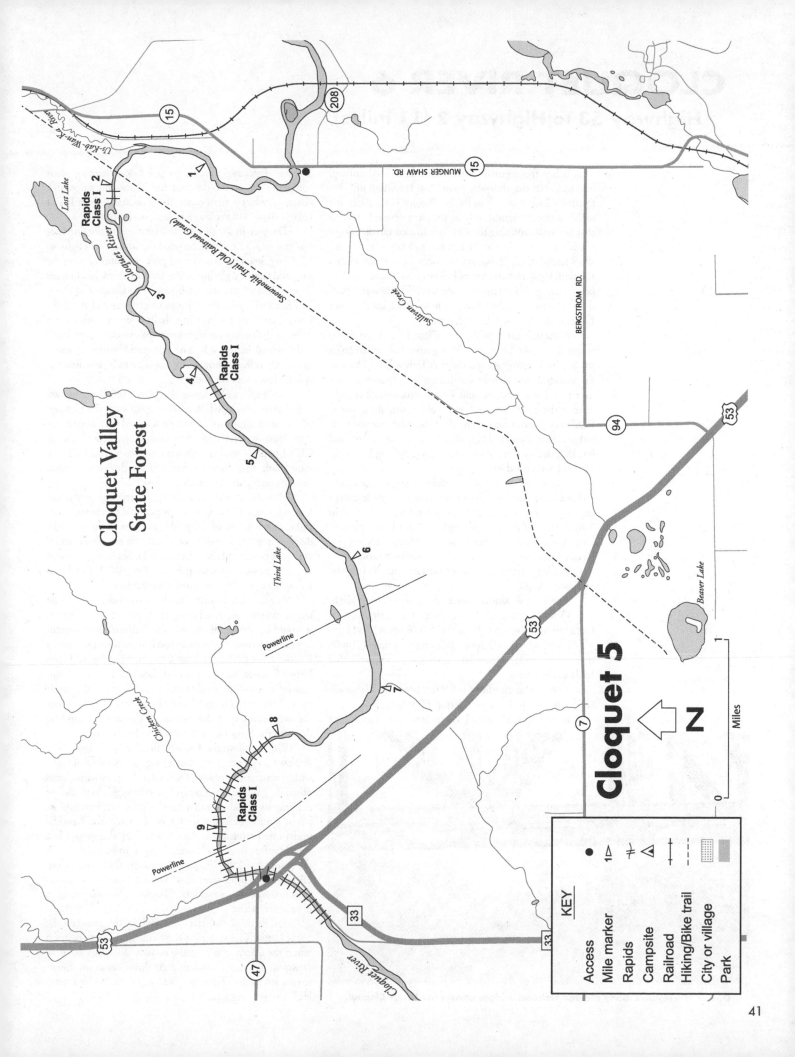

Cloquet Valley
State Forest

Cloquet 5

N

Miles

0   1

KEY

- Access
- 1△ Mile marker
- ≠ Rapids
- △ Campsite
- ┼ Railroad
- --- Hiking/Bike trail
- ▦ City or village
- ▨ Park

CLOQUET RIVER 6
Highway 53 to Highway 2 (11 miles)

When this segment of the Cloquet River is running, it's a really fun ride down frequent Class I rapids. A mile before the Cloquet races into the broad Saint Louis River, the rapids intensify significantly as the river drops 20 feet in that last mile, running through continuous rapids until it reaches the Saint Louis. At low to moderate water levels, this stretch is Class II, but at high water it could rate a Class II+, with big waves and lots of boulders that could pin a canoe, making this a trip for experienced whitewater paddlers. The route to the takeout, a mile farther on the Saint Louis, is down more Class I–II rapids.

Although three bridges, a railroad trestle, and two power lines cross the river in this segment, only about seven small cabins are visible, and the river feels wild and beautiful. Winding past heavily wooded banks, its waters chatter over gravel bars and are split by numerous small islands. Even in the quiet sections, huge boulders stud the channel. Paddlers will almost certainly see wildlife: beavers and their lodges, deer, ospreys, diving mergansers, blue herons, and hawks, possibly a red-shouldered hawk. Fishing for smallmouth bass is good in the pools.

Although there are no established campsites or campgrounds along this stretch of the Cloquet, riverside **camping** is possible on the state forestland that lines about 8 river miles of the Cloquet and the Saint Louis, particularly downstream of County Road 694. In addition, Jay Cooke State Park is about 22 miles from the takeout.

For information on **canoe rentals** and **shuttle service**, see Cloquet 4.

The 14-mile **shuttle route** takes you south on Highway 53 for .1 mile, where you merge onto Highway 33. Go south on Highway 33 (a divided highway) to Highway 2, and west on Highway 2 to a turnoff that is .1 mile before the bridge. Turn left onto the gravel road that leads to the access.

The average **gradient** is 6.9 feet per mile. The gradient for the last mile on the Cloquet is 20 fpm.

For sources of **water level** information, see Cloquet

4. If the Highway 53 bridge gauge is below one foot when you get to the access, the river will be too low to paddle; above three feet is high water. If the discharge from Island Lake is above 340 cfs, you'll have a good paddle.

The **put-in** for this trip is a very well maintained access at the DOT rest area between the bridges on Highway 53. Carry down the steep gravel path and some steps to the river and launch right into riffles that become Class I rapids downstream of the second bridge. The Cloquet is about 100 feet wide, with the copper-colored water of the Saint Louis basin. Its fast-moving shallow water runs over a gravel bed, flowing between low banks wooded with birch and lowland hardwoods. The easy rapid, which is sometimes only riffles, continues for almost a mile downstream. A few islands vary the route.

You'll spot a few cabins along here, but the banks are only lightly developed. After the rapids end, the Cloquet widens for a bit, its streambed punctuated with huge boulders. Then the river narrows again and runs through a short Class I boulder garden with standing waves, followed by a long pool, and then another Class I drop that curves through an S curve and ends at an island.

Shortly after that, at mile 3.2, the County Road 8 bridge crosses, where access is possible on downstream right. Downstream of the bridge the Cloquet flows wide, deep, and quiet. The deciduous trees are now interspersed with jack pines, and the land feels wild. Shallow gravel bars appear occasionally, with the attendant riffles. You'll pass fern-covered islands and marshy lowlands.

At mile 5.4, County Road 7 crosses the river on an old-fashioned iron truss bridge; don't plan on access here as it would be quite difficult. Another half mile downstream is a railroad trestle with dramatic brownstone piers and a bottom truss that carries the Duluth, Missabe, and Iron Range Railway line that runs between Duluth and Mountain Iron. Access is possible on upstream left of the trestle by walking down from County Road 694, which crosses the river immediately downstream of the trestle. From here down to the Saint Louis the shoreline land is public.

Riffles follow the County Road 694 bridge as the shallow Cloquet runs through a long, straight field of huge, widely scattered boulders. Then Class I rapids with chains of standing waves develop as it flows through a long, almost continuous boulder garden laced with gravel bars and islands, a really beautiful stretch of the river. You'll paddle under one power line at mile 6.9 and another power line shortly before the Class II action begins. In its rush to reach the Saint Louis, the Cloquet expends its final burst of energy: a mile-long stretch of solid Class II-II+ rapids with two-foot waves and lots of boulders. You may scrape a little at low water.

Paddle through Class I–II rapids by the island on the Saint Louis. The water on the Saint Louis may be high when the Cloquet is not; the relative difficulty of these rapids would vary accordingly. At the **takeout** on downstream left at the Highway 2 bridge, a concrete boat ramp leads to a parking area.

One of Minnesota's many old iron railroad bridges crosses the Lower Cloquet.

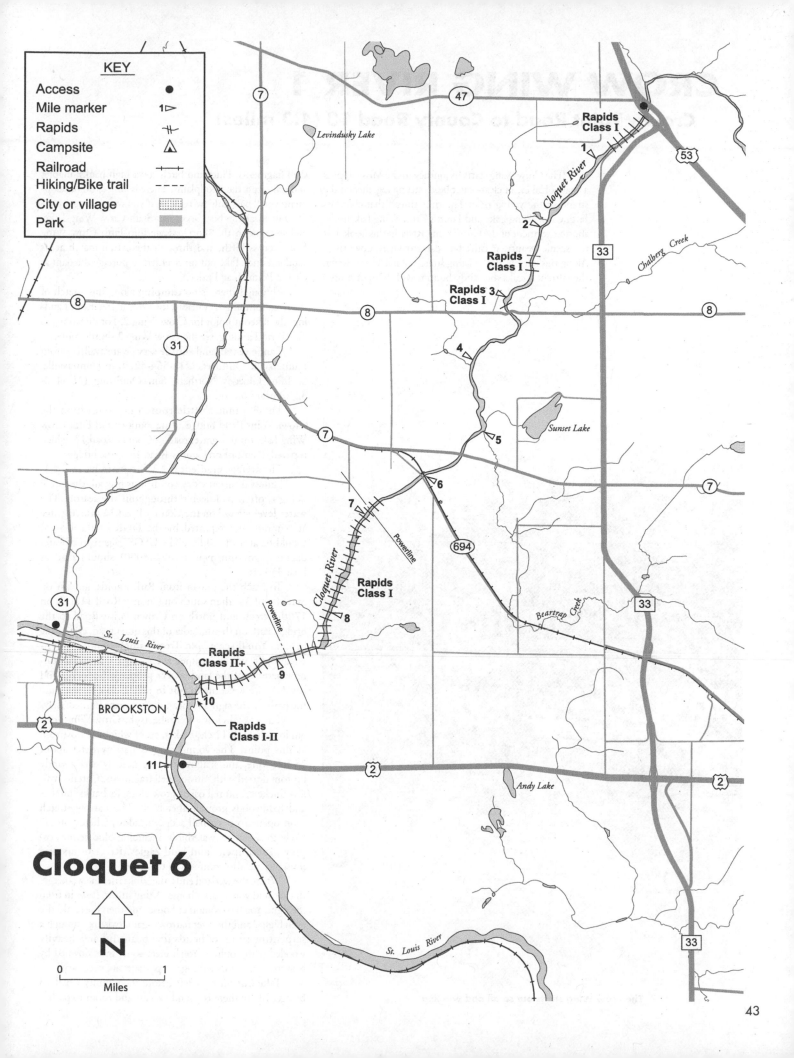

KEY

Access ●
Mile marker 1▷
Rapids ⫢
Campsite △
Railroad ┼┼
Hiking/Bike trail - - -
City or village
Park

Levindusky Lake

Cloquet River

Rapids
Class I

1

2

Chalberg Creek

Rapids
Class I

Rapids 3
Class I

4

Sunset Lake

5

6

7

Powerline

Cloquet River

Powerline

694

Rapids
Class I

8

Beartrap Creek

Rapids
Class II+

9

10

Rapids
Class I-II

BROOKSTON

St. Louis River

11

Andy Lake

St. Louis River

Cloquet 6

N

0 ———— 1
Miles

CROW WING RIVER 1
Crown Point Road to County Road 13 (4.3 miles)

The Crow Wing starts its journey to the Mississippi as a chain of lakes, 11 clear-water beads strung together on the strand of the young river. The river thread that connects Fifth Crow Wing Lake and Fourth Crow Wing Lake is the shortest segment of the Crow Wing River in this book, but for scenic beauty, it can't be beat anywhere downriver. Along this narrow and twisting stretch of lively clear water, the current streaks the sandy bottom with lines of mussel shell fragments. Pines and birch cover high banks; maples and ash forest the floodplains. There is almost no development; you'll pass only two cabins. If you want a longer paddle, put in at the boat access on Sixth Crow Wing Lake, paddle through the short passage into Fifth Crow Wing Lake, across Fifth, and through the cattail marsh at its southern end. Take out on river left to portage the dam at Crown Point Road bridge.

Although there is no **camping** along this stretch of the river, camping is available, for a fee, at Tree Farm Landing, the takeout point for Crow Wing 2. For directions to Tree Farm Landing, see the Crow Wing 2 shuttle route.

Canoe rentals and **shuttle service** are available from Huntersville Outfitters (218-564-4279) in Huntersville, or from Gloege's Northern Sun Outfitting (218-472-3250) near Nimrod.

The 3.5-mile **shuttle route** runs south from the Crown Point Road bridge at the south end of Fifth Crow Wing Lake on this gravel road to County Road 13, which is paved, then east on County Road 13 to the bridge.

The average **gradient** is 2.3 feet per mile.

Unless unusually dry conditions prevail, the Crow Wing is often paddleable throughout the season. The **water level** viewed on the County Road 12 bridge gauge at Nimrod (not reported by the DNR or the USGS) should be at least 3.0 feet. The USGS gage report (water data.usgs.gov/mn/nwis/uv?05244000) should read at least 330 cfs.

To reach the put-in from Park Rapids, go east on State Road 34, then south on County Road 11, east on 170th Street, and north on Crown Point Road to the bridge. Park on the shoulder of this quiet road, east of the bridge. You'll see a "No Trespassing" sign on downstream left, which is aimed at keeping commercial minnow netters off the landowner's property. Canoeists and kayakers are welcome to **put in** here as long as they use the path by the sign and head downstream immediately.

The crystal-clear water reflects the Crow Wing's origin in a chain of 11 clear lakes, six of which are upstream at this point. The young river is narrow here, about 35 feet wide, and shallow, flowing quickly over a sandy bottom dotted with mussel shell fragments. Cattails, willow thickets, and red osiers grow along its banks; birches and hardwoods grow farther back. The narrow stretch soon opens into a small sedge meadow, where you are likely to see many waterbirds, including blue herons, ospreys, sandpipers, and bald eagles. River otters and muskrats are also common in the river.

Where the wetland ends, the banks rise, the woods get thicker, and you'll pass a house. A tiny stream flows in from the right. You'll pass another house, and then the banks rise even higher and the river narrows again, twisting through a serpentine series of bends in a beautiful area heavily wooded with conifers. You'll meet some trees downed by beavers, but, at this writing, no portages are necessary.

Take out on river left before the County Road 13 bridge, where there is a sandy access and room to park.

The Crow Wing starts out small and winding.

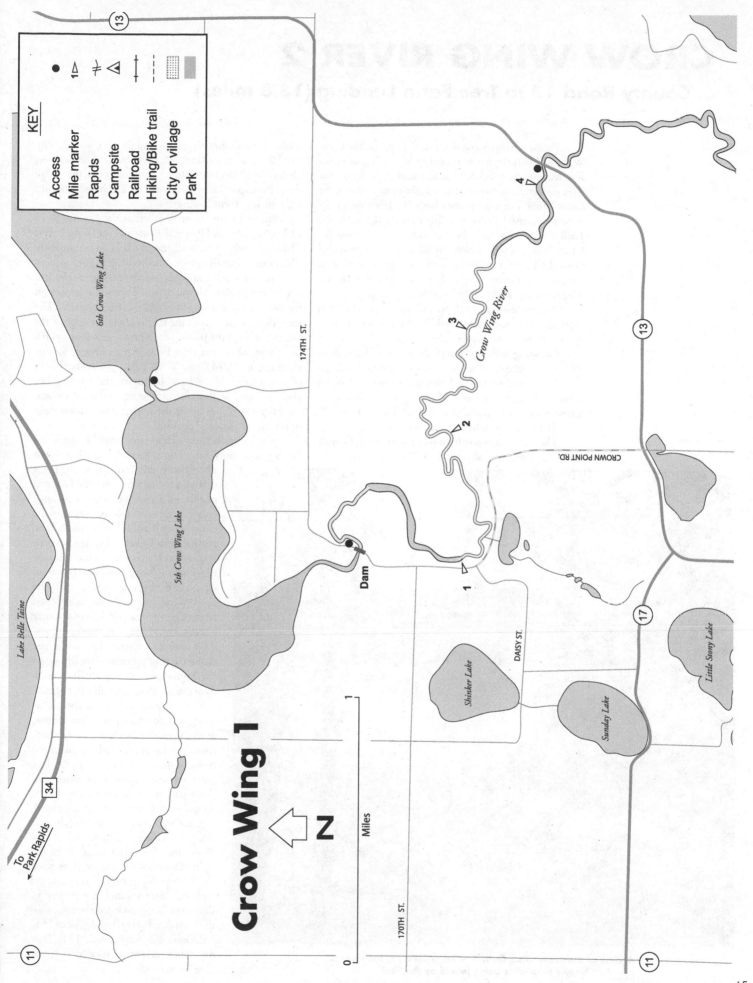

Crow Wing 1

KEY

●	Access
1△	Mile marker
≠	Rapids
△	Campsite
┼	Railroad
┊	Hiking/Bike trail
▦	City or village
▩	Park

6th Crow Wing Lake

5th Crow Wing Lake

Lake Belle Taine

To Park Rapids

Crow Wing River

Dam

174TH ST.

170TH ST.

DAISY ST.

CROWN POINT RD.

Shinker Lake

Sunday Lake

Little Stony Lake

N

Miles

0   1

CROW WING RIVER 2
County Road 13 to Tree Farm Landing (13.8 miles)

Paddlers who choose this peaceful trip on the Crow Wing will visit the last four of the Crow Wing lakes before leaving the chain behind to paddle 4 miles on the river proper. In its riverine reaches, the clear waters of the Crow Wing flow over a sandy bottom strewn with fragments of mussel shells. Flowing in from the west, the Shell River, even more loaded with mussels, joins the Crow Wing 2.7 miles before the takeout. With the added flow, the little Crow Wing becomes a good-sized river. This is a popular trip for paddlers who prefer quiet water; a short portage allows a bypass of the only drop.

Birders will enjoy the 4 miles of river that run through the Crow Wing Wildlife Management Area, where migratory birds often rest.

Camping, with a drinking water well, is available for an $8 fee at the takeout, Wadena County's Tree Farm Landing.

For **canoe rentals** and **shuttle service** and **water level** information, see Crow Wing 1. This segment of the Crow Wing can be paddled at almost all water levels.

The average **gradient** is 0.6 foot per mile.

The 12.4-mile **shuttle route** runs south on County Road 13, which crosses the Shell River just west of the confluence with the Crow Wing and then becomes County Road 25 as it crosses into Wadena County, then east on County Road 18 (380th Street), continuing past the bridge across the Crow Wing, then north on 239th Street (a sand road) to Tree Farm Landing.

Put in on upstream river left at the County Road 13 bridge between Fifth and Fourth Crow Wing Lakes. There's a parking area off the road. The river quickly slides into a cattail marsh, lined with red osier, willow thickets, and marsh marigolds, before opening into Fourth Crow Wing Lake. Although you'll see some houses on the lake, you'll also see loons and great blue herons. The most direct route across the lake is along the edge of the lake grasses past the public access on the east shore; you'll see a sign where the river flows out of Fourth for the short trip to Third Crow Wing Lake. The higher banks of Third Crow Wing Lake are pretty and wooded but also developed, with numerous houses, a float plane, and the Highway 87 bridge at the outlet; downstream right of the bridge, access is possible.

The stream between Third and Second Crow Wing Lakes is also short. Like Third, Second is developed, but when you paddle left around the point that you see as you enter the lake and paddle into the marshy area, a huge beaver lodge signals the beginning of the Crow Wing Wildlife Management Area. For the next 4 river miles, development is sparse and birds—loons, ospreys, bald eagles, great blue herons—are numerous, especially during migration times, as the Crow Wing is in the Mississippi Flyway. At the County Road 109 bridge, you may want to **portage** this short, narrow drop over a rock dam. Take out at one of the piers on upstream river left; across the highway a short path lined with columbine leads down to the river again.

A mile downstream the Crow Wing widens and a power line crosses; at the time this book was researched, there was an active eagle's nest in the power line tower on river right. The river narrows again soon after and flows past scenic steep wooded banks. At mile 11.1, where a tall sandbank topped with conifers and birch rises along the outside of a curve in the Crow Wing, the Shell River enters from the right. The Shell is a bigger river than the Crow Wing before they merge; with the extra volume, the current of the Crow Wing picks up the pace a little. A small tributary flowing out of Mud Lake joins the party at mile 12.8. **Take out** a mile downstream on river left at Tree Farm Landing.

A view of the Crow Wing from Tree Farm Landing; the river is bigger here after being joined by the Shell.

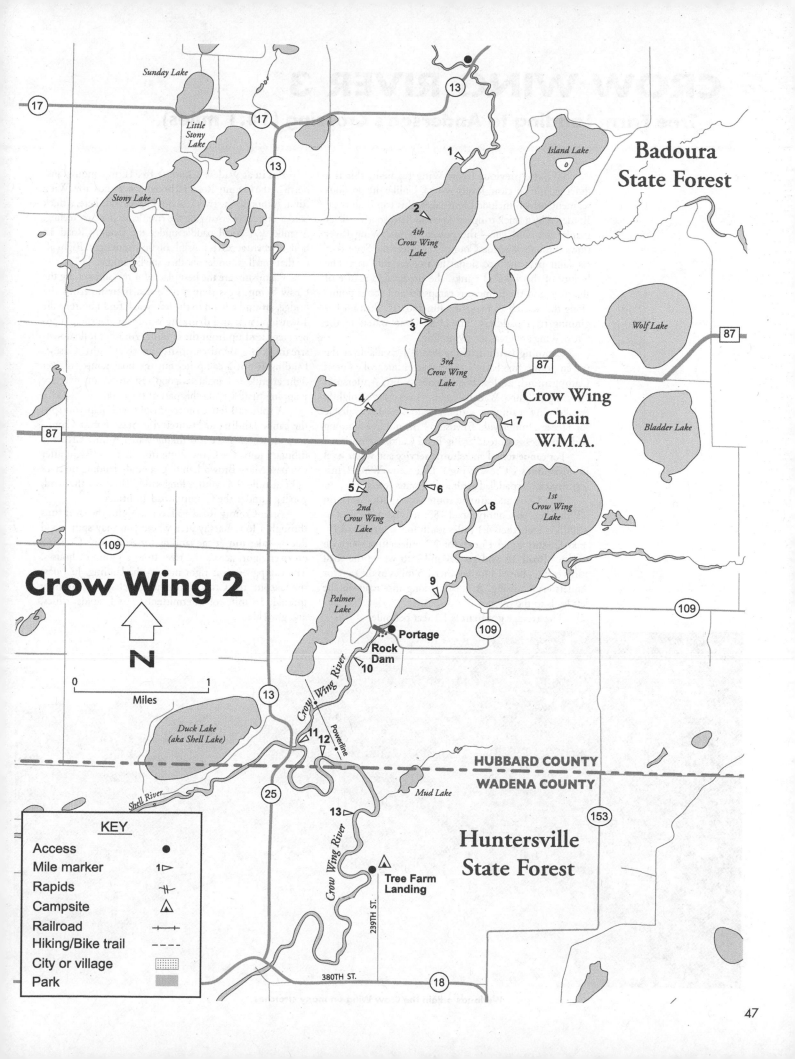

CROW WING RIVER 3
Tree Farm Landing to Anderson's Crossing (14.1 miles)

Like the previous Crow Wing segment, this is a quiet paddle on clear, lovely waters. Unlike the previous segment, which included four lakes, this trip is all river. Bordered by a thick fringe of lowland hardwoods—silver maple, ash, and elm—the peaceful Crow Wing River flows through Wadena County's Huntersville State Forest (and past the occasional house) on this trip. The beauty of the wooded banks, the predictable nature of the river, and the numerous campsites and access points along this stretch all make it a fun and easy float for beginning river paddlers. The clear, clean waters of the Crow Wing are great for swimming.

Camping (with drinking water) is available at the put-in point, Tree Farm Landing; at Huntersville Forest Campground; and at the takeout point, Anderson's Crossing. All three Wadena County sites charge a nightly fee. Primitive camping with access to a road is available for a fee at Huntersville Township Park and free camping with no access to a road at Big Bend Canoe Campsite.

For **canoe rental** and **shuttle service** and **water level** information, see Crow Wing 1. Like Crow Wing 2, this segment can be paddled at almost all water levels.

The 15.6-mile **shuttle route** runs south 1 mile on 239th Street to County Road 18, then 4.2 miles west to 199th Avenue, then 4.1 miles south to County Road 15. Take County Road 15 east for 1.2 miles. Turn south on County Road 14 and go 2.1 miles to where the road turns east. Follow 14 for another 1.5 miles to the sign for Anderson's Crossing. A 1.5-mile-long dirt road on the left leads to the river.

The average **gradient** is 1.1 feet per mile.

Put in at Wadena County's Tree Farm Landing, just north of the County Road 18 bridge across the Crow Wing River. Although the river is about 80 feet wide here, a thick border of trees overhanging the river lends it a cozy feeling. At mile 2.7, you'll paddle under the County Road 18 bridge, where access is possible on upstream right. Right after that you'll go under another, smaller bridge.

Campsites are the best places for rest stops along the Crow Wing. Less than a mile downstream from the bridge, around a bend to the left, you'll find Huntersville Township Park and drinking water on river left. Timber steps lead up from the landing. Another mile downstream is Big Bend campsite, on river right. Casey's Landing is not a campsite, but the boat ramp on river right at mile 6.1 makes a good rest stop. You may see snapping turtles along this part of the river.

A split-rail fence on river right will help you spot the canoe landing at Huntersville State Forest Campground, where there is drinking water. A mile farther, a tributary joins the Crow Wing from the left. Right after you pass Mary Brown Landing, a sandy landing on river right at mile 9.4, with a long sandy climb to the road, you'll go under the County Road 15 bridge.

After County Road 15 is out of sight, the river runs through a low marshy area where you may spot wood ducks. **Take out** at the landing for Anderson's Crossing on river right, across the river from a group of houses. The campground is right next to the landing. Just past the takeout, the Crow Wing changes character, running through 18 miles of intermittent Class I rapids, riffles, and gravel bars.

Wetlands adjoin the Crow Wing on many stretches.

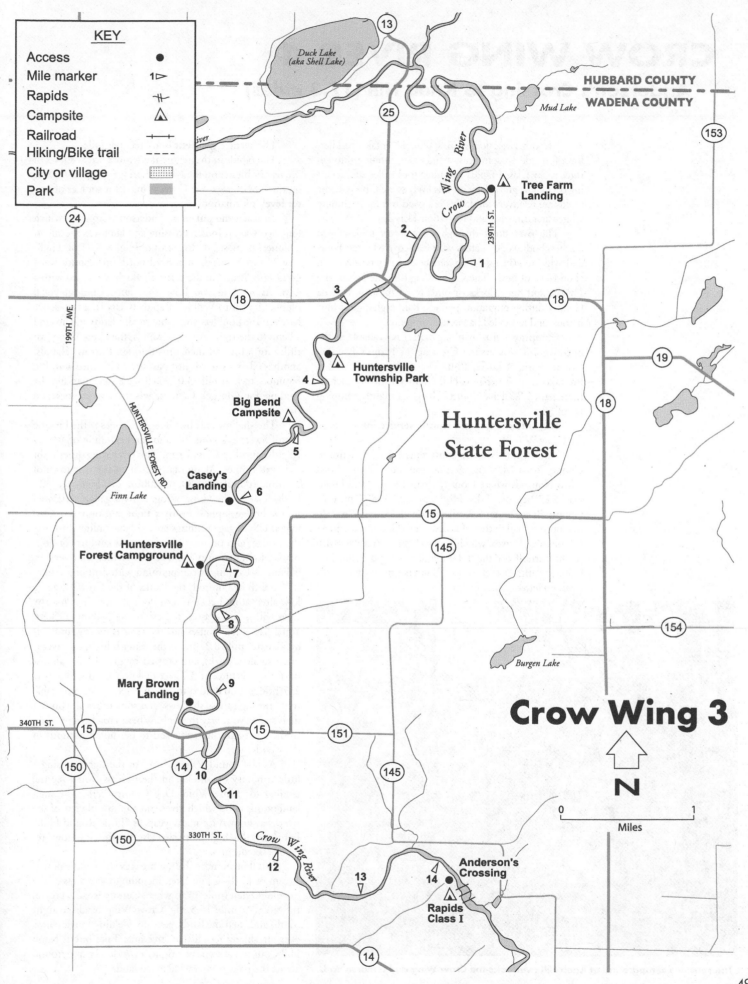

KEY

Access ●
Mile marker 1▷
Rapids
Campsite △
Railroad ┼┼┼
Hiking/Bike trail - - - -
City or village
Park

Duck Lake
(aka Shell Lake)

HUBBARD COUNTY
WADENA COUNTY

Mud Lake

13

25

153

Crow Wing River

Tree Farm Landing

239TH ST.

2

1

24

3

18

18

19

Huntersville Township Park

4

Big Bend Campsite

199TH AVE.

HUNTERSVILLE FOREST RD.

Finn Lake

5

Casey's Landing

6

15

145

Huntersville State Forest

Huntersville Forest Campground

7

18

154

8

Burgen Lake

Mary Brown Landing

9

Crow Wing 3

340TH ST.

15

15

151

N

150

14

10

145

0   1
Miles

150

11

330TH ST.

Crow Wing River

12

13

14

Anderson's Crossing

Rapids Class I

14

CROW WING RIVER 4
Anderson's Crossing to Knob Hill (17.3 miles)

The otherwise docile Crow Wing River takes paddlers for a fun ride on some easy whitewater, running through three rocky Class I rapids and numerous riffles, and scraping over a few gravel bars on this lively stretch. Because the rapids are relatively mild, this is a good trip for beginning whitewater canoeists and recreational kayakers.

The river flows through some lovely undeveloped reaches, both wooded areas with fern-covered forest floors and wide marshlands. The variety of habitats means an abundance of birds. The Crow Wing is in the Mississippi Flyway, and huge flocks of birds travel through Wadena County during migration periods. Bald eagles, great blue herons, and red-tailed hawks are common.

Camping (with drinking water) is available at the put-in point, Anderson's Crossing; at Frame's Landing County Park; at Little White Dog County Park; and at the takeout point, Knob Hill County Park. At each of these parks, Wadena County charges a nightly camping fee of $8.

For **canoe rental** and **shuttle service** information, see Crow Wing 1.

The 18-mile **shuttle route** runs 1.5 miles south to County Road 14, then 3.9 miles south on County Road 14 to Nimrod, where County Road 14 ends and Highway 227 begins. Take Highway 227 for .7 mile to County Road 26; go 4.2 miles south on County Road 26 to County Road 9; then 3 miles east to County Road 138 (Wilderness Drive), which is gravel; and 3.6 miles south to the turnoff for the 1.1-mile dirt road to Knob Hill County Park. At each of two Y intersections on the dirt road, go left.

The average **gradient** is 4.7 feet per mile.

The rapids in this segment are more fun at a level of 3.2 feet or higher on the Nimrod bridge gauge or 460 cfs on the USGS gage. See Crow Wing 1 for sources of **water level** information.

To reach the **put-in** at Anderson's Crossing, which long ago was an Indian crossing and later was the site of a pioneer homestead, drive east of Highway 71 on Highway 227 to Nimrod, then head north on County Road 14 (294th Street) to the turnoff, which is marked with a sign. As soon as you leave the canoe landing, you'll plunge right into Walkin's Rapids (Class I), a fast dance between the boulders and some small islands and around a bend to the right. After the rapids, the Crow Wing just riffles for a bit and then runs through Burrows Rapids, another Class I stretch. Just past the confluence with Big Swamp Creek at mile 3.0, you'll see a sign marking the landing for Gloege's Canoes, which rents canoes and runs shuttles.

The shallow area by Gloege's Canoes is the historic site of Sweeney's Ford. It's also the beginning of Westra Rapids, another Class I run. The river runs quietly for the next 4 miles. Along that stretch, at the tiny town of Nimrod (population 89 in 2000), the Highway 227 bridge crosses the Crow Wing. A river gauge is painted on the bridge support on river right, but only the automated USGS gage readings are available online. Just past the bridge, also on the right, is a good landing for Stigman's Mound County Park. A mile farther, on river left, is Frame's Landing, a campground with drinking water.

South of Nimrod, the banks of the Crow Wing lie low, alternating between fern-floored forest and marshy areas with sedge grasses, red osiers, and willow thickets. You'll pass a few houses but the river is mostly undeveloped. After mile 8.2, unless the water is high, the river is often shallow, rocky and crossed by gravel bars, almost until the takeout. At 3.2 feet or lower on the Highway 227 bridge, you'll need to search carefully for a passable route through these shallows, and sometimes all you can do is scrape your way through. Where a road swings close to the left bank, there are said to be Indian mounds in the woods.

As you round a sharp bend to the right, passing a little tributary on the left in the process, you'll see the landing for Little White Dog County Park. The high land of this park, which gives you a beautiful view of the river, was known for many years as "Little Round Hill." Long ago, this high point was also the site of Ojibwe religious ceremonies.

You'll meet more shallow areas as you paddle downstream of Little White Dog, including rocky flats at the town of Oylen (mile 13.6) where County Road 9 crosses the river. At mile 15.5, the Crow Wing heads straight south, and then the land opens up, yielding longer views over marshland to a distant tree line. **Take out** at Knob Hill County Park on river right, a two-level campground across the river from a wide marshland.

The spacious campground at Knob Hill overlooks the Crow Wing and a marshland.

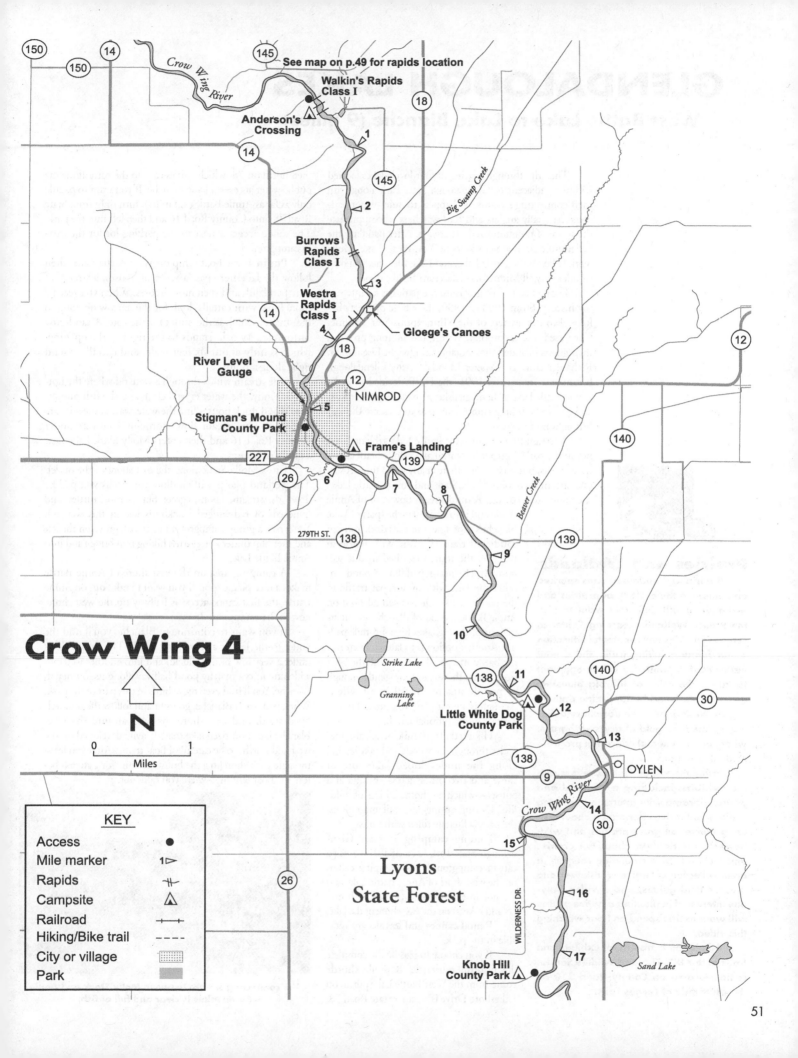

Crow Wing 4

N

0   1
Miles

KEY

Access	●
Mile marker	1▷
Rapids	╫
Campsite	△
Railroad	┼┼┼
Hiking/Bike trail	- - - -
City or village	░
Park	▓

See map on p.49 for rapids location

Walkin's Rapids
Class I

Anderson's
Crossing

Crow Wing River

Big Swamp Creek

Burrows
Rapids
Class I

Westra
Rapids
Class I

Gloege's Canoes

River Level
Gauge

NIMROD

Stigman's Mound
County Park

Frame's Landing

279TH ST.

Strike Lake

Granning
Lake

Beaver Creek

Little White Dog
County Park

OYLEN

Crow Wing River

Lyons
State Forest

WILDERNESS DR.

Knob Hill
County Park

Sand Lake

51

GLENDALOUGH LAKES
West Battle Lake to Lake Blanche (9 miles)

This trip, through a string of four lovely lakes located within or adjacent to Glendalough State Park along with their connecting streams, will appeal to quiet-water paddlers, especially anglers and bird-watchers who appreciate the peace of nonmotorized waterways. After paddling the delightfully clean, quiet waters of West Battle Lake, Molly Stark Lake, Annie Battle Lake, and Lake Blanche, you may wonder why all Minnesota's lakes can't be like these.

Located east of Fergus Falls, the park has an interesting history. From 1903 to 1990, the whole property belonged to the owners of the Minneapolis Star Tribune. They used it as a corporate retreat and hunting preserve; their guests included such notables as Dwight Eisenhower, Richard Nixon, and Walter Mondale. After Glendalough became a state park in 1991, the DNR decided to make Annie Battle Lake a "heritage fishery," banning motorboats and electronic fishing equipment so as to preserve the way fishing was in the past.

A stream flows from West Battle Lake (the outlet is not in the park) into Molly Stark Lake. Molly Stark allows motorboats, but very few are there at any given time. A second stream then joins Molly Stark and Annie Battle Lake, the nonmotorized lake. A third stream flows out of Annie Battle and into Lake Blanche (part of Lake Blanche's shoreline is in the park). You can paddle all the way from West Battle to Blanche, the route described in this section, which means paddling around another big lake with motorboat traffic to the public access. Or you can take out on Annie Battle instead of Blanche, eliminating one of the big lakes for a 4.3-mile paddle. Another option is to launch from Annie Battle and paddle between all the lakes from there; the streams are gentle enough to paddle upstream. All in all, Glendalough is a great place to putter about in a canoe or recreational kayak.

Hiking trails, 10 miles in all, also meander through the woods and prairies and along the undeveloped lakeshore of these and two other lakes—Emma and Sunset—which are home to lots of wildlife. During spring and fall migrations, the park is literally filled with birds.

Finding **camping** is easy: Glendalough State Park (218-864-0110) has a cart-in campground and camping cabins on the west shore of Annie Battle Lake and a canoe-in campground (shared with hikers and bikers) on the east shore of the lake.

Rental canoes and kayaks are available in the park.

If you choose to paddle the complete downstream route, the 8.6-mile **shuttle route** from the West Battle Lake put-in on Lakeshore Drive is west to State Road 78,

then north on 78, which curves east, to the turnoff for the public water access on Lake Blanche. If you want to paddle only as far as Annie Battle (4.3 miles), turn right from State Road 78 onto County Road 16 and then left into the park. The canoe access is next to the parking lot for the cart-in campground.

Put in at the boat ramp on West Battle Lake, then follow the lakeshore past a series of houses, a stretch of state parkland, and then more houses. When you reach a shore lined with cattails, look for the narrow opening to the stream, which is the outlet for the lake. A tan house surrounded by oaks stands to the right of the opening, which is only about six feet wide, and cattails extend right along a point.

The stream winds through a wetland where the bottom is sandy, the water crystal clear, and the fish numerous. Wood duck houses line the waterway, and eagles are common. The stream flows through a culvert under County Road 16 and then enters Molly Stark Lake near a group of houses.

Cross Molly Stark along the east shore to the outlet. The wetland plants will swallow you up as you paddle down the stream. Loons, egrets, blue herons, turtles, and hundreds of red-winged blackbirds live in this wetland. You'll pass a group campground in an oak grove on the left and then slip under a steel truss hiking trail bridge and into Annie Battle Lake.

A camping area on the east shore of Annie Battle makes a nice picnic spot. If you want to **take out** on Annie Battle, the first canoe access is halfway up the west shore, next to the campground.

If you want to continue to Blanche, you'll find the outlet to the left of a swimming beach. The stream flows under a very low bridge (duck!) and into another wetland, widening into a marshy pond halfway along its journey to Blanche. You'll find even more birds in this part of the park. When you reach Blanche, go right and follow the undeveloped south and east shores halfway around the lake. Blanche is a motorized lake that's heavily developed on the west and north, so be careful of boat traffic. After you leave the state park shoreline, the houses resume for a stretch before the boat landing, where you **take out**.

The connecting stream between Molly Stark and Annie Battle lakes is clear and full of fish.

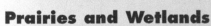

Prairies and Wetlands

If a trip to Glendalough has sparked an interest in the ecology of prairies and wetlands, you'll definitely want to visit the Prairie Wetlands Learning Center in Fergus Falls. This environmental education center features hiking trails and a new visitor center, painted a subtle eggplant to match the color of the big bluestem grass that is found in the prairie pothole region. Next door is the dormitory building, painted the gold of dry switchgrass, where environmental education program students are housed.

Inside the visitor center are fascinating exhibits, including a wetland and prairie diorama with interactive learning stations, extensive information about restoring native tall grass prairies and wildflowers, historic data about the prairies and wetlands of surrounding counties, a great collection of native wildflower and grasses field guides, and a video. Anyone interested in planting a native prairie will want to first spend an hour watching this video.

Admission is free to all exhibits and trails at this U.S. Fish and Wildlife Service center, located on County Road 210 on the south side of Fergus Falls.

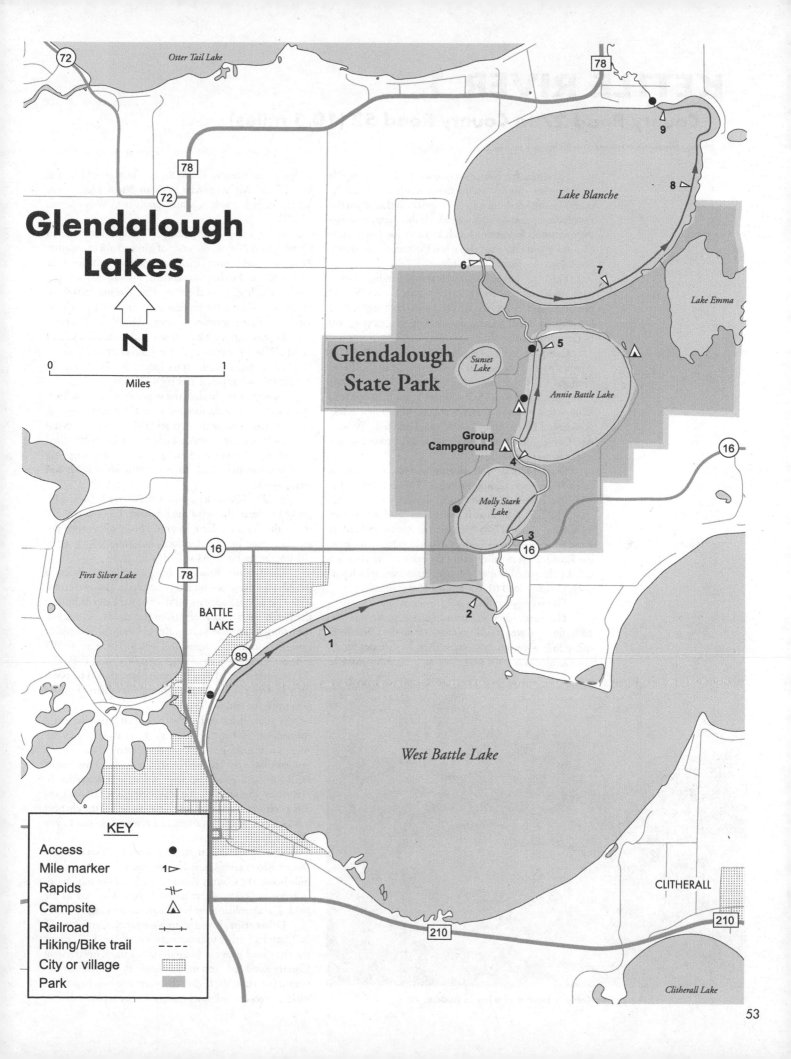

Glendalough Lakes

N

0 — 1
Miles

Otter Tail Lake

72

78

78

72

Lake Blanche

9

8

6

7

Lake Emma

Glendalough State Park

Sunset Lake

5

Annie Battle Lake

Group Campground

4

16

Molly Stark Lake

3

16

First Silver Lake

16

78

2

BATTLE LAKE

1

89

CLITHERALL

West Battle Lake

210

210

Clitherall Lake

KEY

Access	●
Mile marker	1▷
Rapids	╫
Campsite	△
Railroad	┼┼┼
Hiking/Bike trail	- - - -
City or village	▒
Park	▒

KETTLE RIVER 1
County Road 27 to County Road 52 (10.3 miles)

For a fun, fast run down one wavy Class I–II rapids after another, this trip on the upper Kettle River can't be beat. The only downside to this segment is that when the runoff disappears—and on the Kettle this happens fast—the narrow, rocky stream quickly becomes too low to paddle. But if you take your trip when the water is adequate, you'll love this part of the Kettle.

This stretch is scenic as well as fun, winding its way past some beautiful rock outcrops, little waterfalls, and pretty wooded banks. Wildlife, including bald eagles, river otters, and Canada geese, is abundant. Fishing can be good in the numerous pools.

Camp at Moose Lake State Park (218-485-5420) 8 miles east of the put-in on County Road 27/73; at General C. C. Andrews State Forest's Willow River Campground (320-245-2668) just east of the town of Willow River; or along the river at one of two first-come, first-served DNR campsites (miles 6.1 and 6.8). Wilderness Campground (see below) has a campground on the river just west of Rutledge.

Canoe rentals and **shuttle service** are available from Wilderness Campground (218-372-3993);(612-333-5747) from the Twin Cities.

The 13.9-mile **shuttle route** runs east for 5.5 miles on County Road 27 to Moose Lake, south on County Road 61 for 8 miles to County Road 52 (Denham Crossing Road), then .4 mile west to the bridge. Bike shuttlers can use the paved Willard Munger State Trail, which parallels County Road 61, for 8 miles of this shuttle.

The average **gradient** is 7.1 feet per mile.

The Kettle rises and drains quickly, so be sure you have current **water level** information from the DNR (888-646-6367; www.dnr.state.mn.us/river_levels/index.html). You can also look at the river gauge on the County Road 12 bridge by the town of Kettle River, which should read at least 2.5 feet. Medium water levels are 3 to 4.5 feet; above 4.5 feet is high water, at which point the rapids become Class II.

To reach the County Road 27 bridge, drive west on County Road 27 from the town of Moose Lake to the river. Although there is no official access, a long path along the ditch leads to the river on downstream left, and you can park on the shoulder of the road. After you **put in** right in the middle of a narrow boulder garden, you'll be dodging rocks and riding waves right away. The Kettle follows a pool-drop pattern from here down, with numerous Class I rapids. When the river is above 4.5 feet on the County Road 12 bridge gauge, this run edges up to Class II, but the current still isn't as pushy as it is on Kettle 4.

Soon after the bridge, the winding river is undeveloped, its grassy banks forested with birch and edged alternately with willow thickets and fields of ferns. Several large rock outcrops appear, including a beautiful tilted rock bluff, covered with ferns and mosses and dripping with groundwater. Bluffs forested with white birch add scenic appeal.

You'll paddle under a high railroad trestle (mile 4.6), the old route of the Soo Line Railroad. It's now an ATV trail—the Soo Line Trail; its gravel bed makes tough going for regular bicycles, but some mountain bikers use it, sharing the trail with ATVs.

The County Road 46 bridge (mile 5.7) offers a steep but grassy access on either upstream or downstream river left; a house appears on river right. Past the bridge, the Kettle takes a short rest from the rapids. Where you spot a big white pine next to the left shore at Whitepine campsite (mile 6.1), some riffles reappear. Less than a mile downstream is Headwater campsite (mile 6.8), also on river left, nestled in a red pine plantation. The pool-drop pattern reasserts itself, although less intensely, from here until the end of the run.

A short distance downstream, you'll paddle past a spectacular tall red clay bank on the outside of a curve. After a half mile, just past a little stream on the right, a red sandbar covered with small rounded river rocks would make a good rest stop at medium water levels. Following the sandbar the channel splits. At the time this book was researched, the right branch of the channel was blocked by a fallen tree and a beaver dam just before the two branches rejoined.

The Moose Horn River (formerly known as the Moose River) enters quietly from the left, just a quarter mile before the County Road 52 bridge. **Take out** on upstream river right, where a grassy slope leads up to the road. The shoulder is wide enough for parking.

Other trips. If you want a longer run, you can put in 2.5 miles farther upstream at County Road 12 (where the river level gauge is located) or 6.5 miles upstream at County Road 131. You need to know that the farther upstream you start, the higher the water needs to be and the rockier, steeper, and more numerous the rapids are.

The Upper Kettle is swift and a joy to paddle.

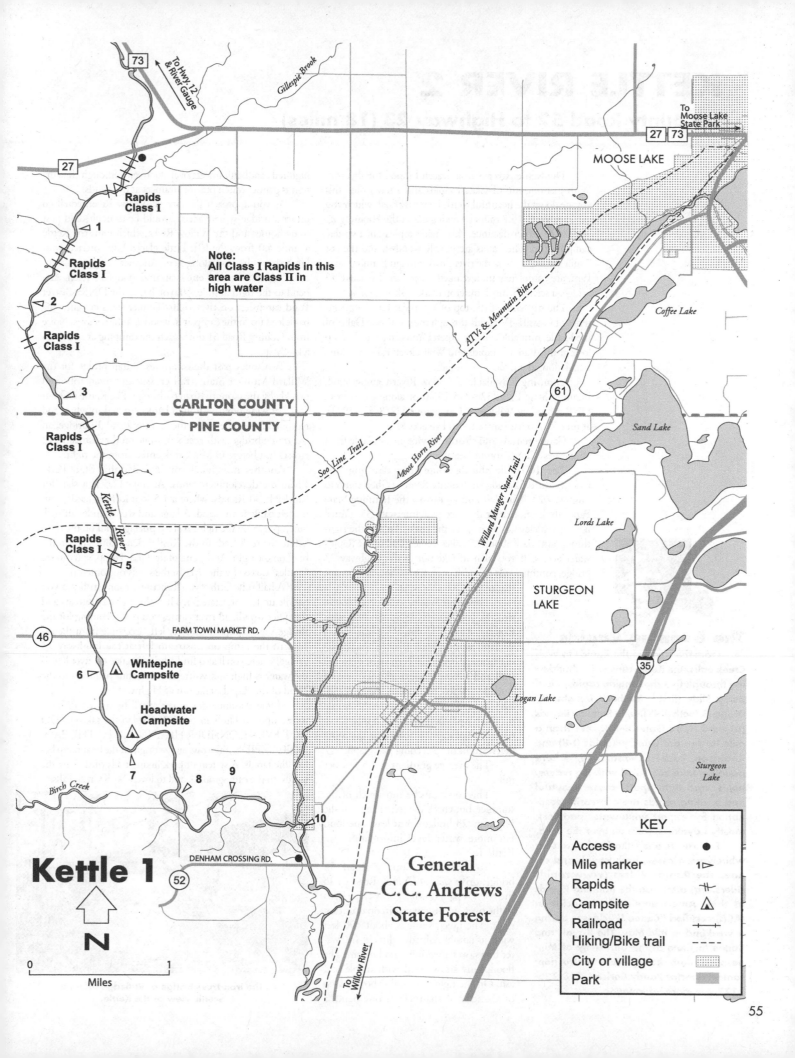

To Hwy 12
& River Gauge

73

27

Rapids
Class I

1▷

Rapids
Class I

2▷

Rapids
Class I

3▷

Note:
All Class I Rapids in this
area are Class II in
high water

Gillespie Brook

To Moose Lake
State Park

27 **73**

MOOSE LAKE

Coffee Lake

ATVs & Mountain Bikes

61

Sand Lake

CARLTON COUNTY

PINE COUNTY

Soo Line Trail

Moose Horn River

Willard Munger State Trail

Rapids
Class I

4▷

Kettle River

Lords Lake

Rapids
Class I

5▷

STURGEON
LAKE

46

FARM TOWN MARKET RD.

35

6▷ △ **Whitepine**
Campsite

Headwater
Campsite

△

7▷

Logan Lake

Birch Creek

8▷   9▷

Sturgeon
Lake

▷10

Kettle 1

⬆

N

DENHAM CROSSING RD.

52

General
C.C. Andrews
State Forest

KEY	
Access	●
Mile marker	1▷
Rapids	╫
Campsite	△
Railroad	┼┼
Hiking/Bike trail	- - -
City or village	▦
Park	▓

0 ———— 1
Miles

To
Willow River

KETTLE RIVER 2
County Road 52 to Highway 23 (18 miles)

The Kettle River is in a peaceful mood for this trip. With just one run of Class I rapids and a few riffles, this voyage down the beautiful Kettle is an easy float, which you can shorten to 16.7 miles by taking out at the Highway 23 bridge. At either distance, this makes a pleasant two-day camping trip. The banks are heavily wooded, and the last 7 miles of river, where the river flows through Banning State Park, are completely undeveloped. Above the Interstate 35 bridge, a scenic bedrock outcrop marks a short rapids.

The trip ends at the top of a popular but dangerous series of Class II–IV rapids through the sandstone Dalles of the Kettle, runnable only by experts. You can get a close-up look at the dramatic rapids and Wolf Creek Falls by hiking a trail along the river.

Camping is available at Willow River Campground, Banning State Park (320-245-2668) or along the river at DNR campsites. Wilderness Campground (218-372-3993), at mile 7, also has campsites and an access.

Canoe rentals and **shuttle service** are available from Wilderness Campground (see above).

The 16.1-mile **shuttle route** runs east from the County Road 52 bridge to County Road 61, then south to Highway 23. Turn left and go east to the Banning State Park entrance, a short distance past Interstate 35. (You'll need a vehicle sticker to enter the park.) Follow the signs through the park about 1.7 miles to the Head of the Rapids water access. If you plan to take out at the Highway 23 bridge, continue past the park entrance to the access on up-stream river left.

This route works well for a **bicycle shuttle.** Just before the intersection with County Road 61, you'll see the paved Willard Munger State Bicycle Trail crossing County Road 52. Turn right onto the trail and follow it south to the town of Rutledge, where the trail no longer parallels County Road 61. Continue the shuttle on the paved shoulders of County Road 61 and Highway 23, following the route described in the preceding paragraph.

The average **gradient** is 1.5 feet per mile.

This route can be run much of the summer, but check the river gauge on the Highway 23 bridge for at least one foot. For more **water level** information, see Kettle 1.

To reach the County Road 52 bridge, drive west of County Road 61 to the river. A path down a grassy slope leads to the river, where you **put in** on upstream right. The quiet Kettle is about 100 feet wide; its tannin-stained, sediment-free water flows over a reddish sand bottom. The floodplains are wooded with maple and ash. On the right is a mini oxbow, a loop of abandoned channel. At one bend, a high red sandbank towers over the river. Although the current is gentle, watch out for strainers at the bends.

As you approach the city of Willow River, you'll go under a bridge (where access would be difficult) and past some houses and the Willow River, which joins the Kettle at mile 4.0 from the left. Little glacial hills forested with birch shape the land along here. Another bridge crosses at mile 5.9, and the river enters an undeveloped stretch. At a bend to the right at mile 7.0, you'll find the DNR's Beaver Pond campsites on river right. Timber steps cut into the bank lead up to the campsites, wooded and spacious. Noise from County Road 61 does reach the camping area, but it's a lovely spot.

Two miles past the campsites, a trail bridge for the Willard Munger State Trail crosses the river, followed quickly by the County Road 61 bridge. The Kettle is about 130 feet wide now, with high banks covered in white and red pine. In another mile, the County Road 39 bridge, an old trestle bridge with access possible on downstream left, crosses just before O'Mix Creek enters from the right.

Another mile takes you into Banning State Park, where the development ends. At mile 12.5 is a sign for Rustler Bend Rapids, where a 1.5-foot ledge extends from the left bank at an island. A large and scenic undercut rock outcrop rises on the right. A steep **portage trail** on the right before the rock leads to the Rustler Bend campsites on the bluff on the right. At the end of the Class I drop, you can see "kettles" carved by the river in the sandstone outcrop.

A half mile farther you'll encounter some riffles as you paddle under Interstate 35. Then the highway retreats and the quiet woodland river carries you past a landing for the Bridge View campsite on river left, accessible from the access, to the ramp on upstream left at the Highway 23 bridge, where you'll also find a bridge gauge on river left. If the water is high and you're uneasy about paddling to the Head of the Rapids, take out at Highway 23.

If you continue downriver, you'll be treated to high, rocky, wooded bluffs in the 1.3 miles to the takeout. DO NOT EVEN CONSIDER HEADING INTO THE BANNING RAPIDS. **Take out** on river right at the boat ramp before the rapids. A system of park hiking trails runs along the rapids, to the campground, and to lovely Wolf Creek Falls.

The Banning Rapids

From the Head of the Rapids to Wolf Creek Falls, the Kettle runs wild, thundering through five challenging rapids: Blueberry Slide (II–IV), Mother's Delight (II), Dragon's Tooth (II–IV), Little Banning Rapids (II), and Hell's Gate (II–III). Less than a mile farther are Quarry Rapids (I–II) and Robinson Park in Sandstone, where paddlers take out. Filled with big waves, holes, and tight spots, these beautiful and exciting rapids are a favorite destination for expert whitewater paddlers, mostly kayakers, from all over the area.

This run is often the final exam for whitewater classes, both kayak and canoe. The Rapids Riders (www.rapids riders.org) often use the Banning Rapids in their American Canoe Association (ACA)–certified "Canoe U" classes during a weekend in mid-May. The Kayak and Canoe Institute at the University of Minnesota–Duluth has private instruction; contact director Randy Carlson, 218-726-6177, for more information.

The iron truss bridge at Rutledge offers a scenic view of the Kettle.

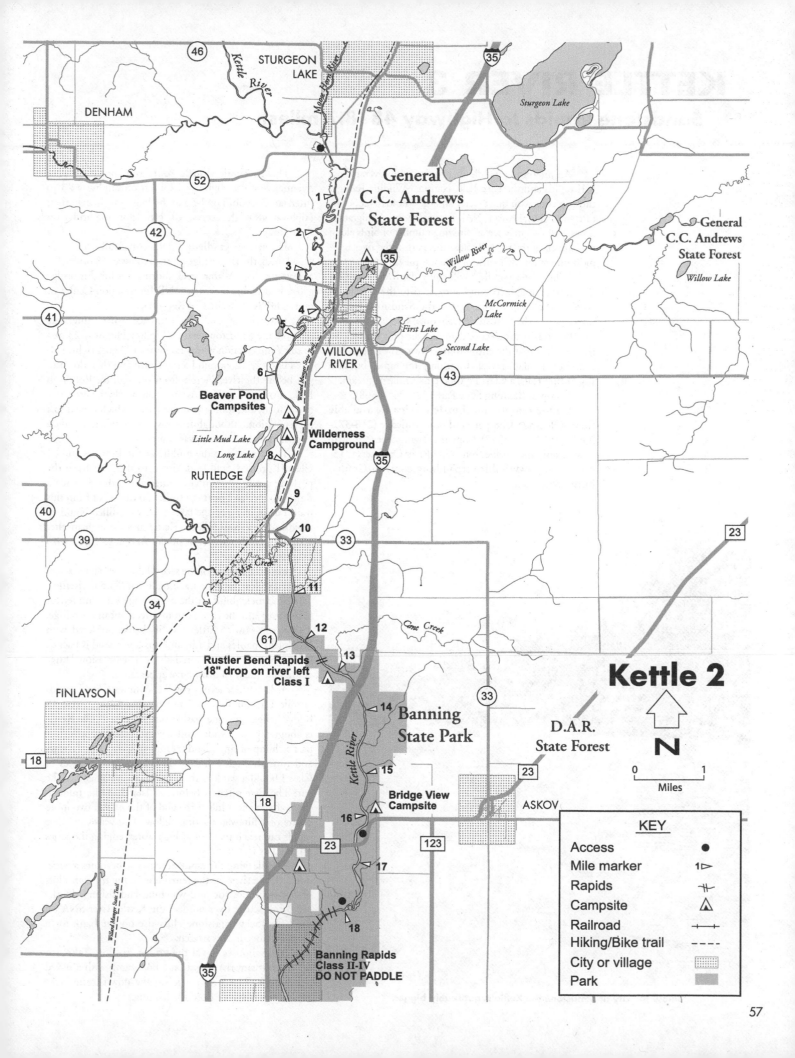

DENHAM

STURGEON LAKE

Kettle River

General
C.C. Andrews
State Forest

Sturgeon Lake

General
C.C. Andrews
State Forest

Willow Lake

Willow River

McCormick
Lake

First Lake

Second Lake

WILLOW
RIVER

Moose Horn River

Willard Munger State Trail

Beaver Pond
Campsites

Wilderness
Campground

Little Mud Lake

Long Lake

RUTLEDGE

O'Mix Creek

Cane Creek

FINLAYSON

Rustler Bend Rapids
18" drop on river left
Class I

Banning
State Park

Kettle River

Bridge View
Campsite

ASKOV

D.A.R.
State Forest

Kettle 2

N

0   1
Miles

Banning Rapids
Class II-IV
DO NOT PADDLE

Willard Munger State Trail

KEY	
Access	●
Mile marker	1▷
Rapids	‡
Campsite	⚠
Railroad	┼┼
Hiking/Bike trail	- - -
City or village	▦
Park	▨

KETTLE RIVER 3
Sandstone Rapids to Highway 48 (8.7 miles)

An interesting paddle that begins with several Class I–II rapids and the Rice Lake National Wildlife Refuge, this trip ends with quiet water and the Kettle River Scientific and Natural Area (SNA). Especially during migration times, paddlers may see an amazing number of birds along this stretch of the river. Because this part of the river is almost undeveloped, a sense of wildness prevails.

Whitewater paddlers will enjoy the lively water on this trip, although it's mild compared to the 4 miles of river mayhem upstream. Where the Sandstone Rapids now cascade, the Sandstone Dam once stood; from 1908 to 1995, this hydroelectric dam was the only obstacle to the free flow that the entire Kettle River now enjoys. Removal of the dam revealed not only the rapids but also Big Spring Falls, a Class IV drop a half mile upstream.

Camp at Banning State Park (320-245-2668).

Canoe rentals and **shuttle service** are available from Wilderness Campground near Rutledge (218-372-3993); (612-333-5747) from the Twin Cities. **Shuttle service only** is available from Wild River Outfitters (715-463-2254; www.wildriverpaddling.com) in Grantsburg, Wisconsin.

The 16.2-mile **shuttle route** runs north on Pine Avenue; west on Highway 123; left on Highway 23 to Interstate 35; south on I-35 to the Highway 48 exit; then Highway 48 to the access, which is before the bridge on the right.

The average **gradient** is 3.9 feet per mile.

Check the river gauge on the Highway 48 bridge for at least five feet. **Water level** information for this bridge gauge is available from the DNR Information Center or on the DNR Web site (see Kettle 1).

To reach the Sandstone Dam access from Interstate 35, take the Sandstone exit and follow Highway 23 east to the Y intersection where Highway 123 goes right. Follow Highway 123 around a right turn and then down to just before the river. Across from the sign for Robinson Park, turn right on Pine Avenue South, which becomes a gravel road, and follow it to the access, which is next to a power station. Although it is easy to see where the dam once stood, the removal was complete.

The access is in the middle of Sandstone Rapids, a Class II drop. A trail leads down to the river from the parking area and then continues along the river for a short distance as a **portage trail**; you can scout from this trail. **Put in** and run the last of the wave-filled bouldery rapids. After a short lull, the Kettle runs through another Class II just downstream of the first, also filled with boulders and waves.

Just past the end of the second drop, you'll see a sign on the left for the Rice Lake National Wildlife Refuge. The close rocky bluffs at the beginning of the run retreat as the river and the river bottom spread out in the refuge. The Kettle slows a little now, its banks bordered with floodplain maples and ash, and this lower land is backed by distant high birch-covered bluffs. The occasional huge white pine makes a distinctive appearance.

At low water levels, you'll encounter Class I rapids at mile 1.4, but above 7.7 feet on the County Road 48 bridge gauge, this one washes out. By mile 3, the Kettle is about 300 feet wide, and several islands appear. Just past a clump of tiny islands at mile 3.7, the river narrows and runs through Friesland Rapids. This is a series of Class I boulder gardens that curves around a bend to the left. The first pitch is before an island in the middle; then, after a short lull at the end of the island, two more bursts of whitewater action follow. The waves in these rapids can reach two feet at high water, edging the series up to Class II.

After leaving the rapids, the Kettle becomes a wide, quiet, docile river for the remainder of the trip, with lots of opportunities for bird-watching and fishing. In the last 3 miles, the river borders the Kettle River SNA on the left. Rocky sandstone cliffs rise on the bank for a short distance in this stretch.

A few houses signal the bridge crossing. **Take out** on downstream river right, at a boat ramp with a paved parking lot. The river gauge on the downstream right bridge pier is visible from the landing.

Below the city of Sandstone the Kettle is noticeably bigger.

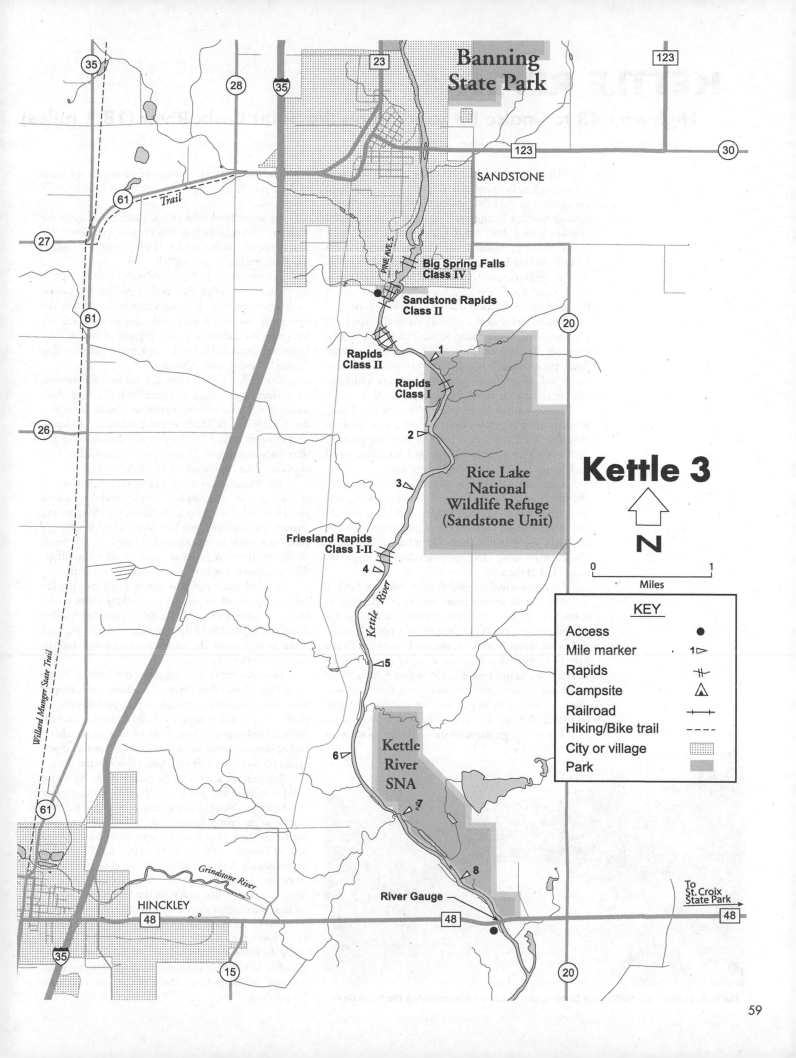

Banning
State Park

35

28

23

I 35

123

123

30

SANDSTONE

61   Trail

27

PINE AVE S.

**Big Spring Falls
Class IV**

61

**Sandstone Rapids
Class II**

20

26

**Rapids
Class II**   1

**Rapids
Class I**

2

3

**Rice Lake
National
Wildlife Refuge
(Sandstone Unit)**

Kettle 3

↑
N

**Friesland Rapids
Class I-II**

4

Kettle River

0   1
Miles

5

KEY

Access   ●

Mile marker   1▷

Rapids   ⊣⊢

Campsite   △

Railroad   ┼┼

Hiking/Bike trail   − − −

City or village

Park

6

**Kettle
River
SNA**

Willard Munger State Trail

61

7

35

Grindstone River

8

River Gauge

To
St. Croix
State Park

HINCKLEY

48   48   48

I 35

15   20

KETTLE RIVER 4
Highway 48 to Snake Bit Landing on the Saint Croix River (18.1 miles)

Whether you like your rivers nice and quiet or a little rowdy, you'll really enjoy all or part of this final trip down the Kettle. For the first 7 miles, the Kettle flows gently through wooded bottomlands, its quiet passage livened only briefly by a short run of Class I rapids. Then, in its rush to reach the Saint Croix, the river races through 6.5 miles of boulder-strewn Class I–II rapids. At high water, the rapids increase to Class II–III. At the end of the Kettle River Slough, the Saint Croix drops over a Class II ledge and rejoins the main channel of the Saint Croix.

Paddlers who want to take a pass on the rapids can take out at the Maple Island access (mile 7). Those who want only the rapids and are willing to do a very long shuttle can put in at Maple Island. Those who want some of the rapids and a short shuttle can put in at Maple Island and take out at Kennedy Brook for a 6-mile shuttle.

This is a beautiful trip through undeveloped land. You may want to explore some of the backwaters of the quiet first 7 miles of river, prime bird-watching territory. You'll spot waterbirds, songbirds, and numerous wood duck houses, as well as otter and beaver slides.

Camping is available at Saint Croix State Park (320-384-6591). From the put-in, go 11 miles east on Highway 48 to County Road 22, then 5 miles south to the park entrance. River's End Forest Service Campground is at the takeout on the Minnesota side of the Saint Croix. There are also several primitive DNR campsites along the river in the second half of the trip.

For **canoe rental** and **shuttle** information, see Kettle 3.

The 32-mile **shuttle route** runs west on Highway 48 to Interstate 35, then south on I-35 to the Pine City exit. Go straight east into Pine City. Turn left on County Road 61 and go to County Road 8. Go right on County Road 8 and follow it to the river. If you want to end up on the Wisconsin side of the Saint Croix, take I-35 to the Highway 70 exit and follow 70 east across the Saint Croix River into Wisconsin. About 1.5 miles past the river, turn left on Soderbeck Road, then turn left on Ferry Road to reach the access.

The average **gradient** for the whole run is 6.4 feet per mile, but between Maple Island and the ledge at the mouth of the Kettle River Slough, the average gradient is 10.65 feet per mile.

For **water level** information, check the gauge at the Highway 48 bridge for a minimum of 6 feet. Above 9.5 feet, the rapids increase to Class II–III. You can also obtain this gauge reading from the DNR.

The turnoff for the boat access is about .1 mile west of the Highway 48 bridge. Park in the paved lot and **put in** on downstream right. The bluffs that are so close to the river in the Banning Rapids gorge have receded, and the river now flows through a wide expanse of bottomland. Quiet and about 200 feet wide, the Kettle is fed in the first 7 miles by several small tributaries.

After Pelkey Creek at mile 2.5, the river widens even more, running deep, dark, and quiet through an area where several sloughs, some visible past the wooded banks, adjoin the channel. At mile 4.0, by several little islands, the Kettle runs through rocky Class I rapids at a shallow bend and then quiets down again. At mile 5, near where Cedar Creek enters from the right, you'll paddle under a power line.

The Maple Island access and canoe campsite are on river left at mile 7.1, across from Maple Island. Both a road and a footbridge over a wetland lead to the parking lot and an outhouse. Right after you leave Maple Island, you'll begin paddling a nearly continuous series of long Class I–II rapids all the way down to the Saint Croix, boulder-filled drops with waves up to two feet high at medium water levels.

At a lull in the rapids at mile 8, you'll spot the Big Eddy campsite, where you can get drinking water, on the left at a bend in the river. At the ledge downstream of Big Eddy, stay right to avoid the chute that ends in a big back roller. In high water, the ledge becomes Class II and the waves could swamp a canoe.

Downstream another 2.3 miles, the dramatic Kettle River High Banks, their sheer red sandstone faces topped with white pines, rise on the left. A state park observation platform is perched at the top of one of the banks. After another 1.2 miles, at the Kennedy Brook canoe access that is tucked into the stream mouth on river left, another observation platform on a cliff gives hikers a view of the river.

Between the access and the mouth of the Kettle the rapids continue and you'll pass the riverside campsites, which can be difficult to spot as the campsite signs are missing. Go to the right of an island where the Kettle flows into the Kettle River Slough of the Saint Croix River. In the mile of slough, you'll run more Class I rapids and pass several islands. An island splits the channel and the slough drops over a wide, steep Class II ledge, forming a two- to three-foot back roller, and joins the Saint Croix proper. To miss the worst of the waves, run this one hard right.

Paddle 3 miles down the scenic island-studded Saint Croix past several campsites to a matched pair of landings where the Riverdale ferry used to cross. **Take out** either on the left at Wisconsin's Soderbeck Landing, or on the right, just past the fast-moving mouth of the Snake, at Snake Bit Landing.

The last reach of the Kettle gets faster and steeper as it approaches the Saint Croix.

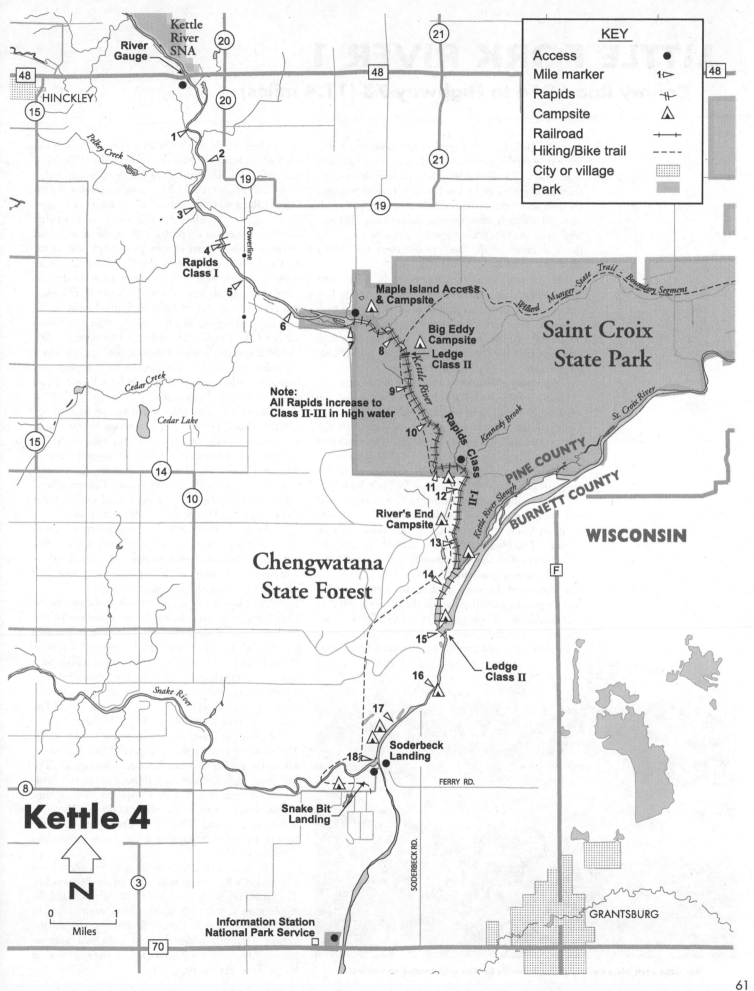

KEY

Access ●
Mile marker 1▷
Rapids ⫨
Campsite △
Railroad ┼┼┼
Hiking/Bike trail - - -
City or village ▦
Park ▧

Kettle River SNA
River Gauge
HINCKLEY
Pelkey Creek

Rapids Class I

Powerline

Cedar Creek
Cedar Lake

Maple Island Access & Campsite

Big Eddy Campsite
Ledge Class II

Note:
All Rapids increase to
Class II-III in high water

Kettle River

Saint Croix State Park

Willard Munger State Trail - Boundary Segment

Kennedy Brook

St. Croix River

Rapids Class I-II

PINE COUNTY
BURNETT COUNTY

Kettle River Slough

River's End Campsite

Chengwatana State Forest

WISCONSIN

Snake River

Ledge Class II

Soderbeck Landing

SODERBECK RD.

FERRY RD.

F

Snake Bit Landing

GRANTSBURG

Kettle 4

N

0   1
Miles

Information Station
National Park Service

70

LITTLE FORK RIVER 1
County Road 914 to Highway 73 (11.4 miles)

The Little Fork lives up to its reputation as a whitewater river on this stretch, racing through two Class I and three tough Class II rapids in the middle of the run. Although several of the Class II rapids can be portaged, the trails are on private land. Experienced whitewater paddlers will definitely enjoy running these exciting and beautiful rapids instead. Whitewater devotees who want a trip that is all rapids, all the time, can take out at the County Road 481 bridge for a 6.9-mile trip.

Along this part of the Little Fork, the banks don't feel as wild as they seem farther downstream. For the first 8 miles, the river runs past farm fields alternating with heavily forested areas where sprinklings of cabins appear occasionally. In the last 2 miles, the development disappears and the trees dominate, offering a taste of what lies downstream, along Little Fork 2 and 3.

Camping is available at McCarthy Beach State Park (218-254-7979) about 21 miles from the takeout. Go south on Highway 73 to County Road 22, west on 22 to County Road 5, then south on 5 to the park. Although there are no river campsites on this trip, if you paddle 2 miles past the takeout, you'll find a DNR campsite on river right followed by an unofficial access .2 mile farther downstream at Highway 1 (see map for Little Fork 2).

The 8-mile **shuttle route** runs north on County Road 914 (Watt Road), east on County Road 500 (Wein Road), north on County Road 668 (Samuelson Road), west on Highway 1 to Highway 73, then south on 73 across the bridge. Watt, Wein, and Samuelson Roads are gravel.

The average **gradient** is 2.4 feet per mile.

Because of the rocky rapids, spring **water levels** are best for paddling this stretch. Like the Big Fork, this river rises quickly after a heavy rain, so good paddling levels are possible later in the season. The river level gauge on the railroad trestle at 2nd Street E and Vermilion Drive in the city of Cook should read 1.9 or above; over 3.0 is high water. You can also get the water level from the DNR (888-646-6367; www.dnr.state.mn.us/river_levels/index.html).

From Highway 53, drive west on Highway 1 to County Road 668 (Samuelson Road), south to County Road 500 (Wein Road), west to County Road 914 (Watt Road), then south to the bridge. Park on the shoulder and **put in** on downstream river right. Disarmingly peaceful for the first 1.4 miles, the copper-colored, sediment-free water of the Little Fork flows quietly past low, flat wooded banks edged with alder thickets. The river is about 80 feet wide, and a few deadfalls may partially block the channel.

Right after you pass a farm on the right, you'll meet the first Class I rapids. The river squeezes through a 20-foot-wide opening between two rock outcrops and over a slight drop for 100 feet of boulder rapids. A quarter mile farther on the left is the confluence with the Rice River, almost as wide as the Little Fork.

Almost immediately, a warning sign on river left signals the Class II rapids. Scout or **portage** left on a steep rocky trail, although you can portage only halfway. The Little Fork roars between two large rock outcrops, over a ledge, and around a bend to the left. A central chute with a back roller is followed by standing waves. Cut left, following the rock outcrop on river left around the bend and down the center of the boulder garden that follows.

The sign for the second Class I rapids appears minutes later on the left. This is an easy Class I, only about 50 feet long, where the Little Fork is squeezed by rock outcrops as it bends left. The banks are higher and steeper now, with some nice groves of big white and red pine.

After a little less than a mile, you'll see the sign for the Class II Twite Rapids on the left. Scout or **portage** halfway on the right on what appears to be an ATV trail. The river bends slightly right and then is split by an island. The main channel is very rocky on the right at first, with a ledge partway down. At the bottom of this first long wave-filled pitch is a short pool; then the river bends sharply left and then right, running through more boulders and waves. The boulders are concentrated on the left of the first bend.

A cluster of houses and a power line appear at mile 4.0; below the power line, a road parallels the river on the left. At Durant Rapids, Class II, scout or **portage** left. The river drops eight feet as it races through the narrow boulder-strewn channel in less than a quarter mile. A huge boulder forms an eddy in the middle of the run. The pitch is steepest at the end. Where Flint Creek enters from the right at the end of the rapids is a house with a footbridge across the creek.

Less than a mile farther you'll reach the County Road 481 bridge, where access is possible on downstream left. The Little Fork is big now, about 150 feet wide, and the terrain more varied, with high banks appearing often. In the 2 miles between the County Road 481 bridge and the County Road 500 bridge the land looks wild, with no houses. Another 2.4 miles take you to the Highway 73 bridge. **Take out** on upstream left.

The Little Fork offers many Class II rapids for the whitewater enthusiast.

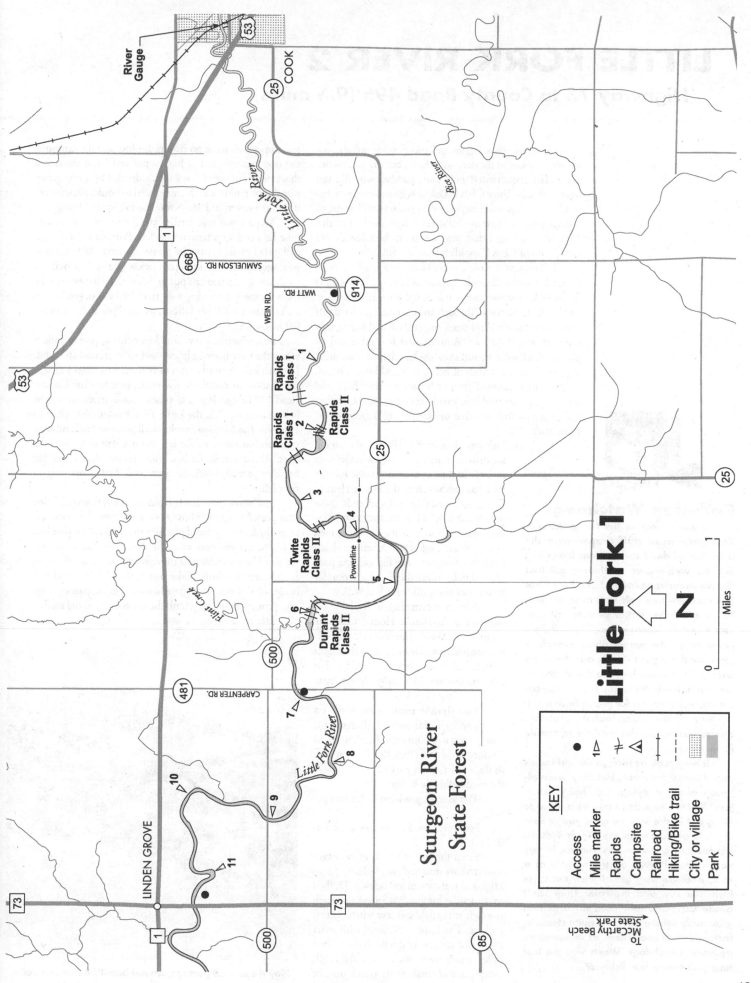

Little Fork 1

Sturgeon River
State Forest

KEY

●	Access
1△	Mile marker
⇥	Rapids
△	Campsite
┼┼	Railroad
---	Hiking/Bike trail
▦	City or village
▨	Park

N

0   1
Miles

River Gauge

COOK

Little Fork River

Rice River

SAMUELSON RD.

WEIN RD.

WATT RD.

Rapids
Class I   1

Rapids
Class II

Rapids
Class I   2

3

4

Powerline

Twite
Rapids
Class II

5

Flint Creek

6

Durant
Rapids
Class II

CARPENTER RD.

7

8

Little Fork River

9

10

11

LINDEN GROVE

To McCarthy Beach
State Park

LITTLE FORK RIVER 2
Highway 73 to County Road 495 (9.5 miles)

The Little Fork begins this trip flowing quietly past wooded banks and the occasional farm, but the quiet water doesn't last. Experienced whitewater paddlers who like fast water will enjoy three Class I boulder beds and two stretches of Class II, but even expert open boaters will want to portage around Hannine Falls. You'll hear the roar of this 15-foot drop long before you see the rocky Class IV–VI falls. A run of Class II rapids follows the falls.

In between the rapids, the Little Fork is still a rocky river, with scattered scenic deposits of large glacial boulders on its bed. Flowing past stands of tall pine, black spruce, and birch, it also passes through an area that must have suffered a blowdown; dead trees, snapped off and falling into the river, line the banks. Another stretch is inhabited by ghostly dead conifers, still standing but draped with drifting grayish-green strands of lichen called old-man's beard. Despite the occasional farm or house, the river feels wild now. Blue herons and bald eagles are common, and anglers will be happy to know that muskie fishing is great on the Little Fork.

The Little Fork was a logging river; in fact, the last big log drive in Minnesota was down this river in 1937 and is captured on movie footage that you can watch at the Forest History Center in Grand Rapids. Deadheads, those mostly submerged logs left over from lumber times, still lurk in the tannin-stained waters of the Little Fork. Hitting a deadhead the wrong way can flip a canoe; paddlers should avoid them. Watch out for fallen trees along this stretch as well.

Primitive **camping** is available on the river at Ax-Handle Hound Campsite (named for an old-time logger), a DNR-maintained campsite located on river right .2 mile before the Highway 1 bridge. For information on McCarthy Beach State Park, see Little Fork 1.

The **shuttle route** runs north on Highway 73 to Highway 1 (Range Line Road), west to County Road 139, north to County Road 495 (Riek Road), then west to the river. You can park at a wide spot in the road before the bridge.

The average **gradient** is 3.5 feet per mile.

For **water level** information, see Little Fork 1.

From the city of Cook, drive northwest a short distance on Highway 53 to Highway 1, then west to Highway 73, then south to the bridge. **Put in** on upstream river left at the public access, where there is parking. The Little Fork, lined with water lilies and rushes, is docile at first. Two miles downstream, you'll reach the DNR canoe campsite (hard to spot) in a grove of pines up a high bank on river right. Just past the campsite, the river narrows and at high water you'll run through a short stretch of easy Class I rapids divided by a tiny grassy island. The rapids, which are reduced to boulder-strewn riffles at low water, end just before the Highway 1 bridge.

About a half mile farther, you'll hear the din of Hannine Falls and see a farm on the left. **Portage** right along a rocky trail made narrow by numerous trees. At low water, **portage** past the rocky rapids below the falls as well. At moderate water, you can put in below the falls and run the Class II rapids. Following a short, quiet section, you'll meet a set of two small Class I drops, which should be run to the left in low water.

At low water, a few bouldery riffles appear at mile 5 where the river narrows briefly and splits around an island. Just past mile 6 another run of boulder-bed Class I rapids, too shallow to paddle at low water, precedes the County Road 139 bridge. If you stop here, downstream river right is best. At mile 7.3, the Little Fork swings fairly close to Highway 1 at Meadowbrook; you'll hear the road and see a transmission tower to the left about a half mile from the river. About a mile farther, small grassy islands and big boulders partially block the river; you'll find an opening on river left.

Just before the Class II rapids at mile 8.9, several fallen trees completely crossed the river at the time this book was researched, but one could pull over the blockage on river left. In high water, two-foot waves fill the rapids, but in low water, you'll have to walk. On the right, about a half mile away, is a modern windmill. **Take out** at the County Road 495 bridge on downstream right (there's a "No Trespassing" sign on upstream right) and climb the grassy bank to the road.

Play it safe and portage around beautiful Hannine Falls.

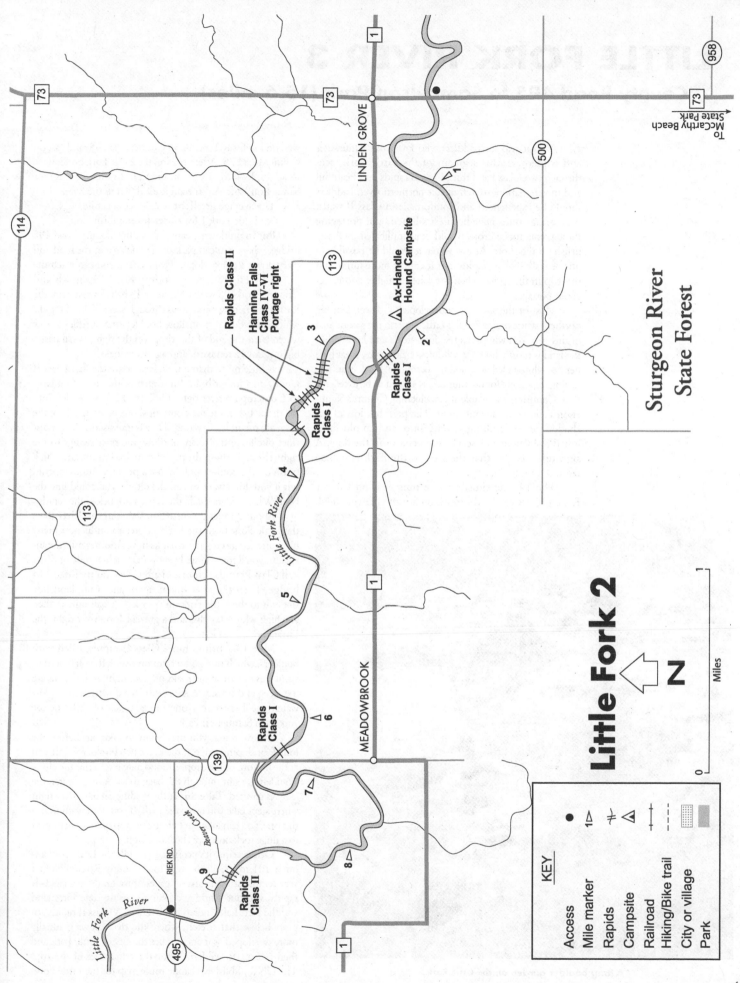

Little Fork 2

N

Miles

0 — 1

KEY

- ● Access
- ⊿1 Mile marker
- ⧺ Rapids
- ⊿ Campsite
- ┼ Railroad
- ┆ Hiking/Bike trail
- ▦ City or village
- ▩ Park

Sturgeon River State Forest

Ax-Handle Hound Campsite

Rapids Class I

Rapids Class II

Hannine Falls Class IV–VI Portage right

Rapids Class I

Rapids Class I

Little Fork River

Rapids Class I

Rapids Class II

Little Fork River

Beaver Creek

RIEK RD.

LINDEN GROVE

MEADOWBROOK

To McCarthy Beach State Park

73

73

73

1

1

1

114

113

113

139

495

500

958

1

2

3

4

5

6

7

8

9

LITTLE FORK RIVER 3
County Road 495 to Samuelson Park (15.6 miles)

A great trip for paddlers who love both whitewater and wilderness, this segment of the Little Fork races through two Class I and three Class II rapids on a beautiful and mostly remote stretch of this northern river. Paddlers should be experienced and comfortable in Class II water. No portage trails have been established, and portaging these scenic rocky drops would be complicated by heavy brush on the shore. At low water, it would be possible to line or walk shallow rapids, but it's much more fun to run this trip in the spring when the water is higher and forget about portages.

Most of the shore is undeveloped and wooded; big northern white cedars line the Little Fork on the second half of this trip. You will pass a few farm fields and houses, but the land is mostly home to wildlife—bald eagles, great blue herons, white-tailed deer, and the occasional black bear. The fishing, especially for big muskies, is alleged to be excellent.

Camping is available at Koochiching County's Samuelson Park, your takeout point. The park has lots of big shade trees, a drinking water pump, and an old-fashioned privy with a crescent moon cutout in the door. A sign tells visitors that the gate to the park is locked from 9 p.m. to 8 a.m.

The 19-mile **shuttle route** runs west on County Road 495 (Riek Road), south on South Greavey Road,

west on Highway 1, north on County Road 65, and east on County Road 75. After crossing the Little Fork on County Road 75, look for a sign on the right (it's hard to see) for Samuelson Park. A dirt road leads down to the river.

The average **gradient** is 2.2 feet per mile.

See Little Fork 1 for **water level** information.

Put in on downstream right at the County Road 495 bridge, where you can park on a wide area in the road and carry down a grassy slope. (From Cook, you can reach the put-in by Highway 1 to County Road 139 north and County Road 495 west.) A mile and a half downstream, the Little Fork narrows and flows through scenic Class I rapids, which are reduced to shallow boulder-strewn riffles at low water. Near the end of this drop, on the right, you'll pass a big meadow, a red barn, and a grove of oaks.

A little more than a mile farther are the first Class II rapids, on another beautiful stretch of the river. At a large rock outcrop on river right, the Little Fork swings left into the drop. Two more rock outcrops, one on each side of the river, are useful for scouting. They frame a series of two distinct pitches and a rocky outflow; the river swings to the right through these drops. The rocky terrain and thick brush on the banks would make a **portage** quite difficult, but if you don't want to run the rapids, you could line the boat. White cedars shade the Little Fork below the rapids.

About 2 miles downstream, the Sturgeon River joins the Little Fork from the left at a pretty confluence; many big white cedars crowd the banks now. Another mile downstream, you'll meet more lively water—a half mile of riffles and Class I rapids before and after the County Road 114 bridge. Then the river quiets again and a big landslide slopes into the Little Fork on river left. A half mile farther, at a high white clay cliff and a gravel bar on river right, the Little Fork curves left.

Mile 13.2 brings more Class II rapids, filled with boulders, which race past a farm on river left; you'll need to scout this one from the rocks on river right as the banks are too steep and brushy. A short distance downstream, at low water, you'll encounter one more stretch of riffles before you reach Samuelson Park.

At low water, you may want to take out before the four-foot sloping ledge at the park; two boulders await you at the bottom of the drop. At moderate levels, run the chute from left to right through the back roller. At high water, the ledge is covered. **Take out** at the landing on hard river right where steps take you up to the park. If you don't want to run this one, you can take out before the drop on river right next to a huge rock outcrop; the bank is quite steep.

Other trips. It's possible to paddle the Little Fork another 101 miles, all the way to the Rainy River. The first very remote stretch runs 44 miles, through three Class I–II rapids, without a bridge crossing, passing state forestland and the Nett Lake Indian Reservation. A Class II rapids appears below that stretch, where the river grows gradually more developed as it approaches the city of Little Fork and then returns to wilderness for the remainder of the trip. The DNR publishes a canoe route map for the Little Fork.

A long boulder garden on the Little Fork.

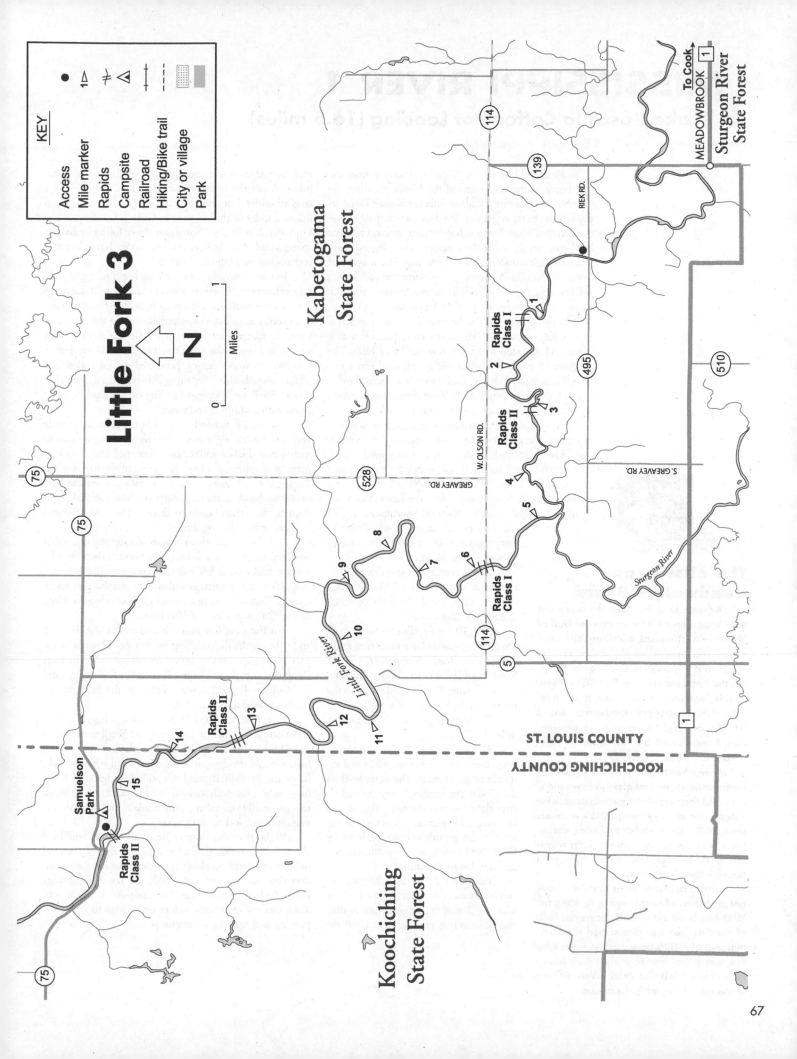

Little Fork 3

KEY

- Access
- Mile marker
- Rapids
- Campsite
- Railroad
- Hiking/Bike trail
- City or village
- Park

N

Miles
0 — 1

Sturgeon River State Forest

To Cook
MEADOWBROOK

Kabetogama State Forest

Koochiching State Forest

ST. LOUIS COUNTY
KOOCHICHING COUNTY

Little Fork River

Sturgeon River

RIEK RD.
GREAVEY RD.
W. OLSON RD.
S. GREAVEY RD.

Samuelson Park

Rapids Class I
Rapids Class II
Rapids Class I
Rapids Class II
Rapids Class II

1
2
3
4
5
6
7
8
9
10
11
12
13
14
15

114
139
495
510
528
75
114
5
1

MISSISSIPPI RIVER 1
Lake Itasca to Coffee Pot Landing (16.5 miles)

What could be a more inspiring canoe trip than one that begins at the headwaters of the Mississippi River, the river Native Americans called the Father of Waters? This journey can also be the beginning of a three-day camping trip on the river. You'll paddle through sedge meadows and wild rice beds, past cattails and rocky outcrops, over a logging dam, and past high wooded banks. If you read The Journals of Joseph N. Nicollet (see Appendix 3) before you paddle, you will probably also feel an affinity for this famous explorer in his map-making adventures on the Upper Mississippi.

Bird-watchers will be fascinated by the number of species they can see; the Mississippi Headwaters Flyway is home and rest stop to an amazing variety of birds. The Audubon Society (651-290-1695) will send you a free map, Great River Birding Trail. Deer, beavers, and otters frequent the marshland as well. If you camp along the river, you may also hear, or even spot, a timber wolf.

On Lake Itasca, the fishing is great for bass, walleyes, northerns, bluegills, and perch. Although anglers probably won't have much luck on the river, they may want to paddle up its tributary, Sucker Brook, to cast for brook trout.

Camp at Itasca State Park (866-857-2757; www.stay atmnparks.com). If the park is full, the Itasca Area Lakes Tourism Association (888-292-7118; www.itascaarea.com) lists area private campgrounds. Primitive camping is available at two riverside campsites, one at the takeout.

Canoe rentals and **shuttles** are available from Terry Larson of Northern Adventures (218-335-2078; 218-766-7543; tlnoadv@paulbunyan.net).

The 10.5-mile **shuttle route** from the public access on Lake Itasca runs north on County Road 38 and then County Road 2, all the way to County Road 40, east to County Road 9, and north to the turnoff on the left for Coffee Pot Landing.

The average **gradient** is 5.0 feet per mile.

The paddling is best in the spring, when the water is higher and wild rice doesn't choke the channel. The **water level** on the Coffee Pot Landing gauge, located on river right just past the footbridge, should be above 1.9 feet; above 3.5 feet is high water. You can get this information from the DNR (888-646-6367; www.dnr.state.mn .us/river_levels/index.html).

Put in at Lake Itasca's public boat access on the east side of the north arm of the lake. You'll need to portage around or drag over (depending on the water level) the rock dam at the outlet and, shortly after that, a low plank bridge across the young Mississippi. This isn't the river's original outlet, but visit the park to hear that story. Then follow 2 miles of shallow river to Gulsvig Landing at the Highway 200 bridge. Naturalists have found freshwater sponges under this bridge, a tribute to the clean water that is characteristic of the headwaters.

Just downstream, wild rice beds begin to appear. Local residents say that this area was an historic wild rice camp for Native Americans. On river left, Sucker Brook, 10 degrees cooler than the Mississippi, flows into the river. Despite the name Sucker, this is a state-designated trout stream, so a visit to this creek could yield you dinner, but be prepared to wade. A tiny protected orchid called bog adder's mouth also lives along this brook. After Sucker Brook, you'll see Wanagan Landing on the right, a canoe access with a campsite and water.

The land is flat and boggy, but the current is steady and you'll move right along. Sedge meadows decorated with willow thickets and red osiers line the banks. You'll see many half-submerged logs, remnants of the logging era. These can be a hazard, so watch carefully as you round the numerous bends in the river. After you have paddled about 7 miles, the terrain begins to change. The banks rise and conifers replace the bog shrubs.

At Vekin's Dam, the remnants of a logging sluice that was used to give logs a downstream boost, a short, brushy portage trail on the left will take you around this scenic drop. It's better to **portage** rather than run this very rocky Class II. Watch for some interesting spikes driven into logs on river left as you leave Vekin's Dam.

For the next few miles, boulders dot the riverbed and riffles make the paddling interesting. This is a lovely part of the trip, even though three bridges cross the river along this stretch: at County Road 37, a footbridge, and the County Road 2 bridge. Between the bridges, the banks are wild and beautiful.

After County Road 2, the Mississippi begins to meander across flat, marshy country again. You'll meet an unusual bridge with triangular railings, a reproduction of the first vehicular bridge across the Mississippi between Lake Itasca and Bemidji. Richard Felt built the original in 1896; his grandson Kenneth Richard Felt replicated it in 1998, although you'll notice that its underside is probably not the same construction as the original.

Right after the County Road 40 bridge, you'll see the collapsed remains of a log cabin on the left. Several oxbows are forming along this stretch to bypass meanders that have meandered a little too far. A footbridge marks Coffee Pot Landing. The campsite is on the left. **Take out** on river right before the bridge to reach the parking area and the water pump.

The Mississippi Headwaters Board

Anyone who has seen the waters of the Mississippi as it flows into the Gulf of Mexico—a chemical nutrient–thickened soup—will marvel at the clean, crystal water that flows out of Lake Itasca. Keeping the headwaters—the first 460 miles—of this legendary river clean is the mission of the Mississippi Headwaters Board (MHB), an eight-county joint powers board mandated by the state of Minnesota in 1980.

A river has to please so many people—from canoeists and anglers to town planners and farmers—that getting people involved has always been MHB's method. With MHB's River Watch program, volunteers from local high schools help monitor and protect the river that runs through their backyards.

Under pressure from the state budget problems of recent years, funding for MHB has been cut in half. However, lack of funding has not diminished the commitment of MHB's board or the folks who live along the river to protect their beautiful river. Visit the MHB Web site at www.mhbriverwatch.dst.mn.us

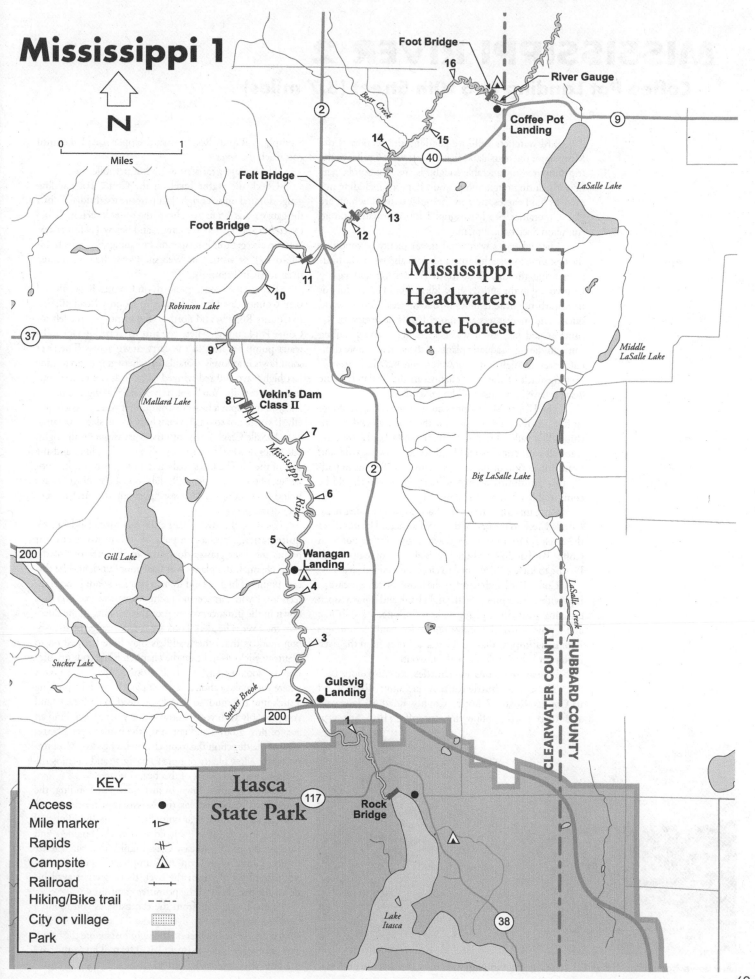

Mississippi 1

N

0 — 1
Miles

Foot Bridge
16
River Gauge
Coffee Pot Landing
2
Bear Creek
14 15
40
9

LaSalle Lake

Felt Bridge
13
12

Foot Bridge
11
10
Robinson Lake

Mississippi Headwaters State Forest

Middle LaSalle Lake

37
9

Mallard Lake

Vekin's Dam Class II
8
7

2

Big LaSalle Lake

Mississippi River

6

200
Gill Lake
5
Wanagan Landing
4

3

LaSalle Creek

CLEARWATER COUNTY
HUBBARD COUNTY

Sucker Lake
2
Gulsvig Landing
Sucker Brook
200
1

Itasca State Park
117
Rock Bridge

38
Lake Itasca

KEY

Access	●
Mile marker	1▷
Rapids	#
Campsite	⚠
Railroad	┼┼┼
Hiking/Bike trail	- - -
City or village	▦
Park	▧

MISSISSIPPI RIVER 2
Coffee Pot Landing to 510th Street (8.7 miles)

Bird-watchers will love paddling this section of the Mississippi; the marshland that characterizes 6 miles of the trip supports innumerable songbirds and waterbirds, particularly during migration periods. Raptors, including numerous bald eagles, nest in the upland areas, which are glacial moraines. See Mississippi 1 for information on an Audubon Society birding map.

May, when it's warm and there's plenty of runoff, is the best time to take this trip, and that's also when the birds are passing through. Waterbirds are nesting and raising their young in the spring, so paddlers should be careful not to disturb the little families of ducks, geese, loons, wood ducks, and mergansers any more than is necessary. In the summer and fall, lower water levels may make paddling through the thick aquatic plants of the wetland more difficult. Even at high water, however, you may have trouble keeping track of the river channel in the wetlands if the beavers have been busy building their dams.

The Upper Mississippi's current moves right along. At first, the river narrows, leaving the wetlands, and sweeps through a valley lined with high sandy banks that are forested with conifers and hardwoods; this is a wild and beautiful section of the river. Because you'll want to paddle this trip during average to high water, you should be comfortable paddling in Class I rapids.

Since this trip is relatively short, consider a side trip up LaSalle Creek to the first of the LaSalle Lakes. The mouth of the creek is just a few miles downstream of your put-in at Coffee Pot Landing and the lake is about a mile upstream. Be sure to leave enough time to cross the wetland area.

Coffee Pot Landing offers the most convenient **camping**, with a water pump on the right bank and a grassy, open camping area with a picnic table, a fire ring, a log shelter, and a privy across the bridge on the left bank. Stumphges Rapids, a campsite that can be reached only from the river, is on river left, .7 mile above the takeout.

For **canoe rentals** and **shuttles**, see Mississippi 1.

The 8-mile **shuttle route** is via County Road 9 east to County Road 27 north. County Road 27 jogs west and then north; follow the turnoff (510th Street or Stumphges Rapids Road) toward Upper Rice Lake until you reach the river.

The average **gradient** is 1.7 feet per mile.

Check the **water level** on the Coffee Pot Landing gauge, located on river right just past the footbridge. When the gauge reads 3.5 feet or above, the water level is high; between 3.5 and 1.9 feet is average, and below 1.9 feet is low. You can also get this information by calling the DNR (888-646-6367), or visiting its Web site (www.dnr.state.mn.us/river_levels/index.html).

From Lake Itasca, go north on County Road 38 and then County Road 2, all the way to County Road 40, east to County Road 9, and north to the turnoff on the left for Coffee Pot Landing, where you **put in**. A parking lot and a water pump are next to the carry-down access. The river soon flows into lovely marshland, where grasses up to nine feet high wave and red-winged blackbirds call their alarms from the cattails. You'll see beaver slides along the banks, and you may spot a beaver swimming if you approach quietly. If you're not so quiet, you'll hear its tail slap a warning.

LaSalle Creek flows into the Mississippi on the right, 2.0 miles downstream from Coffee Pot Landing, and the first of the LaSalle lakes is about a mile upstream. Just upstream of the confluence with the creek, archaeologists have found sites along the Mississippi from the Archaic and Woodland periods.

Finding the river channel in this marshland can require patience and a compass. Watch how the current points the river grasses downstream; if you're out of the main channel, the plants will float more upright. Use distant points of higher land to help you find your general direction; if you can see the point where the tree line dips down in the distance, you're probably looking in the direction the river is headed. Look for red or orange plastic ribbon markers that other paddlers may have left tied on to plants or sticks to indicate the channel. Keep your orientation by looking back and all around. Mark the points where you make a choice between two channels by pushing a stick into the mud, so that if you need to backtrack (and you probably will) you'll know where you've been. Find an area of firm ground and climb up the bank to get a better view of the direction the main channel is headed. Most importantly, allow plenty of time to navigate and to enjoy the birds, beasts, and plants of this beautiful area.

About 6 miles down from Coffee Pot Landing, the marshland maze ends as the Mississippi moves into a wooded valley. You'll hear noisy little springs bubbling and trickling into the river as it flows over the boulders and through the riffles and easy Class I rapids that characterize the last 2 miles of this trip. At Stumphges Rapids, a campsite accessible only from the river, there is water available down the path behind the primitive campsite.

Less than a mile from the campsite, as you round a bend to the right, you'll meet the 510th Street bridge. Watch for a large boulder on the right just before the bridge and **take out** on downstream left. The trail up to the road is a little steep and rocky, but adequate.

Just downstream from Coffee Pot Landing, the morning mist rises to meet the paddler.

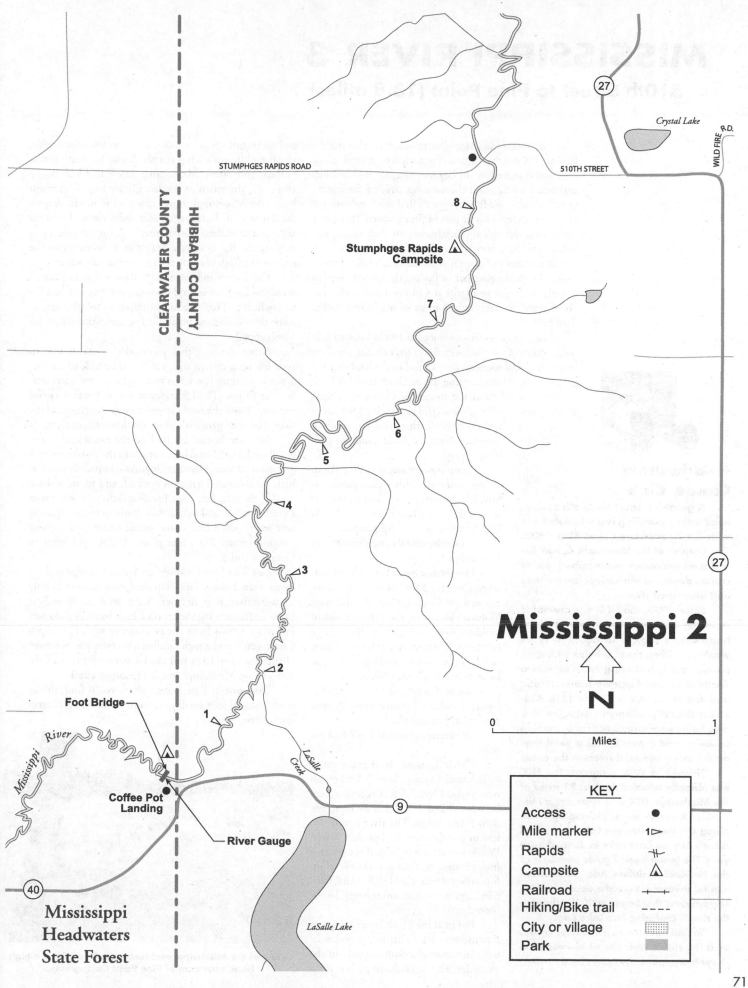

Crystal Lake

WILD FIRE RD.

(27)

STUMPHGES RAPIDS ROAD

510TH STREET

8

Stumphges Rapids
Campsite

7

6

5

4

3

Mississippi 2

N

0 — 1
Miles

2

Foot Bridge

River

Mississippi River

LaSalle Creek

1

Coffee Pot
Landing

River Gauge

9

(27)

CLEARWATER COUNTY

HUBBARD COUNTY

(40)

Mississippi
Headwaters
State Forest

LaSalle Lake

KEY

Access ·
Mile marker 1▷
Rapids ╫
Campsite △
Railroad ┼┼
Hiking/Bike trail - - - -
City or village ▦
Park ▨

71

MISSISSIPPI RIVER 3
510th Street to Pine Point (13.8 miles)

Headwaters Canoe Club

A great introduction to Mississippi headwaters paddling is a scheduled trip with the Headwaters Canoe Club (HCC). This chapter of the Minnesota Canoe Association welcomes nonmembers on its cruises down the Mississippi headwaters and other area rivers.

Since 1990, the HCC has promoted canoeing and protecting the rivers of the headwaters region. In addition to its weekly paddles, the club helps with area canoe races, including the Chippewa Triathlon (www.chippewa-triathlon.com) and the Headwaters Classic (218-335-2526; tjader@paulbunyan.net). The club also holds paddling clinics for beginning canoeists and generally has a good time on the many beautiful rivers in the area.

Through a DNR program, the HCC has officially adopted the first 82 miles of the Mississippi. HCC also sponsors a Mississippi River cleanup, picking up trash along the river between Lake Itasca and Allen's Bay on Cass Lake in June of each year. The group helped guide members of the National Audubon Ark—an environmental awareness paddle down the Mississippi River that began in 2001—through the river's confusing Rice Lake Bog.

To find out how to join a river cruise, visit the club's Web site at www.canoe-kayak.org/pages/hwaters.html

The young Mississippi flows through another marshland area as this trip begins. If water levels are medium or high and if you enjoy the beauties of a marsh—the birds and other wildlife and the amazing array of fascinating grasses, shrubs, and flowers—you'll find this 9-mile stretch of lazy meanders a lovely part of your journey. Trumpeter swans pass through the headwaters on their spring migration and have been spotted here. If the water levels are low, in summer or fall, or if you'd rather minimize the occasionally challenging task of finding the river channel in a wetland, begin your trip at County Road 5 instead. You'll travel through only 3 miles of marshland, rather than 9.

Either way, you'll also enjoy the lovely, forested 4.2-mile section of river between Bear Den Landing and Pine Point. A glacial moraine forms a rise in the land that begins near Bear Den Landing. If you climb the high bank across the river from the mouth of Hennepin Creek, you'll be rewarded by a wonderful view of the Mississippi and the creek. With no riffles or rapids to negotiate along the entire route, the paddling is easy.

Camping is available at Pine Point, a large campsite with water, picnic tables, log shelters, privies, and a good canoe landing. You can also camp at Bear Den Landing or Fox Trap campsite.

For **canoe rentals** and **shuttles**, see Mississippi 1.

The **shuttle route** runs east on Beltrami County's 510th Street and continues east on County Road 27 and then Wildfire Road. At the intersection of Wildfire Road and County Road 3, go north on 139th Avenue (Strecher Forest Road) to Pine Point Landing. If you put in at Beltrami County Road 5 instead, go south on County Road 5, which becomes Hubbard County Road 27 and proceed as just described.

The average **gradient** is 0.7 foot per mile.

Check the **water level** at the gauge at Beltrami County Road 5 bridge, on river right. Over 7.5 feet is high water, between 6 and 7.5 feet is average, less than 6 feet is low. The river is way too low to paddle when it's less than 4 feet. Paddle this stretch in May, if the water is high enough. You can get water level information from the DNR (888-646-6367; www.dnr.state.mn.us/river_levels/index.html).

Put in at the 510th Street bridge on downstream left. This is a gravel road with just enough room to park on the shoulder. The carry-down path is steep and rocky, but adequate. Soon after you leave the bridge, you'll paddle into a big marsh, home to many birds, beavers, and otters. Meandering across this low, boggy area—the aftermath of the last glacier to pass through here—the Mississippi moves along quite nicely, despite the flat terrain. Beaver and otter slides along the banks are evidence of these elusive creatures; if you're quiet, you may see the flat head of a beaver as it swims across the river or the flash of an otter slipping into the water.

The river wanders through these sedge and cattail meadows for 5 miles, and finding your way can be a little confusing. There are lots of things to see, though, so enjoy the wildlife and plant life. For navigational tips, see Mississippi 2.

About the time that you notice several houses to your left on a distant rise, you'll also be able to see evidence of County Road 5 to your right, if there's any traffic. The County Road 5 bridge at mile 6.3 makes a good rest stop. From the roadway you can see the course of the river. The river gauge is located on downstream right.

After the bridge, it's back to the marshland again. You'll see forested land begin to rise in the distance as you get closer to Bear Den Landing. As you paddle past the high, pine-covered bank on your left and round a sharp bend to the left, Bear Den Landing is on your left. From a sandy landing and a dock you climb up to the camping area where you'll find water, picnic tables, and a grassy campsite under big white pines. A dirt road leads to County Road 5.

Past Bear Den Landing, the banks rise high and are closer than before. Fox Trap campsite, accessible only from the river, is on river left, 1.2 miles down from Bear Den. You'll see a log shelter on a high bank. A mile past Fox Trap, across from the confluence with Hennepin Creek, you'll find a high sandbank on river left. A scramble up this steep bank will yield a wonderful view of the meandering Mississippi and of Hennepin Creek.

Take out at Pine Point, which you'll find off the main channel in a small quiet water area. A sign marks the landing.

View of the Mississippi and Hennepin Creek from a high bank upstream of Pine Point Campground.

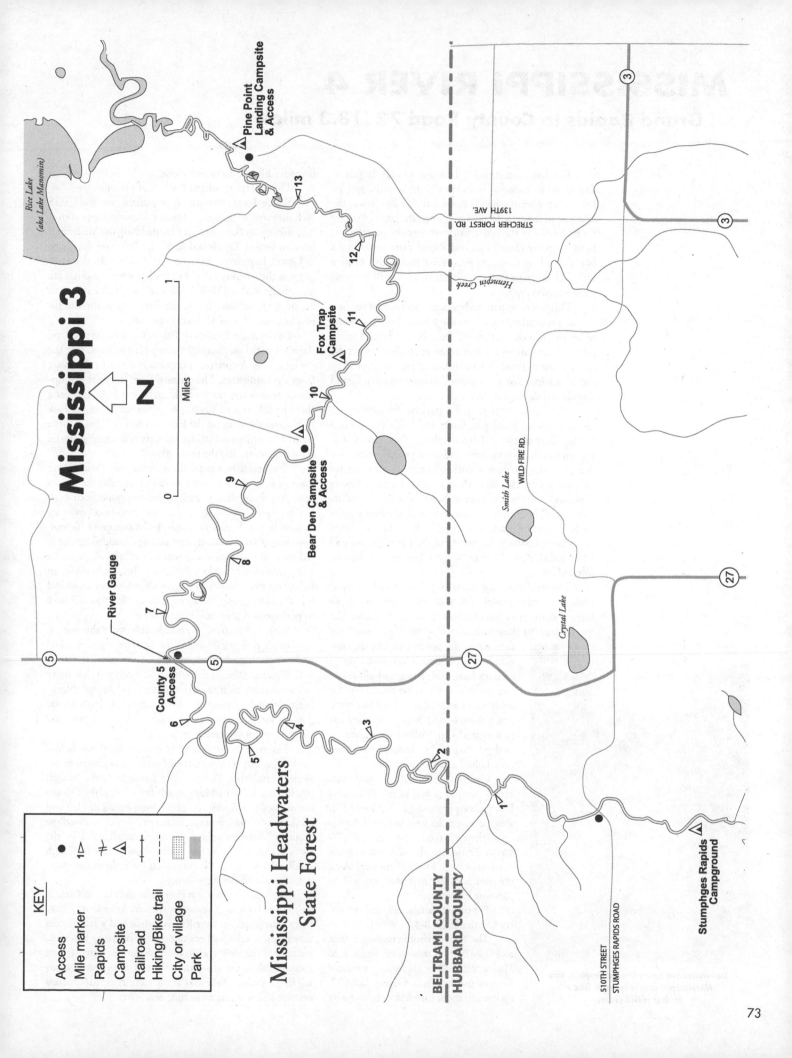

Mississippi 3

N

Miles

0 — 1

KEY

- Access •
- Mile marker 1◁
- Rapids ⊬
- Campsite △
- Railroad ┼┼
- Hiking/Bike trail ----
- City or village ▦
- Park ▨

Rice Lake
(aka Lake Manomin)

Pine Point
Landing Campsite
& Access

13

12

Fox Trap
Campsite

11

10

9

River Gauge

8

7

Bear Den Campsite
& Access

6

County 5
Access

5

4

3

2

1

Mississippi Headwaters
State Forest

STRECHER FOREST RD.

139TH AVE.

Hennepin Creek

Smith Lake

WILD FIRE RD.

Crystal Lake

27

27

BELTRAMI COUNTY
HUBBARD COUNTY

510TH STREET

STUMPHGES RAPIDS ROAD

Stumphges Rapids
Campground

3

3

5

5

MISSISSIPPI RIVER 4
Grand Rapids to County Road 72 (18.3 miles)

The river sometimes called Big Muddy begins to live up to its name as it leaves Grand Rapids. Just an ankle-deep stream when it flows out of Lake Itasca, the Mississippi is now a deep river, stained the color of strong tea by tannin in the water. Pouring over the Blandin Paper Company Dam in Grand Rapids, the water looks like a root beer float, copper-tinted and frothy. Only a little silt hangs in the water here; you can still see your paddle as you dip it.

This is a great trip for beginners and can be the first day of a multiday trip down the Mississippi. You won't meet any rapids, but the current is steady and fairly strong if the water is 2.5 feet or above on the gauge at the Itasca County Road 441 bridge. The Prairie River joins the Mississippi just a few miles downstream from Grand Rapids and doubles its water flow.

The Mississippi is still a narrow, friendly river, though, flowing south past farms and fields and forested banks; silver maple and ash overhang the channel. On upland wooded banks, ferns and spring wildflowers grow densely under the trees. Gentle hills rise, about a quarter mile away from the river. Mostly undeveloped and quiet along this stretch, the river is home to lots of wildlife. Bald eagles, herons, bank swallows, and numerous songbirds, including Baltimore orioles, have been spotted along here. Look for beavers (and their handiwork) and white-tailed deer. Timber wolves live in the heavily forested areas.

The meandering Mississippi is a fickle river. Oxbows—abandoned loops of the channel—have formed as the river has changed its twisting course. The quiet waters of these oxbows are spawning grounds for fish, especially northerns. On the outside banks of some meanders, clumps of trees have slid, roots and all, down the sandy banks into the river. Look for evidence of a past flood about five miles down from Grand Rapids: on river left is a rusted-out Volkswagen carcass, wedged in a gully. Someone whimsically lashed a canoe to its roof.

Camping is available at two river-access campsites and at the Pokegama Dam Campground (218-326-6128), about 2 two miles west of Grand Rapids on Highway 2. For reservations, call 877-444-6777 or visit the Web site at www.reserveusa.com. Much of the land along the stretch of the river that you will be paddling is private.

For **canoe rentals**, call God's Country Outfitters (218-326-9866).

The 15-mile **shuttle route** goes west to Highway 169, then north and east to Highway 2. Follow Highway 2 southeast from Grand Rapids to County Road 72, then south to the turnoff for the access on river left; this is not a bridge access.

The average **gradient** is 0.5 foot per mile.

Water level information is available on the USGS Web site (waterdata.usgs.gov/mn/nwis/current/?type=flow.) The minimum flow necessary for paddling the Mississippi between Grand Rapids and Aitkin is 400 cfs on the gauge at Grand Rapids or 1,000 cfs at Aitkin. On the river gauge at the County Road 441 bridge, where readings are recorded on the DNR Web site (www.dnr.state.mn.us/river_levels/index.html), 1.8 feet is the minimum for paddling and 2.5 to 4.5 feet is optimal.

Put in at the Steamboat Public Water access in Grand Rapids, located on river right, along SE 1st Street, after the dental office. A concrete ramp leads down to the water from a parking area. The outflow from the dam just upstream makes the river a little turbulent here. It's just a short paddle out of town, past Veterans Memorial Park high above the river on the left and Oakland Park on the right. A Continental Bridge steel truss footbridge crosses the river, connecting the two parks.

Two and a half miles downstream, the Prairie River flows in from the left. After another two miles the houses have just about disappeared, as has the noise from both County Road 3 and Highway 2. The river's floodplains are clay, its higher banks are sand; the Mississippi's current, sweeping around its many curves, has mounded up sandy sediment in some areas and washed flat areas clean. Some of the river's sandy banks are dramatically high. You'll see an oxbow on river right; this loop of abandoned channel in a low, flat marshy area invites exploration, but you will have to **portage** into it at most water levels.

Sucher's campsite, accessible only from the river, is just under 6 miles downstream on river right, marked with a brown and yellow sign. This is a good rest area, with a picnic table, a fire ring, and a privy. A few more miles downstream is the County Road 441 bridge (Blackberry Bridge); a ramp on downstream left leads to the parking lot. The river gauge is on a bridge support and visible from downstream right.

The river's course is fairly straight until just before the bridge, but after that, the Mississippi begins some serious meandering. A few miles down from the bridge, you'll actually be paddling north for a half mile. On the outsides of the river's curves are high banks of clay and sand, some of which house bank swallows in vast swallow "condos," fascinating collections of small holes in the vertical banks. Watch for a bold seam of clay in a high sandbank on one of the curves. To the right of the channel, several oxbows have formed.

Herb Beer's access, on river right and close to County Road 3, is your next rest opportunity. After that, Blackberry Campsite, on river left, is a mile and a half farther downstream. Like Sucher's campsite, Blackberry has a picnic table, a fire ring, and an open-air latrine. Stairs lead up a steep bank to the grassy site, which is set in a small clearing in the woods. **Take out** at the County Road 72 access on river left, just one more mile downriver.

Downstream from Grand Rapids, the Mississippi starts to look like a substantial river.

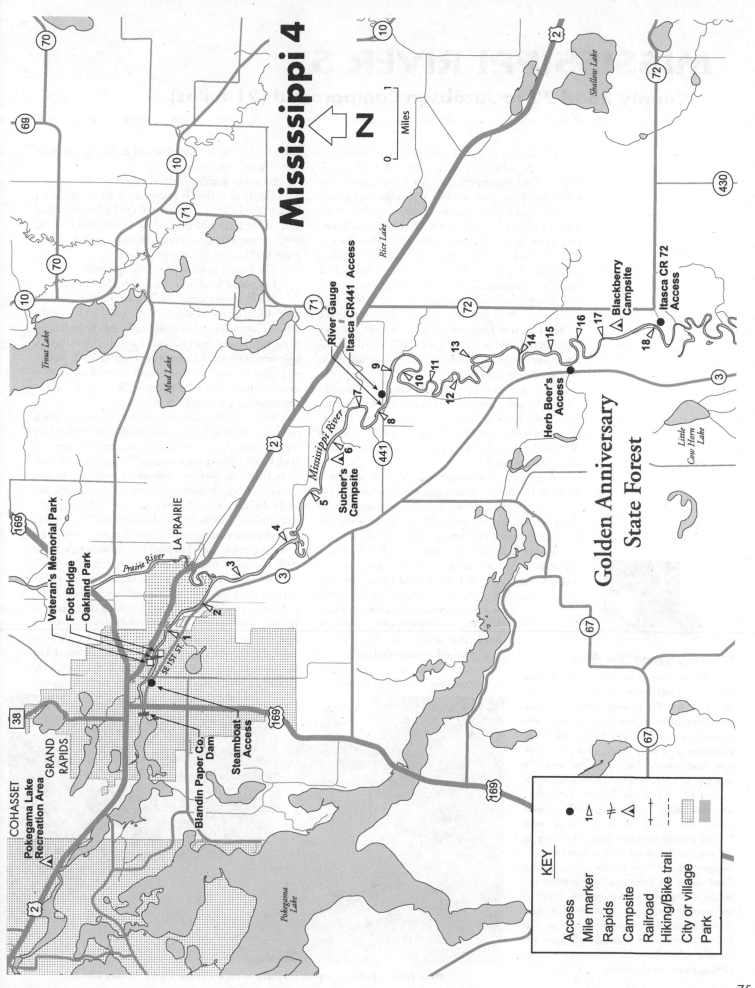

Mississippi 4

N

0 [====] 1
Miles

MISSISSIPPI RIVER 5
County Road 72 to Jacobson Campground (21 miles)

Like the last part of Mississippi 4, this beautiful segment of the Mississippi River flows through heavily forested land, interspersed with a few scattered farm fields. You'll see both wildlife and cattle, but mostly wildlife: bald eagles, waterbirds and songbirds everywhere, white-tailed deer, otters, the ubiquitous beaver population, and maybe even a black bear. When you hear the occasional bellow of cattle, you'll wonder if these are actually wild cattle, as the land seems far from agricultural. Even private land along the river corridor is mostly undeveloped and wild, a lovely habitat for lots of birds and animals. After Split Hand Creek, the low hills that bordered the river farther north fade away. Silver maples, cottonwoods, and ash trees grow thickly on the floodplains, overhanging, shading, and sometimes falling into the meandering channel.

And meander it does: it's only about 12 miles to Jacobson if you're a flying crow, but it's 21 miles if you're a canoeist on the river. Even with all this twisting and turning, though, the current is strong and steady, with only slight riffles, making this segment another good choice for beginning paddlers.

A few fishermen in motorboats use this segment of the river. Deadheads, those soggy, mostly submerged logs that are relics of lumbering days, lurk like crocodiles all along the river. Stay clear of deadheads; they look harmless, but hitting one from the wrong angle can tip a canoe.

Camping is available at Swimming Bear Campsite, a river-access site, and at the Jacobson Campground, an Aitkin County park off County Road 10 on 210th Avenue, on the west side of the river (218-927-7364; www.co.aitkin.mn.us/departments/Land%20Dept/land-dept/camping_information.htm). The campground, which charges a fee, has drinking water and is also accessible from the road. You can buy supplies at the convenience store in Jacobson— across the river on Highway 200 and then north on Highway 65 about a quarter mile.

For **canoe rentals**, see Mississippi 4.

The 18-mile **shuttle route** runs from the access on County Road 72 east and then south to Highway 65, then south to Highway 200, then west to County Road 10 and north a short distance to the campground turnoff. A long gravel road leads to the campground.

The average **gradient** is 0.5 foot per mile.

For **water level** information, see Mississippi 4.

Put in at the County Road 72 access. After you pass what's left of one of the old steamboat landing piers on the left a bit downstream, the next few miles are a beautiful part of the trip. Several small tributaries join the Mississippi. A high vertical riverbank houses bank swallows in a collection of dozens of small holes, the kind of swallow "condominium" mentioned in Mississippi 4. Split Hand Creek, a larger tributary, flows in from the right.

About 11 miles downstream from the put-in, you'll paddle around a big bend to the right and Swimming Bear campsite will appear, perched high on a bank on river left. Look for the yellow and brown sign. With a great view both up and down the river, the campsite is a lovely place to stop for lunch, especially since it's halfway along your trip. You could also stop at the County Line access boat ramp, farther downstream. (You'll cross the real county line another 2.2 miles downriver from the access.) Much of the land on river left is public land, but most land on river right and a small amount on river left is privately owned.

After you cross the county line from Itasca into Aitkin County, the Mississippi runs through several more back-and-forth meanders before depositing you at the **takeout** at Jacobson Campground. Look for a concrete ramp on river right, just before the riverbank rises. At the time this trip was researched, the campground ramp was unmarked, but the missing sign may have been replaced; this is the only ramp along here. A short road leads up to the campground.

Steamboat Traffic

Along the river between Grand Rapids and Aitkin are several spots where you can see the rotting remains of old riverboat landings and piers, relics of the steamboat era between 1870 and 1920. Amazing as it may seem, given the narrow and twisty nature of the river, a number of 85-foot-long steamboats, with names like the Andy Gibson, the Irene, and the Oriole, hustled regularly up and down the river between Aitkin and Grand Rapids in those days, stopping at 25 regular landings and wherever passengers asked them to stop. People who lived along the river would also hang out a flag to signal the boats to stop for passengers or packages, or to deliver their groceries. Because their boilers often exploded, many of these boats burned. Others sank from overloading or after hitting snags in the river.

These folks pulled their kayak on shore to take a break from a 10-day paddle.

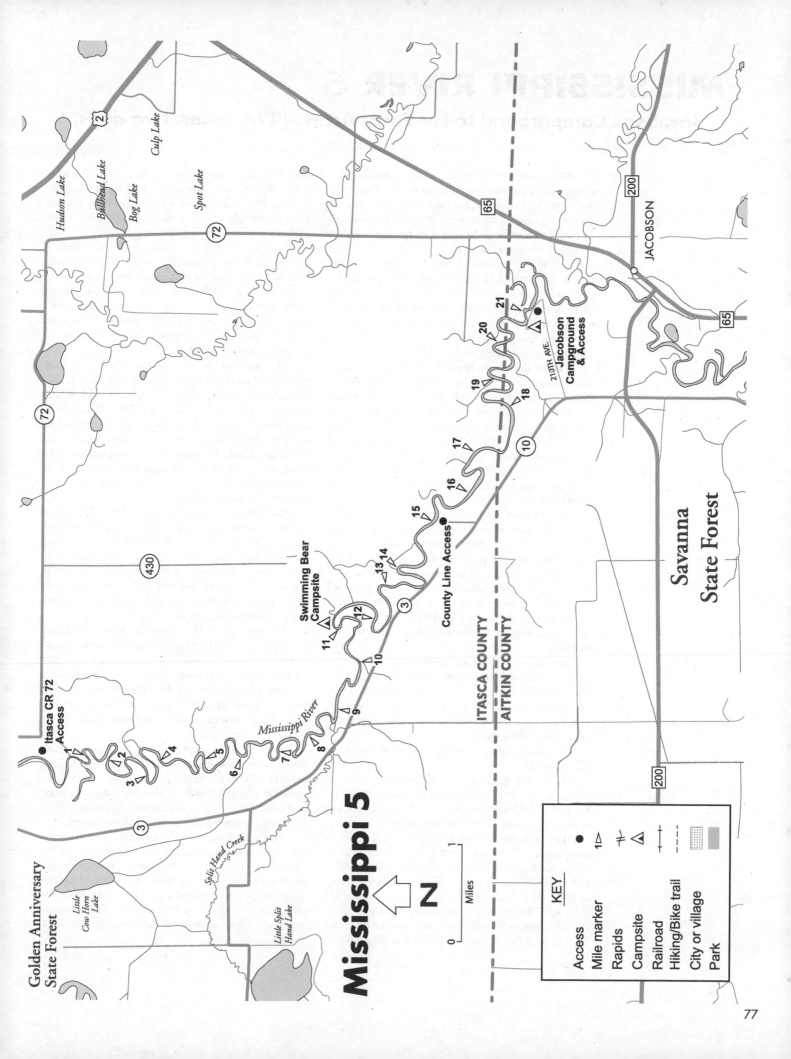

MISSISSIPPI RIVER 6
Jacobson Campground to Lee Ferry Access (29.5 miles, two days)

With enough flow on this stretch of the Mississippi, a strong paddler can finish this trip in one day. Those who like to dawdle, fish, and explore oxbows will prefer to make it a two-day trip and stay at one of the two river campsites. At Pine Rapids (mile 14.8) a small grassy strip of private land on river right separates the river from County Road 10, making this a potential alternate access (with the landowner's permission). A few stretches of riffles punctuate an otherwise smooth, steady flow, great for beginning paddlers who want to improve their boat control. Anglers may decide to explore two state-designated trout streams—Two Rivers Springs and Libby Brook—that feed the Mississippi in the second half of this stretch.

Flowing through the heavily forested land of northern Aitkin County, the river also passes through some agricultural land. The dense forest that lines much of the river is habitat for many different animals and birds. Silver maples and ash grow thickly on the floodplain areas. These hardwood forests also have a beautiful, dense understory of ferns and numerous wildflowers. You will see bald eagles, smaller raptors, great blue herons, geese, mergansers, pileated woodpeckers, and many songbirds. Beavers, otters, and white-tailed deer are common, and you may even hear a timber wolf howl at night.

Broken posts from old boat landings—reminders of the steamboat era of a century ago—are visible in the river between Jacobson Campground, where the trip begins, and the Highway 200 bridge at Jacobson. Towns like Jacobson that sprang up at steamboat landings grew and prospered during the logging era but faded as the logging industry moved away. Jacobson is now working to revive its past vitality by building a community center on river left before the bridge.

For information on **camping** at Jacobson Campground, see Mississippi 5. Camping with all the amenities is also available at the Sandy Lake Recreation Area. For reservations, call 877-444-6777 or go to the Web site www.reserveusa.com. You'll also find two riverside campsites, Willow Wood and Ms. Keto.

For **canoe rental** and **water level** information, see Mississippi 4.

The average **gradient** is 0.6 foot per mile.

The 18-mile **shuttle route** runs south on County Road 10 to Highway 200, then east to Highway 65, and south to the turnoff for the Lee Ferry public water access.

Put in at the Jacobson Campground boat ramp. A short distance downstream, just past the entrance to an oxbow, you'll see what looks like a small building standing high above the river in a farmer's field on river left. It's actually an old railroad car. The rotting remains of the old Hill City Railway (formerly known as the Mississippi Hill City and Western Railway) trestle also cross the river here. You'll see what's left of wooden steamboat landing piers between here and Jacobson. The confluence with the Swan River, a large tributary, appears on river left just before the Highway 200 bridge at Jacobson. The Jacobson Wayside Rest is on the right; at most water levels, access to this park is difficult as the bank is high and steep.

For about a mile below Jacobson, the enclosed river corridor opens up and you'll see houses and farmland. Then the forest returns for a bit, mostly deciduous trees, silver maple and ash with a little birch sprinkled in. About 4 miles from the bridge, you'll find the openings to several oxbows. Even if the mouths of these quiet water loops are blocked by the beaver's handiwork, you can drag your canoe over to explore and fish.

The first river campsite, Willow Wood, is on river right about 9 miles past the bridge, with a picnic table visible. Unless the water level is fairly high, the access to this campsite is a difficult one. Right past Willow Wood, you'll pass a house on river right; then, around a sharp bend to the right, you'll see an unusual geodesic dome house on the left. County Road 10 swings close on river right a few miles down; at the same time you'll meet Pine Rapids, a short stretch of riffles. Access to County Road 10 may be possible here if you ask the landowner.

You'll find Ms. Keto Campsite on river left, about 3.25 miles downriver from Pine Rapids, a quarter mile past a high sandy bank, on a stretch of the river flowing west. Watch for the campsite sign. This wooded site has an easy access. If you visit Ms. Keto in the spring, you'll also find it lavishly decorated with beautiful wildflowers and ostrich and asparagus ferns; moss-covered logs add to the beauty. And yes, there are mosquitoes in these woods.

Downstream of Ms. Keto, the Mississippi flows through more wooded territory. Several stretches of moderate riffles punctuate four scenic miles of shallow, rocky sandbars. Exposed clay banks take on a reddish tint. Four miles down from Ms. Keto is the confluence with the Two Rivers Springs trout stream on the left. At low water levels, the mouth of the stream may be blocked by the handiwork of some busy beavers.

Another 4-mile stretch of rocky shallows and intermittent riffles follows as you paddle past forested, fern-covered banks. Soon after you pass an island on river right, the mouth of Libby Brook, another trout stream, appears on the left. After you pass this confluence, Highway 65 is audible on the left, but only for a very short distance.

Take out on the left at the Lee (aka Libby) Ferry access, a well-maintained canoe access with timber steps up the bank and a short trail to the parking lot. A ferry crossing owned by the Lee family from 1873 to the 1890s, the access has since been part of a parcel of Libby Township public land that also has a river campsite (farther downstream) and is now managed by the Minnesota DNR and Aitkin County.

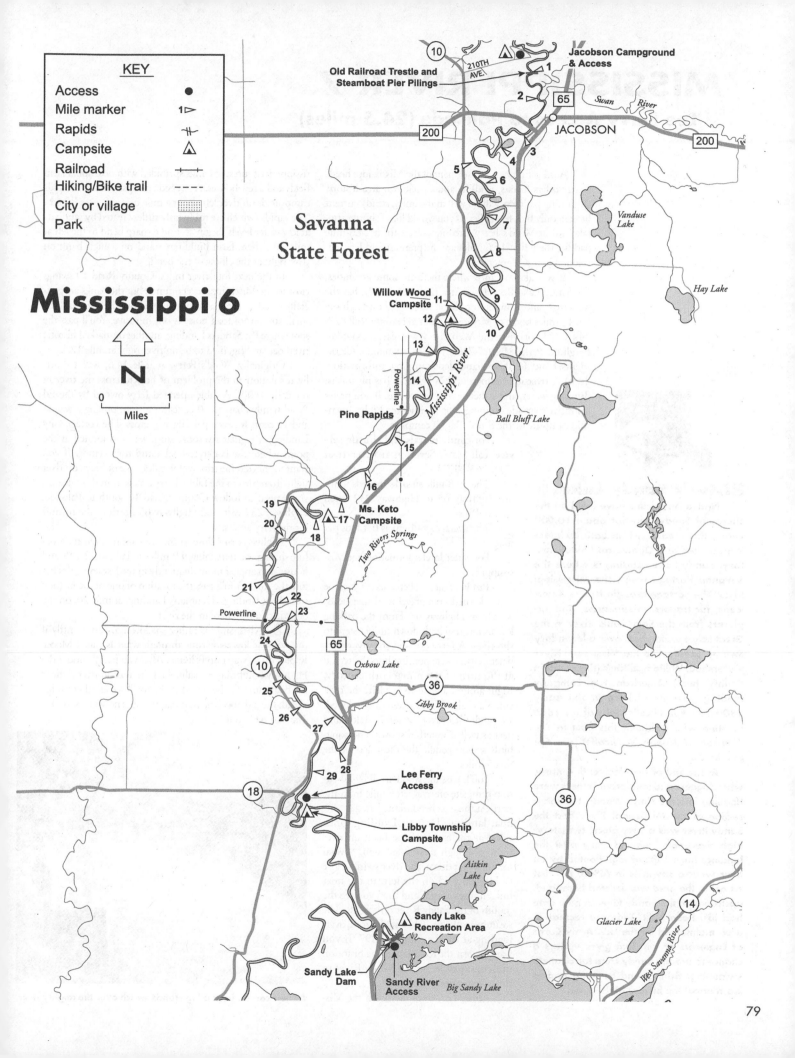

Mississippi 6

KEY

Access	●
Mile marker	1▷
Rapids	#
Campsite	▲
Railroad	+—+
Hiking/Bike trail	– – –
City or village	
Park	

N

0 ——— 1
Miles

Savanna
State Forest

Jacobson Campground
& Access

Old Railroad Trestle and
Steamboat Pier Pilings

210TH AVE.

JACOBSON

Swan River

Vanduse Lake

Hay Lake

Willow Wood
Campsite

Mississippi River

Pine Rapids

Powerline

Ball Bluff Lake

Ms. Keto
Campsite

Two Rivers Springs

Powerline

Oxbow Lake

Libby Brook

Lee Ferry
Access

Libby Township
Campsite

Aitkin Lake

Sandy Lake
Recreation Area

Glacier Lake

West Savanna River

Sandy Lake
Dam

Sandy River
Access

Big Sandy Lake

A peaceful float, this segment of the Mississippi headwaters offers forests, wildlife, and a peek into area history. Beginning paddlers will do well in the quiet, steady current broken only by a few riffles. If you would like a shorter trip, take out at Wold's Ferry Crossing access for a 14.6-mile paddle; these first 14.6 miles are the prettiest and least developed in this segment.

If you like to **camp** where there are some amenities, the Sandy Lake Recreation Area (218-426-3482), has the full range, and a museum to boot. It's located on Highway 65, 13 miles north of McGregor. For reservations, call 877-444-6777, or visit the Web site www.reserveusa.com. Berglund Park (218-927-7364; www.co.aitkin.mn.us/depart ments/Land%20Dept/land-dept/camping_information .htm), a riverside campground in Palisade, has pit toilets, drinking water, and a shelter with a fireplace. If you prefer primitive riverside camping, stop at either the Libby Township campsite or the Scott's Rapids campsite.

For **canoe rentals** and **shuttle service**, call Marty Severson at River Treat (218-765-3172).

The 19.8-mile **shuttle route** is south on Highway 65 to Highway 232, then west to Palisade.

The average **gradient** is 0.4 foot per mile.

For **water level** information, see Mississippi 4.

Put in at the Lee Ferry access, a canoe access located on a gravel road that heads west from Highway 65. From the parking lot, a short trail leads down timber steps to the river. A ferry crossed the river here when settlers were pouring into the region at the turn of the nineteenth century. Right around a bend to the left, the river enters a wetland. This area is undeveloped, so watch for beavers, otters, turtles, and deer as well as waterbirds, owls, and songbirds as you paddle the meanders of the first 5 miles.

You'll pass the wooded Libby Township campsite on river left a mile from the start. At the next bend to the left, a steamboat landing, Doney's Landing, once stood at the elbow of the bend on river right, although there is no sign. Several miles farther down, the river swings close to Highway 65 on the left; in the next mile, houses appear and then you see the mouth of the Sandy River on the left. The steamboat *Walter Taylor* sank from overloading at this landing in 1897. If you want to visit the recreation area's historical museum, paddle up the Sandy River to the campground.

Otherwise, continue down the Mississippi, past forested banks sprinkled with occasional farm fields and a few houses. A riverside campsite, Scott's Rapids campsite, is on river left about a mile before Scott's Rapids. The rapids (which are really only riffles created by sandbars at low water levels) begin around a sharp bend to the left at mile 10, where farm buildings stand on a high bank on river right at the elbow of the bend.

In the next four river miles, County Road 10 swings close to the Mississippi several times, but the banks are generally wooded, the road is not visible from the river, and the small amount of road noise is not intrusive. You'll pass the spot where Pat Sanders Landing, another unmarked historic riverboat landing, used to be on river right at mile 12.5.

Originally, Wold's Ferry, at mile 14.6, was a short-lived solution to the problem of how to cross the river in the early 1900s. A cable-operated ferry owned by the Ed Wold family charged 50 cents for a team pulling a wagon and 10 cents for each passenger to cross. The Portage City Landing, a regular riverboat stop, was also located at the point where the concrete boat ramp now stands. If you want to shorten the trip by 9.9 miles, take out here on river right. To return to the Libby Ferry access from this takeout, you'll need to follow County Road 10 south to Palisade, Highway 232 east, and Highway 65 north to the turnoff for the ferry access.

Highways run close to the river more often than before during the remaining 9.9 miles to Palisade. Fields and houses also appear more frequently in the last few miles before the town. You'll pass the location of one of the historic steamboat landings, Denman's Landing, at mile 20, on the outside of a big curve in the river.

The Mississippi is rather shallow and can be riffly if the water is low as it runs through what is called Moose Rapids on its way into Palisade. After you paddle under the Highway 232 bridge in Palisade, **take out** on river right at the boat ramp for Berglund Park. You'll see another bridge ahead: the old Soo Line Railroad trestle is now the Soo Line Trail, an ATV trail.

Historic Sandy Lake

Native Americans have lived on the shores of Sandy Lake for about 10,000 years; this area is rich in both archaeological sites and Ojibwe and Sioux history. Sandy Lake Landing is where the Savanna Portage meets the Mississippi River. The portage brought Native Americans, fur traders, missionaries, and explorers from the Saint Louis River in the Great Lakes watershed, over a legendary swamp portage, to the Mississippi River watershed. William Aitkin's (this is Aitkin County here) American Fur Company trading post stood here in the early 1800s. Joseph Nicollet tells of an 1836 meeting with Aitkin at this post in *The Journals of Joseph N. Nicollet* (see Appendix 3).

At the end of the nineteenth century, when loggers and immigrant settlers were flooding into the North Woods, this intersection of the Mississippi River and the Sandy River was a busy place: two-story-high riverboats steamed daily past the landing; huge rafts of logs floated by on their way to sawmills in Aitkin; the first school in the area was located here; and, upstream on the Sandy River, a new dam had just been built. Today, a recreation area maintained by the U.S. Army Corps of Engineers at the dam gives visitors a chance to use Big Sandy Lake for boating, swimming, fishing, and camping and to learn about the history of the area.

A chair carved from a log stands watch over the mighty river.

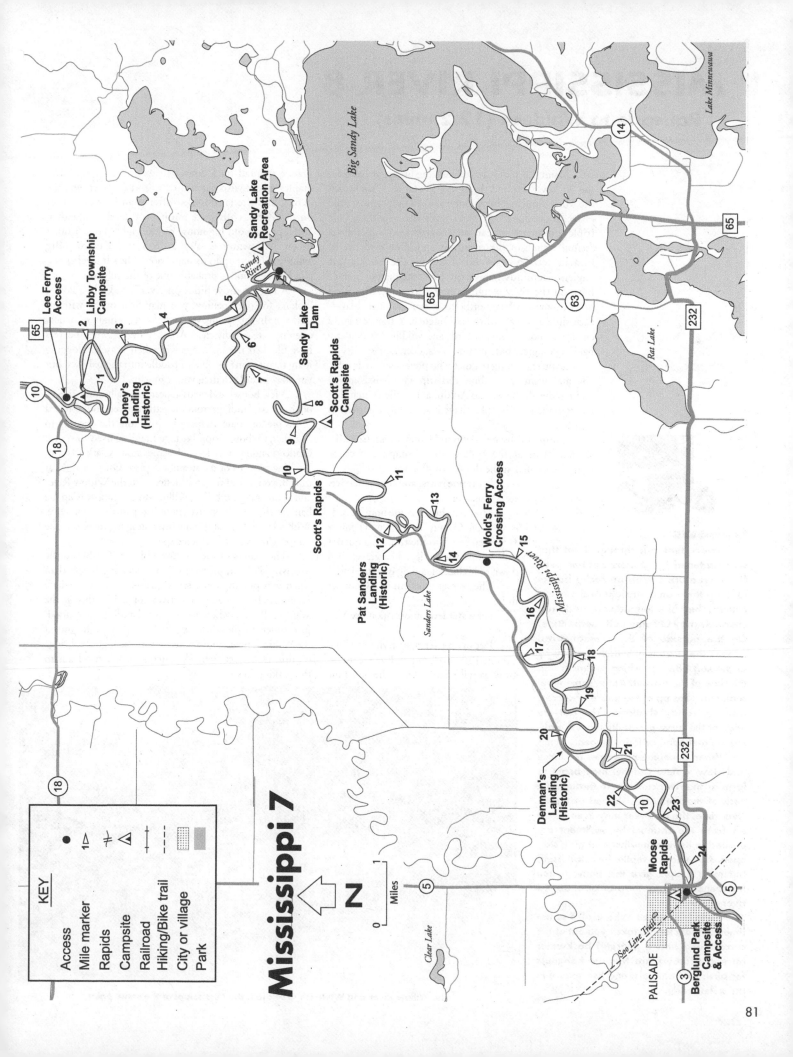

Mississippi 7

KEY

- ● Access
- 1△ Mile marker
- ⚕ Rapids
- △ Campsite
- ┼ Railroad
- ┄ Hiking/Bike trail
- ▦ City or village
- ▨ Park

N

Miles

0   1

Lee Ferry Access

Libby Township Campsite

Doney's Landing (Historic)

Sandy Lake Recreation Area

Sandy River

Sandy Lake Dam

Big Sandy Lake

Lake Minnewawa

Scott's Rapids Campsite

Scott's Rapids

Pat Sanders Landing (Historic)

Sanders Lake

Wold's Ferry Crossing Access

Mississippi River

Rat Lake

Denman's Landing (Historic)

Moose Rapids

Clear Lake

Soo Line Trail

PALISADE

Berglund Park Campsite & Access

MISSISSIPPI RIVER 8
Palisade to Waldeck (12.2 miles)

About 8.0 miles down from the bridge at Palisade, the Willow River and the White Elk Creek Oxbow join the Mississippi at a lovely intersection that captures the peaceful essence of the river along this segment. This triple confluence appears on a heavily wooded, remote-feeling stretch of the river, but appealing evidence of human activity—several chairs on the bank await anglers—reminds you of the fun that people love to have on the river. Anglers may also enjoy exploring other oxbows—where northerns spawn and otters play—accessible upstream of the confluence. You have a good chance of spotting lots of birds and wildlife, particularly bald eagles, great blue herons, owls, deer, and beavers.

If you're a strong paddler who prefers not to dawdle, you may want to combine this trip with Mississippi 9 and paddle all the way to Aitkin, a 31-mile stretch that racers in the Riverboat Heritage Race in July complete in four hours.

Camp at Palisade's Berglund County Park (see Mississippi 7) or at the Willow River campsite, a canoe campsite located at the double confluence.

For **canoe rental** and **shuttle service**, see Mississippi 7.

The 10.2 **shuttle route** from Palisade is west on County Road 3 to Highway 169, then south to the turnoff, a quarter mile before the bridge. The gravel road down to Waldeck Landing is on the left.

The average **gradient** is 0.8 foot per mile.

For **water level** information, see Mississippi 4.

Put in on river right at the Berglund County Park boat ramp in Palisade. Right away, you'll paddle under the Soo Line Trail, a railroad track converted to an ATV trail. Silver maples mixed with paper birches and ash overhang the banks, and the land looks softer than it does farther north. It's not truly wild, but it's not developed, either. You'll pass an old log house on the right about 5 miles down. The water is silty, a deep coffee color—Big Muddy is living up to its name now. The silt level varies, and bank erosion is probably one of the culprits.

A large oxbow hides on river left. Unless you're looking for the opening, you may float on by without noticing. In the spring, when the water is highest, oxbow openings are usually clear. At low water, or when beavers have blocked the openings with their ceaseless logging mania, you won't be able to paddle into the oxbows, but you may be able to drag your canoe in.

A few houses and fields appear, generally at the sites of old riverboat landings from the settlement era, but forested banks predominate. Across the river from the opening to Maydale Oxbow, Tripp Portage Landing used to stand. Clark's Landing was located across from Clark Oxbow. Nothing remains of the steamboat piers. On river right at mile 8, you'll find the confluence with the Willow River and White Elk Creek. The Willow River campsite is up the bank in the woods on river right just past the confluence. With a lovely view and some interesting log furniture, the campsite makes a great picnic spot.

The waters of the Willow add considerably to the Mississippi's flow; the river is now wider and bigger than when you put in. You'll see a sprinkle of houses where Highway 169 parallels the river for a bit; this is the Waldeck Ranch, where John Lyon's Landing once stood. Just under 3 miles downstream from there, **take out** at the Waldeck boat landing, just before the highway bridge on upstream river right. A concrete boat ramp leads to the parking lot.

Oxbows

Rivers that run through land that was flattened by glaciers become very fickle creatures. With no rocky banks to keep them on a straight and narrow course, they like to meander, and their channels may become quite serpentine. On the outside of these meandered curves, the current gradually cuts away at the soft bank, washing sediment into the flow of the current. At the same time, sediment piles up at the inside of curves, forming sandy shallows. The outside edge of the curve gradually moves, making the meander, or loop, bigger.

When a meander becomes too large and slow, a new channel may begin to form as the river cuts a path through the neck of the horseshoe-shaped meander. Over time, the meander may even be cut off from the channel by sediment deposited in its two mouths, or it may stay open. An oxbow is really the cutoff itself, but most people give this name to the horseshoe-shaped loop of abandoned river channel.

Paddling into an oxbow, also sometimes called a logan, takes you out of the current and into a peaceful backwater retreat. Oxbows are favorite hangouts for birds and animals, and fish spawn in the quiet water.

The Willow River and White Elk Creek join the Mississippi at the same point.

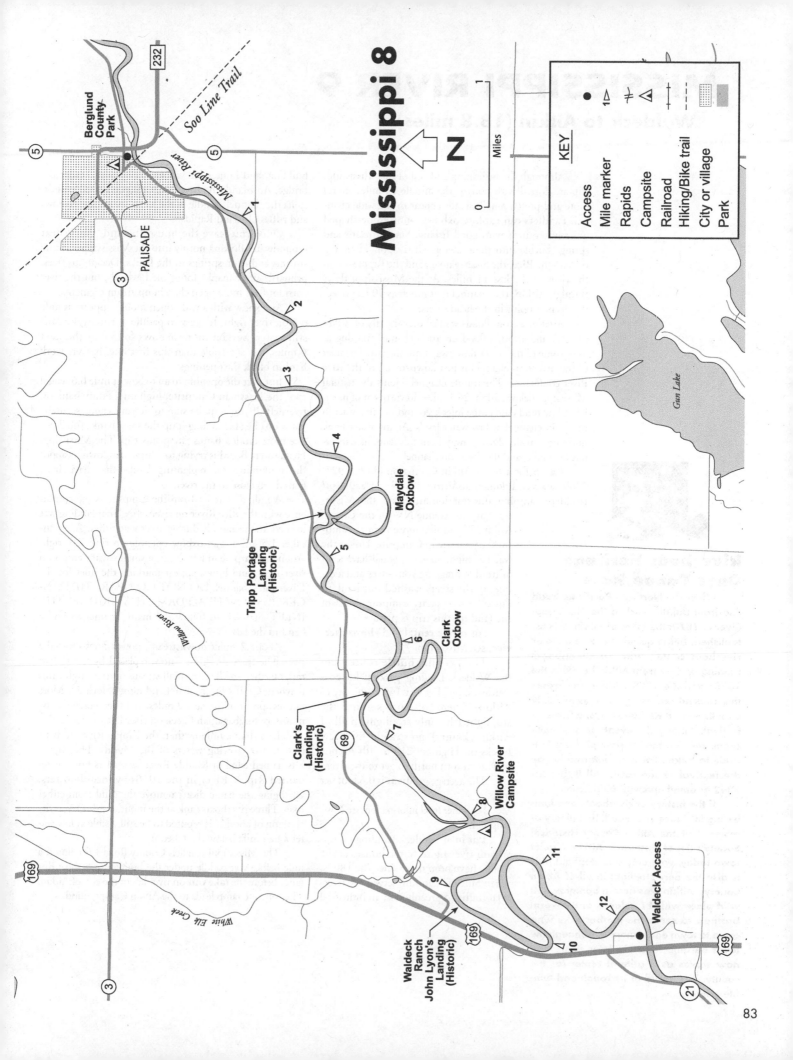

Mississippi 8

N

Miles

0   ½   1

MISSISSIPPI RIVER 9
Waldeck to Aitkin (18.8 miles)

Although the beginning and end of this Mississippi trip are dotted with houses, the middle 12 miles are remote and pretty. Small islands appear in the wide channel. Paddlers can explore oxbows—horseshoe-shaped quiet-water areas with good fishing. Small streams and springs burble into the growing Mississippi. Three big rivers—the Rice, the Sisabagamah, and the Ripple—join the river in the last 11 miles. As the Mississippi flows through Aitkin, the channel is as much as 50 feet deep, the deepest point in the headwaters.

After disastrous floods washed over the city of Aitkin in 1905 and 1950, a flood diversion channel was dug to force some of the river's flow away from the city. The inlet of the diversion channel is just downstream of the Rice River confluence. The 6-mile channel rejoins the natural Mississippi below Aitkin, 24.1 miles downstream of its inlet. A low-head dam at the inlet keeps most of the water in the main channel at low water levels. At any water level, however, you should stay away from this dam, its dangerous hydraulic, and the diversion channel.

Camp for a fee at Aitkin Campground (218-927-7364; www.co.aitkin.mn.us/departments/Land%20Dept/landdept/camping_information.htm), on the Mississippi at 4th Avenue NW in the City of Aitkin. If you like more remote campsites, try Hassman Campsite. Unless the water is high, however, you'll have a lot of trouble dragging yourselves and a canoe up the steep, washed-out bank to this otherwise pretty campsite. Most of the land on this trip is private.

For **canoe rental** and **shuttle service**, see Mississippi 7.

The 12-mile **shuttle route** from the Waldeck Landing parking lot goes southwest on Highway 169 to the city of Aitkin. Where 169 turns south at the stoplight (the only stoplight in all of Aitkin County), go straight for a few blocks on Highway 210 to 4th Avenue NW, then turn north to get to the river.

The average **gradient** is 0.6 foot per mile.

For **water level** information, see Mississippi 4.

Put in at Waldeck Landing on upstream river right. Some houses at the bridge have been there since the 1800s, when Sutton's Landing served the riverboat traffic. A greenhouse, an industrial building, and houses are visible after you go under the bridge. An island, the first of several good-sized islands, splits the channel; paddle to the left to avoid the shallows and riffles of Island Rapids.

Once you leave the houses behind, you'll hear groundwater flowing noisily into the Mississippi, in tiny streams and from springs in the banks. Deciduous trees, primarily silver maple, forest the lowlands, but the river corridor feels more open than in upstream segments.

An oxbow with a wide-open mouth appears at mile 3.5 on river right. It's easy to paddle in and explore the still water. Several more oxbows follow in the next 6 miles, less accessible than this first one: beavers work hard to block the openings.

Just past the opening to an oxbow at mile 6.6, you'll spot the Hassman Campsite, high on a sandy bank on river left. If you stop, be sure to tie your canoe securely; you won't be able to drag it up the steep bank. You'll notice more eroded banks along this trip. The Mississippi Headwaters Board is trying to educate landowners about the importance of replanting banks that have been grazed too close to the river.

A mile downriver from the campsite is the confluence with the Rice River on river left; a boat landing was located at the mouth during riverboat times. After another 1.5 miles is an oxbow opening on river left, right around a sharp bend left. Next, a small stream enters on river right, and buoys appear marking the inlet for the Diversion Channel. DO NOT GO NEAR THE DANGEROUS LOW-HEAD DAM THAT BRIDGES THE INLET. Stay left to follow the main channel around a bend to the left.

About 2 miles downstream, power lines cross the river. The trees are thinner now, replaced by fields. Two miles farther you'll see a small stream on river right: this is where Cluff's Steamboat Landing was located. More houses appear in the next 2 miles, and then you'll see the mouth of Sisabagamah Creek on river left.

Less than a mile farther, the Ripple River adds its flow to the growing waters of Big Muddy. The Ripple was named Mud or Muddy River by settlers but was renamed Ripple River in the 1950s by local boosters. Changing the name didn't remove the mud from either river. Three riverboats sank at the mouth of this river; the skeleton of another is reputed to be still visible at low water a half mile below the takeout.

The Mississippi parallels County Road 1 for almost a mile before you paddle under the bridge just a short distance before the **take out** on river left in the city of Aitkin. The concrete ramp leads to the Aitkin Campground.

Riverboat Heritage Days Canoe Race

When the Northern Pacific Railroad line from Duluth reached the Mississippi River in 1870, the town of Aitkin was established. Aitkin quickly became a major riverboat center, with 14 steamboats running upriver from Aitkin between the 1870s and the 1920s. Aitkin celebrates this colorful era every year in mid-July with Riverboat Heritage Days, a five-day festival. Among the events is a 31-mile canoe race on the Mississippi, from Palisade to Aitkin. For more information on the festival or the race, call 800-526-8342 or email upnorth@aitkin.com.

If the history of riverboats and lumbering intrigues you, you'll find plenty of material at the Aitkin County Historical Society's Depot Museum in Aitkin. A quiet town today, with only one stoplight (this is also the only stoplight in all of Aitkin County), Aitkin was once a boomtown, a wild place with 17 saloons and several brothels to serve the lumberjacks who came to town each summer. Although the town became tamer in later years and now serves as a cultural center for the county, it is proud of its rough-and-tumble origins.

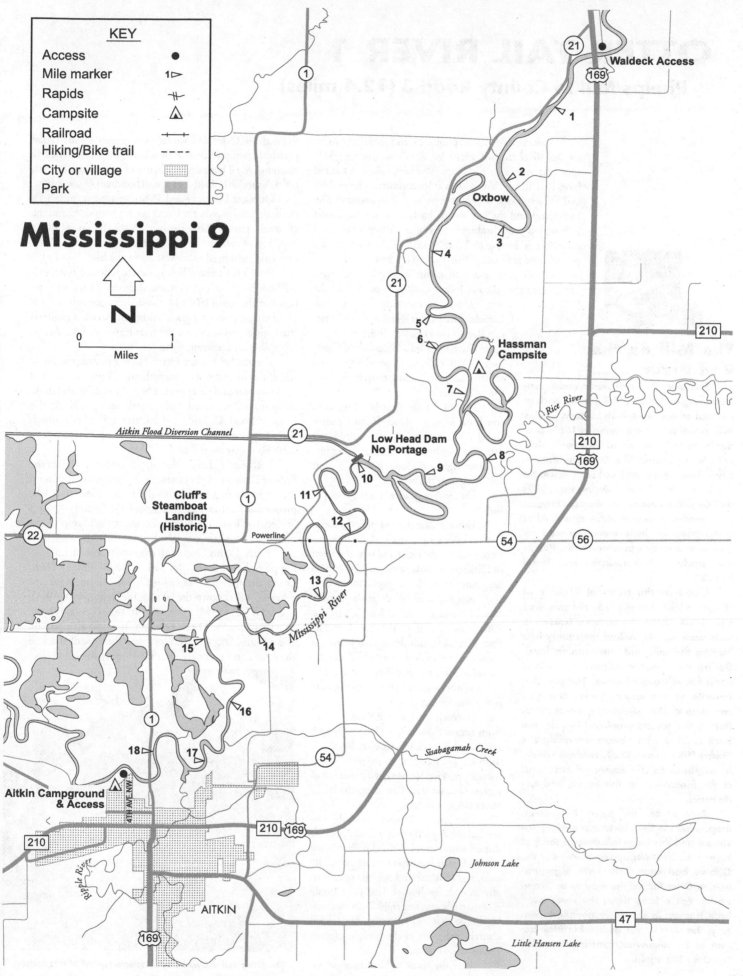

Mississippi 9

KEY

Access	●
Mile marker	1▷
Rapids	⧬
Campsite	△
Railroad	┼┼┼
Hiking/Bike trail	- - - -
City or village	▦
Park	▨

N

0   1
Miles

Waldeck Access

Oxbow

Hassman Campsite

Rice River

210

Low Head Dam No Portage

Aitkin Flood Diversion Channel

Cluff's Steamboat Landing (Historic)

Powerline

Mississippi River

Sisabagamah Creek

Aitkin Campground & Access

4TH AVE. N.W.

Ripple River

AITKIN

Johnson Lake

Little Hansen Lake

OTTER TAIL RIVER 1
Phelps Mill to County Road 3 (12.4 miles)

The Mill on the Red River

This quiet little mill was a major economic engine for Otter Tail County back at the end of the nineteenth century. Phelps Mill, which began operating in 1889, produced up to 75 barrels of flour every day, with lovely names like Gold Foil Patent, Silver Leaf Fancy, and Bakers Choice. So much flour left this mill during the 1890s that Otter Tail County was then the biggest flour producer west of Minneapolis. After water-powered mills were replaced by steam- and electric-powered mills, Phelps Mill gradually lost business and closed in 1939.

Listed on the National Register of Historic Places since 1975, the mill was saved from decay by Geneva Tweten, a local woman who talked the county into buying the mill and surrounding land. During the summer months, the mill is open for self-guided tours. The site is a favorite with photographers, and you can shop at the adjoining general store. During the second weekend in July, the park is filled with visitors attending the Phelps Mill Arts and Crafts Festival, which, in addition to the expected arts and crafts, features food, live music, and turtle races.

And as for the name Red River, mapmakers in the nineteenth century assumed that this large tributary of the Red River was its main upper reach. But the Ojibwe had named the river nigagwanoe, or Otter Tail, all the way up to Grand Forks. For a long time, the river bore both names. In the early twentieth century, the river as far as Breckinridge began to be somewhat consistently called the Otter Tail again.

A nice mix of history, photo ops, and wildlife, this Otter Tail River trip will please paddlers who enjoy a gentle river and some lake paddling. West Lost Lake is a natural lake; Red River Lake, a dam impoundment. Phelps Mill and Friberg Dam are photogenic as well as historic. The marshland and the oak woods habitats of this hardwood hills region provide abundant wildlife. Alternate accesses can shorten the trip to 5.5 or 9 miles. With a visit to the powerhouse at Friberg Dam, the trip is 14 miles.

A great place to **camp** is Maplewood State Park. From the takeout, follow County Road 3 to Highway 59, then go north on 59 to Pelican Rapids. The park is 7 miles east of Pelican Rapids on Highway 108.

The Fergus Falls Chamber of Commerce (218-736-6951), provides current information on **canoe rentals** for the Otter Tail River.

The 11.5-mile **shuttle route** goes south on County Road 45 to County Road 1, then west on 1 to County Road 10. Take a right on 10, then another immediate right on County Road 3, and follow that to the bridge.

The average **gradient** is 0.9 foot per mile.

Although **water level** information is not available for this reach of the river, information for the Otter Tail near the town of Elizabeth is available on the USGS Web site (http://waterdata.usgs.gov/mn/nwis/). If the gauge near Elizabeth (at the County Road 10 bridge) reads at least 5.5 feet or 280 cfs, the level above the dam should be fine. Because it runs through so many big lakes, the level of the Otter Tail is fairly stable all during the paddling season. The DNR is working to determine appropriate flow levels for canoeing.

To reach Phelps Mill County Park from Fergus Falls, follow County Road 1 north and then east to County Road 45. Turn left and follow 45 to the park, where there's a parking lot, shelters, privies, and a grassy picnic area. **Put in** on the backwater below the dam.

The clear shallow waters of the Otter Tail flow quietly over a sandy bottom dotted with mussel shells. The banks are wooded with hardwood trees, especially oaks. Agricultural land appears occasionally, as do a few houses. Less than a mile downstream on river right is an interesting house that is apparently a remodeled church; the front of the building facing the river is all glass.

After the house, a bluff rises on the left and the Otter Tail winds its way into a wide cattail marsh. If you paddle this beautiful stretch in the early morning, you'll have a good chance of seeing deer, beavers, otters, waterbirds, bald eagles, and hundreds of songbirds.

Once the County Road 35 bridge appears (mile 3.5), the marshland is past, the banks rise on both sides, and the channel narrows. After the bridge, the river is split by a huge bed of cattails. Follow the right shore to enter West Lost Lake, and head northwest across the lake.

West Lost Lake is lightly developed, and thick cattail beds line much of its wooded shores. At the narrows between the main lake and its northern portion, a duck blind on the point is a good landmark. An old-fashioned truss bridge crosses where the river leaves the lake. Access is possible on upstream right.

Past the bridge, the Otter Tail is a river again, but it still slides in and out of marshlands. High oak-covered banks appear and disappear. The river is deep and dark, its quiet waters lined with marsh marigolds. At the County Road 43 bridge, the Otter Tail runs through three large culverts. Access is possible up a steep grassy bank on upstream right.

Red River Lake, the impoundment above the Friberg Dam, emerges gradually. More houses appear on the high wooded banks and the river widens into lake proportions. After paddling under the County Road 3 bridge, you'll see the pier and cement boat ramp of the public access where you **take out** on the right.

To see Taplin Gorge and the architecturally interesting powerhouse (see Otter Tail 2) for the Friberg Dam, use an alternate takeout (which involves a **portage**), another 1.5 miles down the lake on the right. STAY AWAY FROM THE DAM. Directions to the access are in the shuttle route for Otter Tail 2. You could also paddle down to the dam to have a look and then paddle back to the more convenient access at the County Road 3 bridge.

The Otter Tail shows its calm nature typical of this section.

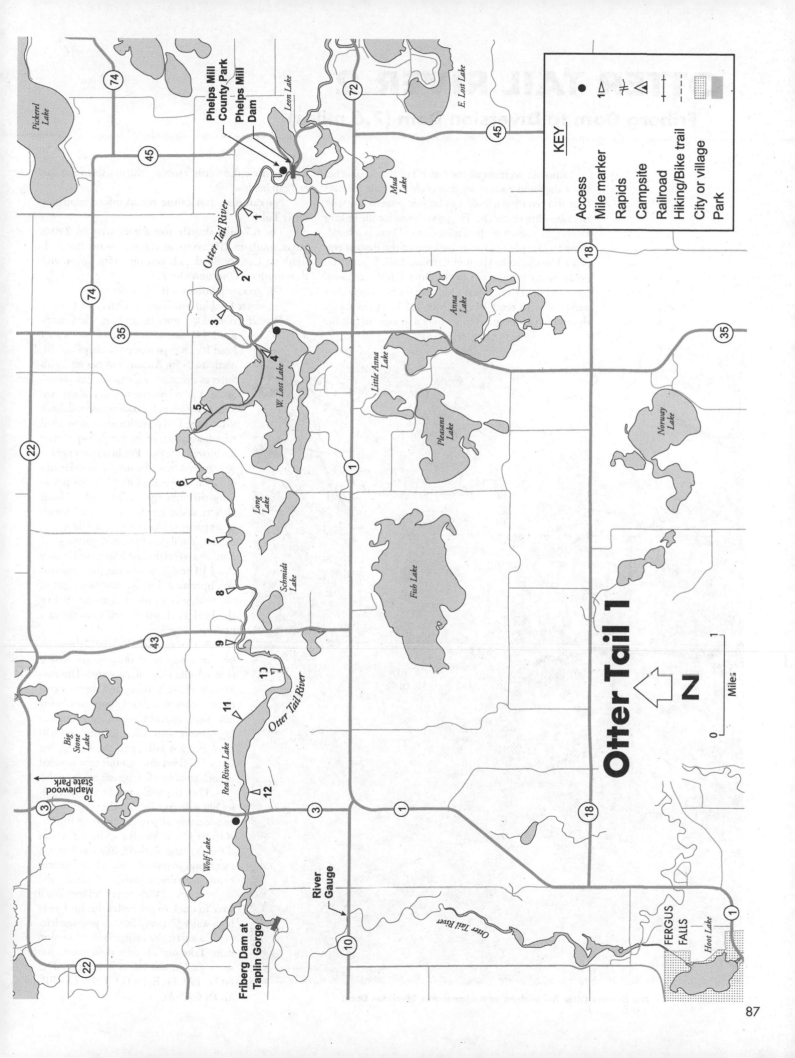

Otter Tail 1

N

Miles

0 _____ 1

KEY

- Access •
- Mile marker 1
- Rapids ⊬
- Campsite △
- Railroad ┼
- Hiking/Bike trail ┄┄
- City or village ▦
- Park ▓

Pickerel Lake

74

45

74

35

22

Otter Tail River

Phelps Mill County Park

Phelps Mill Dam

Leon Lake

Mud Lake

Leon Lake

E. Lost Lake

72

45

18

Anna Lake

Little Anna Lake

Pleasant Lake

Fish Lake

Norway Lake

35

18

1

W. Lost Lake

Long Lake

Schmidt Lake

Big Stone Lake

Red River Lake

To Maplewood State Park

3

43

Otter Tail River

Wolf Lake

Friberg Dam at Taplin Gorge

River Gauge

22

3

1

10

Otter Tail River

FERGUS FALLS

Hoot Lake

1

OTTER TAIL RIVER 2
Friberg Dam to Diversion Dam (7.6 miles)

Another segment of the Otter Tail that begins below a dam and ends in an impoundment, this pleasant float also gives you a look at an historic powerhouse with an interesting precedent. The powerhouse for the Friberg Dam, also known as the Taplin Gorge Dam, is a handsome 1923 replica of the mausoleum of the Roman emperor Theodoric the Great in Ravenna, Italy. With access points recently improved by the Otter Tail Power Company and the DNR, this is a nice trip for beginning river paddlers. This reach of the Otter Tail is free of rapids throughout its length. On a windy day, especially if the wind is from the south, crossing the marshland at the end can be slow.

For **camping** and **canoe rental** information, see Otter Tail 1.

The 6.7-mile **shuttle route** goes west on 290th Street, south on 215th Avenue, east on County Road 10, south on County Road 111, east on 245th Street, and then south on Diversion Drive.

The average **gradient** is 0.5 foot per mile.

For **water level** information, see Otter Tail 1.

To reach Friberg Dam from Fergus Falls, take County Road 111 northeast of town to County Road 10. Then go west on County Road 10, north on 215th Avenue, and east on 290th Street to a parking area near the dam powerhouse. A gravel portage trail around the dam leads to the left of the powerhouse and down to the river. This powerhouse is almost a half mile downstream of the dam; a loop of river lies between the two. **Put in** on river right.

As you leave the steep wooded banks of Taplin Gorge, the Otter Tail runs peacefully through the countryside. About 50 feet wide, its clear waters are sometimes partially blocked by deadfalls in this section. You'll pass the USGS gauging station on river right just before the County Road 10 bridge, which has two large culvert openings. The downstream right of the bridge is a potential access. Below the bridge, deadfalls are sometimes a problem as well.

Amazingly thick beds of live mussels on the sandy river bottom are visible through the clear, deep water. The surrounding land is rolling and the river corridor is quite wooded. Glimpses of lovely hilly fields appear through the overhanging cottonwoods, silver maples, and willows. For 2.4 miles past the bridge, the Otter Tail flows through this cozy wooded tunnel, passing a few houses on the right.

Then the banks recede, the river valley fills with cattails, and the current slows considerably as you get closer to the Diversion Dam. You'll paddle 2.6 miles through a large wetland, filled with marsh plants and waterbirds, and a lake-like area before reaching a cluster of houses and the very low 245th Street bridge. You'll have to duck to get under this bridge; at high water you may have to **portage** left.

Just past the bridge is the diversion dam. **Take out** on river right where you see a gap in the chain-link fence. DO NOT PADDLE INTO THE DIVERSION CANAL.

The narrow Otter Tail widens as it approaches Diversion Dam.

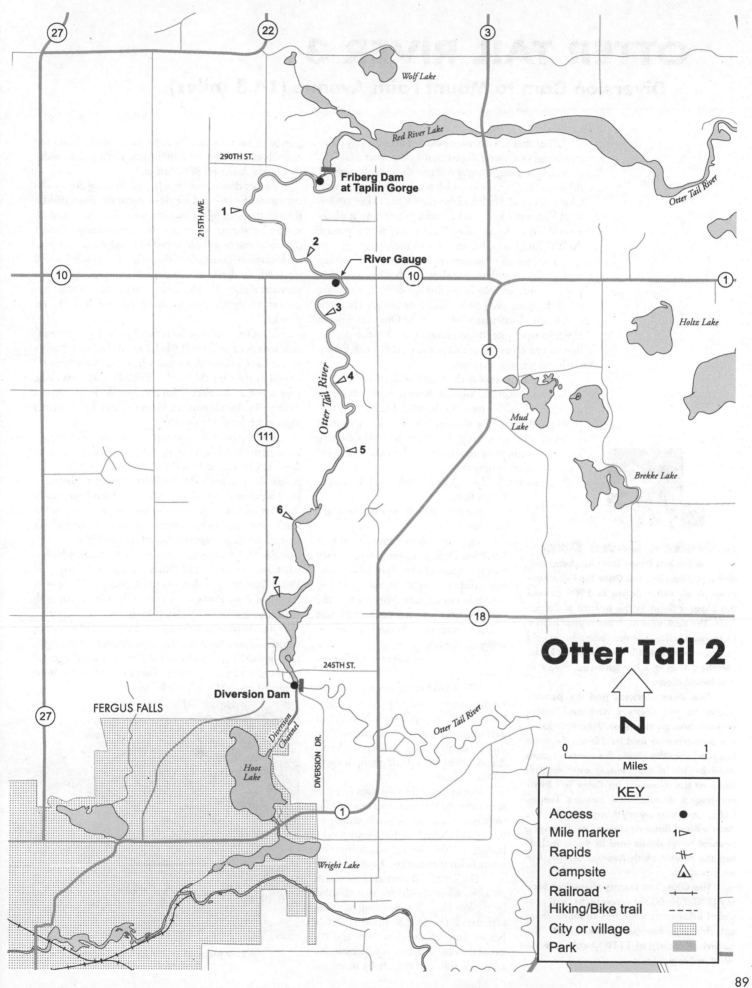

Otter Tail 2

N

0   1

Miles

KEY

Access	●
Mile marker	1▷
Rapids	⧣
Campsite	△
Railroad	┼┼
Hiking/Bike trail	‒ ‒ ‒
City or village	▦
Park	▬

OTTER TAIL RIVER 3
Diversion Dam to Mount Faith Avenue (14.3 miles)

The Otter Tail River runs swiftly through lovely countryside east of Fergus Falls, its crystal-clear water adding to the feeling of a magic carpet ride over the sandy bottom. In the second half of the run, paddlers will race through several Class I–II rapids. The last of these rapids edges close to Class III at high water levels, so be careful to match your whitewater ability to the day's flow. You also may need to portage the Wall Lake Bridge halfway through the trip.

The river also has excellent smallmouth bass fishing; anglers who want the fish and the fun but not the whitewater can fish the holes in the first half of the run and take out at the access just past the Wall Lake Bridge. The DNR established a smallmouth fishery on the Otter Tail River in 1992; its rapid success was proven by a 1999 fish population survey. To maintain this premier smallmouth fishery, catch and release is required.

A marsh meadow in the middle of the run is home to many birds, including ospreys, herons, eagles, and great quantities of smaller birds. In the second half of this trip, you'll paddle through a winding, wooded valley, with thick groves of oaks topping high bluffs. At the end of the long stretch of rapids, you'll also encounter the remains of an old dam with an interesting story.

Camp at Glendalough State Park, 17 miles east of Fergus Falls.

For information on **canoe rentals**, see Otter Tail 1.

The 4-mile **shuttle route** is south on Diversion Drive to County Road 1, then west to Somerset Drive. Turn left on Somerset and then right on Sunset Drive, which becomes Ann Street when the gravel starts. Turn left on East Mount Faith Avenue; the takeout is across the bridge on the left.

The average **gradient** is 4.5 feet per mile.

Water level information is available for the County Road 10 gauge near Elizabeth on the USGS Web site at http://waterdata.usgs.gov/mn/nwis/. Minimum flow should be 280 cfs, and 500 cfs is moderate. A good spring runoff will pump it up to 800 cfs or more.

Put in below the Diversion Dam on river right. A short trail leads down to the river. In the first 4 miles, you'll paddle past houses and an access at the County Road 1 bridge and then into a wooded section where fallen trees can be a hazard.

The Otter Tail then enters a marsh meadow, where the distant view afforded by the low banks is a nice contrast to the high wooded banks that enclosed the river before. Through the clear water and between the ribbon grasses, you'll almost certainly see fish, and deep holes invite anglers to try for those smallmouth bass. Then the banks rise again, boulders litter the bottom, and you'll paddle under the Sophus Anderson Road bridge.

Farther downstream is a line of decaying posts—the remnants of a railroad trestle—across the river; paddle through the opening on river left. Soon after, the hazardous low bridge appears. At high water levels, clearance under the bridge can be as little as two feet, and sharp bolts protrude from the underside of the bridge. (The township will replace the bridge as soon as possible.) **Portage** right when the water is high. The alternate access for those who do not want to run the rapids is just downstream of the bridge on river left.

The Otter Tail now flows into a wooded valley. A half-mile stretch of riffles and Class I rapids begins 1.5 miles past the low bridge. A hazard, which may have been removed by the time this book is published, appears along here: a single wire electric fence crosses the river atop old concrete bridge abutments. Go right, and if the water is high, watch out for the wire!

You'll pass a few houses before the river swings through the blind curve of the Class II rapids. At average flows, large waves form and the current tries to shove you against the right bank. At high flows, the drop pushes Class III. The turmoil ends after the Broken Down Dam, where the river rushes between two huge concrete blocks, the small opening sometimes blocked by debris. If you can't get through safely, **portage** this hazard on river right.

About 1.5 miles downstream, past a railroad bridge, you'll see the Otter Tail Power Company's Hoot Lake Plant. Warning signs alert you to the gnarly and hazardous three-foot drop. **Portage** left along a short grassy trail with steps at both ends. The DNR plans to reduce this drop.

Just downstream, the rest of the Otter Tail rejoins its natural channel from the diversion channel on the right. Do not paddle up this channel; the opening to a dangerous turbine is 0.12 mile upstream. **Take out** on river left at the public access right before the bridge.

A Broken Down Dam

The Broken Down Dam has been quietly crumbling into the Otter Tail River ever since its abrupt collapse in 1909 caused the biggest flood in the history of Fergus Falls. The dam was built just a year before its tragic demise, but the contractor is said to have constructed it over a spring in the riverbed that quickly gnawed away at the foundations.

Two dam workers fled the powerhouse as the lights faded and water leaked through the floor. Moments later, the powerhouse and its 10-ton dynamo tumbled into the river; the massive dam itself broke in the center; and the full force of the dammed-up Otter Tail River rampaged downstream toward Fergus Falls, carrying everything with it. The debris-filled flood destroyed or damaged several other dams and bridges, including the Mount Faith Avenue bridge, but no one died.

The Otter Tail County Historical Society (218-736-6038; www.otchs.org) provided information for this account. If local history intrigues you, visit the historical society at 1110 Lincoln Avenue West in Fergus Falls.

A fast piece of water just upstream of the Broken Down Dam.

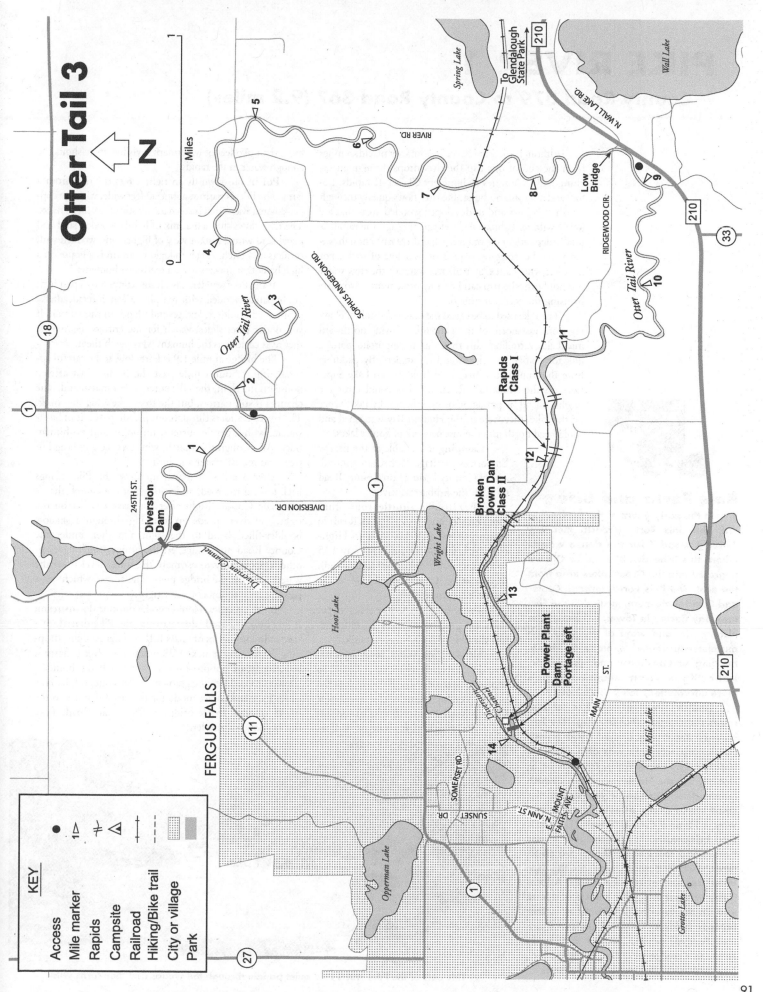

OtterTail 3

N

Miles
0 1 1

KEY

Access	●
Mile marker	1△
Rapids	≠
Campsite	△
Railroad	┼
Hiking/Bike trail	---
City or village	▒
Park	▓

FERGUS FALLS

Otter Tail River

Diversion Dam

245TH ST.

SOPHUS ANDERSON RD.

DIVERSION DR.

Diversion Channel

Hoot Lake

Wright Lake

Opperman Lake

SOMERSET RD.

SUNSET DR.

N. ANN ST.

E. MOUNT FAITH AVE.

Grotto Lake

One Mile Lake

MAIN ST.

Broken Down Dam Class II

Power Plant Dam Portage left

Diversion Channel

Rapids Class I

RIVER RD.

Spring Lake

To Glendalough State Park

N. WALL LAKE RD.

RIDGEWOOD CIR.

Low Bridge

Otter Tail River

Wall Lake

Otter Tail River

PIKE RIVER 1
County Road 379 to County Road 367 (9.2 miles)

Although the Pike River is primarily placid, 3 miles from the end of this trip the river drops through an exciting half-mile series of bouldery Class I–II rapids. Before and after this outburst, the river flows quietly through marsh meadows and undeveloped wooded areas that are lovely wildlife habitat. A good run through the rapids is totally dependent on water level; if there isn't enough water, you'll be dragging your boat over lots of rocks. For paddlers who want either the fast water or the slow water but not both, the trip can be easily broken into two parts by using the access at mile 6.

The Pike used to be called the Lesser Vermilion. Flowing from just north of the Laurentian Divide northward into Lake Vermilion, this river was an important portage link for Native Americans and fur traders. By paddling from the Saint Louis River (which flows into Lake Superior) up the Embarrass River, travelers could cross the height of land by portaging over to the nearby Pike. Once on the Pike, they were in the Hudson Bay watershed and could head north into the vast network of border lakes.

Camping is available at the nearby Embarrass Heritage Park Campground, east of County Road 21 on County Road 615, on the Embarrass River.

The 10-mile **shuttle route** runs south on County Road 379 (Lax Road) to County Road 21, then east to Highway 135. Go north on Highway 135 to County Road 367 (West Saari Road), then west on County Road 367 to the bridge (downstream left).

The average **gradient** is 3.2 feet per mile; the gradient of the 1.28 miles below the bridge is 15.5 feet per mile.

Although no **water level** information is available, the quiet water should be runnable at most levels. If you look at the bridge piers upstream of the access near County Road 303, you'll see that the tannin in the water has left a watermark. If no

more than two feet of watermark is visible, there should be enough water in the rapids.

Put in on downstream right across the river from a farm. The Pike is narrow, about 30 feet wide, with the copper-colored water that is so characteristic of northern rivers. The river flows through a mix of lightly wooded land and marshland with a distant view of higher land wooded with conifers and birch. A half mile downstream is a house on a high bank that appears to be a renovated homestead.

As the Pike wanders east, it sometimes flows past high sandy banks wooded with red pines. Watch for deadfalls, submerged boulders, and several islands in this stretch. If you notice otter slides, watch for the critters themselves; they're as curious as the humans who watch them.

The bridge at mile 1.9 is fairly low, so be careful approaching. About a mile past the bridge, just after a house on the right, the Pike enters a vast marshland. The channel is still narrow, but the trees take a big step back. The river meanders through this marsh, past lots of backwaters, with a gentle current, no noise, and no human trace. All through this marsh, you can't see anything but trees and marsh, water and birds.

After 3 miles of marsh meadow, the Pike swings back toward the road, and you'll spot the church that is near Salo Corner. Right after you pass a trailer on the right, the river speeds up, running through a shallow boulder-filled bend to the right and then under the County Road 303 bridge. At the bridge, you'll have another opportunity to estimate the water level from the watermarks on the bridge piers. The access, which has a parking area, follows on river right.

If the water level looks good, continue downstream. A few hundred yards downstream, the Pike dives into a half-mile-long series of Class I–II boulder gardens, dropping 20 feet in the next 1.28 miles. The river is narrow, reducing your options on routes through the boulder-strewn drops. Then the gradient flattens out and the Pike slides back into quiet mode for the last 1.4 miles to the pretty wooden trestle bridge at West Saari Road. **Take out** on downstream left.

Bois Forte and Sisu

In the early years of the fur-trading era, the Bois Forte (French, meaning "strong wood," for the dense woods where this tribe dwelt) band of Ojibwe migrated into the Great Lakes area from the east. The Bois Forte Heritage Center and Cultural Museum, located at the Fortune Bay Casino in Tower, celebrates the history, life, and ways of the tribe with murals; educational exhibits on ricing, beading, and basketry; and other historical artifacts. For museum hours and more information, call 218-753-6017.

Finnish names on mailboxes and on roads remind you that although the Embarrass River was named by a French missionary, this area was also settled in great part by hardy Finns. You may occasionally see the Finnish word sisu, which means determination. If you stop at the small visitor center at Salo Corner (Highway 135 and County Road 21), you'll find information on Heritage Pioneer Homestead tours of numerous log structures, including three sites on the National Register of Historic Places. A local guide will get into your vehicle and lead you on the two- to three-hour tour. Embarrass holds a Finnish-American Summer Festival on the second Sunday in June. You can contact Sisu Heritage Inc., 218-984-2106, for more information.

This part of the Pike starts as a quiet paddle through the woods and then turns wild.

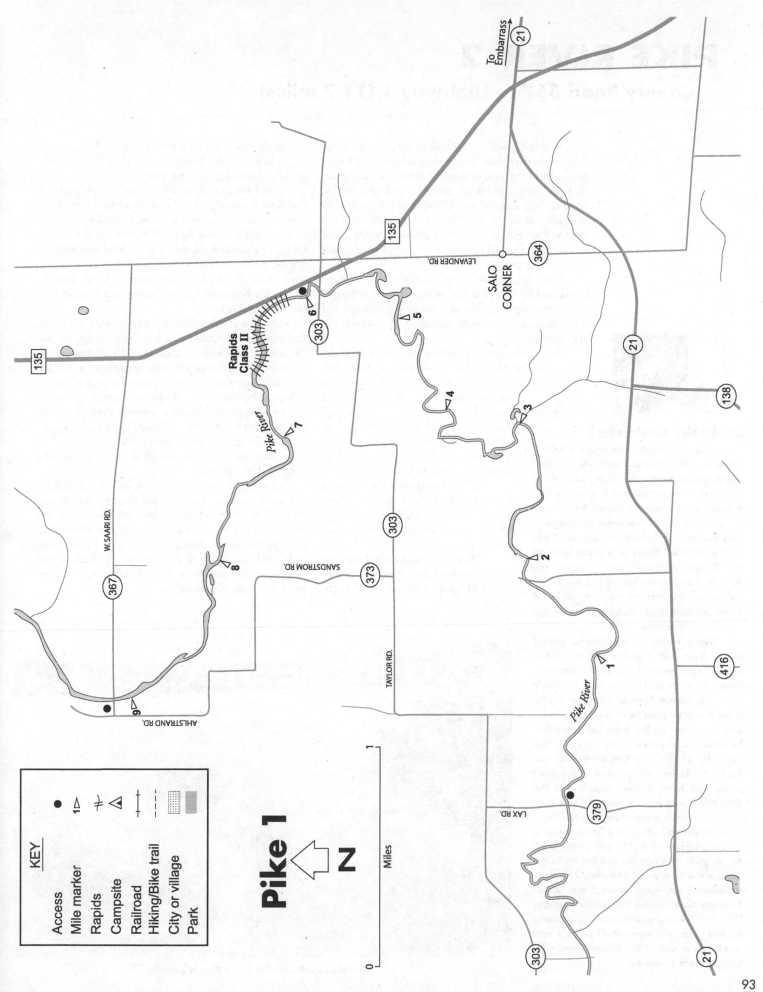

KEY

- ● Access
- 1△ Mile marker
- ⚶ Rapids
- △ Campsite
- ┼ Railroad
- ┊ Hiking/Bike trail
- ▦ City or village
- ▓ Park

Pike 1

N

Miles
0   1

Rapids
Class II

Pike River

Pike River

To
Embarrass

21

135

135

303

303

303

373

367

364

138

21

21

416

379

LEVANDER RD.

SALO
CORNER

W. SAARI RD.

SANDSTROM RD.

TAYLOR RD.

AHLSTRAND RD.

LAX RD.

1 2 3 4 5 6 7 8 9

PIKE RIVER 2
County Road 367 to Highway 1 (11.7 miles)

After the uproar of the rapids in the previous trip on the Pike, the river settles down to its usual quiet style for the remainder of the journey north to Vermilion Lake. Farm fields, lightly wooded areas, marshland, and some heavily wooded bluffs alternate, and the river speeds through a few small riffles along the way. The end of the paddle is across the Pike River Flowage, an impoundment created by a dam downstream of the takeout at the Highway 1 bridge, ending a peaceful and very pretty float.

The sedge meadow at the center of this trip is an excellent bird habitat; great blue herons, ospreys, and eagles are common sightings. You may also see beaver lodges and their inhabitants, mergansers and other waterfowl, and lots of dragonflies.

At a scenic spot just before you paddle into the flowage, the Taconite Trail crosses the river. A snowmobile route in the winter, this 165-mile hiking and mountain biking trail from Grand Rapids to Ely is joined by the Arrowhead Trail just west of the Pike River. The 135-mile Arrowhead Trail, also a hiking and mountain biking route for part of its length, runs north to International Falls.

You'll find **camping** at the Embarrass Campground (see Pike 1) or at Bear Head State Park; follow Highway 1 through Tower to County Road 128, which leads into the park.

The 16-mile **shuttle route** runs east on County Road 367 (West Saari Road), north on Highway 135, and west on High-

way 1. The takeout is on the left before the bridge.

The average **gradient** is 0.8 foot per mile. This route can be paddled at most **water levels**.

Park on the shoulder of this quiet country road and **put in** on downstream left. Less than a mile downstream, just past a small tributary on the right, you'll see wooden pilings on both sides of the river, the remains of a settler's bridge or a splash dam. Yellow pond lilies and wild iris line the shore, as do the dark rocks characteristic of this river. The river spreads out somewhat in this wetland. In the spring, be careful not to disturb duck families that raise their young here.

About 4.2 miles from the put-in you'll reach the County Road 26 bridge. Just before the bridge, on the left among some newer buildings, is an interesting old log home. On upstream left at the bridge is a possible access, although signs are posted prohibiting parking. A mile past the bridge, the Pike narrows briefly to about a quarter of its previous width and sweeps through a short stretch of fast water. About 2.8 miles farther is the Highway 169 bridge, where access would be difficult. The Pike speeds up a little after you go under the bridge, but only for about 50 feet.

At the spot where the river narrows, wooded bluffs rise above the river, and where the Taconite Trail crosses on an arched iron footbridge (mile 10.2) is one of the loveliest places on the river. Just past the footbridge, you'll paddle into the flowage lake. If you head to the left of the island, you'll find the narrows that leads to the Highway 1 bridge. **Take out** on upstream right, where you'll find a gravel parking area.

Duluth, Ontario?

When the Americans and the British were dividing up the North Woods during negotiations for the Treaty of Paris in 1783, the international boundary between Canada and the United States was determined to be "the water communication between it (Lake Superior) and Lake of the Woods." Thirty-one years later, at the Treaty of Ghent, which ended the War of 1812, establishing the actual location of this rather vaguely defined route became a contentious issue in the treaty negotiations.

There were at least three travel routes from Lake Superior to Lake of the Woods: a route that followed the Kaministiquia River from Thunder Bay to Rainy Lake; the Grand Portage route up the Pigeon River; and the Saint Louis route from Duluth Harbor up the Saint Louis, the Embarrass, and the Pike. If the first route had been chosen, a slice of Ontario would now be in the United States. And if the third route had been chosen, Duluth and the BWCAW would now be part of Canada.

The British were voting for the Saint Louis route and made the first survey of Duluth Harbor in 1825. But in the end, the dispute was settled, and the Webster-Ashburton Treaty of 1842 stated that the traditional voyageur route from Grand Portage was indeed the boundary, and that "all the water communications and all the usual portages shall be free and open to the use of the citizens and subjects of both countries."

After the rapids on Pike 1, the Pike is placid.

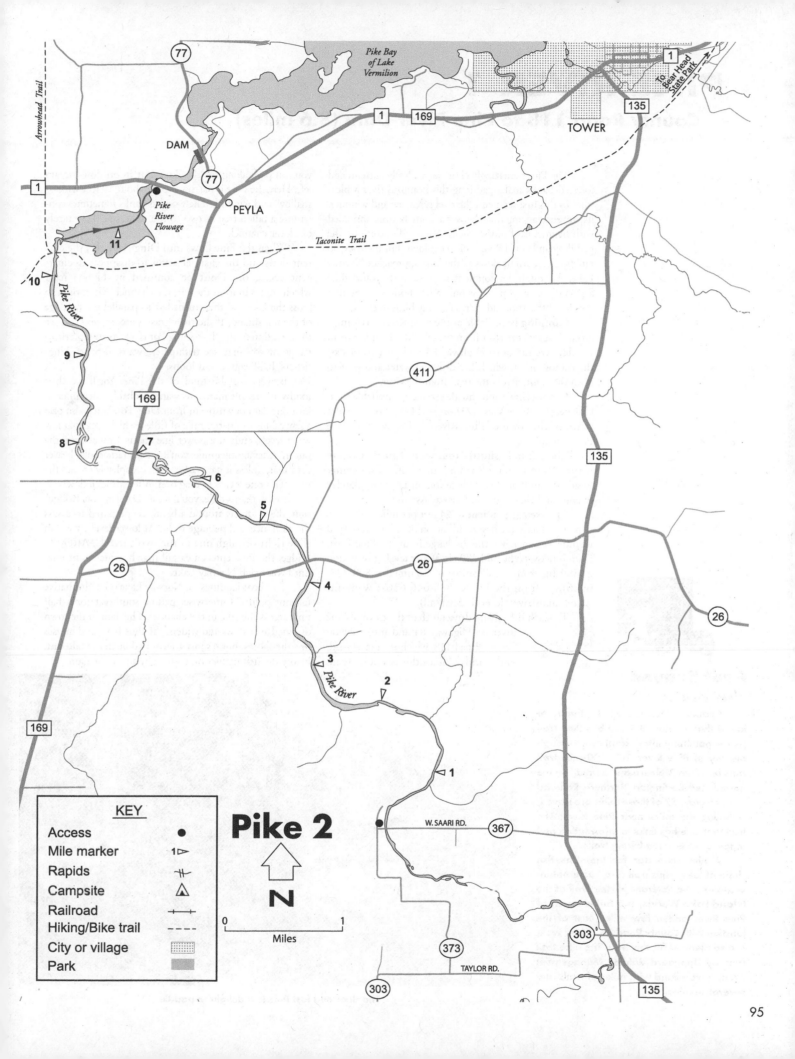

Pike Bay
of Lake
Vermilion

TOWER

DAM

PEYLA

Pike River Flowage

11

Taconite Trail

Arrowhead Trail

Pike River

10

9

8

7

6

5

4

3

2

Pike River

1

411

26

26

26

135

135

135

169

169

77

77

1

1

169

1

135

To Bear Head State Park

W. SAARI RD.

367

373

303

303

TAYLOR RD.

KEY

Access	●
Mile marker	1▷
Rapids	╫
Campsite	△
Railroad	┼
Hiking/Bike trail	- - -
City or village	
Park	

Pike 2

N

0 — 1
Miles

PINE RIVER 1
County Road 118 to Pine River Dam (8.6 miles)

The Pine's amazingly clear waters, lively current, and forested banks make paddling this beautiful river a pleasure. In this first segment, the river is narrow and winding, its current dancing quickly over a sandy bottom sprinkled with fragments of mussel shells. A few riffles spice up the paddling and you'll dodge a few boulders, but there are no rapids. The current slows as the Pine approaches Norway Lake. Although development increases after you paddle across the lake, you'll pass only a few houses in the first 7 miles of this trip, and there are many birds to enjoy.

Camping is available at the Pine River city campground, across the river from the takeout. Turn left from Barclay Avenue onto Highway 84 and go two blocks; the campground, which has drinking water and privies, is on the right, across the road from the river.

Canoe rentals and **shuttle service** are available from Chlebecek's River View (218-587-4112), about 2 miles south of the town of Pine River on Highway 371 (see Pine 2 map).

The 9.2-mile **shuttle route** runs east on County Road 118 to County Road 84, then south on County Road 84 into Pine River, where you turn right on Barclay Avenue and then right on Norway Avenue.

The average **gradient** is 2.4 feet per mile.

You'll have the best paddling on the Pine from April to June, or whenever the discharge from the Pine River Dam is between 80 and 200 cfs. **Water level** information is available from the Chamber of Commerce (800-728-6926), or from the DNR (888-646-6367; www.dnr.state.mn.us/river_levels/index.html).

To reach the put-in, drive north of the town of Pine River on Highway 84 and turn west on County Road 118, which is a gravel road, to the bridge. Since this is a quiet road, you can park along the shoulder. **Put in** on downstream left. Here the Pine is narrow—only about 50 feet wide—shallow, and winding. The wooded banks sometimes contribute a fallen tree or two to the river, but these rarely block the channel.

When the Pine flows into Ding Pot Lake, the current slows and the channel seems to disappear in emergent vegetation. Don't be confused by Lizzy Creek, which comes in from the left; the channel swings right to cross the lake and then turns left to parallel the far edge of the marshland. If the river grasses are up, you can see the direction of the flow. Ding Pot is a favorite waterfowl hangout; you may see trumpeter swans, ospreys, kingfishers, bald eagles, and loons.

Beavers are also fond of the Pine. You'll see their toothy marks on many trees and probably encounter at least one dam downstream from Ding Pot. You'll also pass a few cabins. A quarter mile of riffles, which appear at low water levels, ends at a power line about 3 miles from the put-in. After another mile, you'll reach a rather solid beaver dam that, unless it has washed out, completely crosses the river. This one is easy to drag over. A few riffles follow.

In less than a mile, you'll see a "Danger, Low Bridge" sign; the bridge is around a bend. Be prepared to assess the clearance and **portage** right. At lower levels, you can slide right through one of the two culverts. After the bridge, the Pine enters a cattail marsh, which continues until you reach Norway Lake.

Two boat landings on Norway Lake offer alternative takeout points. Otherwise, paddle southeast for a half mile across the lake to the channel. The dam in the town of Pine River slows and widens the Pine here, and houses line the shores, but it's just a short paddle to the **takeout**, before the fishing pier on river right above the dam.

Paul Bunyan the Biker

Cycling enthusiasts will be happy to know that the Paul Bunyan bicycling trail (www.paulbunyantrail.com) runs through the city of Pine River. This 100-mile trail runs between Brainerd and Bemidji on the abandoned Burlington Northern Railroad right-of-way; 57 of those miles are paved, including the miles near Pine River. The trail Web site has links to information and maps for other area biking trails.

A nice connector for the Whitefish chain of lakes, this trail also has a nature walkway, the Veterans Hiking Trail at the Island Lake Woods, 6.5 miles south of Pine River and a few miles east of the junction with County Road 16. A bog walk is also planned for this trail. The bike trail runs by Uppgaard Wildlife Management Area, a woodland with miles of trails and several small lakes.

The clear and fast Pine is a delight to paddle.

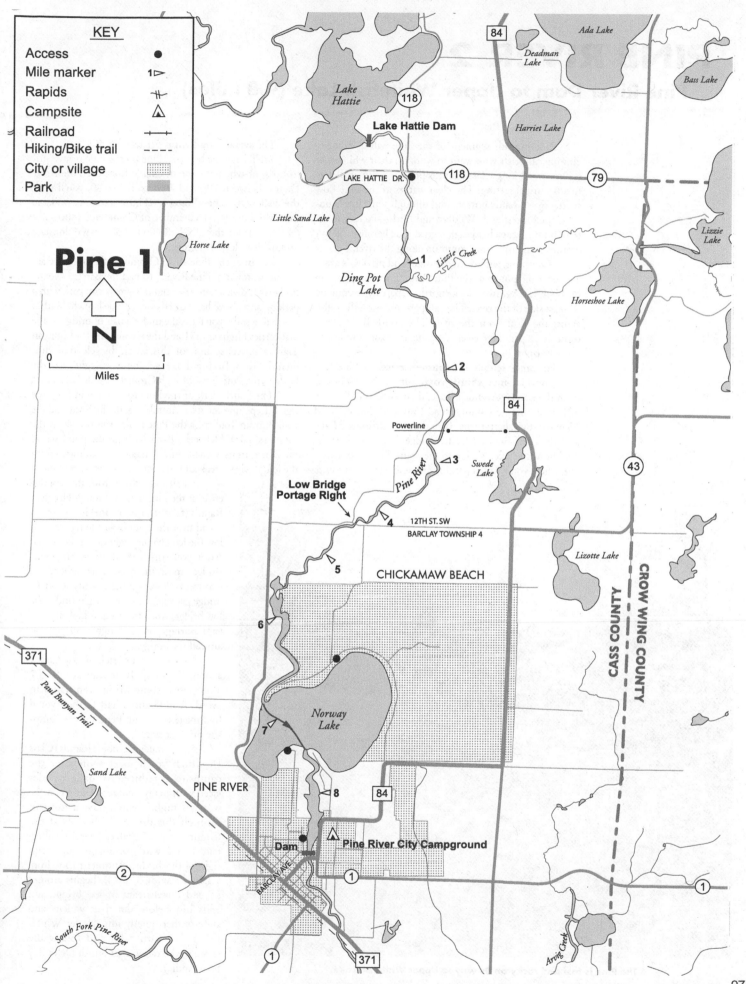

KEY

Access   ●
Mile marker   1▷
Rapids
Campsite   △
Railroad
Hiking/Bike trail   - - -
City or village
Park

Pine 1

⬆ **N**

0   1
Miles

Horse Lake

Lake Hattie

Lake Hattie Dam

Little Sand Lake

LAKE HATTIE DR.

Ding Pot Lake

1▷   *Lizzie Creek*

▷2

Powerline

Pine River

▷3   *Swede Lake*

Low Bridge Portage Right

▷4   12TH ST. SW
BARCLAY TOWNSHIP 4

▷5

CHICKAMAW BEACH

▷6

Norway Lake

▷7

PINE RIVER

Sand Lake

▷8   84

Dam   ⛺ **Pine River City Campground**

BARCLAY AVE.

Paul Bunyan Trail

South Fork Pine River

Deadman Lake

Ada Lake

Bass Lake

Harriet Lake

Lizzie Lake

Horseshoe Lake

Lizotte Lake

CASS COUNTY

CROW WING COUNTY

Arving Creek

84   118   79   84   43   371   2   1   371

PINE RIVER 2
Pine River Dam to Upper Whitefish Lake (9.8 miles)

Paddling this segment of the Pine will delight beginning canoeists who want to work on their whitewater skills: several long Class I rapids provide a fun challenge in a beautiful setting. The clear waters of the Pine flow swiftly over a sandy bottom and through some lovely undeveloped forestland. Wildlife and birds—including otters and muskrats, bald eagles, great blue herons, and numerous songbirds—are common along the river.

Camping, with drinking water and privies, is available near the put-in at the Pine River City Campground on Highway 84, two blocks north of Barclay Avenue on the east side of the river. The campground is on the right, across the road from the river. The South Bend canoe campsite, a primitive river campsite, is at about mile 6.9, on river right.

For **canoe rentals** and **shuttle service**, see Pine 1.

The 11.1-mile **shuttle route** runs west two blocks from the Barclay Avenue bridge, then south on Highway 371 for 6 miles to County Road 15 north. County Road 15 makes two sharp turns. Turn right on Driftwood Lane and then left on Red Cedar Lodge Drive. Follow the "Public Water Access" sign to the South Delta Bay Landing, where you'll find a parking area and a concrete ramp.

The average **gradient** is 5.1 feet per mile.

You'll have the best paddling on the Pine from April to June, or whenever the discharge from the Pine River Dam is between 100 and 200 cfs. Below 80, you'll walk the shallow stretches. **Water level** information is available from the Pine River Chamber of Commerce (800-728-6926), or from the DNR (888-646-6367; www.dnr.state.mn.us/river_levels/index.html).

Put in at the Pine River Chamber of Commerce access in the town of Pine River, just past the Barclay Avenue bridge on downstream river right. A grassy city park with a parking area above has a carry-down canoe launch. Within less than a mile, you'll paddle under a pair of bridges—the first carries Highway 371 and the second, the Paul Bunyan Trail (a paved section of this scenic bicycle trail runs 46 miles from Brainerd to Hackensack). Right after the bridges, the Pine runs through Gromek Rapids (Class I).

The South Fork of the Pine River flows in from the right, deepening the river. At mile 3.3, the highway and the Paul Bunyan Trail cross the Pine again. On the left is the canoe rental, Chlebecek's River View, at the point where the Pine runs its deepest. After Chlebecek's, sliding in from the left, Arvig's Creek adds its water to the growing Pine.

A half mile down from this confluence, as the Pine dances through Hopper's Rapids (Class I), the channel is split by an island near the bottom of the rapids. Follow the left channel right down the center. After you finish the rapids, Hopper's Bridge crosses the river. At water levels of two feet or lower on the County Road 11 bridge gauge, a canoe slips right under the low bridge; when the water is higher, a 10-yard **portage** on river right will get you around the bridge.

Another short stretch of easy Class I action, Kells Rapids, appears at mile 5.7 along with some bridge remnants to avoid. A mile and a half farther, you'll find the grassy South Bend Canoe Campsite on river right.

At low water, Reynolds Rapids (Class I), which you'll meet soon after the campsite, is reduced to shallow riffles laced with many boulders. But when the water is higher, you'll have a fun run through this drop, which ends at the County Road 15 bridge. There's an alternate access with parking on upstream right of this bridge. Another rocky drop, Carlson Rapids (Class I), begins around a bend downstream of the bridge and ends just before the river widens and slides rather quietly into Upper Whitefish Lake. Turn right and follow the shore to the **takeout** at South Delta Bay boat landing.

The Pine is fast and rocky on its way to Upper Whitefish Lake.

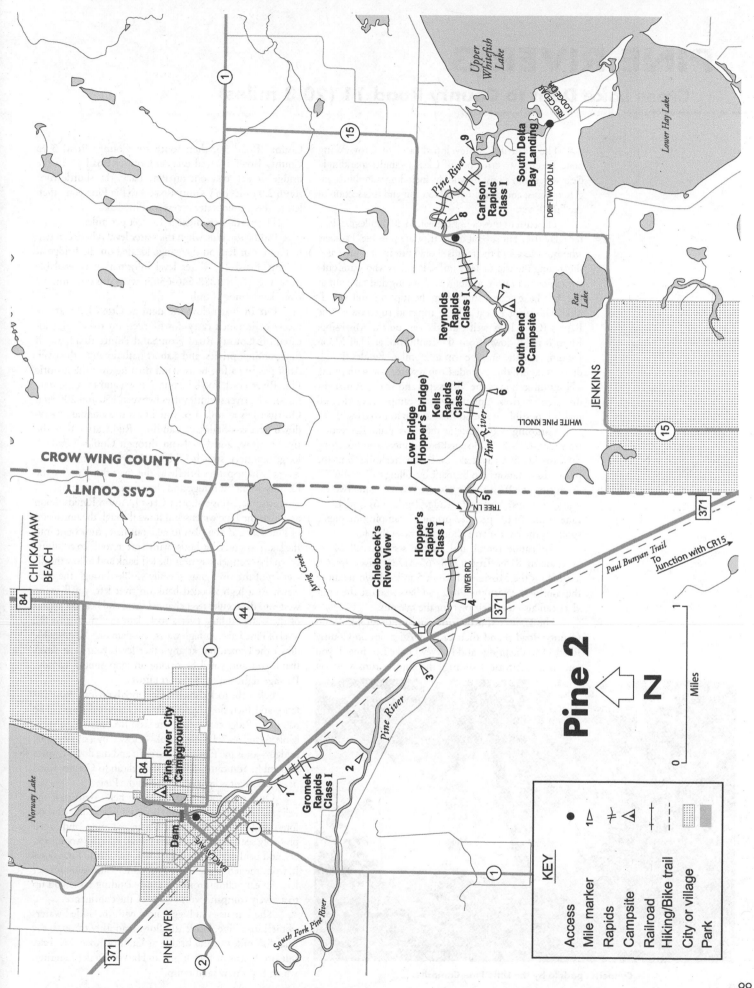

Pine 2

N

Miles
0   1

KEY

Access	●
Mile marker	1△
Rapids	≠
Campsite	△
Railroad	╫
Hiking/Bike trail	-----
City or village	▒
Park	▓

Upper Whitefish Lake

Lower Hay Lake

RED CEDAR DR.
LODGE DR.

South Delta Bay Landing

DRIFTWOOD LN.

9

Pine River

Carlson Rapids Class I

8

7

Reynolds Rapids Class I

South Bend Campsite

Rat Lake

JENKINS

15

Kells Rapids Class I

6

Pine River

WHITE PINE KNOLL

Low Bridge (Hopper's Bridge)

5

TREE LN.

371

Paul Bunyan Trail
To Junction with CR15

CROW WING COUNTY

CASS COUNTY

Chlebecek's River View

Hopper's Rapids Class I

4

RIVER RD.

371

3

Pine River

Arvig Creek

44

CHICKAMAW BEACH

84

1

Norway Lake

Pine River City Campground

84

Dam

BARCLAY AVE.

1

2

Gromek Rapids Class I

1

PINE RIVER

371

2

South Fork Pine River

15

1

1

PINE RIVER 3
Cross Lake Dam to County Road 11 (20.3 miles)

The beautiful undeveloped land of Crow Wing State Forest; two stretches of Class I rapids; sparklingly clear water; and a host of wildlife, including waterbirds, eagles, ospreys, and songbirds, all recommend this section of the Pine River.

The current moves right along, so 20.3 miles can be a nice day trip, but several other trips are possible. Paddlers who want to avoid the rapids should put in on Pine Lake, shortening the trip to 18.5 miles. Paddlers who want only the rapids can put in at Staircase Landing and take out at the Pine Lake access, shortening the trip to 3 miles. Paddlers who want to extend the trip and run Lower Pine Rapids (Class I) as well can take out on the Mississippi River, 8 miles down from the confluence at Half Moon Landing, lengthening the trip to 29 miles. Besides the additional rapids, this extended trip rewards you with seeing a beautiful section of the Mississippi and an eagle's nest visible from the river. A pretty riverside campsite at mile 14.6 makes it possible to extend this last trip to two days.

Camping is available at the Cross Lake Recreation Area (218-692-2025), located on County Road 66, along the east side of Cross Lake and a quarter mile from the put-in. Reservations can be made by calling 877-444-6777 or visiting the Web site at www.reserveusa.com. Two canoe campsites, Mosquito Ridge (mile 5.6) and Little Pine (mile 14.6), provide primitive camping or picnic spots on the river if you choose to travel that far.

For **canoe rental** and **shuttle service**, call Marty Severson at River Treat (218-765-3172). River Treat is located on the Mississippi River, 5 miles downstream of the confluence with the Pine; paddlers who use their services can also use their pier for the takeout.

The 12-mile **shuttle route** runs south for 4 miles on County Road 3 and then east for 7.4 miles on County Road 11 to the bridge and Harvey Drake Landing. If you put in at Staircase Landing, the shuttle runs west on County Road 36, then south on County Road 3 to County Road 11, and east on County Road 11 to the bridge. If you take out on Pine Lake, the shuttle runs south 2.5 miles on County Road 3 to Big Pine Trail, then left to the public water access on Pine Lake.

The average **gradient** is 1.8 feet per mile.

Paddle the Pine when the **water level** is between two feet and four feet on the gauge located on the bridge at County Road 11. Water level information is available from the DNR (888-646-6367; www.dnr.state.mn.us/river_levels/index.html).

Put in just below the dam at Cross Lake at the nicely maintained carry-down access on river right, located off County Road 3 on Sand Pointe Road. You'll find parking, privies, and a short path down to the river. After passing a few houses and floating over the historic Pine River Ford, you'll be out of town and into the state forest. The river's width varies between 150 and 200 feet. On river left at mile 1.6, you'll pass the alternate carry-down access—Staircase Landing. Right after that the river narrows and you'll run through Gould Rapids, a long, bouldery stretch of Class I rapids with standing waves, which pauses briefly as the river flows under the County Road 36 bridge and then resumes.

At mile 2.6 is a shorter Class I, Anton Rapids. Soon after that the Pine widens as it flows through the north end of Pine Lake. If you plan to take out here, turn right into the lake just past a log house with a green roof. To continue down the channel, stay near the left bank and follow the direction of the river grasses, easily visible through the clear water. At a high wooded bank on river left, you'll swing west into the regular river channel again and hear the sound of the water rushing over a rock dam that maintains the level of Pine Lake. At high water, this dam may be runnable down the center, but at any other level, your boat won't thank you and you'll be risking an ignominious capsize. **Portage** right—it's just a short liftover.

Below the rock dam, the Pine speeds up for a short distance and then flows quietly through a cattail marsh. The Mosquito Ridge canoe campsite is on river right, up a steep bank. At mile 8.7, Pelican Brook—crossed by a snowmobile bridge—joins the Pine from the right and the flow increases noticeably. You can paddle up the Pelican to County Road 3, as its current is light compared to the Pine.

Only one house appears along here, right past the Pelican. The terrain alternates between lowland hardwood forest and high banks topped with red pine, and you'll probably see beaver lodges, songbirds, pileated woodpeckers, and bald eagles. Just past where the Little Pine flows in from the left is the Little Pine canoe campsite on river left. An easy climb from the sandy landing takes you up to a lovely campsite with a view of the confluence.

The Pine is even bigger now with the added waters of the Little Pine, but it still flows smoothly through the final 5.5 miles to the bridge at County Road 11. **Take out** on upstream river right at Harvey Drake Landing, which has a new sand ramp.

Canoeists paddle by the Little Pine Campsite.

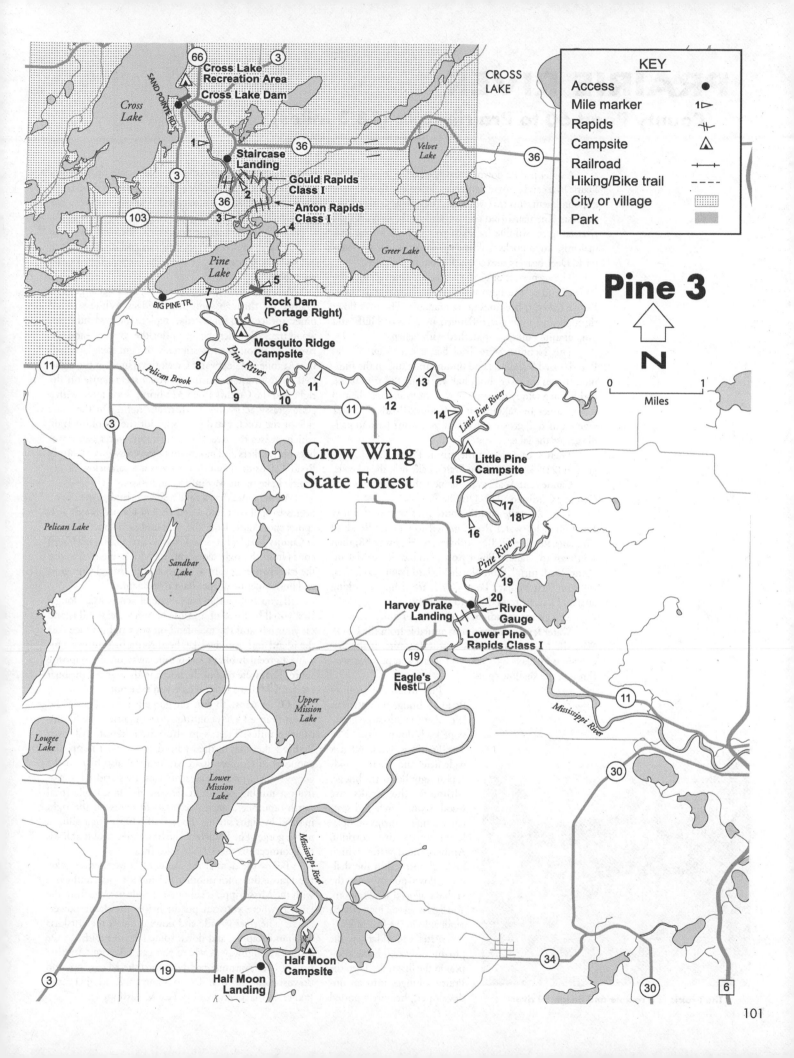

Pine 3

N

KEY

Access	●
Mile marker	1▷
Rapids	⌇
Campsite	△
Railroad	┼┼┼
Hiking/Bike trail	- - - -
City or village	(dotted)
Park	(shaded)

0 ――――――― 1
Miles

Cross Lake Recreation Area
Cross Lake Dam
Cross Lake
Sand Point Rd.
Cross Lake

Staircase Landing
Gould Rapids Class I
Anton Rapids Class I
Velvet Lake
Greer Lake
Pine Lake
Big Pine Tr.
Rock Dam (Portage Right)
Mosquito Ridge Campsite
Pelican Brook
Pine River
Little Pine River
Little Pine Campsite

Crow Wing State Forest

Pelican Lake
Sandbar Lake
Lougee Lake
Upper Mission Lake
Lower Mission Lake
Mississippi River

Harvey Drake Landing
River Gauge
Lower Pine Rapids Class I
Eagle's Nest

Pine River

Half Moon Campsite
Half Moon Landing

PRAIRIE RIVER
County Road 60 to Prairie Lake (13.3 miles)

A quiet paddle down a heavily wooded stretch of the Prairie River and across a lightly developed lake that is a dam impoundment, this trip will appeal especially to nature enthusiasts. The marshland and wooded land that border the river are great wildlife habitats; you may see mergansers, mallards, wood ducks, goldeneyes, orioles, and other songbirds. Deer, beavers, and otters are common as well.

The scenery is beautiful in the riverine reach of the Prairie, and at the narrows between Prairie and Lower Prairie Lakes, it becomes quite dramatic. The river flows through a .3-mile gorge flanked by 30-foot bluffs and pink granite outcrops splotched with lichens.

The Taconite State Trail between Ely and Grand Rapids, used for hiking and mountain biking in the summer, crosses the river about halfway along this trip. If you paddle on a windy day, you may want to shorten the trip to 8.3 miles by taking out at County Road 325, near where this trail crosses; that way you won't have to paddle across the lake.

There is **camping** at the private Prairie Lake Campground (218-326-8486), on Prairie Lake near the takeout.

Canoe rentals are available near the takeout at God's Country Outfitters (218-326-9866).

The 12.7-mile **shuttle route** runs west on County Road 60 (Clearwater Road, gravel) to County Road 49 (Wabana Road, paved), southwest to Highway 38, then southeast to Mallard Point Road. Go past West Mallard Point Road, turn left on North Mallard Point Road, then right on East Mallard Point Road. You'll find a parking area and a short road down to the ramp.

The average **gradient** is 0.4 foot per mile.

Water level information is available from the USGS Web site for the Prairie River near Taconite. If the discharge is at least 240 cfs, you won't scrape your way through the shallow spots.

Put in at the County Road 60 bridge on upstream left, where a fairly steep grassy slope leads down to the river. The Prairie is about 60 feet wide here, and several islands appear right below the bridge. Although the banks are wooded with birch and scattered conifers, there's an open feeling to the river corridor. Amber-tinted water, which looks almost red in the shallows, flows quietly over the visible scalloped sand bottom. You'll pass several high eroded sandbanks in the first mile.

After a small farm at the put-in, only two houses appear in the first mile. Then the Prairie plunges into an undeveloped, heavily wooded lowland area with many oxbows. Depending on the water level, you'll probably be able to explore some of these backwaters, where fishing is often good. The river follows a serpentine course, and low clay banks replace the sandy bluffs. If the many loops confuse you, watch the river grasses to find the channel. Sometimes deadfalls end up in the river, but with the gentle current along this stretch, they aren't a big problem.

At about mile 4, the terrain begins to change. The Prairie cuts through some sandy ridges. White and red pines, spruce, and some cedars replace the lowland hardwood trees. Boulders begin to dot the riverbed, and the river runs through a few stretches of light rock-laced riffles. At mile 7, Clearwater Creek flows in from the right. Less than a mile downstream, you'll see a house on the right and the County Road 325 bridge soon after, with a good grassy access on downstream right. On the same side of the road, you'll see a sign for the Taconite Trail, which crosses the river downstream in winter (snowmobiles only; hikers and mountain bikers cross at the County Road 325 bridge) and then crosses it again below Lower Prairie Lake on its way into Grand Rapids.

A little more than a mile below the bridge, the Prairie begins to spill over into wetlands and lily pad ponds as it approaches Prairie Lake, the impoundment above the dam at County Road 61, below Lower Prairie Lake. Hay Creek enters from the right along this stretch. As the river enters the lake, two long narrow strips of land covered with grass and bushes define the pre-dam river channel.

If you follow this faux channel across MacDougal Bay, you'll be lined up to slide between the small island on your left and the mainland on your right. Once past the island and into the lake, head south by southwest toward a greenish-blue roof .6 mile away on the opposite shore. That's the roof of the house to the right of the boat ramp on Mallard Point where you **take out**.

Other trips. To visit the gorge between Prairie and Lower Prairie Lakes, continue down Prairie Lake for another 3 miles. There's an alternate takeout on Lower Prairie Lake: east of the hydro dam is a boat ramp that connects to County Road 61. You can also hike to the gorge from a parking area off County Road 61 across from a mining operation. Follow the Itasca bike trail north (another branch goes east) to paths on the right marked by signs saying "Foot Traffic Only" that all lead to the gorge. The branch of the Itasca bike trail that leads east connects to the Mesabi Bike Trail.

Below the dam at the outlet of Lower Prairie Lake, the Prairie flows for another 6.5 miles to its confluence with the Mississippi. It's about a .3-mile portage from the lake to where you can put in below the dam's powerhouse. The river is wide and flows through the outskirts of Grand Rapids, and down some Class I rapids, to the bridge at Highway 2, where you can take out. Another option is to continue paddling into the Mississippi and downstream for 6 miles to County Road 441, also known as Blackberry Bridge (see Mississippi 4).

The Prairie is a remote and delightful river.

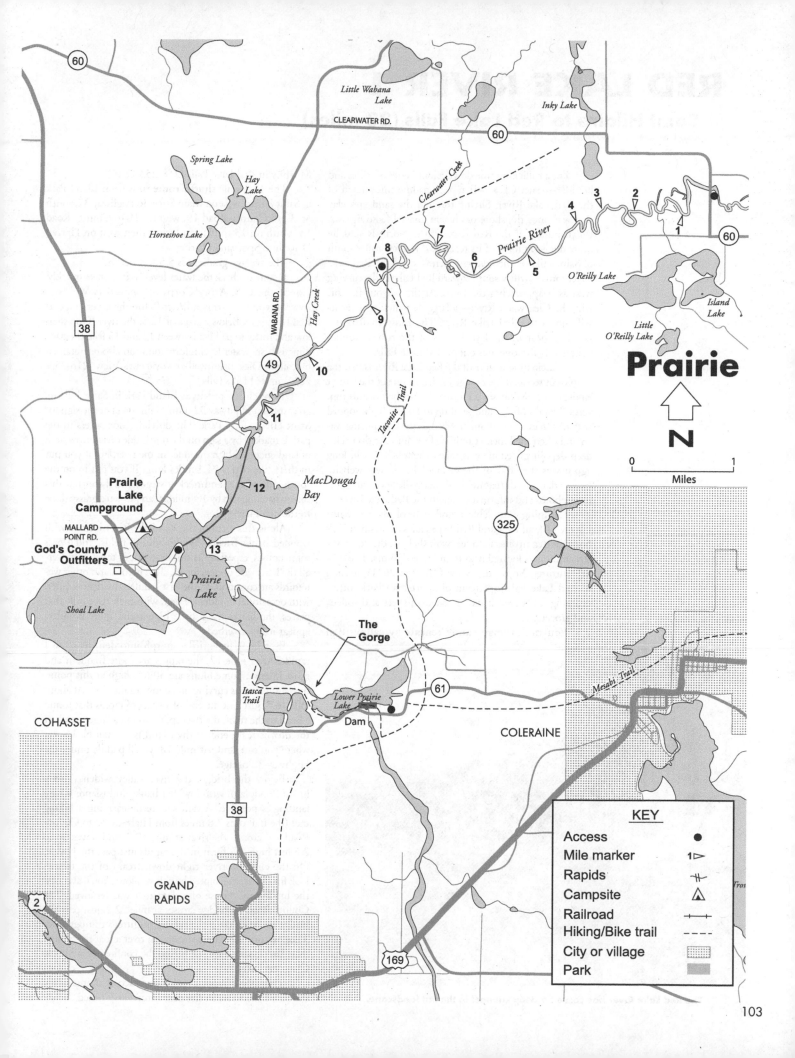

Prairie

↑ N

0 — 1
Miles

Little Wabana Lake

Inky Lake

CLEARWATER RD.

60

Spring Lake

Hay Lake

Horseshoe Lake

Clearwater Creek

Prairie River

3
2
4
1
7
8
6
5
9

O'Reilly Lake

Island Lake

Little O'Reilly Lake

38

WABANA RD.

49

Hay Creek

10

11

Taconite Trail

325

MacDougal Bay

12

Prairie Lake Campground

MALLARD POINT RD.

God's Country Outfitters

13

Prairie Lake

Shoal Lake

The Gorge

Itasca Trail

Lower Prairie Lake

Dam

61

COLERAINE

Mesabi Trail

COHASSET

38

GRAND RAPIDS

2

169

KEY

Access	●
Mile marker	1▷
Rapids	⫲
Campsite	△
Railroad	⊦⊦
Hiking/Bike trail	- - -
City or village	▦
Park	▬

RED LAKE RIVER 1
Saint Hilaire to Red Lake Falls (23 miles)

For a rollicking ride down a long series of riffles and boulder-strewn Class I–II rapids, paddle this stretch of the Red Lake River. Slicing through the sand and clay that was once the shore of ancient Glacial Lake Agassiz, this tributary of the Red River of the North is actually quite docile in most of its reaches. But a few miles south of Saint Hilaire, the gradient increases and the Red Lake River moves swiftly south toward Red Lake Falls, curving west as it approaches the town. At the takeout for this trip, the Clearwater River—a large, fast-moving river itself—joins the Red Lake River. The most challenging rapids appear in the last 7 miles of the run. A tubing concession also operates out of Red Lake Falls.

A fascinating feature of the Red Lake River is that the deeply cut wooded river gorge interrupts one of the flattest landscapes in Minnesota. During the last half of this run, vertical banks of clay and sand up to 80 feet high, topped with oak trees, tower dramatically over the fast-moving water and often shed their crumbling faces into the river. This deep deposit of sediment is called Campbell Beach; long ago it was the edge of the glacial lake. A new website (www.crk.umn.edu/nature-northwest/redlakewebsite/) features photos and information about the Red Lake River.

Camping is available at both ends of this run. Saint Hilaire's Island Park and Red Lake Falls's Sportsman Park both have campsites for a fee, with shelters, drinking water, and toilets located next to the access points. The tubing outfitter, Voyageur's View (218-253-2031), located in Red Lake Falls upstream of Sportsman Park, offers camping for a fee, drinking water, showers and toilets, and groceries.

You can arrange **canoe rentals** by calling Ben Murphy in Red Lake Falls (218-253-2816).

The 12.2-mile **shuttle route** runs from Island Park in Saint Hilaire west on Main Street to Highway 32, south on 32 to County Road 19, west on 19 to County Road 13, south on 13 to Harren Drive, then west on Harren Drive into Sportsman Park.

The average **gradient** is 5.5 feet per mile.

Be sure to check the **water level**, as it changes quickly. Check the U.S. Army Corps of Engineers Web site (www.mvp.usace.army.mil/dcp/) for the river stage at Red Lake Falls. Below a stage of 12.5, the river is too shallow and rocky to paddle. Between 13 and 15 feet, the paddling is best. Water level information can also be obtained by calling Dick Brumwell at Voyageur's View (218-253-2031) in Red Lake Falls.

To reach the **put-in** at Island Park in Saint Hilaire, go east from Highway 32 onto Main Street at the sign for Saint Hilaire City Park. The official canoe access in the park is marked by a sign on the north side of a narrow neck of land encircled by a meander in the river, but if you put in there, the trip is 24.4 miles long. If you put in on the south side of the land neck instead, you'll shorten this somewhat long trip by 1.4 miles. Carry down a grassy slope to the quiet backwater.

Along this section, the Red Lake River is lined with wooded banks backed by agricultural fields. You'll pass some houses, especially as you head out of town, but overall the banks are undeveloped. Blue herons and other waterbirds are common. In the first 7 miles, the river is quiet, with occasional boulders. Then, with each river mile that passes, the banks rise a little higher and more boulders appear in the riverbed.

By mile 9, little riffles morph into definite Class I rapids. After mile 12, the rapids are more frequent and more intense. Some bluffs are 50 feet high at this point, their eroded faces curving down toward the river. At about mile 16.7, just past the end of a series of rapids that round a bend to the right, the river splits around a large island; at the downstream end of the island is a small backwater where you can land. At mile 18, you'll paddle under the Highway 32 bridge.

Below the bridge, the river valley widens into a broad floodplain, with low, flat banks and islands where landing is possible. A railroad trestle carrying a biking trail (the trail runs 3.8 miles from Highway 32 to County Road 19) crosses the river at mile 19.7, and waves up to 2.5 feet high can form in the rapids just past the bridge. On the cliffs on river right downstream of the trestle, look for clay nests sculpted by cliff swallows. You'll also pass the brick powerhouse of a dam that was removed. The County Road 13 bridge crosses at mile 22.2; just past the bridge on river left is the tubing outfitter's campground. **Take out** one mile downstream, on river left at the Sportsman Park boat ramp just before the confluence with the Clearwater River.

The DNR hopes to add more access points along the Red Lake River in the near future; stay tuned.

The Red Lake River has carved a deep channel in the flat landscape.

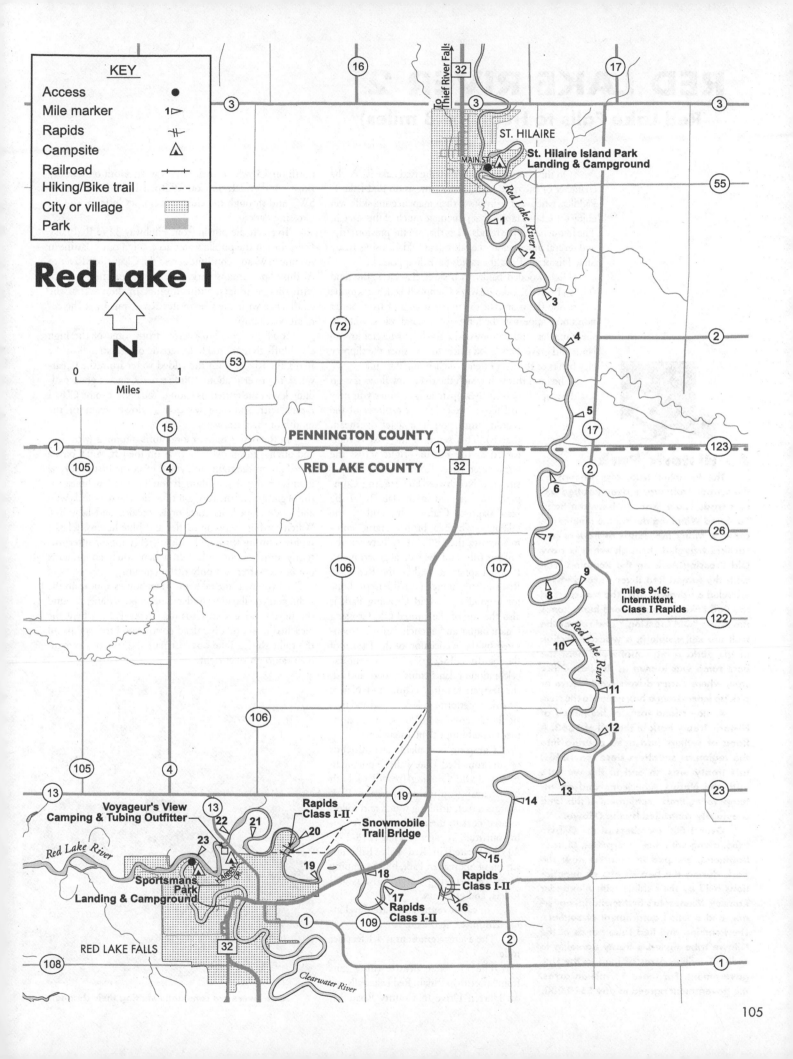

KEY

Access	●
Mile marker	1▷
Rapids	⤙⤙
Campsite	△
Railroad	┼┼┼
Hiking/Bike trail	- - -
City or village	
Park	

Red Lake 1

↑
N

0 ——— 1
Miles

PENNINGTON COUNTY

RED LAKE COUNTY

ST. HILAIRE

St. Hilaire Island Park
Landing & Campground

MAIN ST.

Red Lake River

miles 9-16:
Intermittent
Class I Rapids

Voyageur's View
Camping & Tubing Outfitter

Rapids
Class I-II

Snowmobile
Trail Bridge

Sportsmans
Park
Landing & Campground

Red Lake River

Rapids
Class I-II

Rapids
Class I-II

RED LAKE FALLS

Clearwater River

To Thief River Falls

RED LAKE RIVER 2
Red Lake Falls to Huot (14.8 miles)

On this shorter journey down the Red Lake River, the character of the river is much the same as on Red Lake 1. Paddlers who want to improve their maneuvering skills will enjoy the Class I rapids that punctuate much of this stretch. The frequency of the rapids is less than on the previous trip, and several miles before the takeout at Old Crossing Treaty State Historical Park, the rapids have disappeared.

High wooded banks with sheer clay faces, the sand ridges of Glacial Lake Agassiz's Campbell Beach, continue to provide the drama of the upper stretch of river. Softer notes now appear in the form of ferns, red osiers, willows, silver maples, and cottonwoods. You'll pass several low islands and gravel bars, good places to stop since the slippery clay banks of the river often make landing difficult.

The land through which the river now flows is even less developed than further upstream; at times you may feel like a presettlement explorer of the region (until you hear a jet overhead, that is). This sense of the past is reinforced at the put-in—right across the Clearwater River from the now empty site of a Northwest Fur Trading Company post erected in the late 1700s by Jean Baptiste Cadotte Jr.; and at the takeout—where a bronze statue commemorates the 1863 treaty between the Ojibwe tribe and the federal government. If you happen to paddle the Red Lake River in late August (you'll have to hope for a good rain), Old Crossing Park is also the site of the annual Old Crossing Chautauqua and French Festival, sponsored by the Association of the French of the North (218-253-2270). A four-day celebration of dance, music, food, and art, the festival features Cajun and Native American performers, lots of food and music, kids' activities, a Voyageur encampment, and historical interpretation.

Camping is available at both ends of this run. Red Lake Falls's Sportsman Park and Old Crossing Treaty Park both have campgrounds (Sportsman Park charges a fee), drinking water, and toilets located next to the access points. A tubing outfitter, Voyageur's View (218-253-2031), located in Red Lake Falls upstream of Sportsman Park, offers camping for a fee, drinking water, showers and toilets, and groceries.

For **canoe rental** and **water level** information, see Red Lake 1.

The average **gradient** is 4.1 feet per mile.

The 11.3-mile **shuttle route** runs from Sportsman Park in Red Lake Falls east on Harren Drive to County Road 13;

north on 13, which then curves west; south on County Road 18; then left on County Road 104 (173rd Avenue SW); and through the cluster of houses in Huot to Old Crossing Park.

To reach the put-in from Highway 32 in Red Lake Falls, turn at the public water access sign onto Battineau Avenue NW, and continue across the Clearwater River to Al Buse Sportsmans Park, a spacious community park with shelter, toilets, and camping. In the park, at the confluence with the Clearwater River, **put in** at the cement boat ramp.

You'll be launching across from some of the high clay bluffs that are so characteristic of this stretch of the Red Lake River. With the added water from the Clearwater, the river is about 300 feet wide, and at good paddling levels, the current is strong. You'll meet some Class I rapids with standing waves just downstream of the mouth of the Clearwater.

In the first 3 miles, more bluffs—topped with oaks and birch—tower over the river on the left, you'll pass a gravel pit on the right, and you'll meet the first of several islands on this trip. Although you'll pass a few houses at the beginning of the run, after 5 miles the river feels wild and undeveloped; its corridor is wooded and beautiful. Watch for big snapping turtles and blue herons. Class I rapids running through boulder fields appear intermittently until about mile 9.5, when you'll go under a power line; after that only riffles remain.

As you near the takeout, a few houses appear on the right, and you'll paddle under another power line. Around the next bend is Old Crossing Treaty Park, where the bleached trunk of a big dead cottonwood tree stands on the right shore. **Take out** just past the tree at a cement boat ramp on river right.

An Historic Park

The Pembina Trail, also known as the Woods Trail, was a deeply rutted oxcart trade route that ran between Saint Paul and Winnipeg during the nineteenth century. Many thousands of traders and settlers traveled through what is now Old Crossing Park on the Pembina Trail with the famed Red River oxcarts—two-wheeled ox-drawn carts. The trail crossed the Red Lake River at a ford here, hence the name "Old Crossing," and ruts of the trail are still visible in a wooded section of the park. A big cottonwood near the boat ramp was known as the Post Office Tree, where oxcart drivers would leave or pick up letters from a box nailed to the tree.

A major land transfer happened at Historic Treaty Park in the fall of 1863. A flood of settlers had been pouring into the region as squatters since the 1840s; this treaty was an end to the warfare with the Native Americans and an attempt to legitimize settlement of this land previously controlled by the Ojibwe.

Over 1,600 members of the Ojibwe tribe, along with their interpreter, Charles Bottineau, camped in what is now the park during the two weeks of negotiations held by their chiefs with Alexander Ramsey, Minnesota's first territorial governor, and a small detachment of soldiers. The Pembina and Red Lake bands of the Ojibwe tribe signed a treaty agreeing to cede 11 million acres of land to the U.S. government. For these 11 million acres, the government agreed to pay $510,000.

Some rivers are constantly shifting their channels.

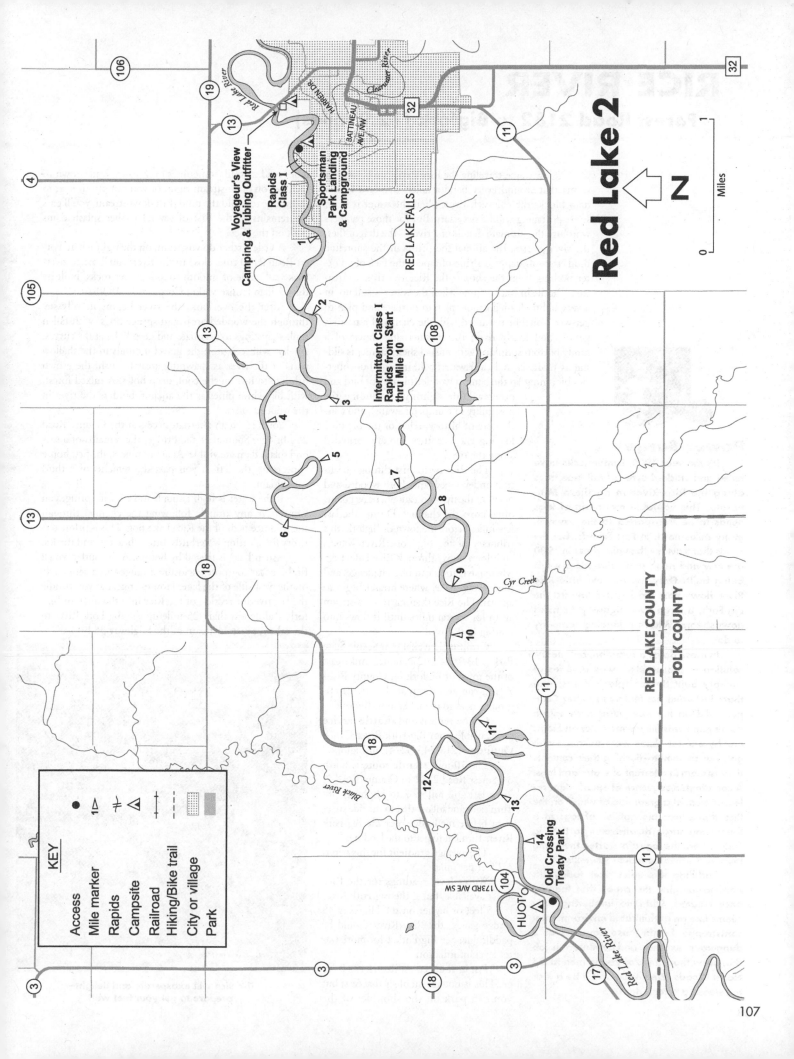

Red Lake 2

N

Miles
0   1

KEY

- • Access
- △1 Mile marker
- ≠ Rapids
- △ Campsite
- ┼ Railroad
- ┊ Hiking/Bike trail
- ▦ City or village
- ▪ Park

Voyageur's View
Camping & Tubing Outfitter

Sportsman
Park Landing
& Campground

Rapids
Class I

RED LAKE FALLS

Intermittent Class I
Rapids from Start
thru Mile 10

Cyr Creek

Black River

Old Crossing
Treaty Park

HUOT

173RD AVE SW

RED LAKE COUNTY
POLK COUNTY

Red Lake River

Clearwater River

Red Lake River

BATTINEAU AVE NW

HARREN DR.

RICE RIVER
Forest Road 2182 to Bigfork (12.9 miles)

Power Surge

It's the year 1900. Lumberjacks have felled and stacked acres of tall pine trees along the Rice River in northern Minnesota. This valuable mountain of logs needs to be transported to the sawmill, many miles north in Fort Francis. But the roads that traverse the wilderness in 1900 are few and poor, and railroads are just being built. Only the narrow little Rice River flows past the loggers toward the Big Fork, a large river highway 12 miles downstream. What's a logging company to do?

In those days, a common, but messy, solution to the problem was a series of cheaply built timber splash dams, and that's just what the Mathieu Lumber Company did on the Rice. After each splash dam's pond was filled with water and logs, one by one the dams were opened—with gates or dynamite—flushing their contents downstream in a torrent of water and logs. A coordinated sequence of splash dam releases created a great tide of water on the Rice that swept big flotillas of logs in a thundering surge downstream to the Big Fork, where the log rafts started their long journey north to Canadian sawmills.

Paddling this quiet river today, it's hard to imagine the chaos that logging once created. Old-time lumbering now seems like an unthinkable environmental catastrophe, but in those days it was a dangerous, exciting, and adventurous job that drew thousands of young men to the North Woods. Well, wouldn't it be a kick to release a splash dam?

At low water, traveling the Rice River can be slow: it seems that around every bend a fallen tree or a beaver dam blocks the channel. Even when the water is high, some portaging will be necessary. But for those paddlers who love the intimate details of a river—the dragonflies, the river grasses, the animal footprints in the shoreline mud, the soft dappled shade of aspen, the face of an otter peeking from the shore—the Rice is a river to treasure. Paddle in May or June when the water is still up, in a very lightly loaded canoe; plan to portage and plan to get wet. You'll be rewarded with the charm of a narrow, gentle, and lovely river; the mesmerizing movie of a sandy bottom sprinkled with mussel shell fragments sliding by under crystal-clear water; wild iris and bunchberries blooming on the bank; a wonderful array of bird and other wildlife sightings (including the possibility of trumpeter swans); and a little taste of history: relics of the big pine logging era a century ago are sprinkled along the river.

The Rice twists first through beautiful undeveloped land, both wooded and open. In the marsh meadows, beaver dams often cross the channel. During the last few miles before the town of Bigfork, this tributary of the Big Fork River widens and flows slowly through Rice Lake Bog, where navigation can be a challenge, and then Aspen Lake, where houses begin to appear. The Rice then narrows, a stream again for several miles until it flows into the Big Fork River.

Camping is available at Scenic State Park (218-743-3362), about 7 miles east of the town of Bigfork on County Road 7. You can also camp at the city campground next to the takeout in Bigfork.

Canoe rentals and **shuttle service** are available from Big Fork River Canoe Outfitting (218-743-3274), in Bigfork.

The 10-mile **shuttle route** is north on Forest Road 2182 to County Road 7. Turn left and follow 7 to Highway 38. Turn right and follow that to the side street right before the bridge over the Big Fork River. Turn left to get to the landing.

The average **gradient** for this trip is 1.2 feet per mile.

Water level readings for the Rice aren't available, but if the Big Fork River is 5.5 feet or higher on the Highway 38 bridge gauge, the Rice River should be paddleable. See Big Fork 1 for more water level information.

Put in at the Forest Road 2182 bridge. This is not an established access, but you can park on the shoulder of the quiet road. A trail, sometimes overgrown, leads down to the river on downstream right, or you can put in next to the bridge to avoid the mud. Just downstream, you'll pass the remains of the first of several timber splash dams built on the Rice.

A little farther downstream, on the right where Forest Road 2180 runs close to the river, you'll see an overlook wall made of smooth rounded river rocks, built by the Civilian Conservation Corps in the 1930s.

After the overlook, the river begins its odyssey through the wooded areas and spruce bogs, with fallen timber crossings to negotiate and deep holes at the curves. Anglers will recognize the gravel mounds in the shallow parts of the river as spawning areas for fish; the grown fish like to lurk in the cool, deep holes. A mixed forest, with big white pines as the anchor, borders the river in the wooded areas.

You'll reach an alternate access at the County Road 254 bridge. Soon after the bridge, the remains of a second splash dam are visible. At about mile 8, the first house appears on the left as you pass the remains of a third splash dam.

If the water is high enough and it's still spring, you won't have any trouble following the channel through the wild rice beds of the Rice Lake Bog. This is prime territory for spotting waterbirds, otters, beavers, and turtles.

Aspen Lake is ringed by houses. At its outlet, you'll find a cedar log post enclosure arranged in a semicircle on the west side of the lake. Houses appear as you paddle the last riverine section of the Rice into the town of Bigfork. Paddle less than .25 mile up the Big Fork River to the **takeout** just upstream of the Highway 38 bridge.

The Rice will exasperate and delight— prepare to get your feet wet!

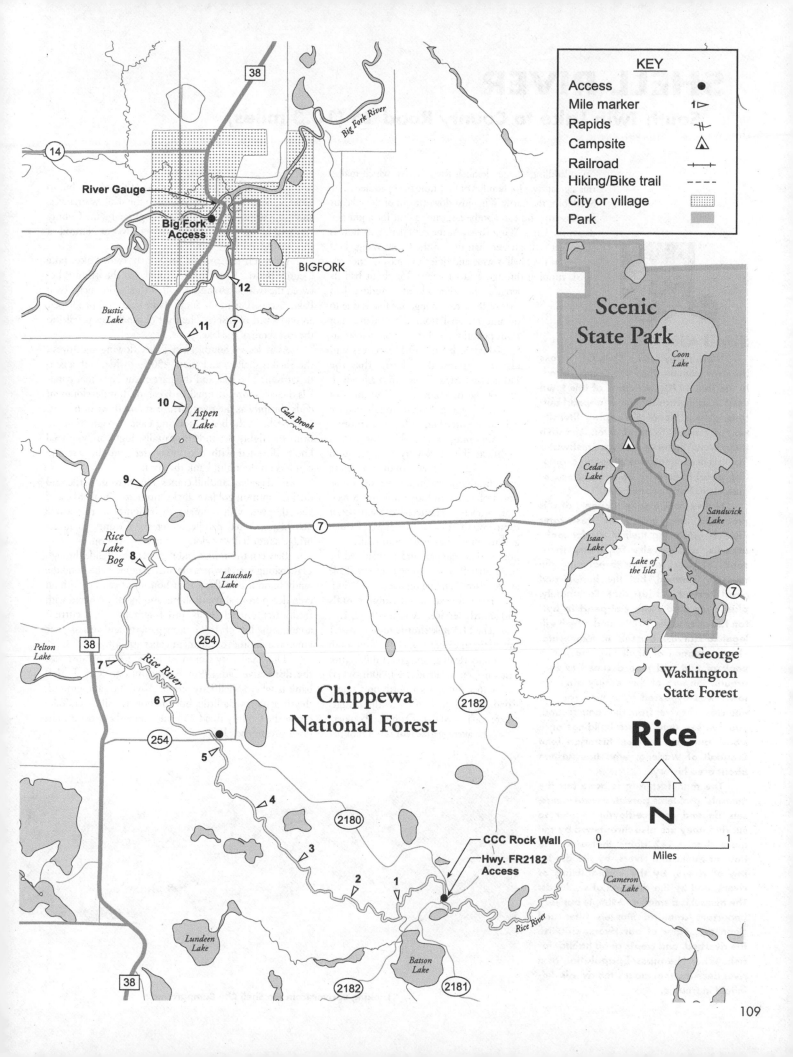

KEY

Access	●
Mile marker	1▷
Rapids	⫲
Campsite	△
Railroad	┼┼┼
Hiking/Bike trail	– – –
City or village	▦
Park	▨

Scenic State Park

George Washington State Forest

Rice

N

0   1
Miles

Chippewa National Forest

River Gauge

Big Fork Access

BIGFORK

Big Fork River

Bustic Lake

Aspen Lake

Gale Brook

Rice Lake Bog

Lauchah Lake

Cedar Lake

Coon Lake

Sandwick Lake

Isaac Lake

Lake of the Isles

Pelton Lake

Rice River

CCC Rock Wall

Hwy. FR2182 Access

Lundeen Lake

Batson Lake

Cameron Lake

Rice River

SHELL RIVER
South Twin Lake to County Road 25 (10.3 miles)

Shell City

There really was a Shell City across the river from the Shell City Campground. In the late 1870s, residents of this town used to manufacture mother-of-pearl buttons, which meant harvesting literally tons of mussels from the river. And then there were the pearl hunters. Freshwater mussels occasionally make pearls, prompting pearl hunters to open hundreds of mussels to find just one pearl.

Native American inhabitants of this area had been eating the freshwater mussels and using their shells for tools, utensils, and jewelry for many thousands of years without threatening the mussels' survival, but the button and pearl harvest did just that. Fortunately, plastic replaced mother-of-pearl in button factories in the 1940s, and now it's illegal to harvest mussels in Minnesota. The population of Shell City reached a peak of 800 and then declined to zero around the turn of the century after the town was bypassed by a new road. If you cross the river from the campground, you can see signs where buildings once stood, put there by local historian John Crandall of Wadena, who has written about area history.

The manufacturing is gone but the mussels' problems persist. Because mussels depend on free-flowing water to survive, they are also threatened by the more than 1,442 dams that slow the flow of Minnesota rivers, by the dredging of rivers, by the channelizing of rivers, and by the draining of wetlands. The mussel is a small and simple but very important creature. Mussels filter and clean the water of our rivers, stabilize the riverbed, and create good habitat for fish. When the mussel population of a river declines, that means the river is definitely in trouble.

Paddling the gentle Shell River is easy, which makes this a great river for families or first-time river paddlers. The Shell joins the Crow Wing just downstream of the takeout for this trip and can also be a starting point for a journey down the Crow Wing River. At the confluence, its flow is actually a little greater than that of the Crow Wing. This section of the Shell is wide and quiet and mostly undeveloped, running through a cattail marsh for about half its length. The water is a little murkier than that of the Crow Wing, but this is due to organic material from the wetland, not from pollution, and the wetland areas attract lots of birds. Bird watchers will also be interested to know that the Huntersville State Forest, through which part of the river flows, has 150 miles of wooded logging trails through diverse habitats—prime bird-watching territory.

Camping is available, for $10 a night, at the Shell City Campground (218-266-2100; www.exploreminnesota.com/listing/index.cfm?id=14296), a mile north of 199th Avenue on 390th Street. This attractive Huntersville State Forest campground, situated in a grove of white and red pines, has water pumps and outhouses. The campground is managed by Itasca State Park. Camping is also available at Tree Farm Landing on the Crow Wing.

For information on **canoe rentals** and **shuttle service**, see Crow Wing 1.

The 11.3-mile **shuttle route** runs 1.1 miles east on County Road 21. Turn south on County Road 23 and go 2.1 miles. Turn east on County Road 18 (380th Street) and go 6.1 miles. Turn north on County Road 25 and go 2 miles to the bridge, where you'll need to park on the shoulder.

The average **gradient** is 0.5 foot per mile.

The Shell can be paddled most of the season, but to avoid being grounded on the sand in the shallow stretches, check the **water level** on the USGS gauge by the County Road 12 bridge over the Crow Wing River at Nimrod; it should read at least 3 feet.

To reach the **put-in** on South Twin Lake, take County Road 21 east from Menagha to the isthmus between the twin lakes and turn off at Russ Commick's Twin Lakes access. Put in on South Twin Lake and paddle left around a bed of rushes. The river channel runs parallel to the east shore of the lake.

As it leaves South Twin Lake, flowing southwest, the Shell is shallow and about 250 feet wide, with a gentle current. The lake and the part of the river that parallels the lakeshore are lined with cabins, but development ends abruptly as the river turns east and flows into a cattail marsh. At the bend, Stocking Lake's stream comes in from the right. Beyond the cattails, high sandy, glacial knolls, forested with deciduous trees on the left and conifers on the right, bank the river.

Bald eagles, sandhill cranes, blue herons, bufflehead ducks, common goldeye ducks, numerous mallards, and Canada geese visit or make their homes in this lovely marshland. You'll paddle under the County Road 23 bridge about halfway along the marshy section.

Between this bridge and the next, you'll slide through a fascinating stretch where the Shell is quite shallow and the sandy bottom is as flat a river bottom as can be, with an even depth from shore to shore, and literally covered with freshwater mussel shells and fragments. The current arranges the bits of shell in flow patterns and you may see long, straight lines of fragment concentrations.

The Shell City Campsite is on the right, just past the distinctive old 199th Avenue bridge. On the left bank is where Shell City stood. After the campground, the river narrows a little, but the flow is still quiet. **Take out** at the County Road 25 bridge on either upstream or downstream river left.

Looking upriver from the Shell City Campground.

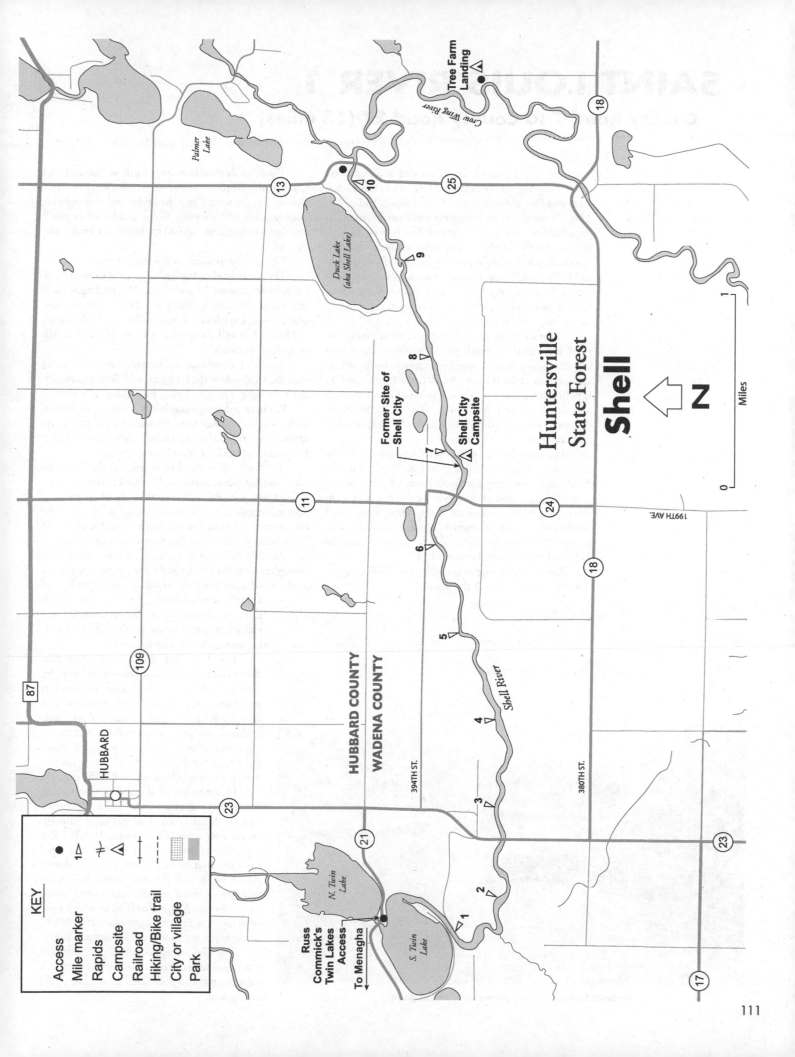

KEY

Access •

Mile marker 1△

Rapids ≠

Campsite △

Railroad —†—

Hiking/Bike trail -----

City or village ▦

Park ▒

HUBBARD

N. Twin Lake

S. Twin Lake

Russ Commick's Twin Lakes Access

To Menagha

87

109

23

21

1

2

3

4

5

6

7

8

9

10

11

13

24

25

18

18

17

23

Shell River

HUBBARD COUNTY
WADENA COUNTY

394TH ST.

380TH ST.

199TH AVE.

Huntersville
State Forest

Shell

N

Miles
0   1

Former Site of Shell City

Shell City Campsite

Duck Lake
(aka Shell Lake)

Palmer Lake

Crow Wing River

Tree Farm Landing

SAINT LOUIS RIVER 1
County Road 7 to County Road 27 (13 miles)

The Upper Saint Louis is wooded and beautiful, and although generally quiet, the first half of this stretch takes paddlers through several Class I rapids and riffles. This is a good trip for beginning whitewater runners to get a little practice in boat control. The flow of this segment of the river is also an interesting study in contrasts. For the first half of the trip, the Saint Louis flows quickly and fairly straight, running through a long series of rocky rapids. In the second half of the segment, the gradient flattens out and the river wanders through a tightly wound series of meanders.

Cedars, birches, silver maples, and white pines grow right down to the riverside on the heavily wooded river corridor. Along several stretches, dramatic banks of clay and sand rise above the river. Much of the land along here is public land, and with the exception of one developed area, there are very few houses. Wildlife sightings are common: white-tailed deer, bald eagles, and lots of ducks and songbirds.

The Saint Louis was a major river highway for the fur trade. Voyageurs paddled from Lake Superior up the Saint Louis, portaging the rapids below Cloquet. Fifteen river miles upstream of the put-in for this trip is the confluence with the Embarrass River. These hardy men would canoe up the Embarrass, portage across the Laurentian Divide to the Pike, and head up into Vermilion Lake and the Hudson Bay watershed.

Riverside **camping** is available at a DNR campsite 3.8 miles downstream of the put-in.

The 6.7-mile **shuttle route** is south on County Road 7 to County Road 27 at the tiny community of Zim, then west to the river. Cross the bridge and turn right on County Road 312 (Norway Ridge Road), where you'll see a sign for the access. A gravel road leads to a small parking area.

The average **gradient** is 2.6 feet per mile.

The **water level** on the Forbes gauge at County Road 7 should be between 2.1 and 6 feet. This reading is available from the DNR (888-646-6367; www.dnr.state .mn.us/river_levels/index.html). At low levels, the rapids will be shallow and the steep clay banks of the river will be difficult to climb.

To reach the Forbes access, turn onto the road leading from the south side of the bridge into the Forbes Cemetery and bear right. The gravel road leads down to a parking area. **Put in** on a sloping sandy beach down a short flight of timber steps. A quarter mile downstream, just past a few riffles, is an impressive old Duluth, Messabe, and Iron Range railroad trestle built on brownstone piers.

The banks are wooded right down to the river with white and red pines, cedars, and lowland deciduous trees. Elbow Creek joins the river from the right at a pretty confluence. At mile 2.4 abandoned railroad trestles cross the river next to a private landing on river left; County Road 788 touches the river here, but there is no road crossing.

About a half mile downstream, you'll begin to run through intermittent riffles and Class I rapids. Just past a sandy island at mile 3.8, the rapids pause. At the base of a high wooded bank, you'll see the DNR campsite on river right. The campsite has several levels (and a privy) up the hillside, and is big enough for four or five tents.

Less than a mile downstream, where East Two River joins the Saint Louis from the right, the river widens and splits around an island. A power line crosses here and the river runs through a bouldery Class I rapids. About a quarter mile farther, where West Two River flows in from the right and several more islands appear, you'll meet more rapids. Go to the left of the islands. This is an especially scenic part of the trip.

Downstream of the double confluence, the gradient decreases, the rapids disappear, and the Saint Louis now meanders through an amazing series of river loops. At mile 7.2, a high ridge of land less than 350 feet wide separates the river from a point 3.5 miles downstream on its own channel. Several houses appear along this circuitous route. County Road 312 (Norway Ridge Road) runs next to the river for a bit and crosses the river at mile 9.6, where access is possible on downstream left.

The Zim access (County Road 27 bridge) where you **take out** is on upstream river right. A long, steep gravel path leads up the hill to the parking area.

The Saint Louis is a lively young river at this point.

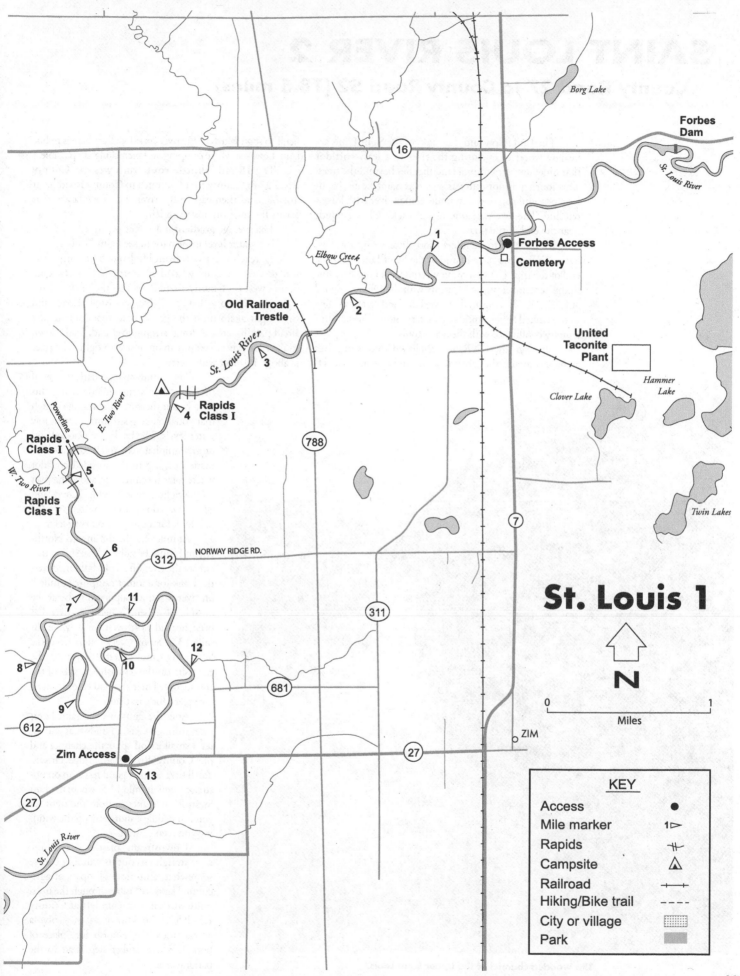

Forbes Dam

Borg Lake

St. Louis River

16

1

Elbow Creek

Forbes Access
Cemetery

United
Taconite
Plant

Old Railroad
Trestle

2

St. Louis River

3

Hammer
Lake

Clover Lake

Rapids
Class I

4

Powerline

E. Two River

Rapids
Class I

788

5

W. Two River

Twin Lakes

Rapids
Class I

7

6

312

NORWAY RIDGE RD.

311

St. Louis 1

11

7

12

8

10

681

9

612

ZIM

ZIM

27

Zim Access

13

27

St. Louis River

0   1
Miles

KEY
Access   ●
Mile marker   1▷
Rapids   ⌗
Campsite   △
Railroad   ┼┼┼
Hiking/Bike trail - - -
City or village   ▦
Park

113

SAINT LOUIS RIVER 2
County Road 27 to County Road 52 (18.5 miles)

The land is low and the banks of the Saint Louis are heavily wooded, enclosing the river in a leafy corridor that hides any agricultural land that lies beyond the trees. This journey is not quite as scenic as Saint Louis 1, but it's a peaceful trip down an undeveloped river with lots of wildlife. The river has one run of rocky Class I rapids near the end of the float.

It's possible to paddle a short distance up the East Swan River, a tributary that joins the Saint Louis near the end of the trip. The East Swan was used as a boundary line in the September 30, 1854, treaty with the Ojibwe, signed at La Pointe, Wisconsin, that ceded the land east of the line to the United States. Another tributary, Stony Creek, forms a pretty confluence with the Saint Louis.

Although the DNR has established three **campsites** along this stretch, they are unmarked, and two are quite difficult to spot. Much of the river corridor along here is public land, however, where camping and picnicking are possible.

The 18-mile **shuttle route** runs west on County Road 27 to County Road 5, south to County Road 52 at Toivola, and then east to the river. The Toivola access is across the river on upstream left.

The average **gradient** is 1.4 feet per mile.

For **water level** information, see Saint Louis 1.

To reach the access from Highway 53 at tiny Cotton, go west on County Road 52, north on County Road 7, and west on County Road 27 across the bridge. Turn right onto County Road 312 (Norway Ridge Road) and then right again onto the gravel road that leads to the small parking area. A long, steep gravel path leads down to the river, where you **put in** on upstream right. The river is about 150 feet wide here.

The tannin-stained dark waters of the Saint Louis run quietly along this stretch, but the current is strong enough that you'll make good time, even at low water levels. The banks are wooded and mostly uninhabited. You'll pass one dramatic opening in the wooded corridor where a farm stands high above the river on the right at mile 2, with cleared land all the way down to the water. At mile 2.5, look for a campsite on river left.

At mile 6.2, the Burlington Northern and Santa Fe railway line, still in use, crosses the river on an old-fashioned trestle. Look for another campsite at mile 9 on river right; it's supposed to be at the outside of a bend where the river has been headed northwest for a while. At mile 13.5, Stony Creek enters from the left. This time, you'll easily find the campsite on the downstream side of the confluence. There's a good landing and a nice place for a rest stop.

After the campsite, the Saint Louis races through Class I rapids that end after a small island splits the channel and the County Road 230 bridge crosses. You'll find another good rest stop on upstream right at mile 14.5, where the East Swan River comes in from the right, or you can paddle a short way up the winding and scenic Swan.

Downstream of the Swan, the river straightens out its winding course somewhat, and more glimpses of agricultural land are visible through the trees. **Take out** on upstream left at County Road 52, also known as the Toivola access (toivola is Finnish for "place of hope"), where timber steps lead to the parking area.

The wooded channel of the Upper Saint Louis.

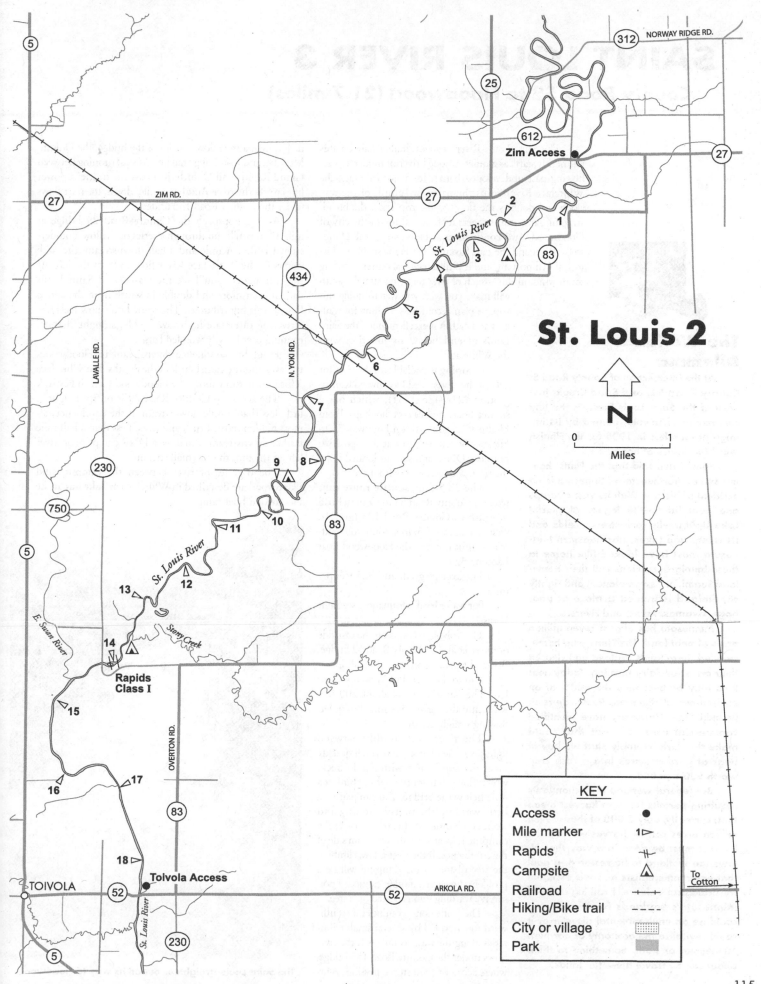

St. Louis 2

KEY

Access	●
Mile marker	1▷
Rapids	⫢
Campsite	△
Railroad	┼┼┼
Hiking/Bike trail	- - - -
City or village	▦
Park	▬

SAINT LOUIS RIVER 3
County Road 52 to Floodwood (21.7 miles)

The Wetlands Dilemma

At the intersection of County Road 5, County Road 52, and Sand Creek, just west of the Saint Louis River, is the tiny community of Toivola, named by its immigrant founders in 1905 for the Finnish word for "place of hope."

Some have said that the Finns' having settled northeastern Minnesota is no accident of history. With its vast swamps and peat lands—the legacy of glacial Lake Upham—its rock-strewn fields and its rivers and lakes, northeastern Minnesota must have looked like home to these immigrants. Finns call their homeland Suomi, or "swampland," and rightly so; Finland is indeed a place of peat bogs, swamps, lakes, and rivers.

Minnesota has almost seven million acres of peat land. The Finns who homesteaded these lands drained and cleared their acres for dairy farming. Today peat land may be becoming the center of an environmental dilemma. Researchers at Bemidji State University have identified commercial uses for peat that could make the dark, crumbly stuff we buy in bags at garden stores into a cash crop worth $30 a pound.

But federal wetland protection laws requiring permits for peat harvest mean that, currently, only 3,000 of those seven million acres can be harvested, and the harvest must be done in a way that allows the wetland to be restored, a goal that environmentalists know is essential for ecological balance. Draining more of Minnesota's wetlands for a cash crop could be an environmental disaster or it could revitalize the economy of northern Minnesota, or both. Something to think about as you travel these flat lands.

The Saint Louis River changes dramatically on this journey. It starts as a quiet, wooded river of moderate size, flowing past undeveloped banks. Its major tributary, the Whiteface River, joins the party two-thirds of the way along and doubles the flow. As the trip ends, the broad, straight Saint Louis meets its first real town, the city of Floodwood. Two confluences at Floodwood, the Floodwood River and the East Savanna, made the small city historically important, and it's still a regional center. A strong south wind on this stretch of river that runs straight south will make you wish you weren't doing this trip, so plan accordingly. Fishing for walleyes and catfish is excellent along the Saint Louis at and below its junction with the Whiteface.

Camping is available on the river for a fee at the city-owned Floodwood Campground (218-476-2751), which has a shower house and electric hookups. From Highway 2, go north on Highway 73 to Hickory Street; turn east at the sign. Two primitive DNR campsites are located along the river, with access only from the river.

The 28.5-mile **shuttle route** runs west on County Road 52 to County Road 5, south to County Road 133 (gravel), west to Highway 73, then south to Floodwood. Turn north at the Floodwood Boat Landing sign.

The average **gradient** is 0.5 feet per mile.

For **water level** information, see Saint Louis 1.

The Toivola access is on the east side of the river at the County Road 52 bridge. Below the parking area, a path and timber steps lead to the river. **Put in** on upstream left. The Saint Louis is about 200 feet wide, and the current is strong but quiet, flowing straight south.

The river runs steadily between lightly wooded banks, and you'll quickly meet the confluence with Sand Creek, which flows in from the right a third of a mile below the bridge. You can paddle a little ways up the pretty winding and wooded channel of this tributary, and a campsite is located on the upstream side of the confluence. If the river is low, climbing the steep bank to the campsite will be a problem, however. Another caution: a poison ivy warning sign is posted on a tree.

The Saint Louis continues its southward journey, fed by several small tributaries along the way. At mile 4.1, the river flows under the County Road 156 bridge, where access or a rest stop is possible. A lit-

tle less than a mile downstream of the bridge, the Duluth, Messabe, and Iron Range rail line crosses, running between Grand Rapids and Duluth. Just past the trestle, a power line crosses the river. Another 2 miles down, the river flows under the County Road 133 bridge.

As you approach the County Road 29 bridge at mile 13.3, you'll run through a series of shallow, boulder-strewn riffles. A mile and a half downstream, the dark waters of the Whiteface River flow in from the left. At the confluence, you'll see the tea-colored Saint Louis darken even more and double in width from the added flow of this big tributary. The Saint Louis now feels like a riverine interstate highway, a wide, straight channel running past heavily wooded banks.

From the confluence downstream to Floodwood, walleyes and the catfish lurk in the depths. See Whiteface 3 for information about the Floodwood Catfish Festival.

The access to County Road 29 is on river right, a little less than a mile downstream of the confluence, almost hidden in the brush and trees. Less than a half mile farther downstream, you'll see a DNR campsite on river left, at the mouth of a small stream.

The 6 miles of river between the campsite and Floodwood are described in Whiteface 3. **Take out** at the Floodwood boat ramp.

The Saint Louis straightens out on its way to Floodwood.

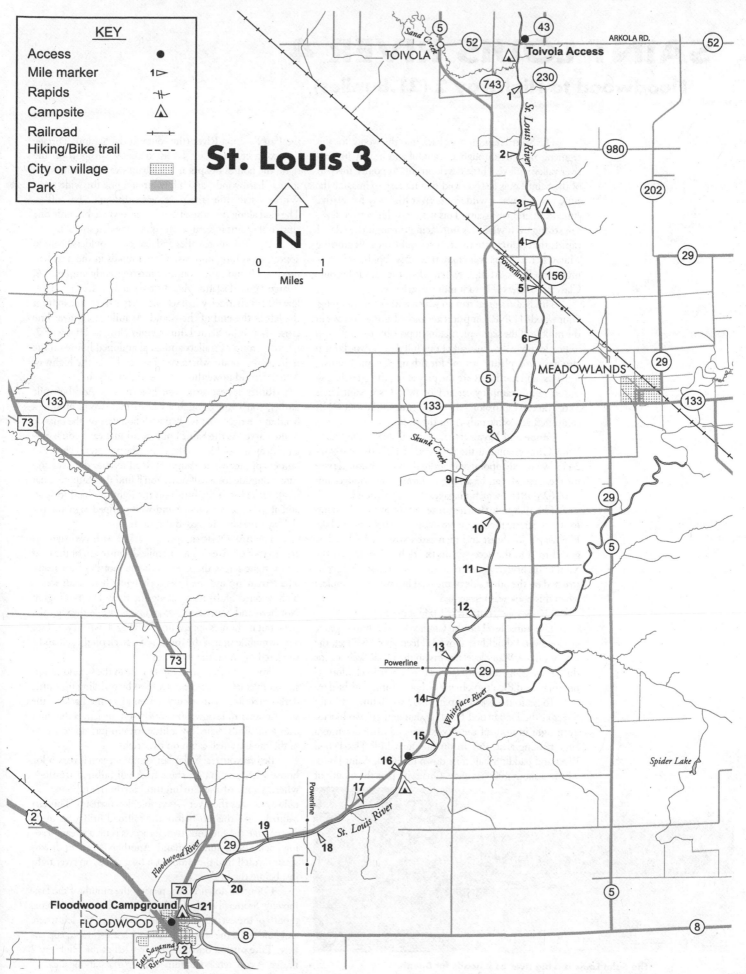

KEY

Access   ●
Mile marker   1▷
Rapids
Campsite   △
Railroad
Hiking/Bike trail   -----
City or village
Park

St. Louis 3

N

0   1
Miles

TOIVOLA

Toivola Access

ARKOLA RD.

MEADOWLANDS

Sand Creek

St. Louis River

Powerline

Skunk Creek

Whiteface River

Spider Lake

Powerline

St. Louis River

Floodwood River

East Savanna River

Floodwood Campground

FLOODWOOD

SAINT LOUIS RIVER 4
Floodwood to Highway 2 (21.8 miles)

The Saint Louis plunges back into the woods for this segment, running through a beautiful and heavily forested river valley with very little development. At points, this part of the Saint Louis feels so wild that it's easy to imagine the time when it was a wilderness river highway for Native Americans and voyageurs. This is a big-volume river, flowing strong even when it's not racing through the Class I rapids that punctuate the run several times. Beginning whitewater paddlers will enjoy these easy rapids, at least at moderate flows. At high water, when the rapids become Class II, paddlers will want more experience.

This is also a great trip on which to do some camping. Four wooded DNR campsites are located along the river in the middle of the segment, making it possible to do the trip in two leisurely days instead of one full day. A two-day trip also gives you plenty of time for fishing. Channel catfish, walleyes, and northerns are the prey along this stretch.

You can **camp** by car at Floodwood (see Saint Louis 3) or you can camp along the river at one of the four DNR campsites, accessible only from the river.

Canoe and kayak rentals are available at the Indian Point Campground at the west end of Duluth (800-982-2453; www.indianpointcampground.com). Shuttle service for these rentals can be arranged through the Munger Inn (218-624-4814), which manages the campground.

The 19.8-mile **shuttle route** runs from the boat ramp to Main Street, then right on Main to Highway 2. Take Highway 2 southeast and then east across the bridge. The gravel road to the access is on the right, .1 mile past the Saint Louis bridge. An entry to the access is also being constructed on the other side of the road but was not complete when this book was researched.

The average **gradient** is 1.0 foot per mile.

The **water level** on the County Road 8 bridge gauge at Floodwood should be above 1.2 feet; above 5.7 feet, the river is unsafe. Water level reports on the DNR Web site for this bridge gauge are only sporadic, so water level information may be difficult to obtain without visiting the bridge.

To get to the boat ramp in Floodwood, turn off Main Street at the Floodwood Landing sign and go two blocks. Turn right in front of the city garage and drive down to a large parking area. **Put in** on the quiet little Floodwood River and paddle a half mile down to the big Saint Louis, which is about 300 feet wide. Once you pass the mouth of

the East Savanna River (the route to the Savanna Portage that connects the Saint Louis to the Mississippi) on the right, the houses disappear. Low banks wooded with some spruce, hardwoods, and a few birches line the wide river. Within a half mile, the river swirls through a few riffles. The land along this stretch is privately owned, but only one cluster of cabins interrupts the quiet wooded shoreline.

At mile 3, more riffles and scattered boulders begin to appear, morphing into easy Class I rapids in the next half mile; rapids and riffles continue intermittently until mile 6. A large wooded island splits the river at mile 4.7; if you follow the left channel, you'll see McCarty River come in from the left at the end of the island. At mile 5, a power line crosses, and the Saint Louis swings close to Highway 2, where a group of trailers and an abandoned house on the right mark a point where you'll see and hear the highway. After a second power line crosses, the rapids end.

Riffles appear again briefly at mile 8. Another mile farther, you'll run through a Class I that sweeps around a bend to the right that is filled with boulders on the outside of the curve. As the Saint Louis continues east, you'll pass an enormous boulder on the right. Shortly after, a cluster of houses appears where Paupores Road reaches the river and runs alongside for a half mile. You'll find the Paupores boat ramp tucked into the brush on the right. It's hard to spot, and if you see an orange-and-white-striped sign on the right, you've already passed the ramp.

The first DNR campsite, marked with two signs, is easy to spot on river left a half mile downstream of the boat ramp, right across the river from the mouth of a stream. The terrain around the river is changing here, with scenic high wooded bluffs rising along the river. The Burlington Northern and Santa Fe Railway line is visible through the trees, but no houses appear until mile 13.4, where you'll see a snowmobile sign at the mouth of a creek on the left and a small red cabin on the right.

From the cabin, it's another mile to the second campsite on river left. This site is accessed by paddling up a little dark-water stream that curves around to the back of the site. Another mile downstream, also on the left, is the third campsite, also reached by a little stream. Just downstream of the site is a small cabin on river right.

Before you reach the last campsite, you'll pass a log house with a sauna on the left. A tall railroad trestle—where a spur of the Burlington Northern and Santa Fe railway crosses the river—is visible downstream. This last campsite, on the left before the railroad bridge, is quite pretty. Like the previous two, its access is up a stream leading back into a quiet wetland. Another 1.8 miles downstream, you'll find the Brookston boat ramp, on river right just before the bridge.

Continue downstream, passing the mouth of the fast-moving Stoney Brook on the right and then the scenic mouth of the even faster moving Cloquet on the left where an island splits the channel. A short Class I–II rapid appears here. **Take out** on downstream river left at the Highway 2 bridge. A concrete boat ramp leads up to a parking area.

The Saint Louis is a big river as it heads for Duluth.

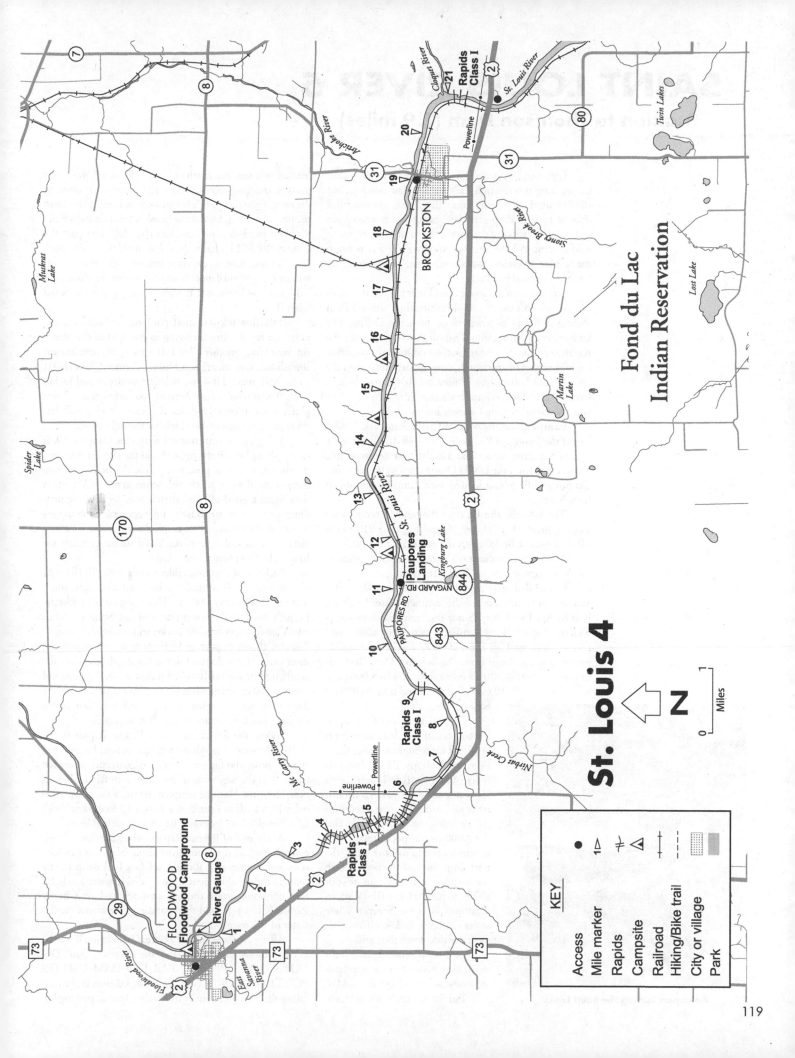

St. Louis 4

Fond du Lac
Indian Reservation

BROOKSTON

FLOODWOOD
Floodwood Campground
River Gauge

Paupores
Landing

Rapids
Class I

Rapids Class I

Rapids
Class I

Rapids Class I

St. Louis River

Cloquet River

Artichoke River

Stoney Brook River

Mc Carty River

Nisbut Creek

Floodwood River

East Savanna River

Muskrat Lake

Spider Lake

Martin Lake

Kingsbury Lake

Lost Lake

Twin Lakes

Powerline

N

0   Miles   1

KEY

●	Access	
1△	Mile marker	
⚡	Rapids	
△	Campsite	
┼┼┼	Railroad	
---	Hiking/Bike trail	
▦	City or village	
▨	Park	

SAINT LOUIS RIVER 5
Scanlon to Thomson Dam (3.9 miles)

For some spectacular Class II–IV whitewater, paddle this exciting run through the dramatic slate outcrops and cliffs of the Lower Saint Louis River bed. Massive tilted slabs of ancient, deep-gray slate, capped with white pines and cedars, tower over the river as the Saint Louis begins its wild descent to Lake Superior, dropping 31 feet between the Scanlon access and the takeout alone. This is not a river for inexperienced paddlers.

Five dams on the lower Saint Louis harness the river's thunderous flow to generate electricity; the Thomson Dam alone is sufficient to power all the homes in Duluth. The University of Minnesota–Duluth (UMD) operates the Kayak and Canoe Institute Outpost on the reservoir, offering whitewater instruction, racing opportunities, and the annual Saint Louis River Whitewater Rendezvous in July. Contact coordinator Randy Carlson (218-726-6177) or visit www.umdrsop.org for more information.

Camping is available at Jay Cooke State Park, 3 miles east of the Thomson Reservoir (218-384-4610). Another option is to camp on an island in the reservoir, accessible by paddling from the UMD Outpost across the reservoir. Do not paddle a boat loaded with camping gear down from Scanlon.

The 4.4-mile **shuttle** from the Scanlon access is via County Road 61, Highway 45, and Highway 210 to the UMD Outpost Building on the east side of the bridge.

The average **gradient** is 8.7 feet per mile; the gradient for the whitewater section is 31 feet per mile.

Controlled by releases from the Scanlon Dam, this section can be run most of the summer. **Water levels** are best in April and May. Since the runnable flow varies widely, choose a level consistent with your ability and your equipment. Call 218-720-2777 for daily flow information on discharge from the Scanlon Dam. It's estimated that 500–1,500 cfs is low flow, 1,500–3,000 cfs is moderate, 3,000–10,000 cfs is high, and over 10,000 cfs is flood stage.

Regardless of the flow, open boaters should paddle a canoe that is outfitted for whitewater with flotation, thigh straps, PFDs, and helmets. When the flow is over 2,000 cfs, the pool-drop pattern diminishes and paddlers are pushed into the next drop without a break. Under 2,000 cfs, the pool-drop pattern means a chance to boat scout the next drop. Stay off the river at high levels unless you're certain of your ability to handle Class III–IV water. A rafting concession, Superior White water (218-384-4637), offers an alternative ride down the rapids.

Another potential hazard is the sharp slate bedrock: wear appropriate footwear and bring a first aid kit. **Put in** at the Scanlon access,

An expert surfing the Saint Louis.

marked by a sign just north of County Road 61. You'll find parking, changing rooms, privies, and an easy carry down to the river. If you first paddle left around the island across from the put-in, you can look at the Scanlon Dam on the left before you head downstream. On river left, just past the County Road 61 bridge, is the site of an old fur trading post.

Pay attention to the river, because right after the interstate bridge, you'll meet Warm-up Rapids. This is a Class I drop at low levels, but at high water, it becomes a solid Class II.

If the flow is low to moderate, you can boat scout the next four rapids. After swinging to the right of the island, run First Hole, another Class I–II. Once you curve around the island, you meet Two Hole, a longer Class II–III with—you guessed it—two holes, at moderate and higher levels. The top hole often forms a good surfing wave. If you prefer to scout from land, use the four-wheeler trail that starts just upstream of Two Hole on the right bank.

At high flow, your route through the Canyon (Class II–III) should be on the right. Avoid the cliff on river left; the current will try to push you into it. Below the Canyon, there's a small rocky beach with access to the ATV trail on river right, a good place to stretch your legs. While paddling, you may be too busy to fully appreciate the rugged beauty of the riverbanks, so climb the rocks here for a nice vantage point and a photo op. You'll almost certainly see bald eagles from here to the takeout.

Back on the river, run Hidden Hole (Class II–III) right of center at low flows and run the hard river right sneak route at flows over 3,000 cfs. This brings you to Electric Ledge, named for the power line overhead. Scout this Class III–IV six-foot falls from the pocket eddy on hard river right. You may choose to **portage** by lowering your boat over the sheer ledge. If you do run this challenging drop, follow the center tongue with right to left momentum. A rooster tail forms at 900 cfs or less when the rock on the right below the drop is exposed. At higher flows, the rock is hidden. If you flip here, you'll swim directly into Rescue Rapids.

Follow the left channel into Rescue Rapids (Class II–III), the longest rapids on this run, named because rescues of those who flip on Electric Ledge happen along the left bank at the beginning of this drop. Run Rescue Rapids right of center. Don't be tempted to follow the right channel, which leads to Boat Beater Falls, a 12-foot Class V–VI falls runnable only by expert kayakers at certain levels.

At the end of Rescue Rapids, when the flow is high enough, paddle upstream around the island to run Upstream-Downstream Rapids, a Class I–II drop in the right channel below Boat Beater Falls. If water levels are low, continue down the left channel to Last Chance Rapids (Class I–II) and then paddle a mile across the flat water of the reservoir.

After you come around Fortress Island, you'll see the UMD Outpost pier on the left of the Thomson Dam. DO NOT GO ANYWHERE NEAR THE DAM AND ITS POWERFUL CURRENTS. From the **takeout** at the pier, follow the path over a rocky rise to the Outpost parking lot.

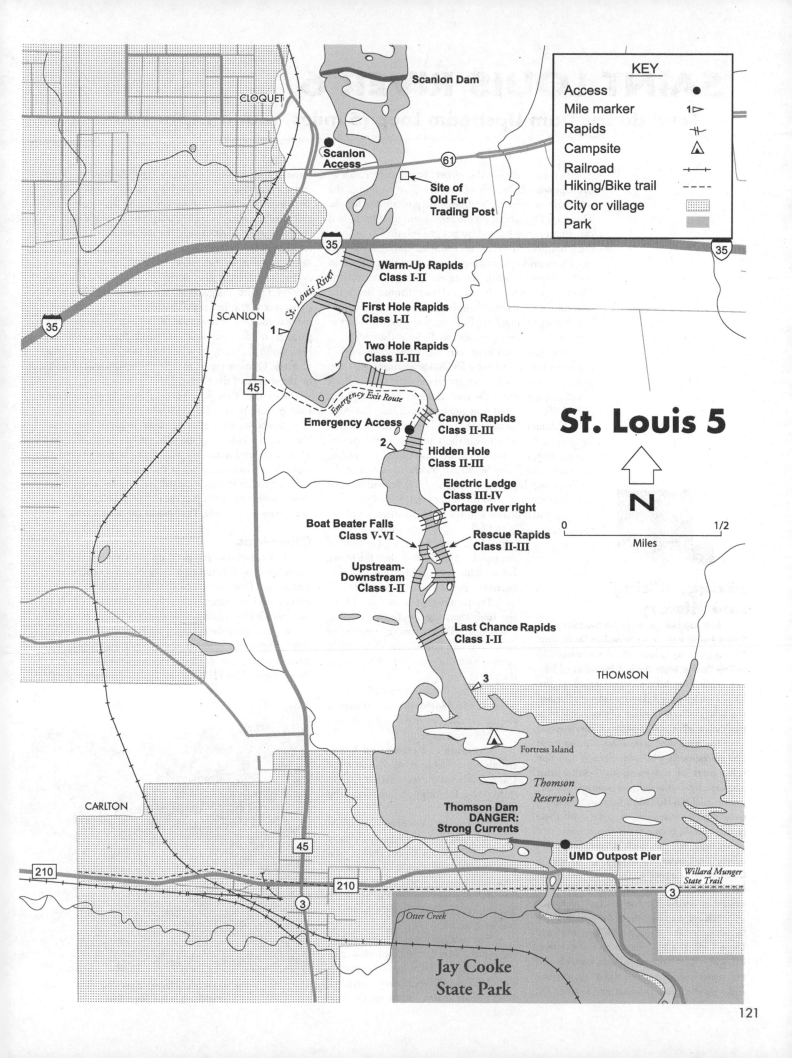

Scanlon Dam

CLOQUET

Scanlon
Access

KEY

Access ●

Mile marker 1▷

Rapids

Campsite △

Railroad

Hiking/Bike trail ---

City or village

Park

61

Site of
Old Fur
Trading Post

35

35

35

Warm-Up Rapids
Class I-II

SCANLON

St. Louis River

First Hole Rapids
Class I-II

1▷

45

Two Hole Rapids
Class II-III

Emergency Exit Route

Emergency Access

Canyon Rapids
Class II-III

2▷

Hidden Hole
Class II-III

Electric Ledge
Class III-IV
Portage river right

Boat Beater Falls
Class V-VI

Rescue Rapids
Class II-III

Upstream-
Downstream
Class I-II

St. Louis 5

N

0 _____ 1/2
Miles

Last Chance Rapids
Class I-II

THOMSON

3▷

△

Fortress Island

Thomson
Reservoir

Thomson Dam
DANGER:
Strong Currents

CARLTON

45

UMD Outpost Pier

Willard Munger
State Trail

210

210

3

3

Otter Creek

Jay Cooke
State Park

SAINT LOUIS RIVER 6
Fond du Lac Dam Upstream Loop (5 miles, round-trip)

For those interested in either historic architecture or hydropower plants, this will be a fascinating trip to the otherwise inaccessible hydroelectric powerhouse for the Thomson Dam, built on the Saint Louis in 1907 to feed the then-energy-starved homes of Duluth. Water from the Thomson Reservoir is channeled through a 2-mile canal into underground pipelines to feed the turbines in the powerhouse, while the excess water pours over the Thomson Dam into the original river channel. Below the reservoir in Jay Cooke State Park, the Saint Louis thunders through Oldenburg Falls, dropping over 300 feet in the 5 miles before the power canal rejoins the river.

For those who have seen the dramatic geology of the Saint Louis riverbed a few miles upstream, this segment of the river will be a surprise: the tilted slate bedrock has disappeared and the river is banked with high red clay bluffs, deposited eons ago by Glacial Lake Duluth.

Although the trip is short and the current fairly gentle at first, when you near the Thomson Development Powerhouse, the outflow can be dangerous if you paddle too close. You'll also be able to paddle upstream of the hydro plant; the distance you travel will depend on your paddling strength and the water level. When you turn around, you'll be just a mile or two downstream of the spectacular rapids and falls that you can see from Oldenburg Point. You can get a great view of the rapids on trails from the Oldenburg Point picnic area off Highway 210, between the park office and the put-in.

The path of the historic Grand Portage Trail, a grueling 7-mile slog that the voyageurs used to bypass the impassable rapids and falls downstream of Swinging Bridge, runs through the parking area at the put-in.

The Jay Cooke State Park Campground (218-384-4610), located west of the access on County Road 210, is a great place to **camp**.

Camping and **canoe and kayak rentals** are available at the Indian Point Campground at the west end of Duluth (800-982-2453; www.indianpointcampground.com).

From the Jay Cooke State Park office, drive 5.5 miles east on Highway 210 to a sign on the right for Grand Portage Trail parking. After you turn in to the parking area, you'll see the water access sign and a trail down to the river. **Put in** at the wooden crib that stabilizes the bank and paddle upstream.

The gradient here is inconsequential and the Saint Louis' flow is slowed by the Fond du Lac Dam just downstream, so paddling against the current is no problem, at least at first. You'll see the road through the birch forest (intermingled with white pines and spruce) that covers the high banks on both sides. Two water towers that stand above the hydro plant are visible as you start the trip. You'll pass two power lines on your way up the Saint Louis; the second one emerges directly from the power plant.

As you near the Thomson Development Powerhouse, the current gets noticeably stronger. The hydropower plant, a large classic revival brick building with two subsequent, less classic, additions, is on the right bank as you paddle upstream. A large danger sign alerts paddlers to stay away from the plant. Buried in the hill behind the plant are the water feed tubes that power the turbines. Outflow from the turbines leaves a trail of foam on the surface of the river.

Past the plant, the current quickly grows even stronger and the river is shallower. At low water, you'll have to choose your path carefully to avoid the rocks. You'll see the tail end of the wild rapids upstream as you approach a bend to the left. Numerous large white cedars grow along this stretch. When you reach the point where it's too difficult to paddle upstream, turn around and return, taking care as you pass the powerhouse again to stay away from the outflow. **Take out** at the same access.

Other trips

Downstream of the Fond du Lac dam, on the Wisconsin side, paddlers can explore the Nature Conservancy's Streambank Protection Area. The Saint Louis River Citizens Action Committee has published a booklet: *The Natural and Cultural History of the Lower St. Louis River*, with annotated maps of the estuary from Fond du Lac to Grassy Point, historic information, and notes about natural features. For a free copy, contact the Saint Louis River Citizens Action Committee (218-733-9520; slrac@stlouisriver.org).

The Saint Louis calms down before
reaching Lake Superior.

Biking, Hiking, and History

The rugged geology surrounding the Saint Louis between Scanlon Dam and Thomson Dam is magnified spectacularly in Jay Cooke State Park. Fifty miles of hiking trails give hikers great views of the river's rocky gorge downstream of Swinging Bridge. Thirteen miles of mountain bike trails also offer out-of-water experiences.

The land that is now Jay Cooke Park has a fascinating human history. You can hike part of the rugged, 7-mile-long portage trail—the link between Lake Superior and the Hudson's Bay watershed—over which voyageurs slogged with their trade goods more than three hundred years ago. You can walk across the park's scenic and squeaky Swinging Bridge, a Civilian Conservation Corps project from the 1930s, and see photographs of an amazing washout in the bridge's history.

Hikers and bicyclists may also want to sample the paved Willard Munger State Trail. The 15-mile section of the trail between Carlton and Duluth, considered the most scenic part of the trail, passes right by the UMD Outpost at Thomson.

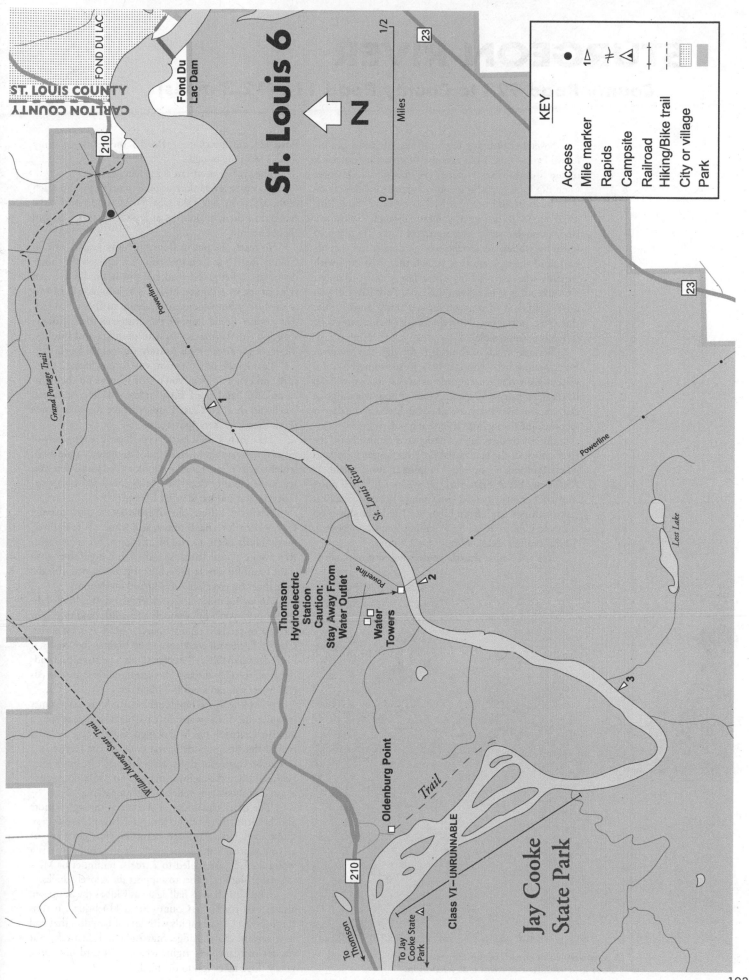

St. Louis 6

N

Miles

0   1/2

CARLTON COUNTY
ST. LOUIS COUNTY
FOND DU LAC

Fond Du Lac Dam

210

23

23

Grand Portage Trail

Powerline

Powerline

Powerline

St. Louis River

Willard Munger State Trail

Thomson Hydroelectric Station Caution: Stay Away From Water Outlet

Water Towers

Lost Lake

Oldenburg Point

Trail

Class VI – UNRUNNABLE

Jay Cooke State Park

To Thomson

To Jay Cooke State Park

210

KEY

- ● Access
- 1△ Mile marker
- ⇌ Rapids
- △ Campsite
- ┼ Railroad
- - - Hiking/Bike trail
- ▱ City or village
- ▬ Park

1

2

3

STURGEON RIVER
County Road 923 to County Road 114 (12.3 miles)

Several challenging Class I–III rapids and a beautiful wilderness make a great combination on the final reach of the Sturgeon River that flows into the Little Fork. (The Big Fork has a Sturgeon tributary, too.) The Sturgeon flows north from near McCarthy Beach State Park for about 38 miles—running mostly through low marshy land, through one 3.5-mile stretch of Class III+ mayhem (great for whitewater kayakers, but it doesn't run very often), and through another stretch that is littered with logjams—before reaching these last scenic 11 miles. The takeout is a mile down the Little Fork River. If you aren't confident of your whitewater skills, don't paddle this river; portaging along the brushy banks would be difficult to impossible.

Because much of the trip is through the Sturgeon River State Forest, you can plan to see some beautiful second-growth northern forest as well as lots of wildlife; bald eagles, hairy woodpeckers, kingfishers, wood ducks, beavers, and river otters are all possibilities. In the deeper sections, the fishing for walleyes is good.

Although there are no designated campsites on the river, much of the land along the river is state forestland where camping is possible. **Camping** is also available at McCarthy Beach State Park (218-254-7979), 10 miles south of County Road 923 on County Road 5; or at Bear Lake Campground: from Highway 1, take Highway 65 south to County Road 52 (Venning Road), go west on 52 for 2 miles, and then south for 2.5 miles.

The 10.7-mile **shuttle route** runs west on County Road 923, north on County Road 5, then east on County Road 114 to the bridge.

The average **gradient** is 2.3 feet per mile.

No **water level** information is available for this reach of the Sturgeon, but if the USGS Web site report for the Sturgeon near Chisholm is at least 2.75 feet, this run should be fine.

To reach the put-in from Highway 1, go south on County Road 5 to County Road 923. Park on the shoulder of this quiet gravel road and **put in** on downstream right by the wood trestle bridge. The Sturgeon is narrow at the bridge but widens downstream to about 100 feet. The copper-tinted flow of the Sturgeon winds quietly through the northern forest of conifers and birches. Watch out for deadheads (mostly-submerged logs).

Less a mile downstream, you'll run through some riffles and shortly after, you'll pass a house on the right. At mile 1.7 Sand Creek flows in from the left. At mile 2, you'll run through Class I rapids where the river bends right, then left, then right again.

Less than a mile farther you'll have a long run of Class II rapids, split by an island. This quarter-mile drop, which tapers off in a shallow boulder bed just before you reach the County Road 107 bridge, is filled with two-foot waves at moderate water levels.

After the bridge, the riverbanks are quite scenic. Covered with ferns, birches, and some white and red pines, bluffs begin to rise on the left. This is Sturgeon River State Forest land. At mile 4.4, a high bluff with some beautiful pines towers over the confluence with the Bear River on river left—a wild and lovely spot.

About 1.4 miles farther, where the river is headed directly north, you'll run through a few riffles and then hear the roar of the next rapids around a bend. A good strong Class II, filled with boulders and up to three-foot waves, it may edge up to Class III in high water. The Sturgeon bends right and then left through this drop, and there are two eddies where you can scout this blind drop.

After leaving the rapids behind, the Sturgeon resumes its quiet life. If the water isn't too high, you may spot a sandbar, a rarity in this land of high, slippery clay banks, at one of the sharp bends in the river. At the Highway 1 bridge on upstream right, access is possible, but a long guardrail along the highway means a long hike up a grassy slope. The shoulder is wide enough for parking.

The quiet remainder of the trip is through remote and beautiful land of the Sturgeon River State Forest. Cedar trees and a few huge, beautiful white pines appear as you approach the Little Fork. At the confluence is a wood duck house nailed to a tree, a reminder of Minnesotans' ongoing effort to support these lovely ducks.

The Little Fork is half again as wide as the Sturgeon, and as you reach the County Road 114 bridge, it runs through fast Class I rapids with lots of boulders that end downstream of the bridge. Stay right and then **take out** on downstream river right, where a 75-yard hike up a grassy slope takes you to the road.

A relatively calm stretch of the Sturgeon, but Class II–III whitewater awaits downstream.

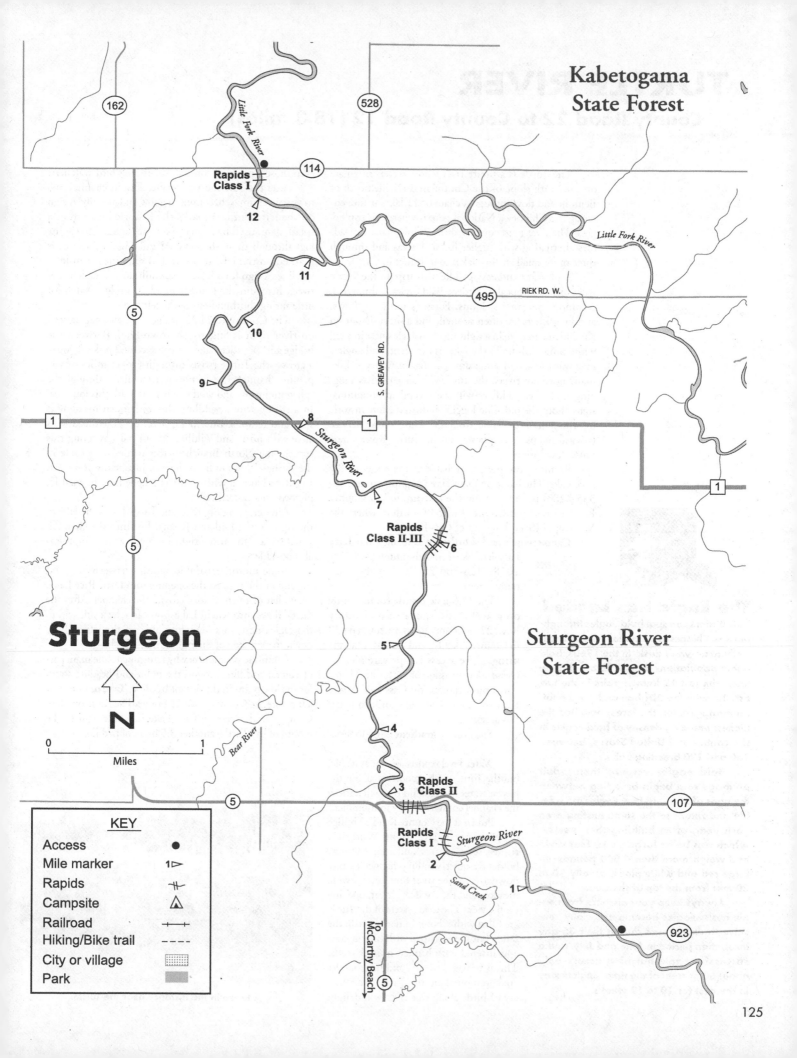

Kabetogama State Forest

Little Fork River

(162)

(528)

(114)

Rapids Class I

12

11

Little Fork River

(5)

495   RIEK RD. W.

10

9

S. GREAVEY RD.

8

(1)   (1)

1

Sturgeon River

7

Rapids Class II-III   6

(1)

Sturgeon

↑ N

0 —————— 1
Miles

Bear River

5

Sturgeon River State Forest

4

3   **Rapids Class II**

(5)   (107)

Rapids Class I   *Sturgeon River*

2

Sand Creek   1

To McCarthy Beach

(5)   (923)

KEY

Access	●
Mile marker	1▷
Rapids	‡
Campsite	△
Railroad	┼┼
Hiking/Bike trail	- - -
City or village	▦
Park	▬

TURTLE RIVER
County Road 22 to County Road 12 (18.3 miles)

The Turtle is a pretty river whose waters originate on the south slope of the Continental Divide north of Bemidji and flow through a chain of 11 lakes before entering the Chippewa National Forest, where this trip begins. The river twists quietly through low marshy meadows alternating with higher forested areas and through three more small shallow lakes to its outlet in Cass Lake.

A pleasant and easy paddle, this trip on the Turtle will especially appeal to birders. Bald eagles, cormorants, common mergansers, loons, Forster's terns, swallows, and kingfishers are often spotted, and a short detour on Kitchi Lake may yield a sighting of an eagle's nest in a tall white pine. Fishing in the lakes is excellent, and anglers may want to spend some time casting for walleyes. Like many northern rivers, the Turtle was once used as a logging highway; paddlers will see several informational signs about the old-time logging industry. More historic information is available from the U.S. Forest Service (www.fs.fed.us/r9/chippewa) on its Turtle River canoe route description.

Primitive **camping** is available at the outlet of Big Rice Lake. The Knutson Dam USFS Campground (218-335-2283) is 4 miles from the takeout: follow County Road 12 east and County Road 39 south to where the Mississippi River flows out of Cass Lake.

Canoe rentals and shuttles are available from Terry Larson of Northern Adventures (218-335-2078; 218-766-7543; tlnoadv@paul bunyan.net).

The 17.6-mile **shuttle route**, mostly on gravel roads, runs east on County Road 22 to County Road 39, south on 39 to County Road 12, and west on 12 to the bridge. The access is a private pier, so please ask permission of the resort. There's also a public access on Cass Lake at the Knutson Dam Campground; to reach this access, see above.

The average **gradient** is 0.4 foot per mile.

Water level reports are not available, but the Turtle can be canoed at all but the lowest water levels. Wild rice will narrow the channel considerably by midsummer.

Put in at the County Road 22 bridge on downstream river right. Wild rice, rushes, sedge grasses, and a mixed forest border the quiet, winding channel. Farther downstream, the river flows into a wide meadow and the conifers retreat, opening up the view. The clear waters of the Turtle are filled with schools of darting fish; the sandy bottom is striped with ribbon grass and littered with broken mussel shells. This is beaver territory, and huge lodges are common along the Turtle. The variety of birds along this river will delight even those who don't consider themselves bird-watchers.

After the Turtle leaves the meadow, its channel narrows several times, becoming shallow and gravelly. A sign on the left at mile 3 marks the historic location of a splash dam, used by loggers a century ago to move pine logs through these shallows. At mile 3.5, a rest area is marked on the left. In a stand of red pines at mile 4, you'll see a sign for a historic sawmill site on the left. Between here and the County Road 20 bridge, watch for little springs burbling out of the left bank.

The County Road 20 bridge is an alternate access; on river right is Sugarbush Town Hall. Between the bridge and Big Rice Lake—a distance of 2 miles if you're a crow—the Turtle twists through 6 river miles of serpentine channel. The channel is deep, slicing through the sphagnum moss and wild rice beds that fill this low area. In a strong wind, paddling this wide-open meadow is slow and tedious. But on a quieter day, the meadow is alive with birds and wildlife. About halfway along this stretch, the North Branch of the Turtle—canoeable in the spring—flows in from the left. Just before you reach Big Rice Lake, a white canvas teepee may be visible, pitched on a distant hill.

After crossing Big Rice, the Turtle leaves the lake to the right of the Hideout Resort. Just into the channel, you'll see a sign on the right for a rest area; camping is also possible.

Some motorboat traffic appears between here and the end of the trip. At the opening into Little Rice Lake, what's left of Burnt Bridge crosses the channel. After the Turtle flows into Kitchi Lake, you can take a side trip to the eagle's nest, in a big white pine on the left halfway down the left side of the right arm of Kitchi.

Continue your journey by returning to the main part of Kitchi, paddling around the point and heading south for the low point in the distant tree line. **Take out** on river left before the County Road 12 bridge. The Knutson Dam Campground access on Cass Lake is 3 miles east of the mouth of the Turtle, another 3.5 miles of paddling.

The Eagle Has Landed

Birders can spot bald eagles throughout the Chippewa National Forest, especially at dawn or dusk. In the 1960s, bald eagle populations dipped to an all-time low, with just 12 known pairs in the forest. But with the DDT ban and good habitat management, the forest now has the highest breeding density of bald eagles in the continental United States, between 160 and 190 breeding pairs.

Bald eagles acquire their adult plumage and begin breeding between the ages of four and five. Eagles mate for life and return to the same nesting area each year, often building their nests—which can be as large as 10 feet wide and weigh more than 4,000 pounds—in large red and white pines, usually 10 to 20 feet from the top of the tree.

Always keep your distance from eagle nests. Eagles become especially sensitive to disturbance during their 35-day incubation period in June and July, and a successful eagle hatching occurs only about 60 percent of the time. Eaglets stay in the nest for 10 to 12 weeks.

A tepee in the distance near the Turtle.

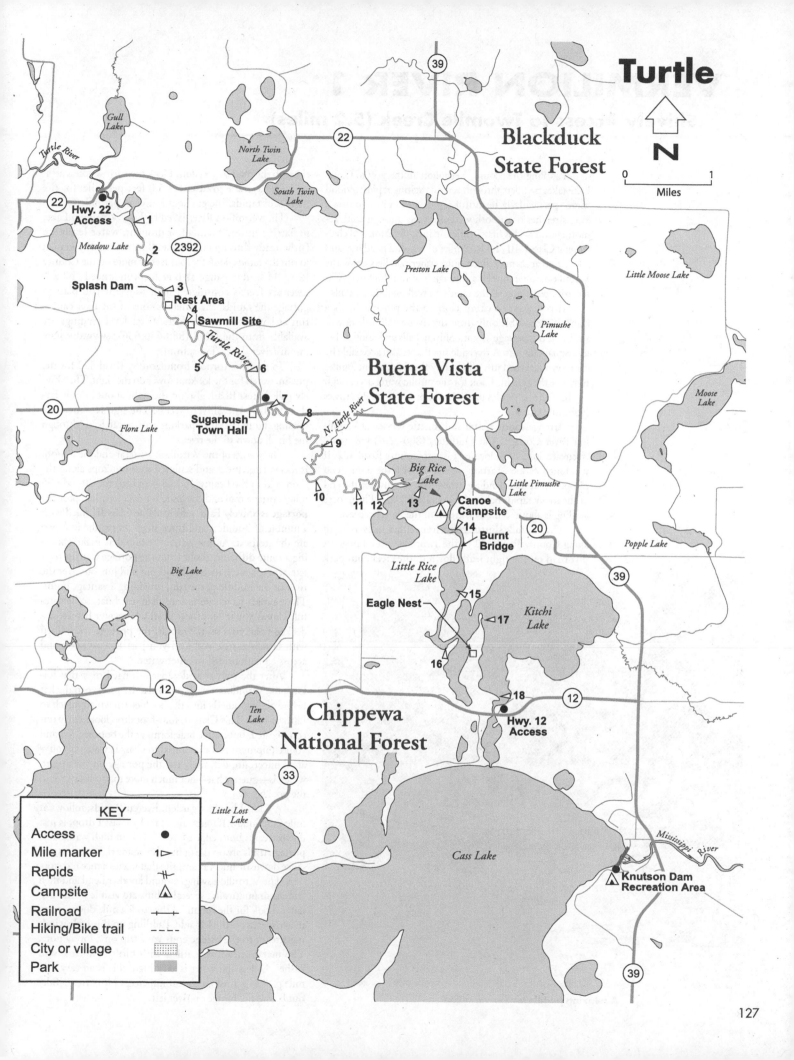

Turtle

N

0   1
Miles

Blackduck State Forest

Gull Lake

Turtle River

North Twin Lake

South Twin Lake

Preston Lake

Little Moose Lake

Pimushe Lake

Hwy. 22 Access

Meadow Lake

Splash Dam

Rest Area

Sawmill Site

Turtle River

Buena Vista State Forest

Moose Lake

N. Turtle River

Sugarbush Town Hall

Flora Lake

Big Rice Lake

Canoe Campsite

Little Pimushe Lake

Burnt Bridge

Big Lake

Little Rice Lake

Kitchi Lake

Popple Lake

Eagle Nest

Chippewa National Forest

Ten Lake

Hwy. 12 Access

Little Lost Lake

Cass Lake

Mississippi River

Knutson Dam Recreation Area

KEY

Access	●
Mile marker	1 ▷
Rapids	‖
Campsite	△
Railroad	+−+
Hiking/Bike trail	- - -
City or village	▦
Park	▬

VERMILION RIVER 1
Shively Access to Twomile Creek (5.2 miles)

Paddling the 39-mile Vermilion all the way to Crane Lake takes paddlers through several exciting rapids; around some spectacularly beautiful rapids and falls; and down long stretches of smooth water flowing through wild, remote country. This first 5-mile trip includes 2 miles of challenging Class I–III rapids, 3 miles of peaceful paddling, and a lot of great scenery. Even quiet-water paddlers enjoy the Vermilion; some travel it as though it were a Boundary Waters trip, portaging all the rapids on well-established trails.

If you want to **camp** close to the put-in, there's a campsite accessible only from the river a half mile downstream at the portage around Shively Falls and another below Squaw Rapids. A riverside site that is also accessible by car is on a dirt road just off County Road 24, about 7 miles north of the put-in. Look for the public water access sign on the right, 1.5 miles past where County Road 24 crosses Eightmile Creek.

Arrange **canoe rental** and **shuttle service** at Vermilion River Cottages and Outfitters (800-628-1438; www .vrcovacation.com), located just off County Road 422. If you rent a canoe or arrange a shuttle with the resort, you can put in at their landing, where you can just see the end of the rocky rapids below the Vermilion Dam. The resort's landing is about .6 mile upstream of the Shively access.

The 1.8-mile **shuttle route** from either access is north along County Road 422 to the Twomile Creek bridge. A dirt road on the right leads down to the creek, but park

A relaxing paddle on the Vermilion.

closer to the road so you don't block the narrow access area.

The average **gradient** is 5.0 feet per mile; for the 2 miles of rapids, the gradient is 23 feet per mile.

The Vermilion River is fed by huge Vermilion Lake, so barring unusual rainfall or drought, **water levels** are fairly steady throughout the paddling season. If you plan to run the rapids, look for four feet or more on the County Road 24 bridge gauge at Buyck (pronounced "bike"). Over six feet is considered high water. If you plan to portage the rapids, the quiet sections of the river can be run at levels below four feet. Water level readings are available from the DNR (888-646-6367; www.dnr.state .mn.us/river_levels/index.html).

To find the turnoff from County Road 422 for the **put-in**, watch for the lookout tower on the right. The Shively Falls Forest Road, also on the right about .5 mile farther, leads to the Shively access. The sign is sometimes missing. From the small parking area, a trail leads through the brush down to the river.

The waters of the Vermilion are clear and the bottom is rocky; large pines and sculpted rock outcrops along the shore add to the beauty. Paddle .5 mile to the 80-rod (.25 mile) portage trail and campsite on river left. Just past the **portage** is Shively Falls, a formidable Class III filled with a jumble of boulders and three steep drops; the first two are the steepest. At low water, the boulders make choosing a route difficult. Scout from the portage trail on river left, where a large rock right off the trail juts out over the river in the middle of the run, providing a vantage point. These rapids have eaten more than one boat, so be careful. Unless you're an experienced whitewater boater in a decked boat, pass on the rapids; the **portage trail**, lined with bunchberries, will lead you past the overlook and across a plank bridge to quiet water.

After the mile of wide, marsh-fringed river that follows, the Vermilion swings around a sharp curve to the left before gliding quietly into the boulder-strewn approach to Liftover Falls. This Class II, four-foot drop looks fairly uncomplicated, but a large hole forms at the bottom. You and your equipment must be suited to Class II water. If you're at all uncertain, definitely use the portage on river right, which is—guess what—not much more than a liftover into the pool below.

A Class I boulder garden, Everett Rapids, follows at mile 2.5. Squaw Rapids, also a rocky Class I drop, is just downstream; both edge up to Class II in high water. The **portage trails** are on the right. Also on the right, a short distance downstream, is a campsite that makes a nice rest stop.

The Vermilion swings around another bend and then widens dramatically; several cabins are visible in the distance. Look for the mouth of the creek a mile downstream in a low area on the left side. Paddling up this little winding stream to the bridge ends your trip on a lovely note. The marsh meadow is filled with birds, wild iris, and rushes. Unless the water is very high, this is an easy 1.5-mile paddle against an almost imperceptible current. **Take out** before the bridge on river left.

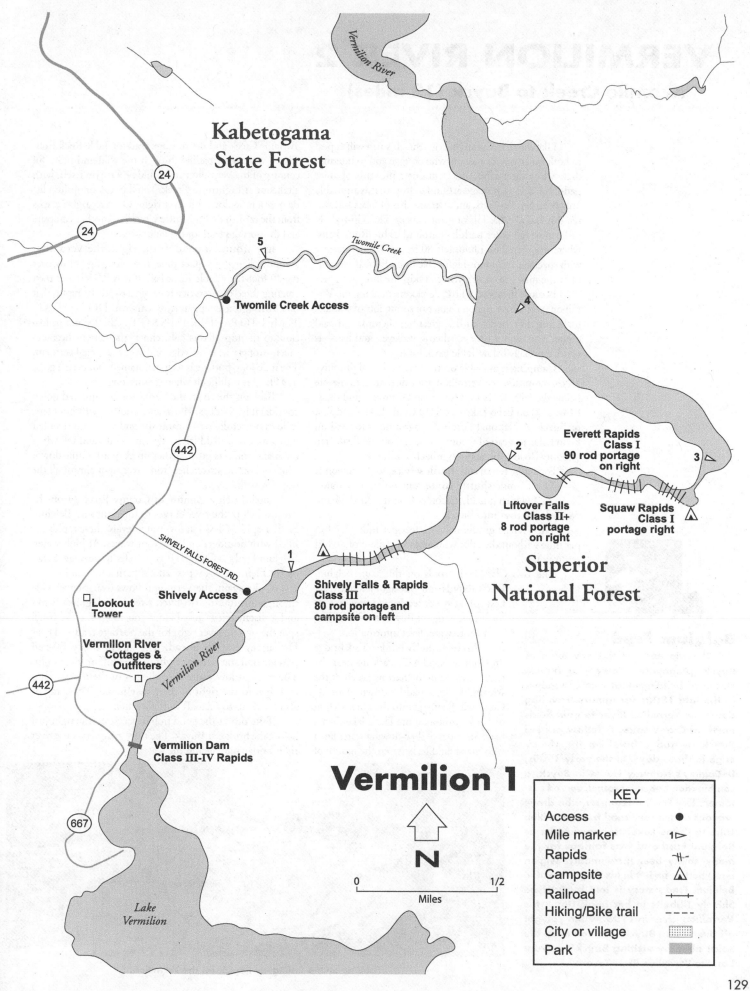

Kabetogama
State Forest

Twomile Creek

Twomile Creek Access

Vermilion River

Everett Rapids
Class I
90 rod portage
on right

Liftover Falls
Class II+
8 rod portage
on right

Squaw Rapids
Class I
portage right

Superior
National Forest

SHIVELY FALLS FOREST RD.

Shively Access

Shively Falls & Rapids
Class III
80 rod portage and
campsite on left

Lookout
Tower

Vermillion River
Cottages &
Outfitters

Vermilion River

Vermilion Dam
Class III-IV Rapids

Lake
Vermilion

Vermilion 1

N

0   1/2

Miles

KEY	
Access	●
Mile marker	1▷
Rapids	─╫─
Campsite	△
Railroad	─┼─
Hiking/Bike trail	- - - -
City or village	▦
Park	▬

VERMILION RIVER 2
Twomile Creek to Buyck (12 miles)

Like the first Vermilion segment, this trip will appeal to both quiet-water canoeists who portage and to intermediate whitewater canoeists. Featuring a nice mix of quiet paddling, a long portage around a drop that is runnable only by expert kayakers, and two stretches of Class I–II water, this run also has lots of great scenery. The 330-rod (1-mile) portage takes paddlers around Table Rock Falls, where the Vermilion plummets 80 feet in 1 mile, starting with spectacular 20-foot-high Table Rock Falls. If you put in at the mile 7.4 access, you can skip the long portage.

Because there's very little development along the Vermilion, you'll have a good chance of seeing lots of wildlife, including deer, otters, turtles, great blue herons, and bald eagles. The fishing—for northerns, walleyes, and bass—is good, especially below Table Rock Falls.

Camping is available on the river at several primitive DNR campsites. See Vermilion 1 for directions to the site below the falls. Trail's End Resort and Campground (888-844-2257) on Echo Lake is at 6310 Crane Lake Road, east of Buyck. A National Forest campground is located on Echo Lake, just east of County Road 24, off the Echo Trail (County Road 116), about 6 miles from Buyck.

For **canoe rental** and **shuttle service**, see Vermilion 1.

The 12-mile **shuttle route** runs north on County Road 422, which quickly becomes County Road 24 and parallels the river into Buyck.

The average **gradient** is 8.1 feet per mile (1.7 feet per mile without the falls, which has a gradient of 80 feet per mile).

The two Class I–II rapids on this trip, Belgium Fred's Rapids and DeCagney Rapids, are best run at **water levels** over four feet on the bridge gauge at Buyck. See Vermilion 1 for more water level information.

Put in at the Twomile Creek bridge on County Road 422. Park up near the road, away from the narrow access at the stream. A short paddle down Twomile Creek will float you into the quiet section of the Vermilion, more like a lake than a river. Six miles of slow-flowing water lined with marshland lie between the mouth of Twomile Creek and the **portage trail** for Table Rock Falls. This is a peaceful paddle through the wild and beautiful country of the Vermilion and could be a trip in itself, with a takeout at Eightmile Creek. You'll pass a campsite a little over a mile down on river right. On river right, across from the mouth of Eightmile Creek, is another campsite and the **portage trail** for the falls.

Just around a bend to the right, the Vermilion abruptly changes its quiet tune, first plunging noisily over the 20-foot-high Table Rock Falls (Class IV–VI) and then entering three-quarters of a mile of Class III–IV rapids that race through a deep, narrow canyon. DO NOT ATTEMPT TO PADDLE THIS STRETCH. Do not paddle close to the top of this falls, either; the current becomes much stronger near the edge and you risk a fatal accident. The mile-long portage is well maintained, but even a good trail like this is difficult when it's this long.

Back on the river, the Vermilion has quieted down considerably. Wide, shallow, and studded with boulders, it flows peacefully past a campsite and access on river left into a narrows. Wild irises edge the banks and tall white birch and conifers grow farther up. A quarter mile down, a line of boulders stretches from river right almost all the way across the river.

You'll catch a glimpse of County Road 24 on the left just before the river curves to the right into Belgium Fred's Rapids. Class I at low water levels, these rapids are filled with boulders and one-foot waves. At high water, Belgium Fred's is Class II. If you prefer to **portage**, a trail on river left takes you past an old barn and a cabin.

Quiet again, the Vermilion flows straight and wide through a cattail-marsh-lined stretch with grassy banks and a distant view. Just before you reach Buyck, you'll spot the sign on river right for the **portage trail** and hear DeCagney Rapids ahead. The steep, rocky 60-rod portage trail starts to the right of the bluff on river right. The route at low water is to the left of the rocky island and then to the right of the grassy island. These rapids also move up to Class II in high water.

Take out at the good public access on the right just before the bridge at Buyck. The river gauge is on the river right bridge pier, facing the water.

Belgium Fred

The trip ends at the tiny town of Buyck (pronounced "bike"), a remote cluster of buildings that was a stopover in the late 1800s for miners traveling down the Vermilion River to gold fields north of Crane Lake. A fellow named Buyck owned a hotel on the river's edge in those days. In the early 1900s, DeCagney's Halfway House in Buyck, a combination bar and brothel, served customers like Fred, a teamster who drove wagons on the cord road from Vermilion Lake to Crane Lake. He was known as Belgium Fred and was famous for the many empty beer (presumably Belgian beer) bottles he left in his wagon's wake. Belgium Fred's story is told by Adelyne Shively Tibbetts in her book *Down the Vermilion River in 1908*. When you get off the river at Buyck, you can keep the spirit alive by visiting Buyck's current bar, the Vermilion River Tavern.

Looking up the DeCagney Rapids on the Vermilion.

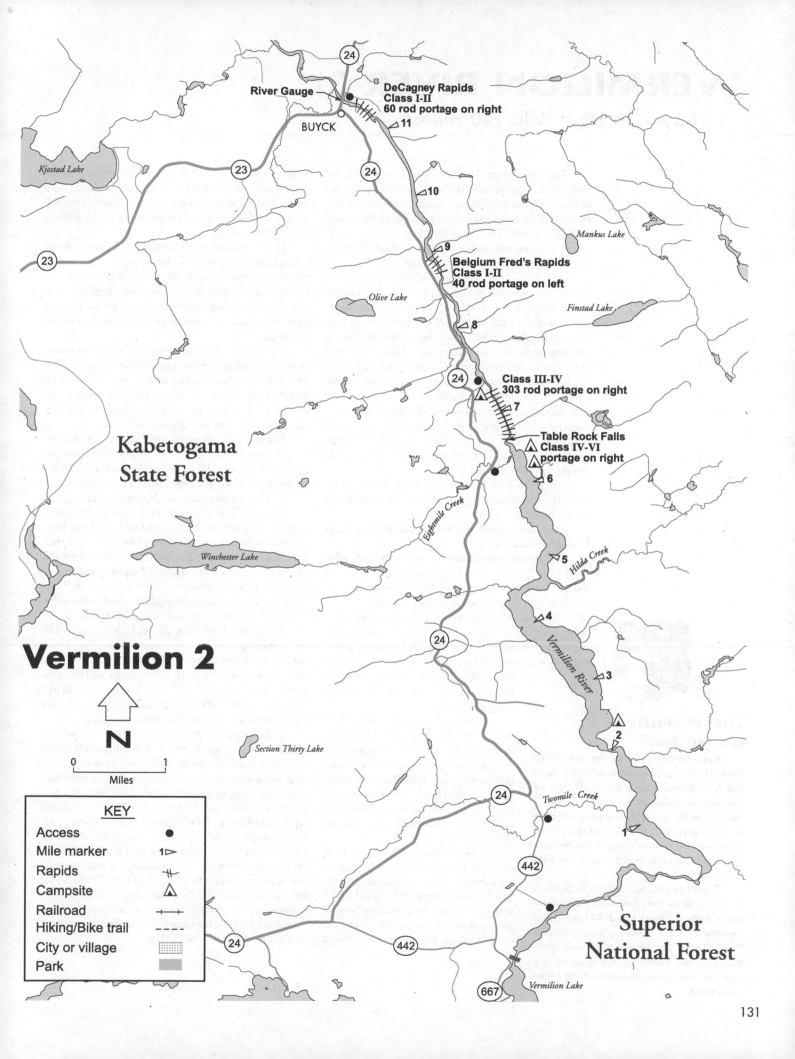

Vermilion 2

River Gauge

DeCagney Rapids
Class I-II
60 rod portage on right

BUYCK

Belgium Fred's Rapids
Class I-II
40 rod portage on left

Class III-IV
303 rod portage on right

Table Rock Falls
Class IV-VI
portage on right

Kabetogama
State Forest

Kjostad Lake

Olive Lake

Mankus Lake

Finstad Lake

Winchester Lake

Eighmile Creek

Hilda Creek

Vermilion River

Section Thirty Lake

Twomile Creek

Superior
National Forest

Vermilion Lake

N

0   1
Miles

KEY

Access	●
Mile marker	1▷
Rapids	╫
Campsite	△
Railroad	┼┼┼
Hiking/Bike trail	- - -
City or village	▦
Park	▨

VERMILION RIVER 3
Buyck to High Falls (20 miles)

The most remote stretch of the Vermilion lies between Buyck and spectacular Vermilion Falls, also known as High Falls, with only one intermediate access point. By midsummer, wild rice makes passage to this access nearly impossible. Three river campsites make this an excellent camping trip. Unless you run the Class II rapids, you'll also be hiking a short portage trail.

This land is home to white-tailed deer, moose, otters, turtles, beavers, timber wolves, and black bears. Great blue herons, loons, and bald eagles are common, and an eagle's nest is visible in a tall white pine. The varied terrain is alternately marshy and densely wooded, with banks that are sometimes high and rocky. The walleye fishing is excellent in the second half of the run. A single stretch of Class II rapids, Chipmunk Falls, punctuates the otherwise smooth, steady flow. At High Falls, the Vermilion undergoes a startling personality change as its considerable volume roars, twists, and falls through a narrow, sluice-like opening in the granite bedrock, dropping 25 feet in about 100 yards. An observation deck just off the portage trail overlooks this dramatically beautiful falls.

Three DNR campsites are accessible only from the river. For additional **camping** possibilities near Buyck, see Vermilion 2.

For **canoe rental** and **shuttle service** and **water level** information, see Vermilion 1.

The **shuttle route** is north from Buyck on County Road 24 to Forest Road 491, then west across the river to the left turn for the Vermilion Falls Recreation Area.

The average **gradient** is 1.0 foot per mile.

Put in at the public access at Buyck on upstream right, where there's a parking lot and a concrete ramp. For the next 6 miles, the river is placid, flowing quietly through marshy areas and deciduous forest. An occasional high, aspen-covered bluff varies the scene. You'll probably see beaver lodges along this stretch.

At mile 4.7, the Pelican River flows in from the left. A quarter mile up the Pelican is a campsite on river right, where you can portage 80 rods around some rapids and paddle to the base of a waterfall. The river channel downstream from the campsite is divided by a median strip of wild rice, making the Pelican look like a divided highway.

As you approach Chipmunk Falls, the Class II rapids, the right bank, pine trees draped over its edge, rises abruptly. The Vermilion swings left around a huge rock and into the long, shallow boulder garden. If you plan to run this blind drop, scout from the beginning of the 60-rod

portage trail on river left and from the rocks at the downstream end, because you can't see the rapids from the trail. If the water is too low, if you have a canoe full of gear, or if you just don't want to run it, the portage trail is short and easy.

Just downstream are the remains of a logging industry railroad bridge. The banks rise high along this stretch, their pine trees a reminder of the vast forests of huge white and red pines that covered this land before the logging era. At rows of timber pilings in the river, logs were loaded onto train cars. These barely submerged pilings can be a canoeing hazard.

After a log cabin on the left, the Vermilion swings around a bend into Snowshoe Narrows, a scenic spot where rock outcrops backed by high wooded bluffs jut into the river. A campsite on river right has wooden steps up the bank. Three miles farther down is another, slightly smaller campsite, also on river right.

On a stretch where the river bottom spreads out into a wetland, a tributary flows through the wide-open expanse of marshland. Flanked by distant bluffs, this is a magnificent vista. At about mile 15, an eagle's nest perches atop a white pine on a big bluff on the right.

After the confluence with Flap Creek, you'll enter a long, straight section thickly lined with wild rice beds. About .5 mile past a small resort, Holmes Creek, a shallow stream through the rice beds, enters from the right. In the spring when the channel is open, paddling up Holmes Creek will take you to the access at the Gold Mine Road bridge. Later the wild rice grows so thick that it's hard to even see the stream, much less paddle it.

As you near High Falls, the rice beds are replaced by rocky outcrops, and the slow-moving river flows into a narrows. Go left of the rocky island that divides the channel and **take out** on river left at the portage trail up to the parking lot. DO NOT ENTER THE RAPIDS THAT LEAD TO THE 25-FOOT-HIGH FALLS. You can get a good view of the falls from the observation deck.

Other trips. Two beautiful Class III–V stretches, the Chute and the Gorge, follow the Forest Road 491 bridge and can be seen from portage trails. The Chute is a 10-foot drop over a ledge, with a strong current and two undercuts. The Gorge drops over two ledges and runs through a narrow canyon with sheer 50-foot walls where there's almost no chance of rescue. Only highly trained whitewater paddlers should attempt these challenging pitches. The University of Minnesota–Duluth's National Kayak and Canoe Institute teaches whitewater paddling on these exciting runs. Contact director Randy Carlson (218-726-6177) for more information. The River Ramblers, an affiliate of the Minnesota Canoe Association (www.canoe-kayak.org) run Table Rock Falls and the Gorge (see Vermilion 3) every year on a rafting trip at the end of May.

The Vermilion Gorge Trail

For another view of the Vermilion River from some scenic overlooks, hike this 1.5-mile trail above the Gorge, where the river is squeezed by granite before it flows into Crane Lake. The trail, winding through aspens, birches, and red pines, rewards you with a view of the Vermilion River flowing into Crane Lake and views of the Gorge.

From the takeout at High Falls, it's a short drive to the community of Crane Lake. Follow Forest Road 491 east and County Road 24 north, going left at Crane Lake. The parking lot and trailhead for the Vermilion Gorge Trail are past the Voyageurs National Park office on the left.

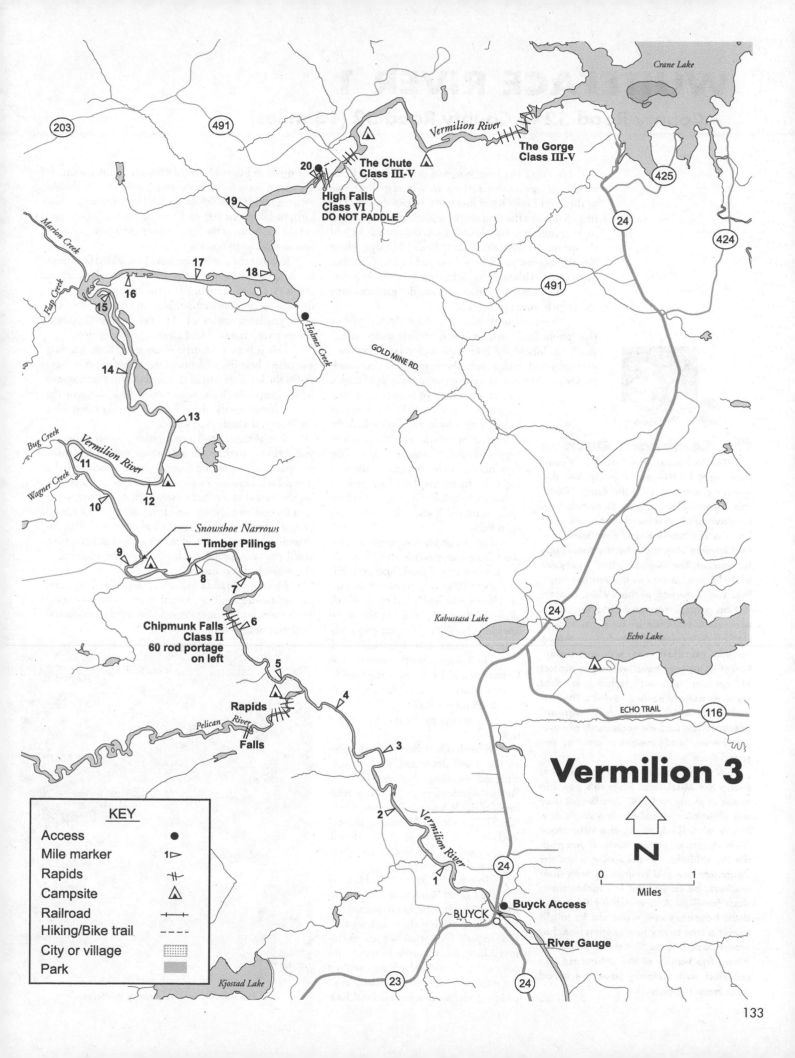

203

491

Vermilion River

The Gorge
Class III-V

Crane Lake

425

24

424

491

20

The Chute
Class III-V

19

High Falls
Class VI
DO NOT PADDLE

Marion Creek

17

18

Flap Creek

16

15

Holmes Creek

GOLD MINE RD.

14

13

Bug Creek

Vermilion River

11

Wagner Creek

12

10

Kabustasa Lake

24

Echo Lake

Snowshoe Narrows
Timber Pilings

9

8

7

Chipmunk Falls
Class II
60 rod portage
on left

6

ECHO TRAIL

116

5

Rapids

4

Pelican River

Falls

3

Vermilion 3

2

Vermilion River

N

1

0   1
Miles

24

Buyck Access

BUYCK

23

River Gauge

24

KEY

Access	●
Mile marker	1▷
Rapids	╬
Campsite	△
Railroad	┼┼┼
Hiking/Bike trail	- - -
City or village	▦
Park	▨

Kjostad Lake

WHITEFACE RIVER 1
County Road 52 to County Road 52 (15 miles)

The copper-colored waters of the Whiteface River wind their way southwest from the Whiteface Reservoir to the Saint Louis River just north of Floodwood. The first 15 miles of the river are the wildest, and that narrow, rocky section is navigable only when the water is high in the spring. South of the County Road 52 bridge, where this trip begins, you'll be able to paddle the Whiteface more often. Although the Whiteface is relatively gentle by nature, numerous riffles and boulder gardens along this stretch spice up the paddling.

This section of the river runs through more private than public land, but, because it's mostly undeveloped, you'll see lots of wildlife: bald eagles; common mergansers; wood ducks; great blue herons; pileated woodpeckers; owls; white-tailed deer; several species of turtles; a great abundance of beavers (and their handiwork); and possibly, if you're very lucky, a timber wolf. The clay banks of the Whiteface are overhung with grass and heavily wooded, with silver maples on the floodplain, and birches and conifers on higher banks; the river has a cozy, enclosed feeling along much of its length. You'll see some scattered houses and farms with open fields.

The closest car **camping** is at various private campgrounds near Markham, at the south end of the Whiteface Reservoir, about 19 miles northeast of the put-in. There are no established campgrounds along the Whiteface, so if you plan to canoe camp, be prepared for primitive conditions, and please camp only on public land.

The 8.5-mile **shuttle route** runs on County Road 52 west across Highway 53 to the County Road 52 bridge. Use downstream left for the access.

The average **gradient** is 3.1 feet per mile.

Water levels are best in the spring after the runoff. To be sure you'll be paddling and not hiking, check the Minnesota Power daily elevation and discharge readings for the Whiteface Reservoir (218-720-2777; www.shorelandtraditions.com/levels.htm). A discharge of 100 cfs will mean a good trip, and 50 cfs is enough to get by with some scraping.

To reach the put-in from Highway 53, take County Road 52 east from Cotton to the bridge. **Put in** on downstream left; the shoulder is wide enough for a vehicle to park. The narrow Whiteface's current is lively, and although the water is the color of tea, there's little sediment and you can see the sand and gravel riverbed. You'll paddle under a Canadian National Railway trestle and through several stretches of riffles, alternating with quiet sections in the first 3 miles. At the confluence with Bug Creek (which sounds like a tiny stream, but isn't), paddle about 100 yards up the creek to a good rest stop on the banks of the Bug. The current is brisk, so you'll have to work to go upstream.

Just past the confluence, full of the added flow from the Bug, the Whiteface sweeps rapidly through a narrow, bouldery Class I section. After another mile, you'll run through more Class I action. Just after a short stretch of riffles, you'll pass under the Jenkins Road bridge. On downstream river left, you'll find another good rest stop.

This is beaver country; many trees, both standing and fallen, bear the evidence of the beaver appetite. Several of the small tributaries that feed the river are home to beaver lodges. You'll also notice wood duck houses on the banks. If you paddle the Whiteface during migration, you'll see waterbirds everywhere.

Several houses and a transmission tower appear as you get closer to the town of Cotton. In the next 2 miles you pass under a second County Road 52 bridge and a power line. Then the Highway 53 bridges appear, crossing the river at two rather widely separated points, as the northbound and southbound lanes diverge. The northbound lane parallels the river for about a half mile. Although a trail from the road means a possible access here, you'll probably prefer a takeout with less traffic than this major highway carries.

About a mile and a half after you pass a tributary on the right—the similarly named Paleface River— you'll reach your third County Road 52 bridge. The **takeout** is on downstream left.

The Comeback Duck

The iridescent wood duck is a common sight in Minnesota today, but this wasn't always true. In the early 1900s, this beautiful bird was disappearing. Landowners had cleared vast areas of its favorite habitat—wooded river bottoms—and hunters shot them by the thousands for market. The Migratory Bird Treaty Act of 1918 put an end to the market hunting. Then, starting in the 1930s, conservation groups responded to the bird's precarious situation by building and installing thousands of wood duck nesting houses, an effort that continues today. Forest managers have learned to protect old-growth trees with rotted holes that serve as natural nesting cavities. The critical factor today, however, is wetland preservation and management; protecting the wetlands means protecting the wood duck.

Wood ducks migrate in great flocks. Along the Mississippi River, it's possible to see as many as 1,500 woodies (as they are affectionately called) on a single day. Many also flock along the Whiteface River during migration times. If you paddle the Whiteface in the spring when the fledglings are still swimming with their mothers, be careful not to frighten these duck families. And watch for the wood duck houses; some wood ducks might prefer a tree cavity to a nesting box, but wood duck houses like those you'll see along the banks of the Whiteface are credited with helping save the wood duck from extinction.

The remote, fast, and rocky Whiteface.

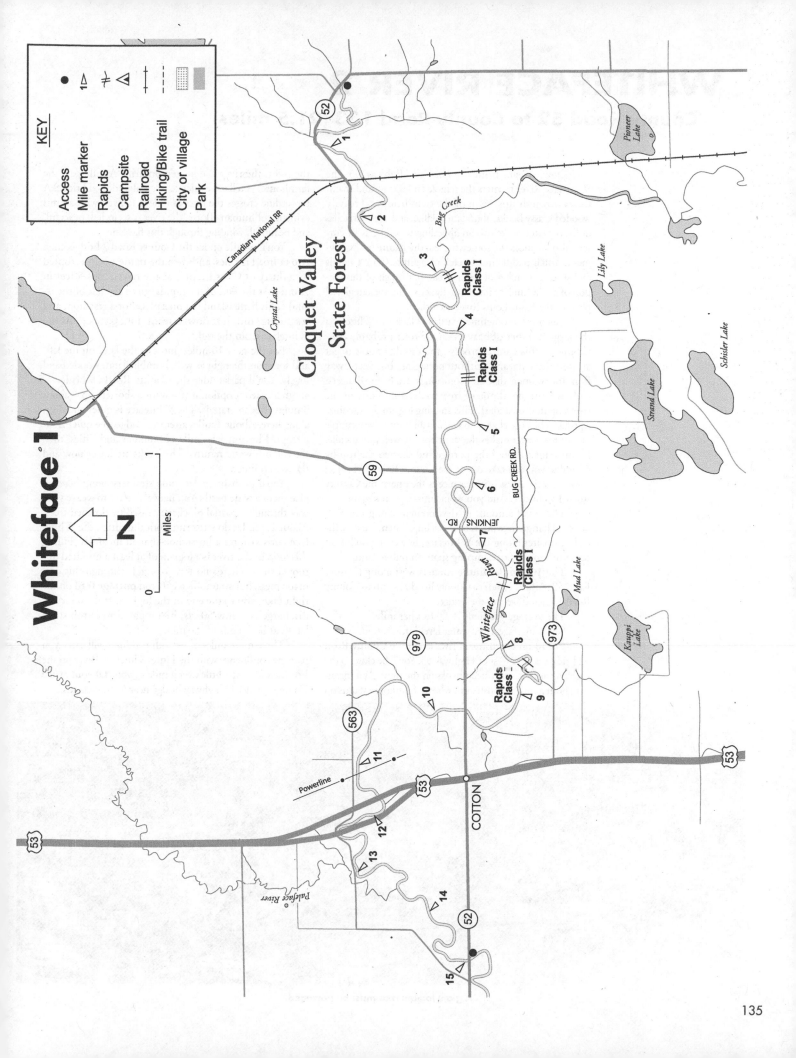

Whiteface 1

KEY

- ● Access
- 1△ Mile marker
- ≠ Rapids
- △ Campsite
- ┼ Railroad
- ┊ Hiking/Bike trail
- ▦ City or village
- ▨ Park

N

Miles
0 — 1

Canadian National RR

Cloquet Valley State Forest

Crystal Lake

Pioneer Lake

Lily Lake

Schisler Lake

Strand Lake

Mud Lake

Kauppi Lake

Bug Creek

Rapids Class I

Rapids Class I

Rapids Class I

Whiteface River

Rapids Class I

Rapids Class I

Paleface River

Powerline

COTTON

52

1

2

3

4

5

6

7

8

9

10

11

12

13

14

15

59

52

53

53

53

563

979

973

BUG CREEK RD.

JENKINS RD.

WHITEFACE RIVER 2
County Road 52 to County Road 133 (21.5 miles)

Downstream from the noise of Highway 53, the Whiteface River reenters the remote and scenic land that it flows through upstream of the twin bridges. Heavily wooded grassy banks, abundant wildlife, and a few stretches of lively water make this an appealing trip. The swift current also balances the somewhat lengthy nature of this segment. You'll paddle one stretch of definite Class I rapids and several stretches of lesser riffles, but much of this section of the Whiteface flows quietly across the ancient glacial plain of the Saint Louis River watershed.

Fallen trees sometimes partially block the Whiteface; the large number of beavers on the river probably contributes to this natural process. You should be able to get around these hazards without portaging, but keep away from the strainers that they sometimes create. You'll meet a truly monumental pile of trees wedged into one of the river's tightest meanders. This amazing logjam does require a portage, but the chance to see such an impressive example of nature's power makes the short portage well worthwhile. If you want to avoid the portage and shorten the trip by 10 miles, you can take out at the County Road 29 bridge; however, this access is not as nice as the one at the County Road 133 bridge. And you would miss a great logjam.

The small amount of development along the river doesn't change its wild, remote feeling. There are no official campsites along the Whiteface; however, you'll find some nice picnic or **camping** spots on public land.

The 16.8-mile **shuttle route** is west along County Road 52 (Arkola Road) to County Road 7, south to County Road 133, and west to the bridge.

The average **gradient** is 2.0 feet per mile.

See Whiteface 1 for **water level** information.

Put in on downstream river left at the County Road 52 bridge, a mile west of Highway 53. You'll be close to the highway at first, with steep banks on the right. At a meander about a mile downstream, where a farmhouse stands on the right, the river widens temporarily. A mile past the farmhouse, you'll see evidence of an abandoned bridge. A power line crosses the river at mile 4.1. Even with all this evidence of human efforts, the river is secluded, peaceful, and beautiful, winding through this flat land.

You'll paddle under the County Road 7 bridge, then two railroad trestles, and then the flatness is interrupted by a flurry of Class I rapids as the river drops 5 feet in .3 mile. At the end of the rapids, go to the left of the island. This little island is a nice place for a rest stop, and it's public land. Just downstream, Joki Creek joins the Whiteface from the right.

For the next 10 miles, most of the land on the left, and some on the right as well, is public land, wooded and lovely. You'll pass under the County Road 29 bridge—another takeout option if you want a shorter trip—about 3 miles after the rapids. The Whiteface is quiet and deep along here. About 3 miles after the bridge, the quiet is interrupted by a quarter mile of boulders and riffles, then the smooth water returns. The banks are lower now and the trees thinner.

You'll probably meet some strainers along here, so give them a wide berth. You may also have to weave your way through a partial blockage caused by downed trees. About 2.5 miles downstream from the riffles, the Whiteface curls around a horseshoe-shaped meander. Filling this loop in the river is a logjam of at least a hundred uprooted trees. There's no way to wiggle through this dramatic mess, but an unofficial 50-rod **portage trail** on the right takes you to the end of the logjam. If the reservoir discharge is below 50 cfs, be prepared to climb steep banks at both ends of the trail.

Three more miles of smooth paddling will carry you past the confluence with the Little Whiteface River on the left; then it's just a little over a mile to your **takeout** at the County Road 133 highway bridge near Meadowlands.

A giant logjam that must be portaged.

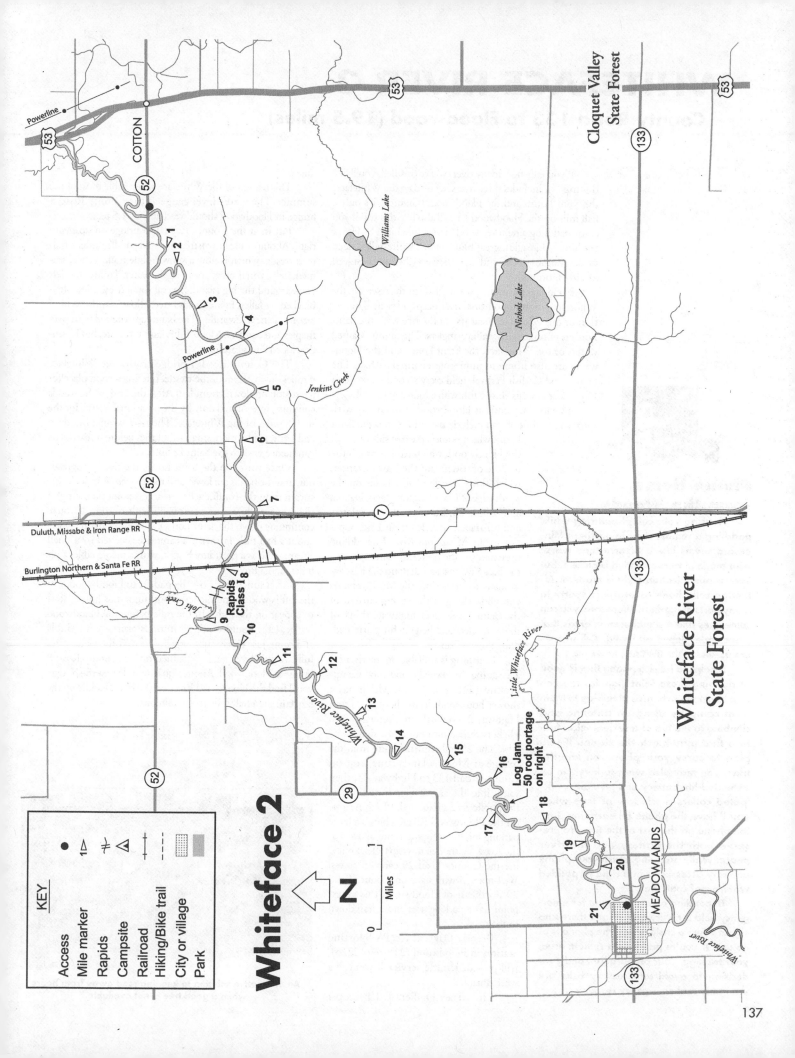

Whiteface 2

N

Miles

KEY

- Access
- Mile marker
- Rapids
- Campsite
- Railroad
- Hiking/Bike trail
- City or village
- Park

Powerline

53

COTTON

52

1
2
3
4

Powerline

Jenkins Creek

5

6

7

53

Williams Lake

Cloquet Valley
State Forest

133

Nichols Lake

Duluth, Missabe & Iron Range RR

7

Burlington Northern & Santa Fe RR

133

9 Rapids
Class I 8

10

Johs Creek

11

12

13

14

15

16

Little Whiteface River

Whiteface River

Log Jam
50 rod portage
on right

17

18

19

20

21

29

52

Whiteface River
State Forest

MEADOWLANDS

133

Whiteface River

WHITEFACE RIVER 3
County Road 133 to Floodwood (19.5 miles)

If you tally how many rivers you've paddled, you'll like this trip—it includes three rivers in one day: the Whiteface, the Saint Louis, and the Floodwood. (Granted, it's only a half mile on the Floodwood.) You'll also like this trip if you enjoy paddling a remote, wooded river inhabited by lots of wildlife: bald eagles, great blue herons, white-tailed deer, turtles, various ducks, and many beavers (these are best seen in early morning).

No longer the narrow stream that left the reservoir, the Whiteface is now a good-sized river, deep and swift. The section of the Whiteface near its confluence with the Saint Louis is popular with walleye anglers. The tannin-stained waters of the Whiteface, the Saint Louis, and the Floodwood are also home to numerous channel catfish. The Floodwood Catfish Festival, held every second weekend of July, celebrates this elusive fish with a four-day festival.

The journey ends at Floodwood, a small city with three rivers (four, if you include the Whiteface): the Saint Louis, which borders the east side of town; the Floodwood, which runs through the middle of town; and the East Savanna, which flows into the Saint Louis on the south edge of town. Centuries ago, Dakota and Ojibwe Indians, and later explorers and fur traders, traveled from Lake Superior to the Mississippi River by paddling upstream on the powerful Saint Louis to the East Savanna, and then up the East Savanna to a portage into the Mississippi. As you glide along in the strong current of the Saint Louis river highway, think of these travelers and be grateful you're paddling downstream.

Camping is available on the river for a fee at the city-owned Floodwood Campground (218-476-2751), which has a shower house and electric hookups. From Highway 2, go north on Highway 73 to Hickory Street; turn east at the sign.

The 25-mile **shuttle route** from the bridge at Meadowlands runs west on County Road 133 to Highway 73, then south into the city of Floodwood, where the public access is located off 7th Avenue on the Floodwood River. There's a large parking lot, but camping is not allowed at the access. To shorten this trip to 13.4 miles, use the County Road 29 carry-in access. Well-marked with signs on County Road 29 northeast of Floodwood, this access point has a parking area and a trail down to the river.

Brenda Davis at R&B's Sporting Station in Floodwood (218-476-2225), will provide **shuttle service** if you call a week ahead.

The average **gradient** is 1.1 feet per mile.

This section of the Whiteface is runnable most of the summer. The **water level** gauge at the County Road 8 bridge in Floodwood should read at least 1.5 feet.

Put in at the County Road 133 bridge on upstream right. About a mile downstream, you'll paddle under a railroad trestle, which is now a snowmobile trail. Almost immediately, you'll meet some lively water. Follow the left bank around the big island. Several small tributaries, often blocked by fallen branches and trees, flow into the Whiteface in the next few miles. The banks are forested with river maples and conifers. Most of this land is private, but it's undeveloped and peaceful.

The County Road 5 bridge crosses the Whiteface 4 miles downstream of the trestle, offering a good place for a rest stop on downstream left. After the bridge, the woods continue, interrupted only by the occasional house, for the final 8 miles of the Whiteface. The river is quiet but deep and swift, fed by more small tributaries before it reaches its confluence wwsith the Saint Louis.

Once you're on the Saint Louis, the riverbed spreads out, and the banks are lower and more open. A mile downstream from the confluence is an access point on the right; the sign for this access point is difficult to spot. If you're continuing down the Saint Louis to Floodwood, on the left about a half mile farther is a campsite accessed by a small stream. This is a great lunch spot, with a picnic table, a pit toilet, and a fire ring.

After lunch, it's a 6-mile paddle to Floodwood. On the left is wooded public land, but numerous houses start to appear on the right. In the mile before the Floodwood bridge, large boulders appear in midstream—some visible and some just barely submerged—so read the water carefully. A river level gauge is painted on the County Road 8 bridge at Floodwood. About a quarter mile past the bridge, you'll find the Floodwood River on the right. Paddle up the lazy current a half mile to the **takeout**.

Phone Home from the Woods

Hearing your cell phone ring while paddling a remote river in northern Minnesota seems like a bizarre time warp: your mode of transportation is ancient, but your communication style is modern. Although cell phone coverage is spotty in many parts of northern Minnesota, you can sometimes find a signal even in areas that seem undeveloped and wild. Cell phones are useless in the BWCAW, however.

It helps to have a phone that is good at nabbing those faint signals. You can also boost your chances of talking to Mom from camp by using an antenna and climbing to the top of any geological feature that may block the signal. If you plan to carry your phone on lengthy trips, you may also want to invest in an extended-life battery and give any anticipated callers a window of time when you'll have the phone on each day. Turn the phone off the rest of the time, to preserve both the battery and the river peace. While paddling, stash your phone and any accessories in a rigid or padded waterproof container.

Depending on a cell phone for emergency help is a very bad idea; if there's no signal when a crisis arises, the phone is of no use. If you're paddling a remote area, your training, your preparation, and your decision to avoid unnecessary risks are your only real emergency resources.

An alternative solution to keeping food away from bears when a good tree is not available.

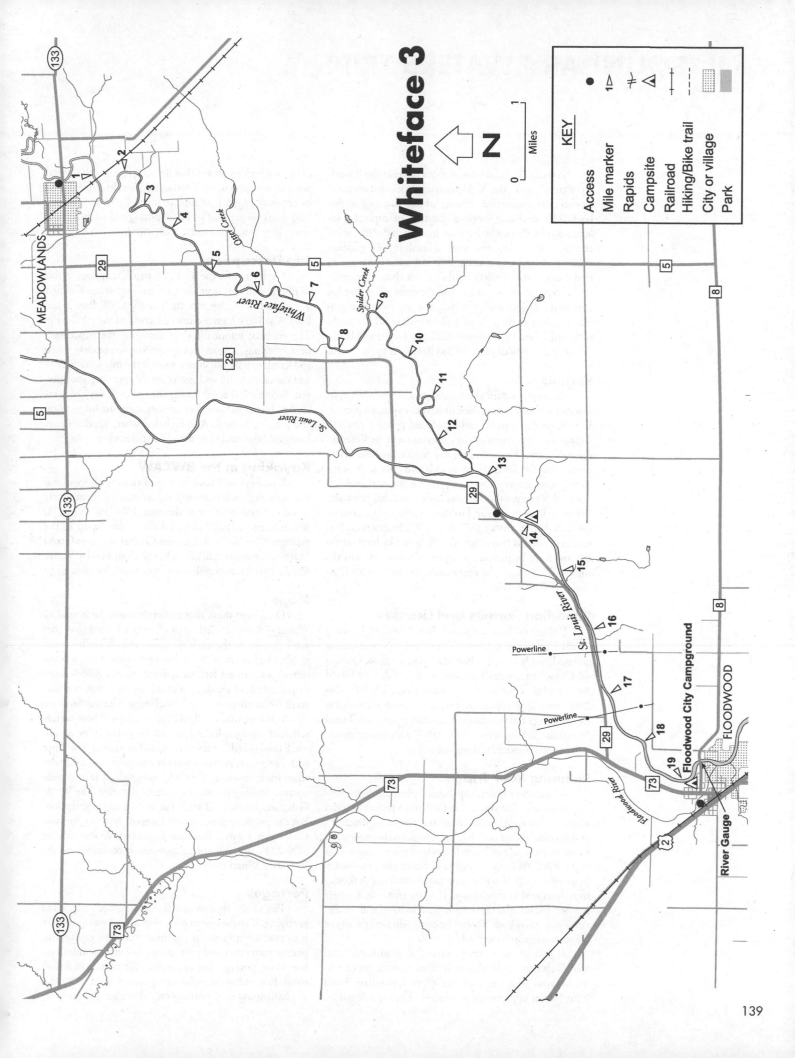

II. BOUNDARY WATERS TRIPS

So much has been written about travel in the Boundary Waters Canoe Area Wilderness that it seemed unnecessary to offer exhaustive coverage of this vast area in this book. This section is simply a summary of important information for those who have not traveled in the area or for experienced travelers who want a brush-up. All paddlers thinking about a trip into the BWCAW are encouraged to read some of the excellent books written about this amazing wilderness and to understand the great effort that has gone and still goes into preserving the area for future generations. As a starting point, paddlers who read the works of Sigurd Olson (*The Singing Wilderness* is one) will be inspired by the spirit of this land and the efforts to preserve it.

Permits

All travel within the boundaries of the BWCAW, whether on foot or by canoe or kayak, requires a permit. Permits for day trips are unlimited, and paddlers can self-register for a day trip without a reservation at the time and point of entry. Overnight camping permits are limited to a certain number for each day at each entry point. At some entry points, a reservation for a permit is almost essential to ensure that you get the date and entry point that you want. For more information and to make a reservation, contact the U.S. Forest Service (877-550-6777; bwcaw.org). Permits are issued at Forest Service offices and by local outfitters and must be picked up in person before you start the trip; you'll also have the opportunity to view a video illustrating BWCAW rules.

Canadian Permits and Licenses

Unless you have a Remote Area Boundary Crossing (RABC) permit, also known as a CANPASS, you cannot go into Canada except at boundary portage trails. Contact the Canada Immigration Centre, Suite 108, 221 Archibald Street North, Thunder Bay, Ontario P7C 3Y3; 807-624-2158; www.queticopark.com/rabc, for more information on these passes. If you fish in Canadian waters, you'll need a Canadian fishing license (800-955-8795; www.permitme.com/nonres_canadianfishing_form.htm).

Planning Your Trip

A Boundary Waters trip requires planning, at the very least to be sure that you're able to obtain a permit to travel where and when you want. Read over the routes described in this book to find one that fits your goals. Because you'll be out of reach of medical help (and cell phones don't work in the BWCAW), you'll need to be healthy and reasonably fit to enjoy a trip. You may want to start with one of the day trips described in this section. If you're planning a longer journey, the number of days you want to travel and the distance you travel each day can be easily adjusted for any of the multiday trips described.

If you plan to camp overnight, read books and visit Web sites to develop a detailed equipment checklist for your trip, and then use it (see appendixes 3 and 5 for lists of appropriate resources). The remote nature of the wilderness means that if you forget to take a vital piece of equipment or if something breaks, there won't be any way to get it or replace it until you paddle out. And don't forget that you'll be portaging, so don't take along items that you won't really need.

Trip Descriptions

The format for the BWCAW trip descriptions in this section is different from that for the river trips. The first day of each multiday trip, such as BWCAW East 2 and BWCAW West 2, gives a brief overview of the whole trip. The essential information for arranging the trip comes next: camping facilities the night before you launch, canoe and kayak rentals, the shuttle route if the trip is not a loop, and the entry point and exit point for reserving your permit. Following that are descriptions of each day's trip, including highlights, portages, scenery, campsite suggestions, and possible hazards. Also included where applicable are historical notes and ideas for additional reading.

Kayaking in the BWCAW

Kayakers will find here two trips with minimal portages and maximum big water, making them nicely suited to kayaking. One of the trips, BWCAW West 3-1, which begins at Fall Lake, also allows wheels on all the portages. One outfitter, Superior Coastal Sports in Grand Marais, rents the PakYak, a kayak designed by Vetter Kayaks (www.vetterkayaks.com) specifically for portaging.

Maps

Don't even think about venturing into the Boundary Waters without detailed maps of every lake and river that you'll paddle. In the intricate and seemingly endless maze of lakes and rivers, with no roads for many miles, it is extremely easy to get lost. In addition to this guide's route map for each of the days of travel on your chosen route, you'll definitely need navigational maps. The standards are W. A. Fisher maps and McKenzie maps. These water-resistant topographic maps contain all the information you'll need (in addition to a compass) to navigate your trip, with campsites, portages and their lengths, and other details clearly marked. They are also gridded in one-mile squares, making it easier to estimate distance. The W. A. Fisher maps you need are listed in each trip description. You can purchase these maps at camping stores in the Twin Cities area, by mail from the Boundary Waters catalog (800-223-6565; www.piragis.com), or at outfitters near the Boundary Waters entry points.

Portages

Part of the rhythm of a Boundary Waters trip is the portaging. If you're new to portaging, a good way to prepare is to practice at home. If you have your own equipment, portage your canoe and your gear packs a quarter mile to see how many portages you can realistically include in a day's travel. Remember that wilderness portages are at least twice as challenging as a portage on sidewalks. By the way, portages are calculated in rods, a measure that is roughly the length of a canoe, or 16.5 feet; so a quarter mile is 80 rods. The lengths of all portages in this book are given in rods.

Camping and Outfitters

Campers who are new to the Boundary Waters should learn about the unique demands that portaging everything places on equipment choice and camping technique. Many great books have been written on canoe camping, but my favorite is *Roughing It Elegantly*, by Patricia J. Bell. If you aren't sure of yourself or your equipment, one good way to try out Boundary Waters camping without buying an expensive pile of new equipment is to rent everything you need from an outfitter. Outfitters charge reasonable rates, and they can provide partial outfitting or everything but your personal items. A list of outfitters for the western region of the Boundary Waters is available from the Ely Chamber of Commerce (800-777-7281; www .ely.org), and for the eastern region from the Gunflint Trail Association (800-338-6932; www.gunflint-trail.com) or the Grand Marais Chamber of Commerce (218-387-9112; gmcc@boreal.org).

Drinking Water

The lakes in the Boundary Waters are very clean, and some campers scoop their water right out of the middle of the lake, in the deep water. But because of the danger of giardiasis, many boil, treat, or filter their drinking water.

Bears

Black bears are a campsite reality on most lakes in the Boundary Waters. Although they're not usually aggressive and shouldn't be actively feared, they will sometimes wander right into camp even while people are clearly present. In such situations, bears are definitely seeking food, not humans, but any human–animal confrontation carries the potential for trouble. Your main tasks are to keep food out of your tent, keep a clean campsite, and protect your food pack, but the experts don't agree on the food protection question. The Forest Service advises campers to deal with bears by hanging the pack in a tree or using a "bear-proof" container. The book *Roughing It Elegantly* also describes a slick way to hoist your food pack up into a tree out of the reach of these pesky animals. In his book *Canoeing and Camping: Beyond the Basics*, the well-known outdoor writer and speaker Cliff Jacobson, who disagrees with the hanging food pack concept, recommends lining the food pack in heavy plastic to keep the odors contained and hiding it in the bushes far away from your tent.

No Cans or Bottles

As part of your planning, you'll be faced with a ban on cans and bottles into the Boundary Waters. This necessitates the use of alternate methods of food storage, which is not as hard as it sounds and needn't be expensive. Many good books have been written on the subject of camp food, one of which is *NOLS Cookery* (National Outdoor Leadership School), by Claudia Pearson. Another is Pat Bell's *Roughing It Elegantly*. If you heed their advice, you won't have to get by on freeze-dried food, beef jerky, or ramen noodles, and most of the supplies you need can be found in the grocery store or at a food co-op.

Leave No Trace

Maintaining a pristine campsite and leaving it in that condition is a concept that most paddlers embrace. In a wilderness that has as many visitors as the Boundary Waters, however, it's especially important to pack out everything you bring in, including any items left by previous campers. Leaving the area cleaner than you found it is one sure sign of a considerate camper.

Quiet

The Forest Service limits groups to nine people and four watercraft in order to minimize impact on the campsites and to reduce the noise that often accompanies larger groups. Do your part to respect others' solitude. You'll also see more wildlife.

Fires

Once you've seen the aftermath of the forest fires that careless campers have started in the Boundary Waters, you won't have to be persuaded to be careful with campfires. Take along a small camp stove for your cooking, especially when fire danger is high. It's more reliable anyway. Campfires are prohibited in certain areas; check with the Forest Service when you pick up your permit.

A view from an overlook above Rose Lake; Canada is in the distance.

BWCAW EAST 1
Bearskin Lake–Rose Lake Loop (8 miles, 6 portages, round-trip)

This beautiful day trip has an interesting portage—and a hiking trail. Paddling the lakes is the joy of being in the Boundary Waters, but a trip to the BWCAW needn't be all paddling. Hiking trails crisscross this rocky, forested land, often traversing the tops of the dramatically high cliffs that characterize many lakes in the tip of Arrowhead Country. The trip takes you over a spectacular portage that makes a 170-foot descent from little Duncan Lake into big Rose Lake. The trail is so steep that the Forest Service installed stairways, but not just for the ease and convenience of portagers; they protect this popular route from erosion. This is a challenging portage; be sure you're able to carry a canoe safely and remember that you'll also be portaging back up the 170-foot climb later in the day.

The portage trail crosses the Border Route Trail that leads to the high cliffs to the east and an amazing view of Rose Lake and the Quetico, the vast Canadian wilderness on the far shore of Rose. These cliffs are part of the Rove Formation, the Precambrian slate that delineates the long, narrow border lakes. From this overlook, you'll hear the stream flowing from Duncan into Rose, crashing through a falls where the hiking trail's bridge crosses. Hidden in a dark mossy glen just off the trail, Rose Falls begs to be photographed. Huge white pines and cedars shade the portage and the campsites on the shores of Rose.

This is a day trip that will make you want to return, and in fact many people feel this way. Day use requires only a free self-issued permit. If you plan to extend this beautiful trip with a night on Rose Lake, remember that Duncan is a well-used entry point, especially in July and August.

Drive north on the Gunflint Trail (County Road 12) from Grand Marais. **Camping** is available at the Flour Lake Campground, east of the Gunflint Trail on County Road 66. During July and August, or on weekends, reserve a campsite (877-444-6777; www.reserveusa.com). You can also camp at Hungry Jack Lodge and Campground (800-338-1566; www.hungryjack lodge.com), 2 miles east of the Gunflint Trail on Hungry Jack Road (County Road 65). If you camp at Hungry Jack Lodge, you'll wake up just a half mile from a put-in point at West Bearskin Lake.

Canoe rentals are available through numerous outfitters on the Gunflint Trail (218-387-9112; gmcc@boreal.org; 800-338-6932; www.gunflint -trail.com). Hungry Jack Outfitters (800-648-2922; www.hjo .com) is located on the south side of Hungry Jack Lake.

Your **entry point** is Duncan #60 and you'll need **Fisher map F-13.**

A waterfall along the portage from Duncan Lake to Rose Lake.

The Route

Put in at the public water access on Bearskin Lake, east of Hungry Jack Lodge on Menogyn Trail, which goes left at a Y intersection in the road. Signs lead to the access, where another sign points left to West Bearskin (there is also an East Bearskin Lake) and right to Hungry Jack. A parking lot has space for about eight vehicles; extras can park on the side of the road. There is also a toilet.

Fill out a day-use permit and **portage 8 rods** to Bearskin Lake. Across Bearskin is the **75-rod portage** into Duncan Lake and a sign marking your entry into the BWCAW. A beautiful stand of large white pines, including one with its roots wrapped around a huge boulder, is on the easy portage trail.

Duncan is a pretty lake, with lovely bluffs at its south end, but not a big, grand lake. You find its beauty in its details, particularly on a calm day: the water grasses softening the shores of the narrow north end, reflections of cedars leaning over still water, a rocky inlet on the south shore with interesting rock formations. The narrow northeast end of the lake leads to the sandy landing for the **80-rod portage** into Rose Lake.

The portage trail starts under a grove of big cedars and climbs a rocky rise to the intersection with the Border Route hiking trail. The hiking trail goes right, across a small footbridge over Rose Falls, and climbs, a steep and rugged climb with some deep crevasses, for about .25 mile to a spectacular overlook. The portage trail goes straight and widens about 2 rods farther along, allowing room to leave a canoe if you hike the short distance to the overlook. If you don't want to do the hike, continue on the portage trail that curves to the right; the hiking trail goes left at this point.

After descending 28 wooden steps, the portage trail does a switchback around a rock outcrop. If you stop for another look at Rose Falls on the right, this is a wonderful vantage point for a photograph. Then it's back to the portage trail: 91 more wooden steps, several stone ledges, six timber and earthen steps, and a rocky slope down to Rose; the sound of the stream keeps you company all the way down. The end of the portage is spacious, but be considerate about the amount of time you spend resting there.

Your paddle around Rose, on either the wide-open water or the more protected and narrower west end, may include a lunch stop under the cedars and white pines of one of the seven campsites along Rose's south shore. The second campsite to the west of the portage is in a lovely grove of white birch. Return to the **takeout** by the same route.

If you didn't hike up to the overlook on your outbound trip, be sure to make this wonderful climb on your way back. If hiking still seems fun after your return to the takeout at West Bearskin, add a trip to Caribou Rock. As you leave the parking lot, drive a short distance east on Hungry Jack Road to the trailhead of the Caribou Rock hiking trail on the right. A .25-mile climb to Caribou Rock will reward you with another beautiful overlook from 200 feet above Bearskin Lake.

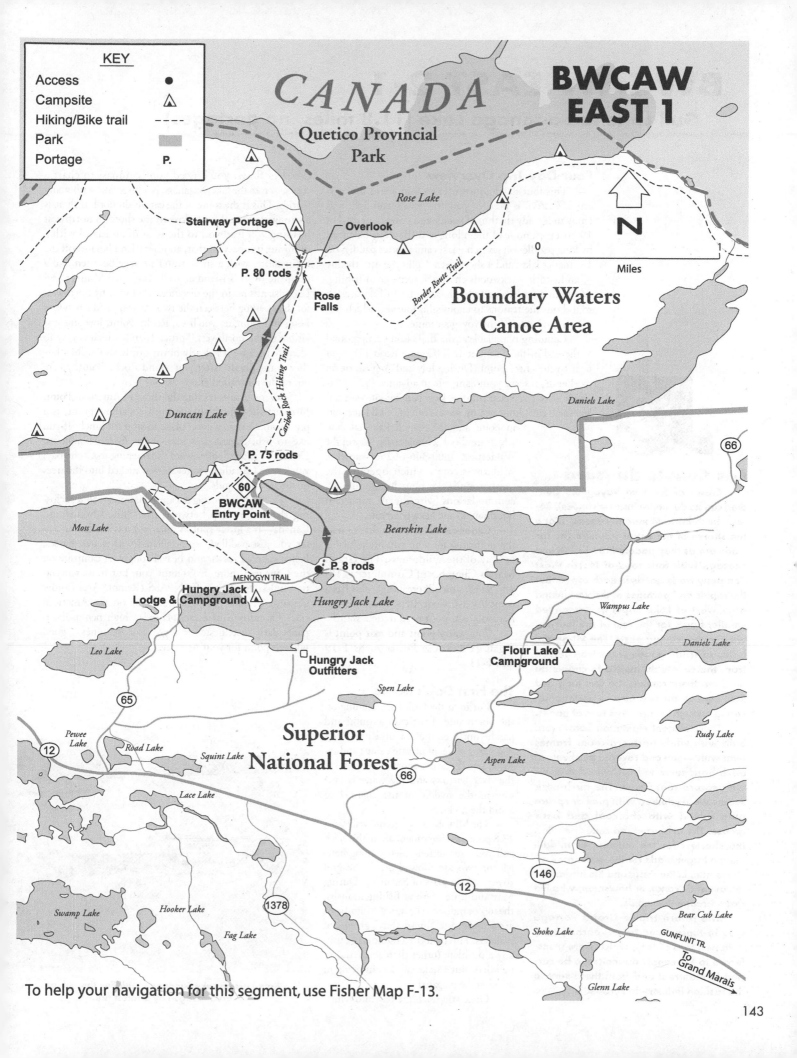

KEY

Access	●
Campsite	△
Hiking/Bike trail	– – –
Park	▨
Portage	P.

CANADA

Quetico Provincial Park

BWCAW EAST 1

N

0 ——— 1
Miles

Stairway Portage

Overlook

Rose Lake

P. 80 rods

Rose Falls

Border Route Trail

Boundary Waters Canoe Area

Daniels Lake

Caribou Rock Hiking Trail

Duncan Lake

66

P. 75 rods

60
BWCAW Entry Point

Moss Lake

Bearskin Lake

P. 8 rods

MENOGYN TRAIL

Hungry Jack Lodge & Campground

Hungry Jack Lake

Wampus Lake

Daniels Lake

Leo Lake

☐ Hungry Jack Outfitters

Flour Lake Campground

Rudy Lake

65

Spen Lake

Pewee Lake

Road Lake

12

Squint Lake

Superior National Forest

Aspen Lake

66

Lace Lake

12

146

Swamp Lake

Hooker Lake

1378

Fag Lake

Shoko Lake

Bear Cub Lake

GUNFLINT TR.

To Grand Marais

Glenn Lake

To help your navigation for this segment, use Fisher Map F-13.

BWCAW EAST 2-1
Gull Lake to Saganaga Lake (11.8 miles, no portages)

Four-Day Trip Overview

This four-day loop trip, a nice sampler of the eastern BWCAW, is best for paddlers who travel light and enjoy the steady rhythm of paddle and portage. A total of 19 portages, none of them long or difficult, is balanced by long paddles on seven big lakes and shorter paddles on 14 smaller lakes and a short river. A glimpse into the life of an historic backwoods character, some great fishing, two hiking trails, a pictograph, and a beautiful waterfall round out the reasons to choose this journey, which follows a short part of the voyageur route.

Camping is available at the Trail's End Campground at the end of the Gunflint Trail (County Road 12), right next to the entry point. During July and August, or on weekends, reserve your campsite in advance (877-444-6777; www.reserveusa.com). A large parking lot, with toilets and a pay phone nearby, serves both the Gull Lake put-in point and the Seagull Lake takeout, which are about .25 mile apart. Way of the Wilderness (800-346-6625; wayofthewilderness.com), which operates the campground, also rents bunkhouse accommodations (with the all-important hot showers) and has a good cafe.

Canoe rentals and complete or partial outfitting for your trip are available at Way of the Wilderness. The Grand Marais Chamber of Commerce (218-387-9112; gmcc@boreal.org), also has a complete list of outfitters. Since this trip is a loop, you won't need to do a shuttle.

Your **entry point** and **exit point** is Saganaga #55. Use **Fisher maps F-19 and F-11**.

The First Day's Route

Put in at the Gull Lake landing on the north side of the campground and paddle north on the Seagull River. After you pass a series of private cabins and resorts, you'll reach a short stretch where the river narrows and the water is fast; stay in the middle of the channel to avoid the rocks.

The Minnesota state record walleye—17.8 pounds—was caught along this river, and you'll see anglers aplenty along here. Motorboats are allowed on the Seagull River and on parts of Saganaga. During May and June, the best fishing months, the motor traffic can be heavy. Motorboats are also used to "jump-start" groups of paddlers. This motorized traffic is not usually a problem (other than aesthetic) to paddlers, but a wake can be annoying to avoid, so be prepared.

Once you reach the bay into which the river flows, you'll need your compass to chart a course across the lake; Saganaga is a huge lake with many islands. This is the route of the canots du nord. If there is a strong west wind, stay close to the shore. A northwest heading will lead you to the west of an island with a campsite; just beyond that, another island lies just off the main shore, with a small water passage between and a campsite on this island as well. You'll see Munker and Long Islands far in the distance; head west by northwest for the opening between the two. As you paddle between Long and Munker, you'll see Rocky Point, low and just visible to the northwest. Spruce Island, which is easy to identify because it's clearly burnt off, is also visible, farther to the north. After you round Rocky Point, you're out of the motorized area.

Several campsites line the shore of American Point. Just past the fourth site, around a shallow point, is a pretty sand beach, a good place to stop for lunch. If you like to fish, Saganaga is known for its large walleyes. Down this shore, look toward the opening to Cache Bay; you'll see a Canadian ranger station tucked into the trees on one of the islands.

The point where big Saganaga narrows—almost closing the watery gap between the United States and Canada—is a lovely spot. A quiet contrast to the big water you just paddled, it's populated with water grasses, lichen-covered rocks, and beaver lodges. A campsite on the Canadian shore may tempt you, but resist temptation unless you have a CANPASS (Remote Area Border Crossing permit); two good sites lie on the American side. The second of these, behind a high peninsula, is particularly nice, nested in a grove of red pines, a good **takeout** point for your first day.

Kayakers on Lake Saganaga paddling through an area ravaged by a forest fire.

Les Canots du Nord

Crews of fourteen voyageurs paddled canots du maître (master canoes), 36-foot birch-bark Montreal canoes, along the shores of the Great Lakes in the fur trade era as they paddled toward Grand Portage with four tons of North West Company trade goods in each canoe. But the rapids and portages of the vast inland area west of Lake Superior demanded smaller boats for the rest of the journey west to the trading posts. The 90-pound bales of trade goods were transferred from the canots du maître to canots du nord (northern canoes), 26 feet long and light enough for two men to portage but strong enough to carry two tons of goods.

These elegant eight-man boats were built with white northern cedar frames bent with steam and covered by sheets of birch bark sewn to beechwood thwarts with spruce root fibers. The birch-bark seams were caulked with pine or spruce gum mixed with charcoal and bear grease. The men used red cedar paddles, the shortest for the milieux, or middle men; a larger blade for the gouvernail, or steersman, in the stern; and the largest for the avant de canot, or bowsman, who led them through the rapids.

The return trip to Grand Portage was in these same boats, each loaded with two tons of furs, which were transferred to the canots du maître to be carried to Montreal and from there sent to the fashion industry in Europe.

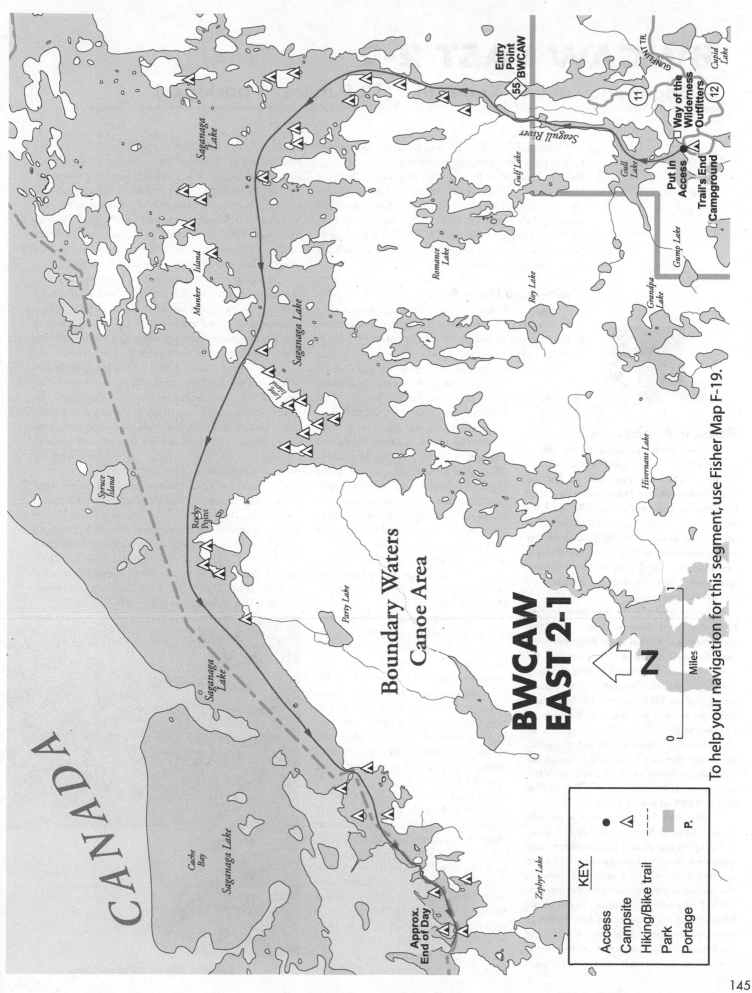

CANADA

Saganaga Lake

Cache Bay

Spruce Island

Rocky Point

Munker Island

Long Island

Saganaga Lake

Saganaga Lake

Party Lake

Zephyr Lake

**Approx.
End of Day**

Boundary Waters
Canoe Area

BWCAW
EAST 2-1

N

Miles

0   1

Gulf Lake

*Romance
Lake*

Roy Lake

Hivernant Lake

*Grandpa
Lake*

Gump Lake

*Grull
Lake*

Seagull River

GUNFLINT TR.

*Capid
Lake*

**Entry
Point
BWCAW**

55

11

12

☐ **Way of the
Wilderness
Outfitters**

**Put in
Access**

△ **Trail's End
Campground**

To help your navigation for this segment, use Fisher Map F-19.

KEY

●	Access
△	Campsite
– – –	Hiking/Bike trail
�box	Park
P.	Portage

BWCAW EAST 2-2
Saganaga Lake to Knife Lake (12.9 miles, 3 portages)

After a day of all paddle and no carries, the rhythm now changes: three portages today will get you warmed up for the second half of the trip. You'll be paddling along the international border all day, following the historic route of the voyageurs as they headed west, their canots du nord full of trade goods. The border route can be a busy place during the favorite months of July and August, but if you visit in September, it's just as beautiful and not nearly as busy. There won't be any bugs left, either.

The Second Day's Route

Begin with the carry from Saganaga into Swamp Lake, just a rocky **5-rod liftover** that bypasses a tiny stream flowing east out of Swamp. Watch the **put-in** on Swamp; it's rocky and awkward.

As you cross Swamp Lake, go to the right of the peninsula that lies due west of the portage; if you go left, you'll end up portaging into Ashdick Lake instead of Ottertrack. Further confirmation that you're in the right place is a boardwalk that starts the **80-rod portage** by crossing the mucky landing. Three steel monuments, one each at the beginning, middle, and end of the trail, mark the international border and give the portage its imposing name: Monument Portage. The dirt trail rises steeply at first, with a set of steps. After a rain there are several soggy sections about halfway along. The trail ends with 15 earthen/timber steps down a steep rocky slope to Ottertrack Lake.

Ottertrack is long and skinny, with lichen-stained high-rise cliffs ranging along the Canadian shore. Reindeer moss, which is not a moss but a lichen, grows profusely on many of the rocks, softening their angularity. Reindeer moss is the preferred food of caribou, and its tiny fronds actually resemble the caribou's antlers. White cedars line the shores of Ottertrack, interspersed with white and red pines as the bluffs rise from the lake.

About 1.5 miles from the end of Monument Portage, a large, irregularly shaped peninsula juts from the American shore. On one of the Canadian cliffs across the lake from this peninsula, down near the water level, you'll find a weathered plaque dedicated to Benny Ambrose, who lived on the American side of Ottertrack until 1982. Remnants of a rock crib that supported his pier remain by the shore, and traces of his homestead are still visible on the low hill above the lake. A sign surrounded by a cairn of found items reminds visitors to please treat the area with respect. Benny Ambrose's place makes a lovely lunch stop, but please remember that no camping is allowed.

By the time you reach Little Knife Portage, you may be eager for another chance to hike instead of paddle, but it's just a short **5-rod portage** over a rock ledge to avoid a little waterfall. The lead-up to the portage is a short stream, with long, thin dead trees lying on the bottom that look like pickup sticks in the clear water.

If you didn't stop for lunch at Benny's, you'll find two campsites on the American side about a mile and a half past the portage. The second is on a point, with a wide-angle view, and makes a nice rest stop. A mile past the campsite, Knife Lake slips through a narrow opening that frames a beautiful view across the lake.

You'll want to start looking for a **campsite** as you approach Thunder Point another 2.5 miles down Knife, and there are several campsites around the point. The campsite situated on a small north-facing point is especially spacious and beautiful. A large rock outcrop provides a handsome base for the fire ring and there is room for several tents. If the wind is quiet, you'll hear the sound of running water from across the lake.

If you're feeling adventurous after you set up camp, paddle to the southwest tip of the point to find the landing spot that marks the base of the Thunder Point Trail. A quick scramble up the rocks, about 150 feet up, will win you a beautiful, unobstructed view west over Knife Lake. The trail isn't always well maintained, but since it's only about a quarter mile long, you can pick your way over any deadfalls. If you'd rather fish, Knife Lake supports healthy populations of walleyes, lake trout, and northerns.

Benny Ambrose

Benny Ambrose went to the North Country to prospect gold when he was 23 years old. He never left. He built a one-room cabin on Ottertrack Lake that he lived in the rest of his life, and he prospected and trapped until these activities were banned in 1978. One of the last permanent residents of the Boundary Waters, Benny worked as a fishing guide after that; among his clients was Hubert Humphrey.

Benny had a wife and two daughters who lived there with him until the girls reached school age; then his wife took the girls away to live in the city. He built a three-bedroom house, with a gravity-feed water system for indoor plumbing, on his homestead to lure them back. He hauled dirt from his home state of Iowa to plant lilacs. The daughters returned every summer, but not his wife. He never did live in the big house himself; he preferred his little cabin with the kitchen tent. Benny died in a fire in that tent in 1982 at the age of 86.

After the funeral, there was talk among Benny's high-up friends of memorializing his home, but his daughters and the forest service knew he wouldn't have wanted that, so right after the funeral, the cabins were burned and the site reverted to nature. Nothing remains of Benny's cabins now but a few footings and the remnants of a pier. If you visit the homestead, please respect the memory of this remarkable wilderness man.

Canadian cliffs on Ottertrack Lake.

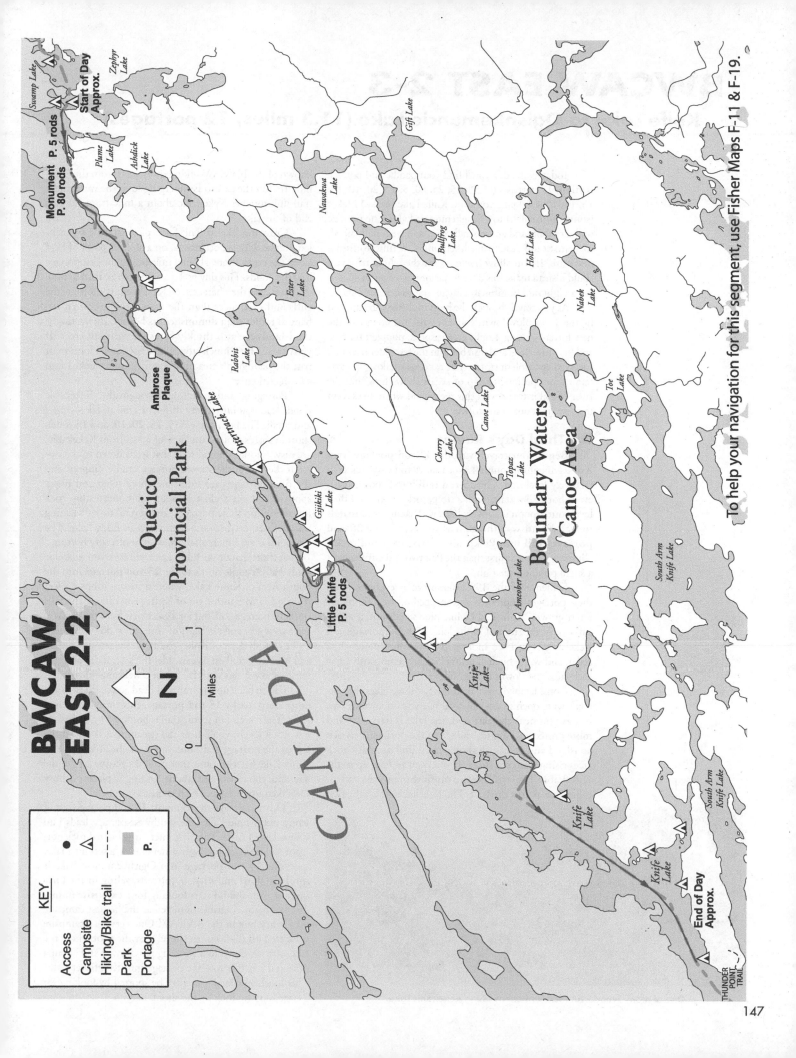

BWCAW EAST 2-2

KEY

- **Access** ●
- **Campsite** ◬
- **Hiking/Bike trail** – – –
- **Park** (gray shading)
- **Portage** P.

N

Miles
0 ... 1

Quetico
Provincial Park

CANADA

Boundary Waters
Canoe Area

Start of Day
Approx.

Monument P. 5 rods
P. 80 rods

Swamp Lake

Zephyr
Lake

Plume
Lake

Ashdick
Lake

Gift Lake

Nawakwa
Lake

Bullfrog
Lake

Holt Lake

Nabek
Lake

Ester
Lake

Rabbit
Lake

Ambrose
Plaque

Otterrtrack Lake

Gijikiki
Lake

Little Knife
P. 5 rods

Cherry
Lake

Canoe Lake

Topaz
Lake

Toe
Lake

Ameober Lake

Knife
Lake

South Arm
Knife Lake

Knife
Lake

Knife
Lake

South Arm
Knife Lake

End of Day
Approx.

THUNDER
POINT
TRAIL

To help your navigation for this segment, use Fisher Maps F-11 & F-19.

BWCAW EAST 2-3
Knife Lake to Ogishkemuncie Lake (11.3 miles, 12 portages)

Today is the day you'll find your paddle and portage rhythm; 12 portages (of 33, 25, 25, 80, 5, 15, 20, 10, 15, 15, 15, 15 rods) take you from Knife Lake across 11 lakes (some quite small) to Ogishkemuncie Lake. The portage trails are short and are generally even and well-maintained, so you should reach Ogishkemuncie in time to find a campsite. If you allow five days for the whole trip, you could instead make this day's route into two days by spending a night on beautiful and interesting Kekekabic Lake.

As you travel through the heart of the region flattened by the 1999 blowdown, you can sense the energy of the new forest—young, bright green aspens; popples; birches; and firs grow thick and lush beneath the few older trees that survived the violent storm. The exposed shallow root system of an uprooted clump of cedars shows how thin the layer of soil is that covers this rocky land where trees seem to grow right out of the rocks.

The Third Day's Route

Begin your travel with the **33-rod portage** from Knife Lake into Bonnie Lake, a short and easy trek on a relatively level trail. The **25-rod trail** into Spoon Lake is even shorter but starts with a steep, rocky climb and then levels out. Spoon is a lovely lake, with a cluster of islands to wend your way through as you cross. The **25-rod portage trail** into Pickle also starts steep and rocky, climbing higher at first than the first two and curving past a small pond on the right.

Evidence of the 1999 blowdown is everywhere on these portages—uprooted and snapped-off trees, lush new forest growth. A thick old white pine stands out, a sturdy survivor of the storm. On the longer **80-rod portage** into Kekekabic, you'll see more survivors: white pine, white cedar, and white birch. This trail is fairly even, with a few rocky ups and downs in the middle.

Considerably larger than the last three lakes, Kekekabic's wide-open spaces can challenge you on a windy day, but as you near the east end, the lake is narrower and more protected. About a mile from the portage, between an island and the south shore, you'll find dramatic rock faces rising from the shore. If you want to hike up to the Kekekabic Trail, follow the south shore to the ranger cabin that marks the trail. The Kekekabic Trail, the best known of the BWCAW hiking trails, runs from the Gunflint Trail in the east to Fernberg Road in the west, and a trail link touches Kekekabic about a mile from the east end of the lake.

Cross the lake to look for a pictograph, a six-inch-long canoe with six occupants, on a shallow point of land along the north shore, about a mile before the first portage into the ponds. This tiny rock painting can be hard to find.

Because the character of Kekekabic is more in the cliffs and rock faces than the trees, the blowdown enhanced rather than diminished its beauty. Interestingly, the islands are still thickly forested with tall trees. If you're ready for a lunch stop, a nice site can be found just past the pictograph area on the north shore, tucked into a C-shaped cove.

Portaging and paddling through the Kekekabic ponds lead you into a very different kind of lake—quiet and small. The five portages (**5, 15, 20, 10, and 15 rods**), short bypasses around the flow of water from Kekekabic, are easy. A long, sloping rock that leads down to the water at the end of the second portage can be slippery, and the final portage into Eddy has some steep and rocky spots. You'll get a close look at some interesting rock formations on these portages, and several tiny, charming waterfalls entertain you on your way to Eddy Lake. The last pond is extremely shallow, with a soft, silty bottom.

A short detour on Eddy Lake will take you to scenic Eddy Falls. Paddle north to the **25-rod portage** into the South Arm of Knife Lake, where a stream drops 75 feet from Eddy to South Arm of Knife. You can see the falls from the portage trail, but for a great view from the bottom, leave your gear and portage just your canoe down the steep trail to South Arm of Knife, paddle to the stream's outlet, and hike up a trail on its east side. If it's a hot day and you want a shower, this waterfall can be a welcome side trip.

Climb back up the trail and head across Eddy to another steep, rocky **15-rod portage**, this time into Jenny Lake. The rough but scenic trail is bordered by cedars. At low water levels, you'll hear the stream that flows on the left of the portage trail, but you won't be able to see it. Jenny Lake has two campsites, so if it's getting late in the day and you're worried about finding a place on busy Ogishkemuncie Lake, you'll want to stop here.

Otherwise, take the southeast **15-rod portage** out of Jenny into Annie Lake (the southwest portage leads into Calico Lake.) Annie Lake has interesting big red rock outcrops and is ringed by lovely water grasses, a soft little lake.

The **15-rod portage** into Ogishkemuncie Lake is similarly short and easy. If you're traveling in the busy months, you should start looking for a **campsite** immediately because Ogishkemuncie has the highest campsite occupancy rate in the BWCAW. One very nice campsite is located on the western shore, past the spot where the lake narrows down to a winding passageway and about a mile and a half before the portage into Kingfisher Lake. This southwest-facing site can be spotted by looking for a large, sloping rock by the shore.

One of many wonderful rock formations along Kekekabic Lake.

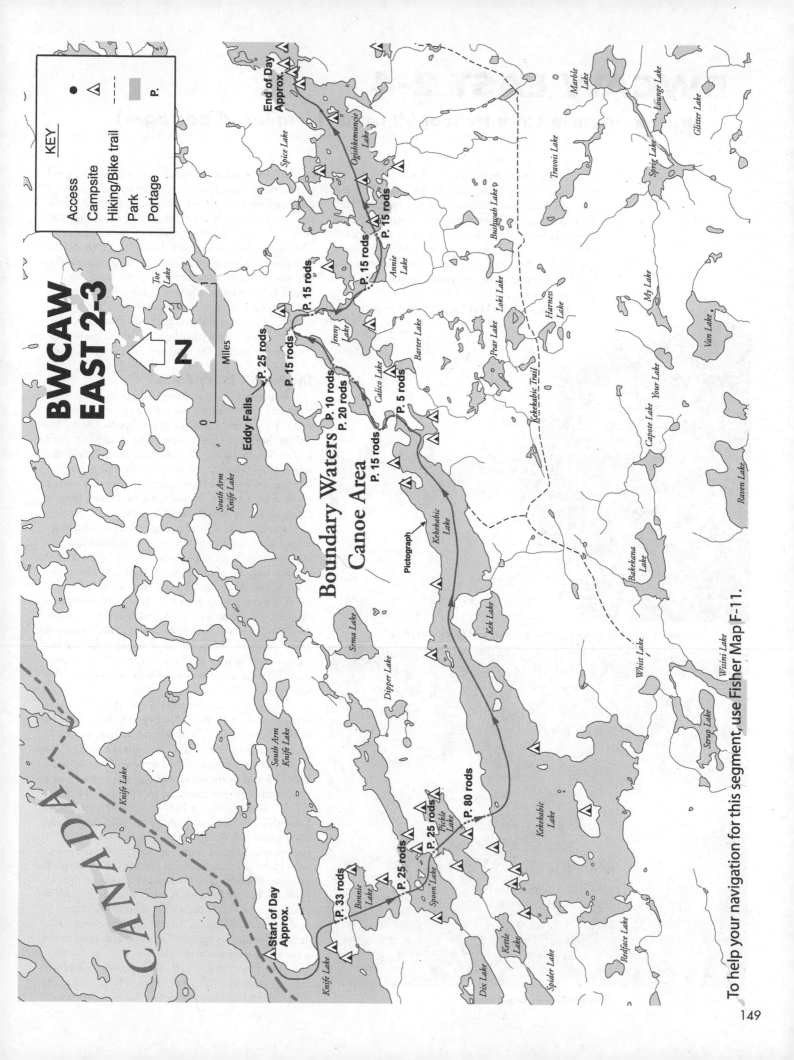

BWCAW EAST 2-3

KEY

- Access •
- Campsite △
- Hiking/Bike trail - - -
- Park (shaded)
- Portage P.

N

Miles

Boundary Waters
Canoe Area

CANADA

Start of Day
Approx.

End of Day
Approx.

Eddy Falls

Pictograph

P. 33 rods
P. 25 rods
P. 25 rods
P. 25 rods
P. 80 rods
P. 15 rods
P. 5 rods
P. 15 rods
P. 20 rods
P. 10 rods
P. 15 rods
P. 25 rods
P. 15 rods
P. 15 rods
P. 15 rods

Knife Lake
Bonnie Lake
Spoon Lake
Pickle Lake
Kettle Lake
Dix Lake
Spider Lake
Redface Lake
Kekekabic Lake
Kek Lake
Serna Lake
Dipper Lake
South Arm Knife Lake
South Arm Knife Lake
Toe Lake
Spice Lake
Jenny Lake
Calico Lake
Barter Lake
Ogishkemuncie Lake
Annie Lake
Bushyab Lake
Loki Lake
Pear Lake
Harness Lake
Travois Lake
Marble Lake
Lounge Lake
Glitter Lake
Sprig Lake
My Lake
Van Lake
Raven Lake
Your Lake
Capote Lake
Bakekama Lake
Whiss Lake
Wissini Lake
Srup Lake
Kekekabic Trail

To help your navigation for this segment, use Fisher Map F-11.

BWCAW EAST 2-4
Ogishkemuncie Lake to Seagull Lake (11 miles, 4 portages)

A mere four portages (38, 25, 45, and 105 rods) will make your last day in the BWCAW feel like Easy Street, especially since these portages are all well-worn and fairly level. You may still want to get an early start if you'll be driving home directly from the takeout or if a northeast wind is blowing. Seagull Lake, the final lake before the takeout, has a lot of fetch (distance over which wind can build waves) and is on a northeast heading; the wind generally gets heavier as the day goes on.

You won't be looking for a campsite tonight, how-

![Seagull Lake photo]

Seagull Lake has many interesting islands and inlets to explore.

Ready to cross Jasper Lake.

ever, so if the winds are favorable, you may want to spend part of the morning exploring Ogishkemuncie Lake or fishing for the walleyes and northerns that lurk in its waters. Ogish, as you may hear it called, probably gets its name from the Ojibwe Ogishkimanissi, kingfisher or Okishkimonisse, fisher. Partly because it's a lovely lake with good fishing opportunities and partly because it's a relatively short distance from the heavily used access at Seagull Lake, many people visit Ogish every summer, so you won't have the lake to yourselves. However, numerous islands, inlets, and portage trails into other lakes make it an interesting lake. An inlet next to the portage into Mueller Lake on the lake's east shore is worth a visit.

The Fourth Day's Route

Begin your day by paddling to the first portage at the north end of the lake. (If you reach a portage that heads west at the end of the lake, you've gone too far.) At the **38-rod portage** from Ogishkemuncie into Kingfisher, you'll find shallow rapids that flow into Kingfisher. If the water level is not too high or too low, you can walk or line this short stream instead of portaging. On a hot day, wading can be more appealing than carrying, but be sure to scout the rapids first as it's not a difficult portage.

An even easier **25-rod portage** takes you from Kingfisher Lake into Jasper Lake, another popular lake. Six campsites offer lunch stop possibilities. Just off the **45-rod portage** trail out of Jasper, you'll be able to admire the beautiful falls on the stream that flows into Alpine.

Only one portage away from Seagull, Alpine Lake is studded with campsites. If you didn't lunch on Jasper, Alpine will certainly have a campsite available around noon, and you can restore your strength for the last portage and the long paddle across Seagull. The campsites also provide landmarks to help you navigate this sometimes confusing lake.

The portage into Seagull Lake on the east shore of Alpine has an easily visible landing. The blowdown hit heavily here, and this trail is lined with new growth. Small trees and shrubs flourish with the energy of a young forest amid the uprooted remains of the old forest. This **105-rod portage** trail starts generally level and is worn, with a few low spots that are mucky after a rain.

If a northeast wind is blowing when you cross Seagull Lake, this will be a long paddle, and you'll be grateful if you started early. Navigation can be challenging as well. Use your compass to set headings from the numerous campsites.

Threemile Island is easy to identify; it was burned off in a prescribed burn in 2001 and only a few of the old-growth white and red pines, and some ancient white cedars, remain. Follow the western shore of this charred island to guide you toward the takeout. Two campsites located at the narrows between Threemile Island and several other islands are good landmarks.

A short paddle down an inlet leads to a public landing. The **takeout** is just a short distance from the parking lot where you left your vehicle four (or five) days before.

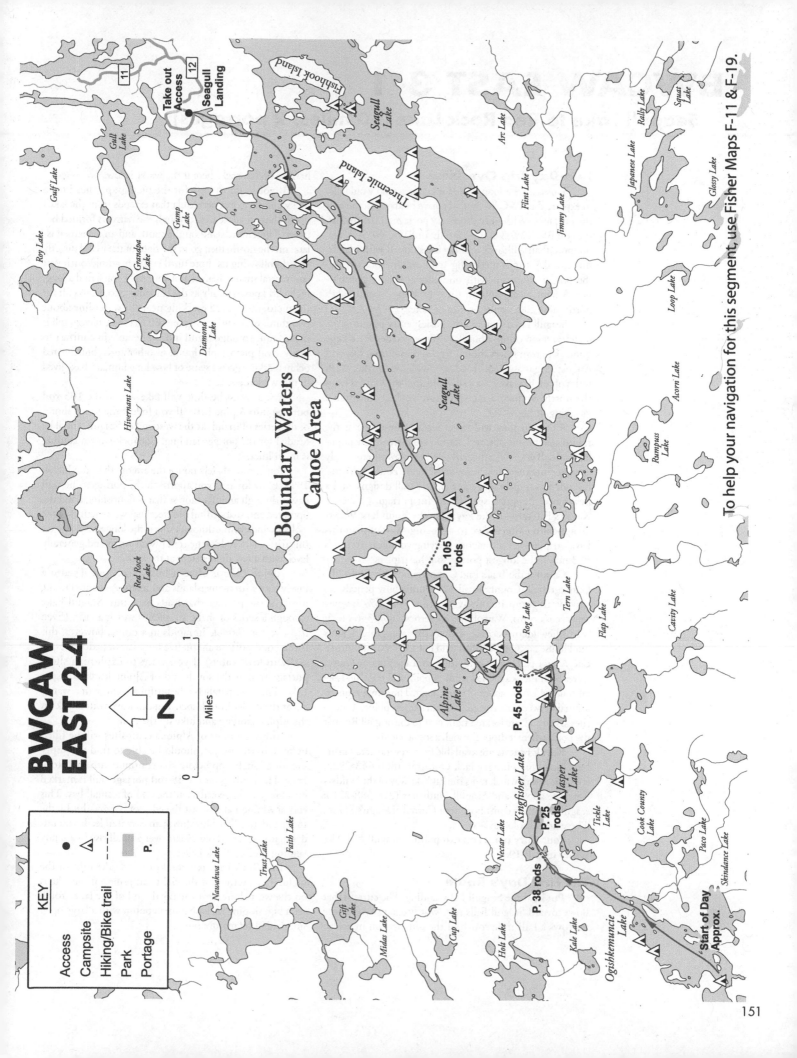

151

BWCAW EAST 3-1
Seagull Lake to Red Rock Lake (10 miles, 2 portages)

Two-Day Trip Overview

This is a great loop route for kayakers who would like to explore the BWCAW but who have hesitated because of the portages. With only three easy portages, (105 and 48 rods on BWCAW 3-1 and 10 rods for BWCAW 3-2), one no more than a liftover, and big lakes dotted with islands, this two-day trip is a relaxing and beautiful journey into the border country—with outstanding fishing possibilities. A faint pictograph on the cliffs along Seagull Lake's north shore adds an historical side note.

Seagull Lake is one of the busiest entry points in the eastern region of the Boundary Waters, so despite a large quota, a permit reservation is a good idea during July and August. Saganaga Lake is a huge, wide-open lake. With miles of fetch, waves can really pile up if the wind is from the northern quadrants, so be sure you're comfortable kayaking in big waves.

Although they will never replace the canoe as the traditional means of travel, kayaks are increasingly popular in the BWCAW, especially on big lakes where windy weather means a less seaworthy craft could be wind bound. Kayak portage yokes, lighter hull designs, and a new kayak designed specifically for portaging—Vetter Kayak's PakYak—make kayaking the Boundary Waters an appealing alternative to canoeing. As you plan this kayak trip, however, practice carrying your gear 105 rods (0.3 mile), the longest portage on this trip.

Camp at the Trail's End Campground at the end of the Gunflint Trail (County Road 12). During busy periods, reserve your campsite in advance (877-444-6777; www.reserveusa.com). Way of the Wilderness (800-346-6625; wayofthewilderness.com) operates the campground, rents bunkhouse accommodations (and hot showers), and runs a cafe. A large parking lot, with toilets and a pay phone nearby, serves both the Seagull Lake put-in point and the Gull Lake takeout, which are about .25 mile apart. The campground is located between the two public water access points. Campsites 18 and 19 are located right next to the Seagull River at the point where it drops through a scenic rapids.

Kayak rentals are available from several area outfitters, including Hungry Jack Outfitters (800-648-2922; www.hjo.com), which rents the PakYak; Way of the Wilderness (see above) and Seagull Outfitters (218-388-2216; seagulloutfitters.com) both rent Current Design's Storm. These are all solo kayaks.

Your **entry point** and **exit point** is Seagull #54. Use **Fisher map F-19**.

The First Day's Route

Put in at the Seagull Lake landing. The current that flows toward Seagull Falls runs swiftly against you at the narrows a half mile south of the put-in; you may also have to dodge rocks here if the water is low.

If you want to look for the pictograph, head for a rocky cliff face on a peninsula that extends from the lake's north shore. Paddle west through the narrows formed between Threemile Island on the south and an unnamed island on the north, then go to the right of the island directly ahead, following its shore until you're heading southwest past several smaller islands. On your right you'll find a long, high cliff known locally as the Palisades. Scout this cliff for the pictograph, a red marking near the water line about two-thirds of the way along the cliff face. The pictograph is quite faint, smudged, and indecipherable in contrast to many vivid pictographs found in other areas, but this red ochre marking gives a sense of how long humans have lived in this wilderness.

A southwest heading will take you to the **105-rod portage** into Alpine Lake. If you follow the south shores of the series of islands at the west end of Seagull, you'll be headed for the portage landing. The rock-strewn landing is in an inlet.

You'll immediately notice the aftermath of the July 4, 1999, blowdown as you approach the portage. The trail passes through an infant forest that is flourishing amid the uprooted and snapped-off old trees that were victims of the violent windstorm. Although this is the longest portage on this trip—105 rods—the trail is well-worn and generally level, with a few timber steps at the end.

Alpine Lake is often a busy place, but it's also a lovely lake with many islands and inlets. A channel to the north of the portage that leads back into Seagull Lake through a series of shallow rapids is worth a visit. (Even if you're comfortable in rapids in a canoe, however, this isn't a good portage alternative for a kayak paddler, especially in low water.) If you want to explore, a short portage trail at the south end of Alpine leads to Jasper Lake. This trail parallels a beautiful stream with a waterfall at the outlet from Jasper. You can leave your kayaks at the Alpine landing and hike up the trail.

Although most of Alpine's campsites will be filled by midafternoon, you should be able to find an empty site for a lunch stop before you continue into Red Rock Lake. The landing for the **48-rod portage** trail is marked by a grove of large cedars at the end of a small bay. This end of Alpine Lake is past the edge of the area hit by the Independence Day blowdown; an easy trail leads you under many beautiful old cedars over a small rise to a sandy landing on Red Rock Lake.

Red Rock Lake is a good place to **take out** for the night. The prettiest of the eight campsites on the lake is on the west shore near the north end of the lake. You'll see a big, sloping rock on a small point, with a large open site shaded by mature pines.

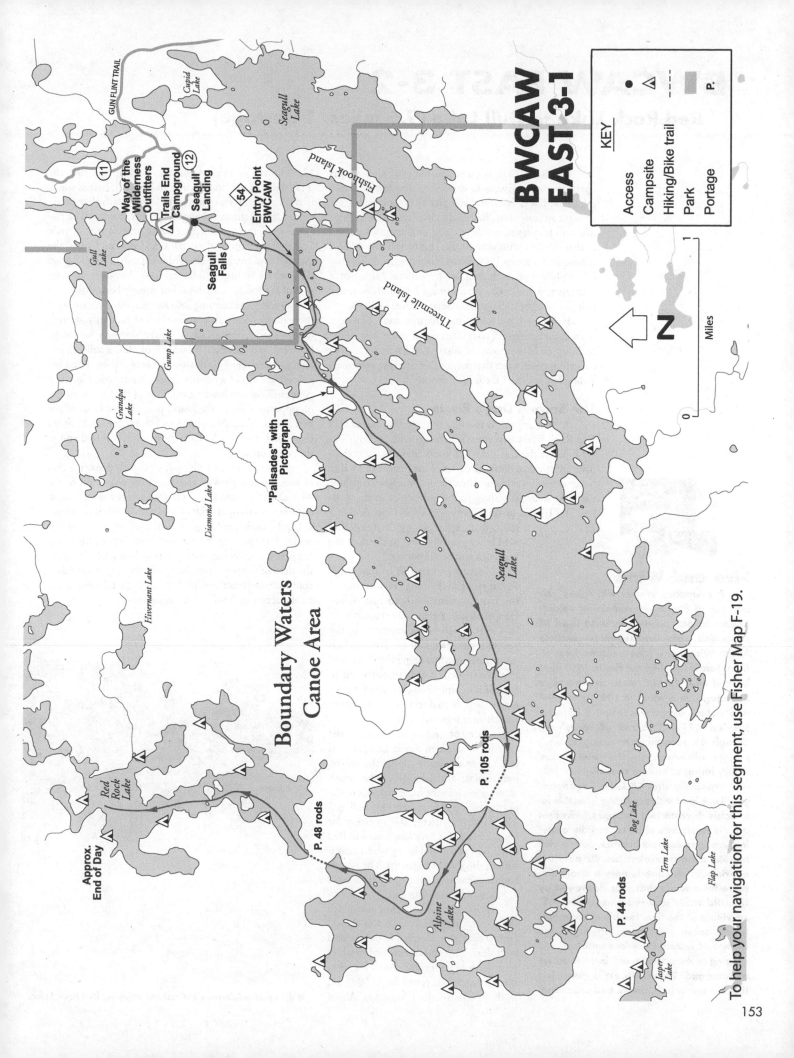

BWCAW EAST 3-1

BWCAW EAST 3-2
Red Rock Lake to Gull Lake (9.5 miles, 1 portage)

Red Rock Lake is quiet and the campsites are far apart, so you may want to enjoy the solitude of a morning in the BWCAW, but if you plan to do any fishing today, get an early start. Red Rock Lake has a natural population of walleyes, northerns, and smallmouth bass and is also stocked with lake trout. The wonderful walleye fishing in Saganaga Lake draws many anglers to this big lake in hopes of catching a trophy walleye. Minnesota's state record walleye, a mammoth 17-pound, 8-ounce fish, was caught in Saganaga's Seagull River in 1979.

Fishing from a kayak may require some practice; www.kayakfishingstuff.com offers tips if you're new to the techniques. Motorboats are allowed on Saganaga, east of American Point, a fact that may detract from the wilderness feeling but not from the fishing opportunities.

The Second Day's Route

As you approach the tiny portage into Saganaga's Red Rock Bay, you'll cross a shallow inlet filled with water lilies on the east side. The rocks that dot these shallows are streaked with the colors of the many canoes that have scraped over them when the water is low, so paddle carefully to avoid adding your kayak's color to the medley. The **10-rod portage** runs over a rocky rise next to a short, rocky water passage. You may find wild irises growing next to shore at the Saganaga end of the portage.

Near the north end of Red Rock Bay, if you paddle along the west side of the large unnamed island just before Cooper Island, a peninsula extends from this island, offering a lovely stopping point for either a rest or an early lunch. A campsite lies farther along the shore, and if it's occupied, you may not want to stop. If it's empty, however, you'll have a nice view in both directions and room to stretch your legs with a hike.

Once you paddle out into the vast expanse of southern Saganaga Lake, you can either continue along the inlets, peninsulas, and islands of the south shore or explore the bigger islands to the north, fishing their margins for walleyes. The wind may decide this question for you. If you didn't have lunch back in Red Rock Bay, you'll find many island campsites in this part of Saganaga. The islands and their campsites are useful landmarks as you navigate this big lake.

If you choose to follow the south shore, a startling sight awaits you. As you pass to the right of a small island covered with dead trees and one surviving white pine, look to your right. You'll see what the Romance Lake forest fire of 1995 did to the forests south of Saganaga. About 12,600 acres of forest were destroyed in that fire; the rocky ridge of the land is still studded with charred stubs. If you've ever been tempted to leave a campfire unattended, this sight will change your mind forever. The fascination of this landscape is being able to see the pale bones of the land; with its tall trees burnt and gone, the exposed ancient bedrock of the Canadian Shield gives the country an utterly different look than does the softness of the forest—different, but equally beautiful.

Finding the opening into the Seagull River is easy if there is any boat traffic, motorized or human-powered, heading out of its mouth. If you're alone on Saganaga, however, and confused by what looks like a solid shoreline, use a campsite on the south side of an island that lies just off the tip of a peninsula as a landmark. Confirm your position and heading with one of the two campsites on opposite sides of the island that lies southeast of the first island. A southeast heading from that island toward the highest point of land on the horizon will lead you to the river's opening.

Dramatic rocky hills, carpeted with dense patches of young forest growth, rise above the river. Follow the wide channel south into a narrows where the oncoming current tries to fight you; stay in the center of the channel and paddle hard to get past this short stretch of fast water. After passing the narrows, you'll spot a building, the first since you left, with a dark brown roof. Paddle to the right of the point on which this building stands; then continue upstream to Gull Lake and the **takeout** at the public access by Trail's End campground.

Fire and Wind

A Boundary Waters trip takes you into one of the largest remaining wildernesses in our country, a wild land of rocks and water and seemingly endless forest. With that wildness comes the reality of forest fire, like the fire in 1995 that burned over 12,000 acres around Lake Saganaga. And wind: in 1999, a sudden and violent windstorm called a derecho leveled 477,000 acres of trees. Although it's sometimes tempting to wish that the wilderness stay the same, nature is indifferent to human wishes.

Especially around Lake Saganaga, you'll see land still recovering from this inevitable devastation: charred trunks that are the reminders of a fire; rapidly growing young trees; pale bedrock clearly visible, like a forest exoskeleton. But nature is capricious: on islands only a short distance from forest that was destroyed by fire, old white and red pines stand tall, survivors of the fire. The blowdown flattened some portages, leaving huge clumps of uprooted cedars with soil still clinging to their dead roots, but left others undamaged. The old forest is gone, but the new one is lush, green, and promising.

A group of wilderness enthusiasts enjoying Red Rock Lake.

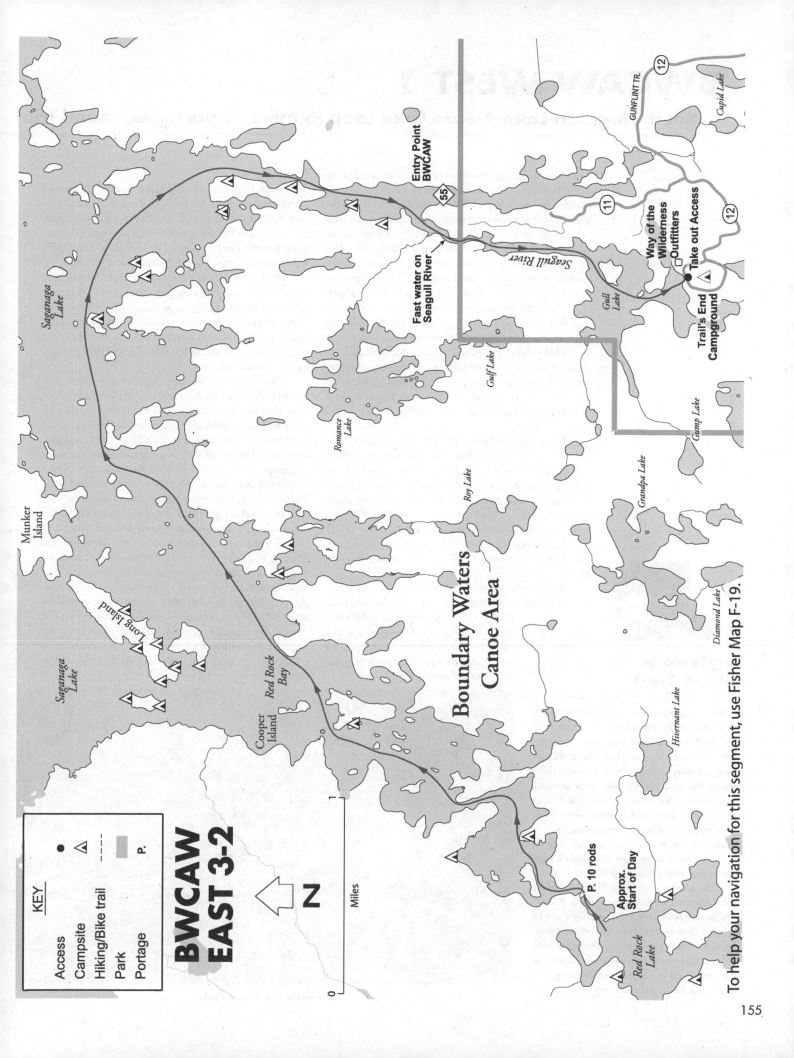

BWCAW EAST 3-2

N

KEY
●	Access
△	Campsite
‑ ‑ ‑	Hiking/Bike trail
(gray)	Park
P.	Portage

Miles

Saganaga Lake

Munker Island

Long Island

Saganaga Lake

Cooper Island

Red Rock Bay

Romance Lake

Roy Lake

Boundary Waters Canoe Area

Gulf Lake

Gull Lake

Gump Lake

Grandpa Lake

Diamond Lake

Hivernant Lake

Red Rock Lake

P. 10 rods

Approx. Start of Day

Fast water on Seagull River

Entry Point BWCAW

55

Seagull River

11

12

GUNFLINT TR.

Cupid Lake

12

Way of the Wilderness Outfitters
☐ Take out Access

Trail's End Campground

To help your navigation for this segment, use Fisher Map F-19.

An easy day trip, this short paddle to visit some of the finest Native American pictographs in the BWCAW will also give first-time Boundary Waters paddlers a taste of the wilderness that lies beyond these three small lakes. The trip begins with an 80-rod (.25 mile) portage. If you want to take a multiday trip but have never paddled the BWCAW, you should definitely decide whether the beauty and the solitude are worth the work of the carries. The easy portage into South Hegman is not a true test, but it's at least a quiz.

These pretty lakes are often visited on a day trip, and they also lead to the Angleworm Portage, a much more challenging 460-rod (1.4 miles) portage to Angleworm Lake and to the remote country that BWCAW enthusiasts seek. If you have a full day for this trip, consider hiking the portage trail to a spot high above Angleworm Lake for another taste of the wilderness. You won't have to portage the canoe; just leave it off to the side at the portage landing.

Camping is available at the USFS Fenske Lake Campground (218-365-4966). From Ely, travel east on Highway 169 north for 1 mile; turn left on County Road 88 and travel 2 miles to the Echo Trail (County Road 116); turn right on 116 and travel 7 miles to the campground entrance on the right. Reserve a campsite by calling 877-444-6777 or online at www.reserveamerica.com.

Canoe rentals are available in Ely. The Ely Chamber of Commerce (800-777-7281; www.ely.org) has a list of area outfitters.

Because this is a day trip, you won't need a reservation and there is no quota on day-use visits, but you must fill out a free day-use permit at the **entry point**. Self-issue permit forms are in a box near the beginning of the portage trail. Your **entry point** is South Hegman #77. Use **Fisher map F-9**.

The Route

South Hegman Lake is 3 miles north of the Fenske Lake Campground on the Echo Trail (County Road 116). Turn right at the sign; you'll find parking by the portage trail. Follow the **80-rod (quarter mile) portage** trail down to the **put-in**. The trail is wide, well-worn, and downhill, with 16 timber steps down the steep bank at the end.

It's about a mile to the **short portage (5 rods)** that leads from South Hegman Lake into North Hegman Lake and then another mile to the narrow north end of North Hegman. The pictographs, a group of red ochre figures painted on pink-hued granite, are on a rock face midway along the west or left side of this narrow passage, well above the water level.

These magical rock paintings are the reason that many paddlers visit this lake, and they've been undisturbed since their discovery. Please don't touch the pictographs; oils from human hands may speed the disintegration of the pigments. No one knows exactly who painted these pictographs or how old they are, but scientists think that most pictographs in the BWCAW were painted by the Ojibwe people within the last three hundred to four hundred years. To the Ojibwe, these paintings are sacred; you should respect the spiritual significance of this site by treating the pictographs as you would paintings from your own religion.

You may want to spend some time inspecting the floating bog between North Hegman and Trease: the pitcher plants, other wildflowers, and the composition of the bog itself are fascinating to observe. To reach the Angleworm Portage trail—whether to hike or just to stop for a rest or lunch—continue north .6 mile to the end of Trease Lake. If you hike the trail, stow your canoe out of the way so that other travelers may pass. Or you may choose to paddle back to South Hegman for a stop at one of its three campsites before you **take out** at the entry point.

Angleworm Hiking Trail

The 14-mile-long Angleworm is one of many hiking trails that wind through the Superior National Forest. From the Echo Trail, this rugged path heads northeast for 3 miles—entering the BWCAW along the way at Entry Point 21—and then swings through an 11-mile loop around Angleworm Lake, Whiskey Jack Lake, and Home Lake. The land is hilly, with high rocky ridges and scenic overlooks. Stands of red and white pine, moose sightings in the Home Lake area, and pink lady's slippers in the spring also lure hikers.

The Angleworm has 10 campsites, which hikers share with canoeists. A BWCAW permit is required for overnight use in summer. One needn't hike the whole thing, however. The Angleworm is also accessible by the Angleworm portage trail, making a short day hike a nice adjunct to the pictograph paddle. Use Fisher map F-9.

Beaver dam on Hegman Lake.

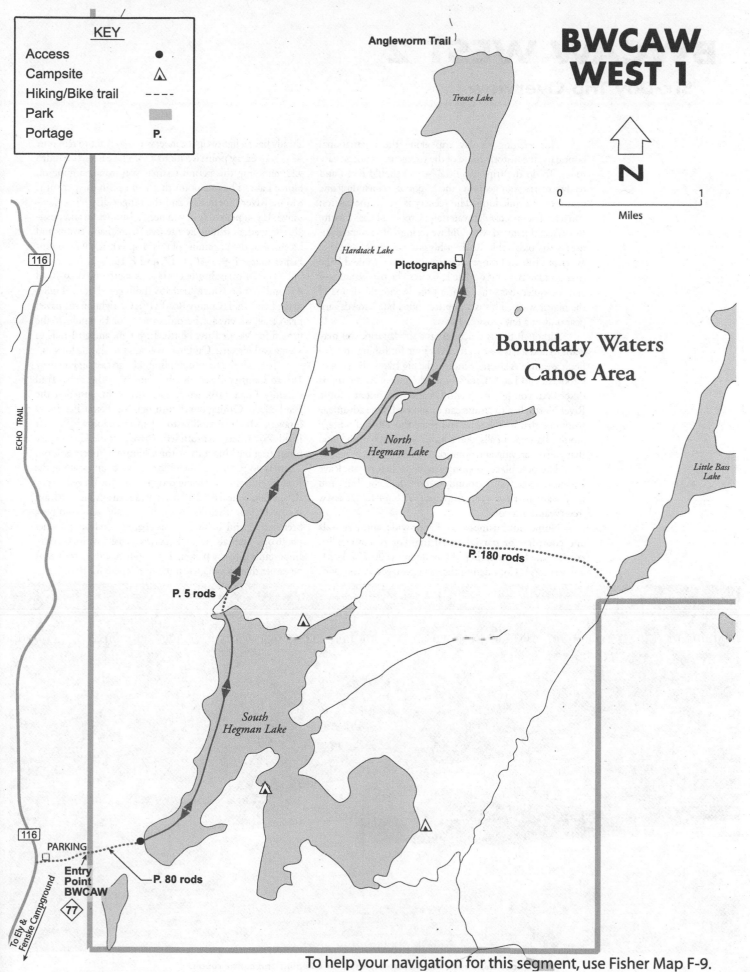

KEY

Access ●
Campsite ⚠
Hiking/Bike trail - - - -
Park ▨
Portage P.

Angleworm Trail

BWCAW WEST 1

N

0 _____ 1
Miles

Trease Lake

Hardtack Lake
Pictographs

Boundary Waters Canoe Area

North Hegman Lake

Little Bass Lake

P. 180 rods

P. 5 rods

ECHO TRAIL

116

South Hegman Lake

116

PARKING

Entry Point BWCAW

P. 80 rods

77

To Ely & Fenske Campground

To help your navigation for this segment, use Fisher Map F-9.

BWCAW WEST 2
Six-Day Trip Overview

This exciting six-day trip along the international boundary, the historic route of the voyageurs, is not an easy route. To do the trip comfortably, you should be fit and ready to carry your gear over the 17 portages, including one that is over a mile long. The scenery is worth the carries; you'll see five spectacular waterfalls; Crooked Lake's Picture Rock, a cliff painted with Ojibwe pictographs several hundred years old; Table Rock, a historic voyageur campsite; Warrior Hill; and more pictographs—on Crooked Lake near Sunday Bay and on Lac la Croix. The trip begins and ends on quiet rivers that contrast nicely with the drama of the bigger water. This is a popular route, but "crowds" appear only at a few crossroad areas.

Although this is described as a six-day trip, you may want to add a day or two to allow time for fishing and difficult weather. A strong wind on the big lakes—Basswood, Crooked, and Lac la Croix—may delay you. As the trip is described, you put in at Mudro and take out at Moose River North, but the route can be reversed. One advantage would be that by the time you reach the 340-rod portage around Basswood Falls, you'll have eaten much of the food that you're carrying and your load will be lighter.

The best place to **camp** the night before you leave is Fenske Lake Campground, just off the Echo Trail. You may want to reserve a campsite (877-444-6777; www.reserveamerica.com).

Numerous businesses in Ely provide **canoe rentals** and **complete or partial outfitting**. For a complete list, contact the Ely Chamber of Commerce (800-777-7281; www.ely.org). Considering the long portages, if you don't already have a lightweight canoe, you may want to rent one.

Your **entry point** is Mudro #23. There is also a Mudro #22; choosing this permit restricts you from camping on Horse Lake. The exit point that you list on the permit is Moose River North #16 and the ranger district is Kawishiwi. If you plan to fish, you need a Minnesota and possibly a Canadian fishing license (see "Canadian Permits and Licenses" at the beginning of this chapter). You'll need four **Fisher maps: F-9, F-10, F-17, and F-16**.

The 24-mile **shuttle route** runs south on Forest Road 457 and west on Forest Road 459 (both gravel) for 7.4 miles to the Echo Trail (County Road 116). Go right on the paved Echo Trail, which soon becomes gravel, for 15.4 miles to the turnoff for Moose River North. Turn right and go 1 mile to a large parking area. Outfitters will run this shuttle for you.

To reach the entry point from Ely, go east on Highway 169 to County Road 88, then north to the Echo Trail (County Road 116), where you turn right. Just past the Fenske Lake Campground, turn right on Forest Road 459 (gravel), which you follow to a T intersection with Forest Road 457, where you turn left. Drive past the USFS entry point to a parking area at the Chainsaw Sisters Saloon. There is no parking at the official entry point or along the road, so unless you're being dropped off, you'll need to pay the Chainsaw Sisters $2.50 per day (due in advance) to leave your vehicle in their lot. A small store also sells cold pop, beer, snacks, and T-shirts; a rusty chainsaw in front provides photo ops. They also rent canoes (www.chainsawsisters.com). Important: if you're parking here, your first day's start can't be earlier than 8 a.m., when the store opens for payment.

The famous table rock that voyageurs used for camping and canoe repair.

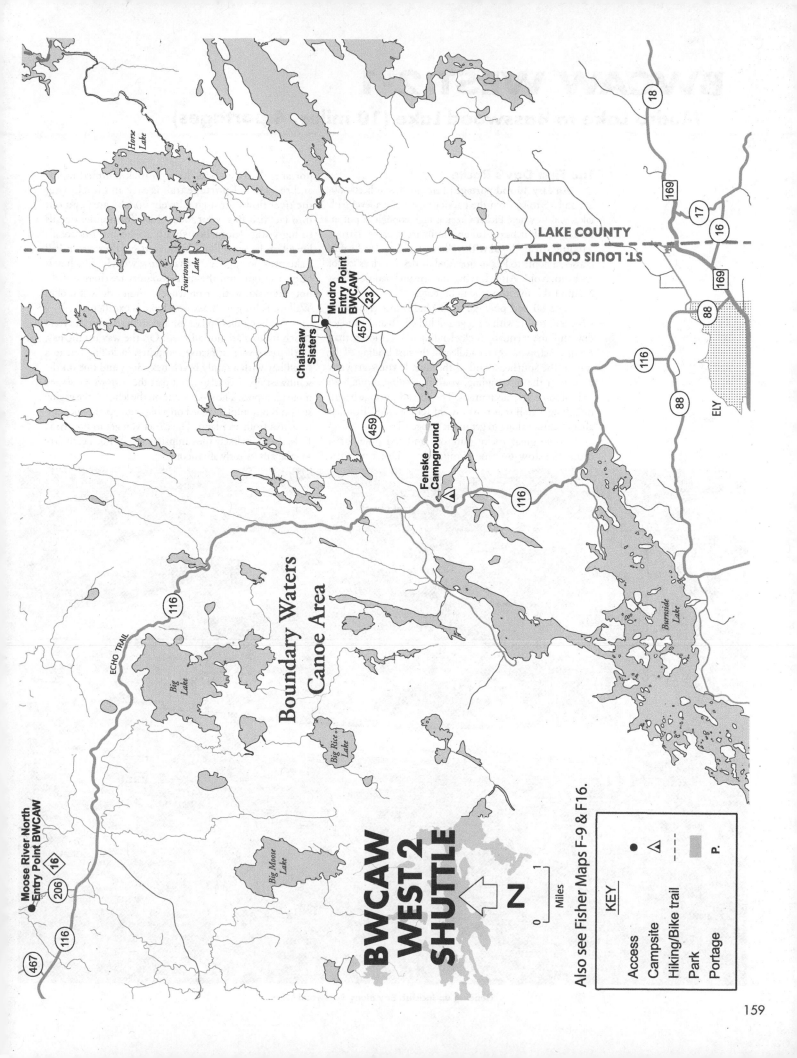

BWCAW
WEST 2
SHUTTLE

Boundary Waters
Canoe Area

Horse Lake

Fourtown Lake

LAKE COUNTY
ST. LOUIS COUNTY

Mudro Entry Point BWCAW

⬦ 23

457

Chainsaw Sisters

459

Fenske Campground

116

116

Echo Trail

116

Big Lake

Big Rice Lake

Big Moose Lake

Moose River North Entry Point BWCAW

⬦ 16

206

116

467

116

88

88

116

169

88

ELY

169

16

17

169

18

Burnside Lake

N

Miles
0   1

KEY

Access   ●

Campsite   △

Hiking/Bike trail - - -

Park   ▨

Portage   P.

Also see Fisher Maps F-9 & F16.

BWCAW WEST 2-1
Mudro Lake to Basswood Lake (10 miles, 4 portages)

The First Day's Route

An easy **30-rod portage** (there are three others—80, 20, and 15 rods) from the parking area along a level path takes you to where Picket Creek is high enough to put in. Picket Creek is beautiful and intimate, a slow, narrow, winding stream lined with yellow pond lilies and water grasses, a home to lots of frogs and turtles as well as lots of rocks to avoid. After leaving the stream, paddle across Mudro Lake, following the right shore.

The **80-rod portage** from Mudro into Sandpit is steep and rocky, with a rugged uphill climb and a longer downhill to an equally rocky landing, 63 feet lower than Mudro. Across Sandpit, paddle past the first landing all the way to the southeast end of the lake. If you start your portage at the first landing, you'll be wading through 15 rods of some very deep muck. The **20-rod portage** begins on a longer trail that runs toward Range Lake. Turn left about halfway along to get to the Range River.

Some great rocky outcrops and red pine forest flank the slow-moving Range River. Don't pass the portage; the river runs through rock-jammed rapids and the **15-rod portage** trail is easy and level. After the river flows through a lovely marshy area and out into Jackfish Bay, your focus shifts from quiet details to big vistas. Motorboats with 25-hp motors are allowed on Jackfish Bay; the boaters get there from Fall Lake over portage trails that allow wheels. The bay is huge, though, and the motorboaters are there to fish, not water-ski, so their presence does not detract much. Walleye fishing in Basswood Lake is excellent.

Paddle 6 miles up Jackfish Bay to the narrows, beyond which motors are not allowed. On the way up the bay, you'll pass several attractive campsites, including one in a small bay with a sandy beach next door and one on the southwest tip of an island, but past the narrows are several more nice spots. The second one on the left past the gaging station is beautiful, perched on a big outcrop of pink granite across from an island. The closer you get to Basswood Falls, the more likely the campsites will be filled early. Try to **take out** by early afternoon.

Heading up Jackfish Bay along Basswood Lake.

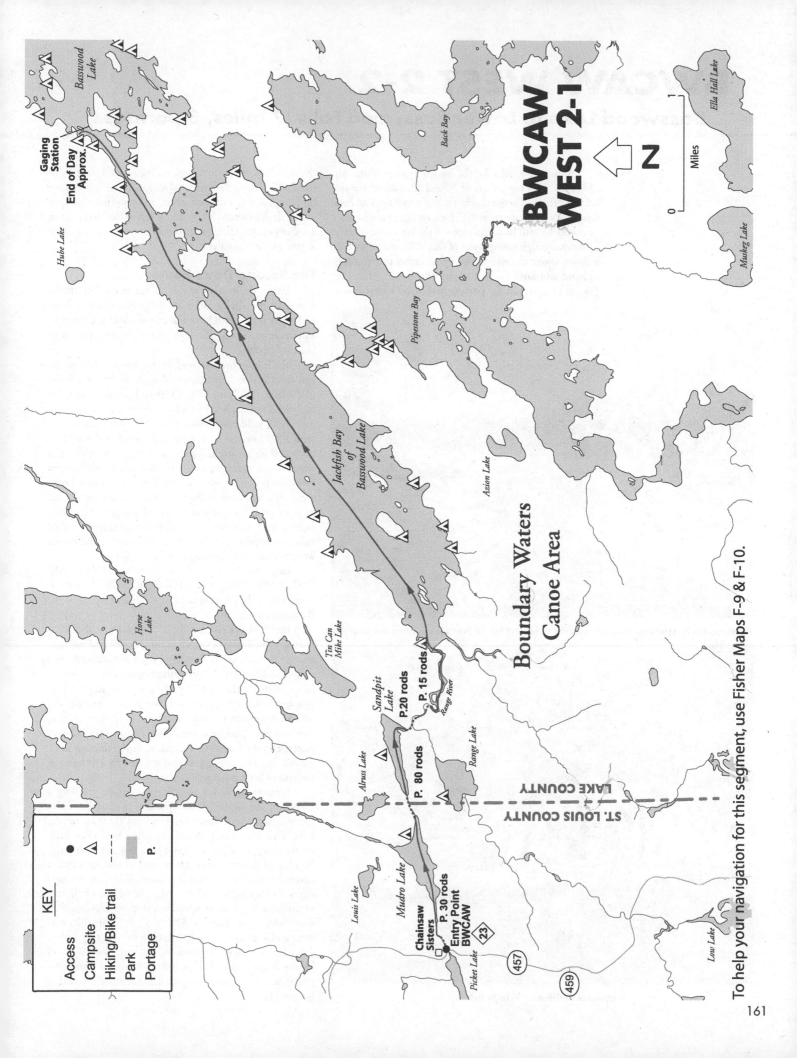

**BWCAW
WEST 2-1**

N

Miles

0   1

Boundary Waters
Canoe Area

Basswood Lake

Gaging Station

End of Day Approx.

Hula Lake

Back Bay

Pipestone Bay

Jackfish Bay of Basswood Lake

Azion Lake

Tin Can Mike Lake

Horse Lake

Ella Hall Lake

Muskeg Lake

P. 15 rods

Sandpit Lake

P. 20 rods

Range River

Alruss Lake

P. 80 rods

Range Lake

ST. LOUIS COUNTY
LAKE COUNTY

Louis Lake

Mudro Lake

Chainsaw Sisters

P. 30 rods

Entry Point BWCAW

23

457

459

Picket Lake

Low Lake

KEY

Access	●
Campsite	△
Hiking/Bike trail	––––
Park	▒
Portage	P.

To help your navigation for this segment, use Fisher Maps F-9 & F-10.

BWCAW WEST 2-2
Basswood Lake to Lower Basswood Falls (7 miles, 3 portages)

Although you'll hike the longest portage of the trip (340 rods, with two others of 30 and 32 rods) on the second day, this is also the shortest day of paddling. The Basswood Falls trail, known as the Horse Portage, has a number of overlooks with beautiful views of the Basswood River as it rushes through a long series of drops. Wheelbarrow Falls follows, where the river drops again, rather precipitously, around an island. Whether you choose the American portage or the Canadian portage, you'll have a great view of

Basswood Falls starts its descent, with the mile-long Horse Portage awaiting the paddler.

the twin falls once you're back on the water. Lower Basswood Falls, where the river tumbles spectacularly over a big drop, is probably the most scenic, and most popular, spot on the day's itinerary. It's by the mouth of the Horse River, another popular route to the border, so you won't be alone as you admire the falls.

The Second Day's Route

This is definitely a good day for an early start: the temperatures will be cooler, the bugs may still be asleep, and fewer people will be out to crowd the Horse Portage. **Put in** on Basswood Lake, leave your campsite behind, and head for the falls.

You'll hear the roar and see the horizon line of the first drop as you approach a well-worn landing to the left of the falls that leads to the **340-rod portage** trail. It's fairly level at first, lined with bunchberries, ferns, reindeer moss, and wild roses. After a long downhill grade, you cross a few low, wet spots covered by boards followed by a steep and rocky finish. Along the way are two wide areas where you can rest without blocking traffic. Unless you finish the portage in one trip, you'll have a chance to sightsee on the side trails to the river as you return for the rest of your gear. The best trail near the beginning of the portage leads to a huge flat rock outcrop below the initial falls. A campsite is visible across the water to the northwest. Several other trails also lead to campsites.

Important: DON'T BE TEMPTED TO SKIP THE LAST PART OF THE PORTAGE. Many canoeists have drowned in the fast water and rapids of the Basswood River.

Just a short paddle from the end of the Horse Portage, you'll take out again for an easy **30-rod portage** around another drop. It's a little steep at both ends, but generally level. After launching again, you'll pass two nice campsites that would make good rest stops before you reach the Wheelbarrow Portage. You can take the **50-rod American portage**, which is a little hard to spot, but best is to paddle around the island to the **32-rod portage** on the Canadian side that leads you through some balsam firs. The convergence of the two rocky chutes at the end of both portages is a lovely sight.

Before you reach Lower Basswood Falls, you'll see a nice campsite on the left on a point of land to the east of the mouth of the Horse River, one of three above the falls. This is one of those crossroads where the traffic sometimes gets heavy, so if you take this site, there may be a lot of action in your front yard. If you can't find a campsite, portage Lower Basswood Falls (see portage notes on Day 3). Several more sites lie within a half mile of the falls. Don't be tempted to camp on the Canadian shore unless you have a CANPASS (see "Canadian Permits and Licenses"). Stopping here for the night gives you plenty of time to appreciate the stunning beauty of Lower Basswood Falls, a popular subject for photographers. Walleye and smallmouth bass fishing is also said to be good here.

A group of Girl Scouts in high spirits.

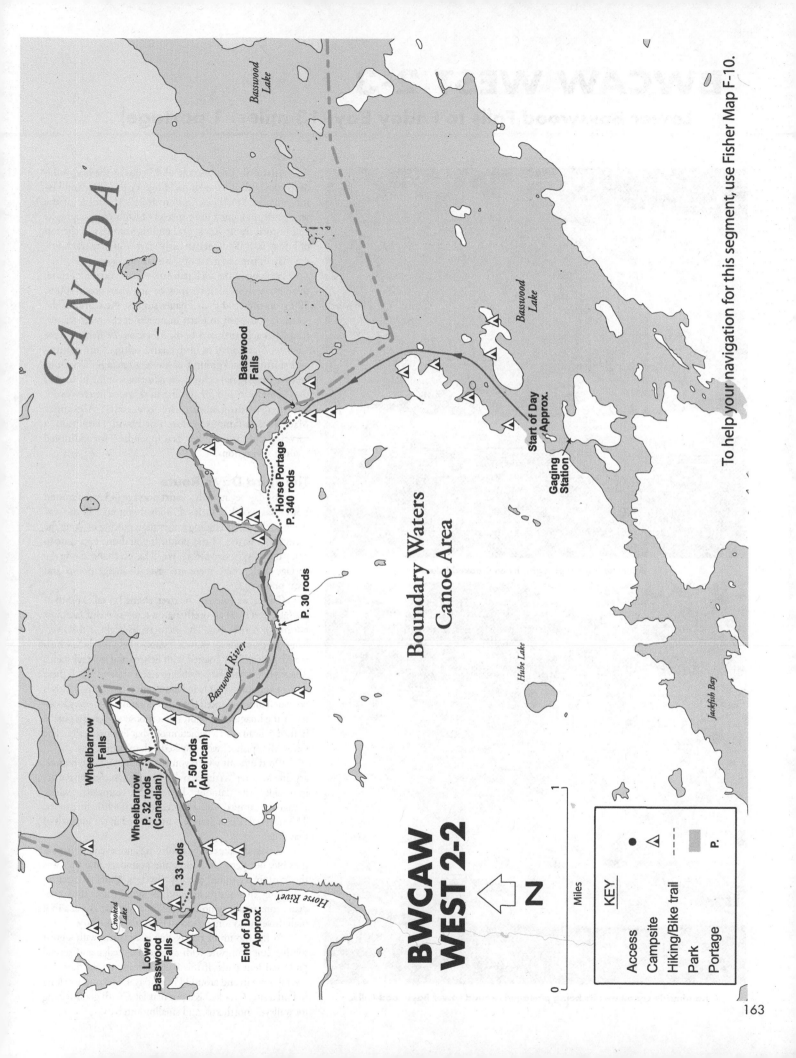

CANADA

Basswood Lake

Basswood Lake

Basswood Falls

Horse Portage
P. 340 rods

P. 30 rods

Basswood River

Start of Day
Approx.

Gaging Station

Boundary Waters
Canoe Area

Hube Lake

Jackfish Bay

Wheelbarrow Falls

Wheelbarrow
P. 32 rods (Canadian)

P. 50 rods (American)

P. 33 rods

Crooked Lake

Lower
Basswood
Falls

End of Day
Approx.

Horse River

**BWCAW
WEST 2-2**

N

Miles

1

0

KEY

- Access
- ▲ Campsite
- - - - Hiking/Bike trail
- ▨ Park
- P. Portage

To help your navigation for this segment, use Fisher Map F-10.

BWCAW WEST 2-3
Lower Basswood Falls to Friday Bay (13 miles, 1 portage)

Appreciating the pictographs on Crooked Lake.

A handmade canoe awaits being portaged around Lower Basswood Falls.

After only one portage of 43 rods at the beginning of the day, this is a day of paddling, or paddling and history, that is. You'll continue to follow the route of the voyageurs, passing a long spread of Ojibwe pictographs and historic Table Rock, and ending your day at the top of Friday Bay. If you get an early start, you may reach Friday Bay in time to get a nice island campsite.

Looking at the rock paintings takes you out of time; these mysterious pictures may be anywhere from 100 to 300 years old, and their images suggest the world of the spirit. If you want to learn more about the pictographs, read Michael Furtman's book *Magic on the Rocks: Canoe Country Pictographs* to understand some of the cultural and spiritual background of these amazingly tenacious and fascinating red ochre rock paintings. If the history of the exploration and fur trading in this area interests you, consider reading about the voyageurs; Alexander Mackenzie, a famous explorer; or David Thompson, a surveyor and cartographer. See appendix 3 for additional reading suggestions.

The Third Day's Route

The day begins with a **short portage (43 rods)** around Lower Basswood Falls. It's 43 rods if you hike all the way down to the sandy landing rather than putting in along the rocky shore at the 33-rod point. If you didn't take time to enjoy the falls the day before, you'll have a chance along the portage trail, where there are several vantage points and great photo ops.

On the west side of the river, about 1.5 miles north of the falls, you'll see an overhang on a massive cliff face, just north of a narrow bay. The pictographs begin at this overhang and continue for quite a distance along the rock, which is also spectacularly colored with lichens and mineral stains. Although it would be possible to reach out and touch these ancient and somewhat faded drawings, please don't. The oils on your hands will speed their deterioration. Just enjoy looking at the imaginative figures of a moose smoking a pipe; a horned pelican; and a depiction of what Furtman calls "The Great Missepishu," with a spiked tail, to name a few.

On the point where you turn west along the boundary line to enter Wednesday Bay, you'll pass, on the American side, the famous Table Rock campsite, where voyageurs camped and repaired their birch-bark canoes. This unusual slab of granite is mentioned in the journals of that time.

Crooked Lake can be confusing and several routes are possible, but generally follow the boundary line that was the "customary route" of early travelers. Numerous campsites along the route make good rest stops. Along the Canadian shore, you may notice small iron obelisks about a foot high driven into some rocks to mark the boundary.

At the mouth of Friday Bay is an island with a great south-facing campsite with a large rock ledge and several protected tent pads. If this site is already taken, there are several more in and around Friday Bay. Don't wait too long to find a site; Crooked is a popular lake, with good fishing for walleyes, northerns, and smallmouth bass.

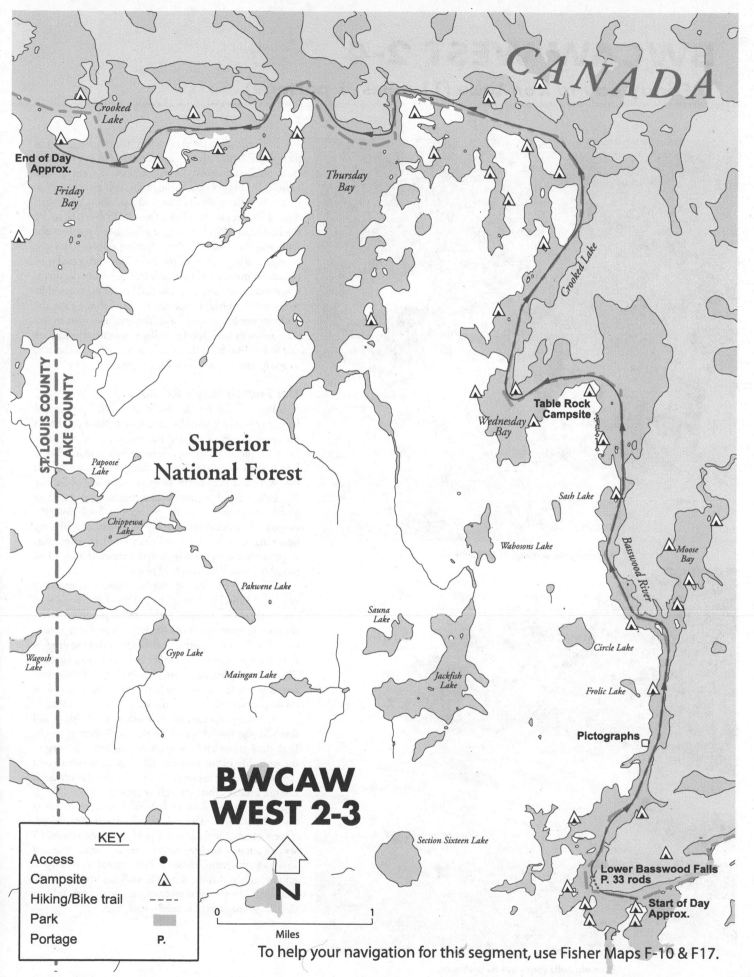

CANADA

Crooked Lake

End of Day Approx.

Friday Bay

Thursday Bay

Crooked Lake

ST. LOUIS COUNTY
LAKE COUNTY

Superior National Forest

Papoose Lake

Chippewa Lake

Pakwene Lake

Sauna Lake

Wabosons Lake

Table Rock Campsite

Wednesday Bay

Sash Lake

Moose Bay

Basswood River

Wagosh Lake

Gypo Lake

Maingan Lake

Jackfish Lake

Circle Lake

Frolic Lake

Pictographs

BWCAW WEST 2-3

N

Section Sixteen Lake

Lower Basswood Falls
P. 33 rods

Start of Day Approx.

KEY

Access	●
Campsite	▲
Hiking/Bike trail	- - -
Park	▓
Portage	P.

0   1
Miles

To help your navigation for this segment, use Fisher Maps F-10 & F17.

BWCAW WEST 2-4
Friday Bay to Iron Lake (11 miles, 1 portage)

Beginning the portage at Curtain Falls.

This easy day's travel takes you past another group of pictographs (although they are not nearly as impressive as those on the Basswood River) and around dramatic and beautiful Curtain Falls. Through this falls and the rapids that follow, the waters of Crooked Lake thunder down a drop of 29 feet into Iron Lake. From 1939 to 1965, before the Boundary Waters became a wilderness area, Curtain Falls was the home of Zup's fishing resort. After the portage, you'll paddle into Iron Lake, large and dotted with islands, some with old-growth trees growing on them. Once you set up camp, you can paddle past high rock cliffs to the northern edge of the lake to visit Rebecca Falls, the northern outflow of Iron Lake. You may also want to fish the outflow of both falls for walleyes; smallmouth bass are said to be plentiful in the lake. Rebecca Falls is in Canada, so you'll need a Canadian fishing license.

The Fourth Day's Route

From Friday Bay, head west along the international boundary line past Saturday Bay. A large island that lies in the open mouth of Sunday Bay offers a good rest stop. Look for the south-facing campsite that is marked by a large high rock outcrop. You can then paddle north around the island and head north along the west side of Sunday Bay. Follow this shore toward a peninsula that is almost an island if you want to find the pictographs. Look along the east side of the peninsula, north of the notch, for a faint red figure that may be a canoe. Michael Furtman writes that, surprisingly, these pictographs were unnoticed until 1980, probably because they are hard to see.

The roar of Curtain Falls announces its presence where the shoreline rises high, and you can see the mist from way across the lake. Although it's possible to start the portage from just above the falls, it's probably best to stay away from the current at the edge of this big drop. A slightly longer trail begins farther back, at a rocky landing. The **140-rod portage** is a smooth, gradual downhill, with several nice side trails over to look at the falls. The view of this impressive falls is worth the little bit of extra hiking.

Crossing Iron Lake to the south of Three Island will take you past two campsites on the south shore of the island; the first, which faces south, is quite nice. Crossing to the west side of the lake will take you to another good campsite, the second one down from the Bottle Portage. If that one is taken, there are eight other sites on Iron Lake. If you decide to visit Rebecca Falls, it's best to set up camp first to be sure you get a good campsite. From Three Island, it's only about 2 miles round-trip. From the west shore, it's about a 4-mile round-trip to this Canadian spot, a pleasant afternoon diversion. Rebecca Falls' tumultuous drop is split by an island as the water of Iron Lake rushes into the Namakan River. Stay away from the top of both sides of the falls, as the current is quite strong.

Curtain Falls roars out its presence.

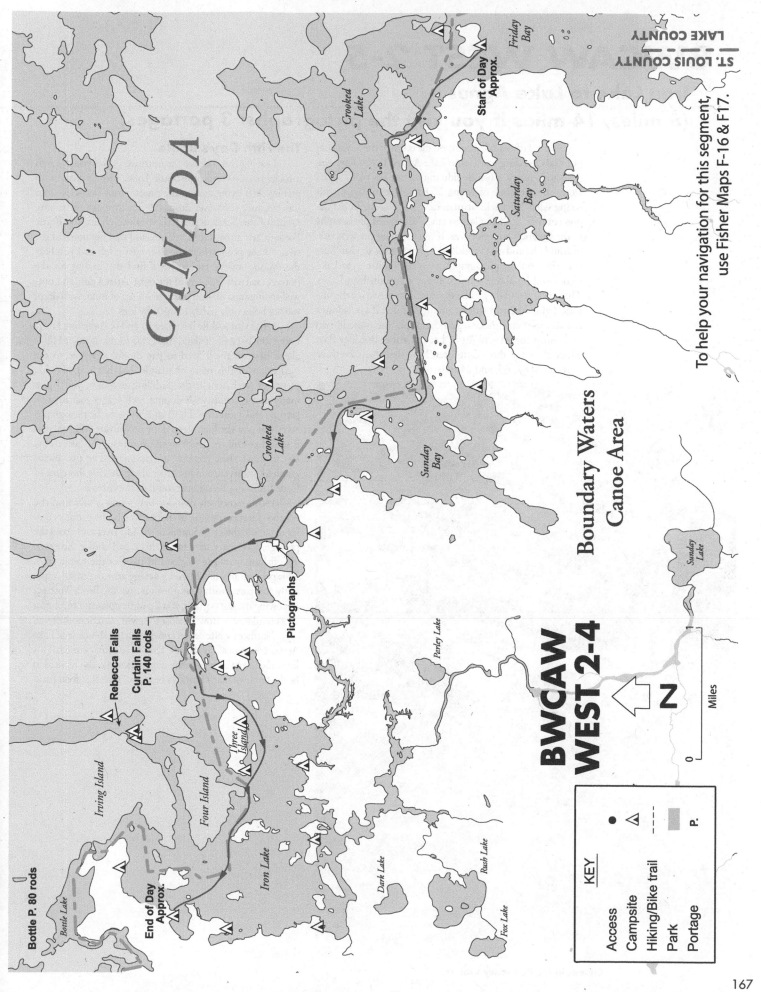

CANADA

Crooked Lake

Friday Bay

Saturday Bay

Start of Day Approx.

Sunday Bay

Crooked Lake

Pictographs

Perley Lake

Rebecca Falls

Curtain Falls
P. 140 rods

Irving Island

Three Island

Four Island

Iron Lake

Dark Lake

Rush Lake

Fox Lake

Sunday Lake

Bottle P. 80 rods

Bottle Lake

End of Day Approx.

To help your navigation for this segment,
use Fisher Maps F-16 & F17.

Boundary Waters Canoe Area

BWCAW WEST 2-4

N

Miles

0

KEY

Access	●
Campsite	△
Hiking/Bike trail	- - -
Park	▨
Portage	P.

BWCAW WEST 2-5

Iron Lake to Lake Agnes
(8 miles, 14 miles if you visit the pictographs; 3 portages)

This day's paddle begins on the route of the voyageurs but ends heading south into Lake Agnes. If you have the time and energy, a 6-mile side trip to visit the pictographs along the shoreline of Irving Island will reward you with seeing what Michael Furtman calls "the best art in the canoe country" and the largest single display of pictographs in the Quetico-Superior area. If you camp on the west side of Iron Lake and don't paddle the extra 6 miles to visit Warrior Hill and the pictographs, your day's journey to Lake Agnes will be about 8 miles. If you camp on Iron Lake's Three Island and do paddle the extra distance to see the historic sights, the trip will be about 14 miles. If you allow a rest day in your itinerary, you could split the route in two and camp the first night in Lac la Croix's Boulder Bay, where there are three campsites. Note that there are three portages of 80, 65, and 24 rods.

The Fifth Day's Route

Leaving Iron Lake to the northwest takes you through a rocky narrows and into Bottle Lake, a lovely place with granite cliffs rising among the pines. From Iron Lake into Lac la Croix the water drops 33 feet through the raging rapids of the Bottle River. To avoid this chaos, the Bottle Portage cuts across the Canadian land that lies north of the river. At the point where the river curves left and you hear the thunder of the rapids, you'll find the landing for the portage trail in a little bay to the right. After a rain, this not-well-maintained **80-rod portage** is a sea of mud, with deep, mucky holes only partly bridged by logs.

Once you paddle into the east end of sprawling Lac la Croix, the back of the land mass that forms Warrior Hill is ahead of you. You'll need to pay careful attention to the navigation in this maze of islands. Lac la Croix also has plenty of fetch, but if the paddling is rough, you'll pass many rocky islands with sloping rock ledges that invite a landing and a rest stop. The 3-mile route to the pictographs takes you past the high steep slope of Warrior Hill, where it is said that Ojibwe youth would run from the lake to the top to prove their courage and strength. The two pictograph locations are a mile farther along the east shoreline of Canada's Irving Island, just south of the narrows.

Paddle south to Boulder Bay, where you'll find the **65-rod portage** into the Boulder River. Some paddlers prefer to paddle the extra 3 miles of shallow river and avoid the portage; low water may make this a bad choice, however. The fishing is said to be good in parts of the scenic river. This portage and the **24-rod portage** are uneventful, especially compared with your previous one, the Bottle Portage. Following the last portage, you'll paddle upstream through a short bouldery narrows against the swift current of the river.

Northern white cedars growing on the shoreline of Lake Agnes are conical, as though they have been pruned. This large and lovely lake has many campsites and is also reputed to be the home of many bears, so be careful with that food pack.

Canoes in the Boundary Waters.

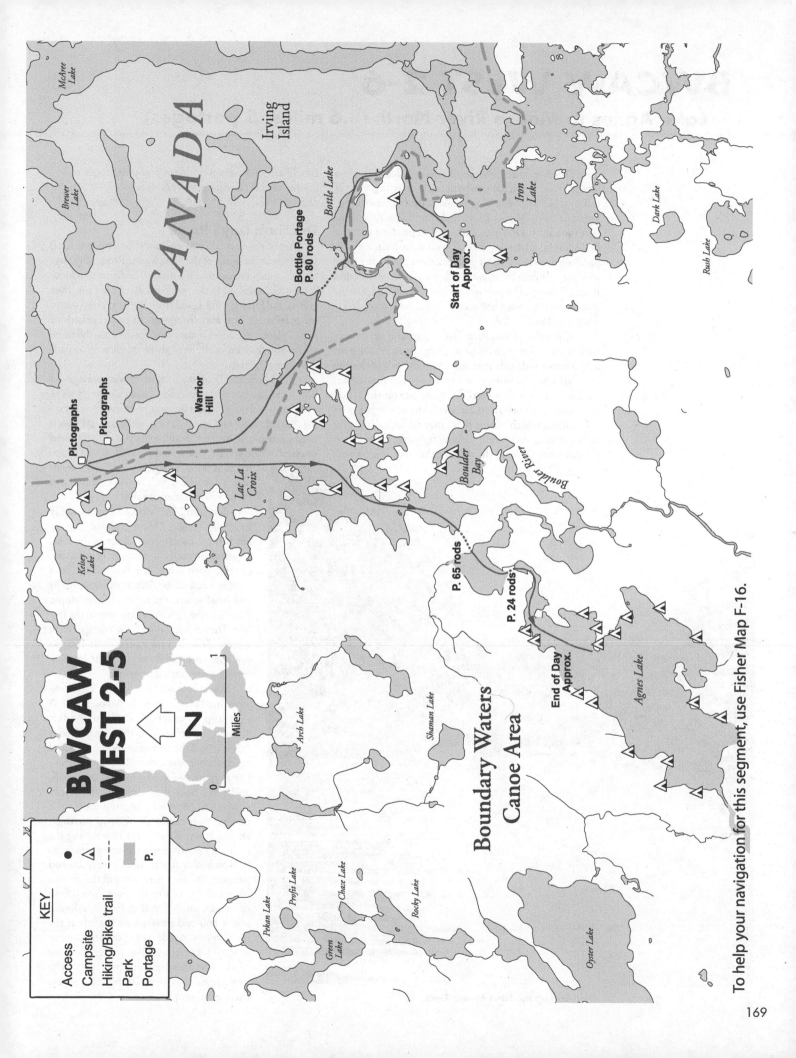

KEY

Access •
Campsite △
Hiking/Bike trail – · – · –
Park ▨
Portage P.

BWCAW
WEST 2-5

N

Miles
0 1

McAree Lake

Brewer Lake

CANADA

Irving Island

Bottle Lake

Bottle Portage
P. 80 rods

Warrior Hill

Pictographs □

Pictographs □

Pictographs □

Lac La Croix

Kelsey Lake

Start of Day
Approx.

Iron Lake

Dark Lake

Rush Lake

Boulder Bay

Boulder River

P. 65 rods

P. 24 rods

End of Day
Approx.

Agnes Lake

Boundary Waters
Canoe Area

Shaman Lake

Arch Lake

Pekan Lake

Profit Lake

Chase Lake

Rocky Lake

Green Lake

Oyster Lake

To help your navigation for this segment, use Fisher Map F-16.

169

BWCAW WEST 2-6
Lake Agnes to Moose River North (8.6 miles, 5 portages)

Traveling south now, away from the border route, you return to the protected environment of rivers for most of today's paddling; Nina Moose Lake is the only open crossing. The Nina Moose River and the Moose River flow north toward Lake Agnes, and you'll be paddling up these beautiful and interesting rivers. Unless water levels are high, paddling upstream is not a problem; these are marshy rivers with very gentle current, and portage trails take you around the rocky drops. The portages are not difficult, and, like the shorter ones, the final half mile portage trail is also not difficult, just long.

Along the Moose River, you'll pass a sheer, smooth rock face the size of an office building; you can drag your canoe into a little side trail and climb the side of this hill for a view of the otherwise low-lying area. Sometimes shallow enough that you'll bottom out on the sandy streambeds, the two rivers are also home to a large beaver population, which means there may be little dams over which to drag your canoe. Moose sightings are common on this route through the muskeg that they love so well.

People are also common; this is a popular route to the border lakes. The trip has five portages of 96, 70, 25, 20, and 160 rods.

The Sixth Day's Route

Leave the conical cedars of Agnes behind and head southwest to the outlet of the Nina Moose River. After days of open water, the contrast is a delight. Suddenly the focus is once again shifted to the gentle details of lily pads, river grasses, wild irises, turtles, and frogs. Distant trees bound the marshland. You may see moose. In the wide beds of marsh plants, a channel is not always visible, but the route is easy to follow, especially since there are often other paddlers along the river.

A 1.5-mile paddle up the river, the **96-rod portage**—a little rocky but not steep—parallels a noisy and lovely series of rapids, which you can also see most of the time you're hiking the trail, lined with bunchberries, wild roses, and several huge white pines. Another .5 mile takes you to the **70-rod portage**, where you'll spot the landing to the left of where the river flows through a steep field of boulders, a dramatic sight. The trail ends next to a pretty falls that starts the river's descent.

Just into Nina Moose Lake is a sandy beach on the right. On the peninsula that extends from the northeast shore of the lake, an attractive campsite with lots of wildflowers and lovely white cedars is marked by a large squared-off boulder at the landing. As you head south, the mouth of the Moose River is at the right-hand low spot in the tree line. The left-hand river is the Portage River, a more difficult route to the Echo Trail, so use your compass to set the right heading from the peninsula if necessary.

More beautiful vegetation, including arrowhead plants, lines the Moose River. If you stop to climb the hill on the left 1.5 miles upstream from the lake, pull your canoe out of the way of other travelers and be careful on the climb. The river is shallow in spots as it winds through the marsh, and your boat may drag on the sandy streambed. A sandy landing along the narrow river marks the **25-rod portage**, an easy carry. Note: If you're reversing the route, it's possible to miss this portage, so be watchful. After an equally easy **20-rod portage**, the river narrows, and the current increases for a short distance. You'll find the wide, sandy landing for the takeout and a **160-rod portage** on the left at the bottom of a rapid. Along the trail, moss-covered logs from a fallen tree give a sense of the size of old-growth pine trees. The portage ends at the parking area, where there are also toilets.

Heading up the Nina Moose River.

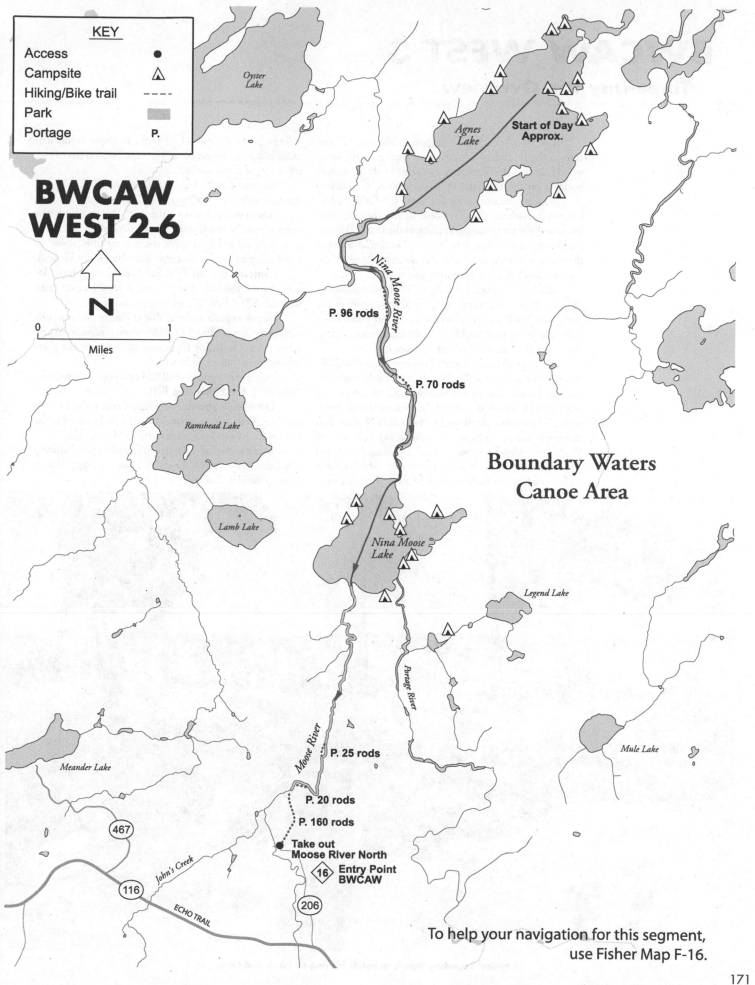

BWCAW WEST 2-6

KEY

Access ●
Campsite △
Hiking/Bike trail - - -
Park
Portage P.

N

0 _____ 1
Miles

Oyster Lake

Agnes Lake

Start of Day Approx.

Nina Moose River

P. 96 rods

P. 70 rods

Ramshead Lake

Lamb Lake

Boundary Waters Canoe Area

Nina Moose Lake

Legend Lake

Portage River

Mule Lake

Meander Lake

Moose River

P. 25 rods

P. 20 rods

P. 160 rods

● **Take out Moose River North**

◇16 **Entry Point BWCAW**

467

116

John's Creek

ECHO TRAIL

206

To help your navigation for this segment, use Fisher Map F-16.

BWCAW WEST 3
Three-Day Trip Overview

If you're a kayaker who longs to paddle your favorite craft in the Boundary Waters, you'll appreciate big Basswood Lake and the fact that you need hike only three short portages on this three-day, 37.3-mile route. In addition, these portages are among the few in the BWCAW that allow portage wheels (if you choose to add them to your load), and a truck portage is available at the Prairie Portage. Another good technique is to "leapfrog" loaded kayaks over the portage, moving one for a short distance, then walking back for another, alternating until you reach the end.

Much of Basswood lies along the international boundary, and thus you'll be traveling the historic route of the voyageurs. You'll see several scenic rapids and waterfalls—including lovely Basswood Falls—tall pines, ancient cedars, and many more ancient bedrock outcroppings.

Although this is a relatively busy part of the BWCAW, it's quite possible to paddle this trip in mid-July, traditionally the busiest time of the summer, and see only a few other groups once you're out of the motorized area. Boats with 25-hp motors are allowed on Fall Lake's Newton Bay, Basswood Lake's Pipestone Bay, Basswood Lake east of Washington Island, and Sucker Lake, Newfound Lake, and Moose Lake. In case this makes you wonder whether this is really a wilderness trip, be reassured. Unless you want complete isolation, the motorboat traffic is simply mildly irritating and not a big problem. The entire second day of this trip is out of the motorized area.

Basswood is the biggest lake in the BWCAW, and strong winds may challenge you. If you haven't kayaked much rough water, stay along the shore and use islands and inlets as windbreaks. If you're an experienced kayaker, however, your decked boat gives you the enviable ability to travel safely in weather that may leave canoes wind bound.

Camping is available at Fall Lake Campground, located by the Fall Lake Entry Point. Reserve a campsite in advance (877-444-6777; www.reserveusa.com).

Kayak rentals are available at Piragis Northwoods Company in Ely (800-223-6565; www.piragis.com) and River Point Outfitting Company (800-456-5580; www.elyoutfitters.com/packs.htm).

Your **entry point** is Fall #24 and your **exit point** is Moose#25. Use **Fisher map F-10**.

The 15-mile **shuttle route** is on County Road 182 to Fernberg Road (County Road 18), east on Fernberg to the turnoff for Moose Lake, then north to Moose Lake.

To reach the Fall Lake put-in from Ely, take Fernberg Road east to the turnoff for the Fall Lake Campground on County Road 182 north.

A typical Boundary Waters campsite fire ring on Basswood Lake.

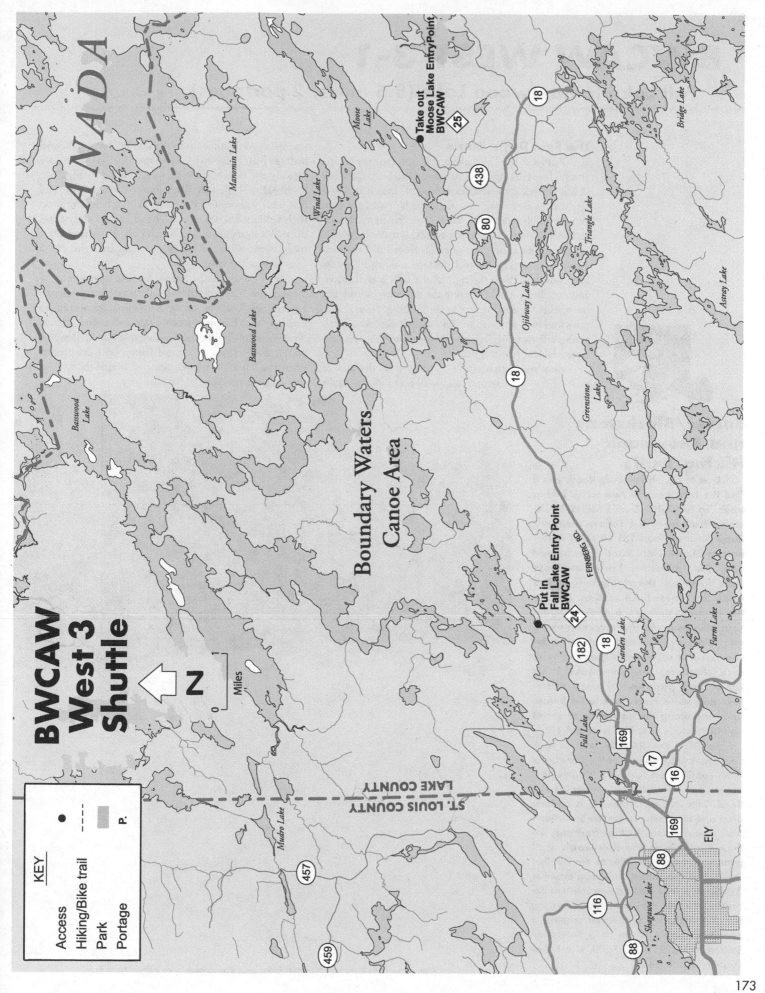

BWCAW West 3 Shuttle

KEY

- Access
- ‑ ‑ ‑ Hiking/Bike trail
- Park
- P. Portage

N

Miles
0

CANADA

Manomin Lake

Moose Lake

Wind Lake

Basswood Lake

Basswood Lake

Take out
Moose Lake EntryPoint
BWCAW
25

438

80

18

Triangle Lake

Ojibway Lake

18

Greenstone Lake

Astrey Lake

Bridge Lake

**Boundary Waters
Canoe Area**

FERNBERG RD.

Put in
Fall Lake Entry Point
BWCAW
24

182

18

Garden Lake

Fall Lake

Farm Lake

169

17

16

Mudro Lake

457

459

**ST. LOUIS COUNTY
LAKE COUNTY**

169

ELY

88

116

88

Shagawa Lake

BWCAW WEST 3-1
Fall Lake to Basswood Lake (8.5 miles, 2 portages)

The First Day's Route

Put in at the Fall Lake access, just past the campground by a parking lot. A northwest heading, to the left of Mile Island, the island across from the launch area, will take you through a narrows and toward Newton Falls. Stay away from Newton Falls; you may see fishermen in motorboats anchored above the rapids, but the current is strong and it's a long, rocky rapids from Fall Lake into Newton Lake. The **80-rod portage** trail into Newton Lake, which starts to the right of the falls, is level, wide, and easy, but you'll be sharing the trail with motorboats on wheels, so don't linger at the landing. Several side trails lead over to the scenic falls and rapids; take a break from your carrying, leave your kayak on the side, and have a look at Newton Falls.

Another dramatic falls awaits you at the end of Newton Lake; you'll hear Pipestone Falls roaring as you paddle up to the landing for the **90-rod portage** into Basswood Lake's Pipestone Bay. There are actually two possible landing spots, fairly close together, to the right of the falls. They join to form a single trail that takes you around Pipestone Falls, a beautiful drop with wild rapids. Like the Newton Falls portage trail, the trail is more like a road than a trail. A side trail and a rocky overlook to the left of the main trail give you a great view of the falls.

Start looking for a campsite for your **takeout** early in the afternoon. At the north end of Pipestone Bay, you'll pass a particularly lovely site on the east shore at the opening to a narrows with big pines, lots of space, and a good landing. If you want to leave the motorboat traffic behind, however, paddle 2 miles farther toward Basswood Lake proper, where you'll find several sites clustered around the narrows that leads into the lake.

Secret/Blackstone and Snowbank Hiking Trails

East of Ely, off Fernberg Road, you'll find the trailheads of two scenic hiking trails. To reach the 5-mile Secret/Blackstone Trail from Ely, follow Fernberg Road (County Road 18) 20 miles northeast to Moose Lake Road (Forest Road 438). The trailhead is 3 miles up Moose Lake Road on the right, before you reach the Moose Lake landing. Park at the landing; then it's a two- to three-hour hike on moderate terrain along the west sides of Blackstone Lake and Secret Lake to a rock cliff (popular with rock climbers) that overlooks Ennis Lake. You'll pass several small waterfalls and some lovely overlooks before returning along the east sides of Secret and Blackstone. Use Fisher map F-10.

To hike the 24-mile loop around Snowbank Lake known as the Snowbank Trail, continue on Fernberg 2 miles past Moose Lake Road to Snowbank Lake Road. Turn left; it's 2 miles to a parking area and the trailhead for the Snowbank Trail. Two miles south of the trailhead, the Snowbank joins the Kekekabic Trail (which runs east 40 miles to the Gunflint Trail). The combined trails run east for 3 miles to a spur trail leading south to Becoosin Lake. At this point, you enter the BWCAW; camping on the trail requires a permit, available at the USFS Kawishiwi Station in Ely, 218-365-7600. Use Fisher maps F-10 and F-11.

Pipestone Falls between Newton Lake and Basswood Lake's Pipestone Bay.

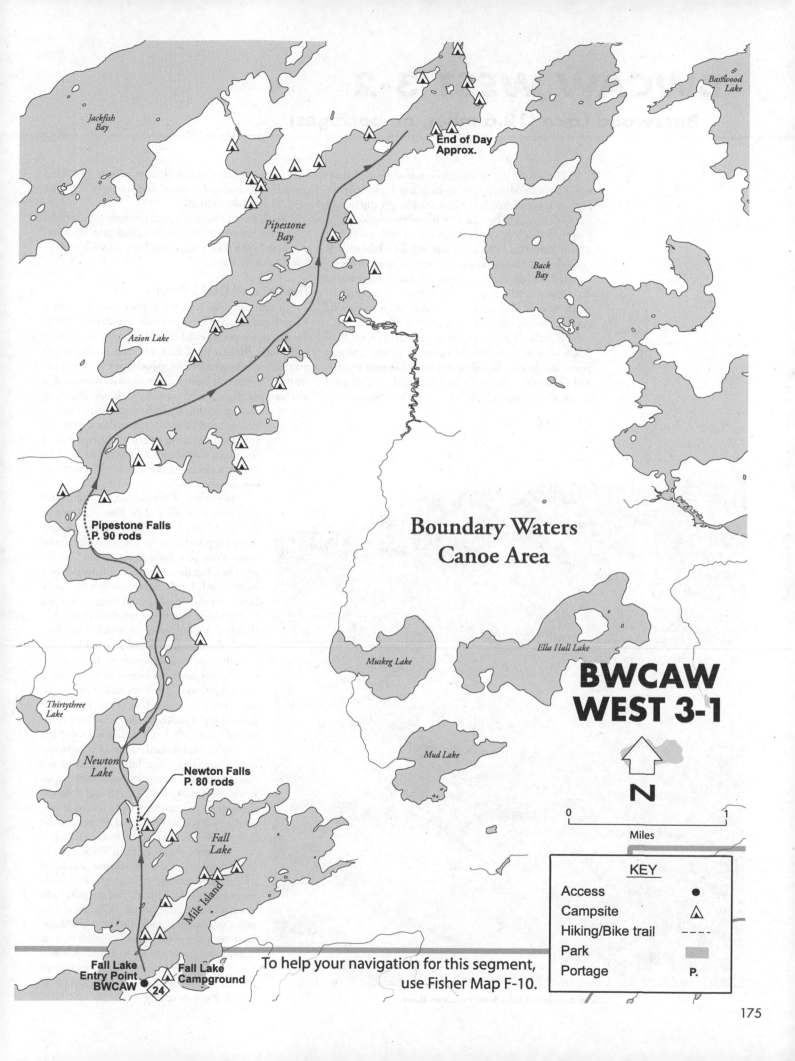

Jackfish Bay

Pipestone Bay

Azion Lake

End of Day Approx.

Basswood Lake

Back Bay

Boundary Waters Canoe Area

Pipestone Falls P. 90 rods

Ella Hall Lake

BWCAW WEST 3-1

Muskeg Lake

Thirtythree Lake

N

Mud Lake

0   1
Miles

Newton Lake

Newton Falls P. 80 rods

Fall Lake

Mile Island

Fall Lake Entry Point BWCAW

⬦24

Fall Lake Campground

To help your navigation for this segment, use Fisher Map F-10.

KEY	
Access	●
Campsite	△
Hiking/Bike trail	– – –
Park	�largeblock
Portage	P.

BWCAW WEST 3-2
Basswood Lake (12.6 miles, no portages)

The second day of this trip is marvelous—all Basswood Lake, all day. You won't meet any motorboats or portage any gear. Paddlers who want a longer trip should consider spending two days on Basswood, exploring its shores from a base camp. If you depart early enough, a stop at Basswood Falls in the morning for a hike (minus gear) along the scenic falls still leaves time to reach Washington Island by early afternoon. If you want a shorter day, skip the falls and just enjoy the cruise along the south shore of Basswood. Several nice campsites provide good rest stops; one even has a sandy beach.

Wind is always an important consideration on Basswood: with miles of fetch on Basswood in which to gain power and speed, a northeast wind will slow your progress and add to the risks on this leg of the trip, another good reason for starting early. Wind from the northwest can be dicey on the first leg also as it blows from your side. Wind generally rises in the afternoon, so if you wake to a brisk wind, be especially cautious.

You'll want to stake out your campsite for the night by early afternoon. If you paddle farther than Washington Island, you'll be competing for sites with motorboaters as well.

The Second Day's Route

If time and weather permit, **start** your day with a 4.5-mile paddle up to Basswood Falls. Leave your kayak at the start of the **portage** and hike at least part of the mile-long Horse Portage. You'll find side trails leading to the river that offer beautiful views, especially in the first quarter mile. When you launch again to cross Basswood, a southeast heading will keep you close to the few islands on the 2-mile crossing back to the south shore of Basswood. A campsite that makes a great rest stop is on the north end of a long oval bay on the south shore, with a view across the lake from a rocky promontory decorated with old weathered cedars.

Regardless of the weather, it's best to stay close to shore as you paddle down Basswood to the tip of United States Point. A ridge of land along the point, densely forested with red and white pines, rises dramatically as you near the tip. On a hot day, if you're in the mood for a swim, watch for the campsite with the sandy beach. At the tip of United States Point is a C-shaped bay that forms two little points. On the tip of each little point a low rocky area where bleached cedars grow would be good for a rest stop; there are no campsites there, however.

Farther down the eastern shore of United States Point, you'll pass some rocks that are a favorite perch for gulls. They're easy to see; gull guano has painted them white. Stay away from the gulls; especially during nesting times they can be quite unfriendly, and you won't want to disturb their nesting. Other little islands along this shore, uninhabited by noisy birds, invite exploration. Nestled into the inlets and bays along this shore are several campsites that may tempt you, especially if you want to avoid the noise of the motor traffic allowed past Washington Island.

However, if you can reach Washington Island for an early afternoon **takeout**, you'll find a big, beautiful site on the second rocky point of the eastern tip of the island. This campsite looks inaccessible at first; you must paddle around the point to a sandy landing on the south shore. From the point you'll have an excellent view up Basswood and east to Ottawa Island. A sign at the point informs travelers that no motors are allowed beyond this point. If this site is taken, several others are nearby.

View of Basswood Lake from the south shore.

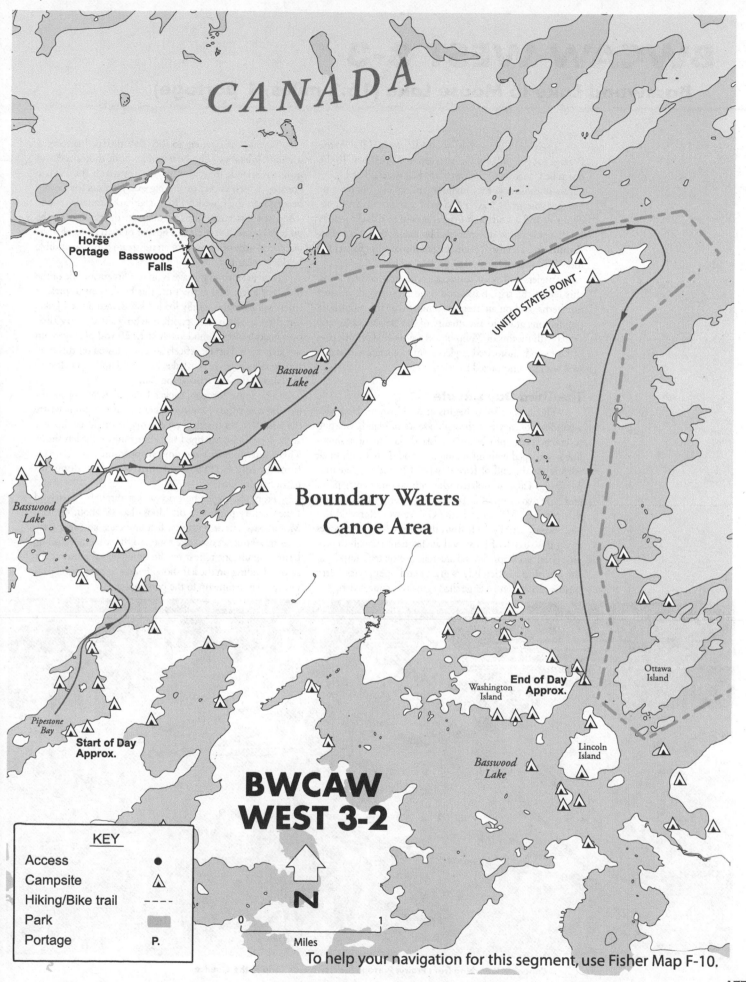

CANADA

Horse
Portage

Basswood
Falls

UNITED STATES POINT

Basswood
Lake

Basswood
Lake

Boundary Waters
Canoe Area

Ottawa
Island

Washington
Island

End of Day
Approx.

Lincoln
Island

Basswood
Lake

Pipestone
Bay

Start of Day
Approx.

BWCAW
WEST 3-2

N

KEY

Access   ●

Campsite   ⛺

Hiking/Bike trail   - - - -

Park

Portage   P.

0   1

Miles

To help your navigation for this segment, use Fisher Map F-10.

BWCAW WEST 3-3
Basswood Lake to Moose Lake (16.2 miles, 1 portage)

The paddle down Basswood Lake toward the Prairie Portage roughly follows the international boundary. To the north lie Canada and the vast Canadian waters. The big expanses of those bays may invite you to explore, but remember that you need a CANPASS to hike and camp on Canadian soil and a Canadian fishing license to fish the waters on that side of the international boundary. See "Canadian Permits and Licenses" at the beginning of this chapter for more information.

Anglers will want to spend some time fishing along this leg of the trip. Basswood is noted for walleyes and northerns, and on an average summer day, the motorboat populations attest to the quality of the Basswood fishery. Boats with motors of 25 hp or less are allowed on this part of Basswood; motorized anglers seem to coexist reasonably well with nonmotorized travelers.

The Third Day's Route

The day's traveling **begins** at Washington Island with a winding journey east through a series of islands. Starting several miles east of Washington Island, the American shoreline is scalloped with intriguing bays and dotted with small islands. At the end of Rice Bay is a 120-rod portage into Manomin Lake, an isolated lake with no other entry point and only two campsites. (Portage wheels are not allowed on this portage.) Manomin is the Ojibwe word for wild rice and means, literally, "gift from the creator." The campsites along this stretch of Basswood are frequent enough to provide good rest stops. Several are quite pretty; the campsite at the opening to Rice Bay is grassy and open, with berry bushes, daisies, and a large shady grove of white cedars.

Beyond the opening to Rice Bay, the lake narrows as it enters Inlet Bay. The boat traffic, both motorized and nonmotorized, increases as you approach the Prairie Portage, which is one of the big entry points for canoes headed into the Quetico Provincial Park, Canada's canoe wilderness. As you reach the takeout, the reason for the portage becomes very clear. The roar of twin flows of rushing water—the outflow from an upstream dam—is audible before you land.

The motorized portage is on the American side of the flow. For a fee, $10 at the time this book went to press, a truck will transport a fully loaded kayak into Sucker Lake. On the Canadian side, paddlers who want to carry their own boats traverse a moderately steep **20-rod portage** with wooden steps. Portage wheels are also allowed on this trail. As you launch on Sucker Lake, be careful not to get close to the current flowing toward the dam.

The route through Sucker Lake takes you by an eagle's nest, if winds have not taken it. At the point where the lake narrows (marked on the map), you'll see the nest at the top of a big snapped-off white pine on the left shore. This white pine isn't the only snapped-off tree. Damage from the July 4, 1999, windstorm is evident along this part of your journey.

From the eagle's nest on Sucker through Newfound Lake to entry point #25 on Moose Lake is about 4 miles. Motorboats carrying canoes, fishing boats, and many canoes travel the Moose Lake route, so the wilderness feeling beats a significant retreat by the time you **take out** at the second landing on the left shore. Follow a short gravel path under a white pine up to the parking lot.

Canoeists launching from Prairie Portage for a two-week trip in the Quetico.

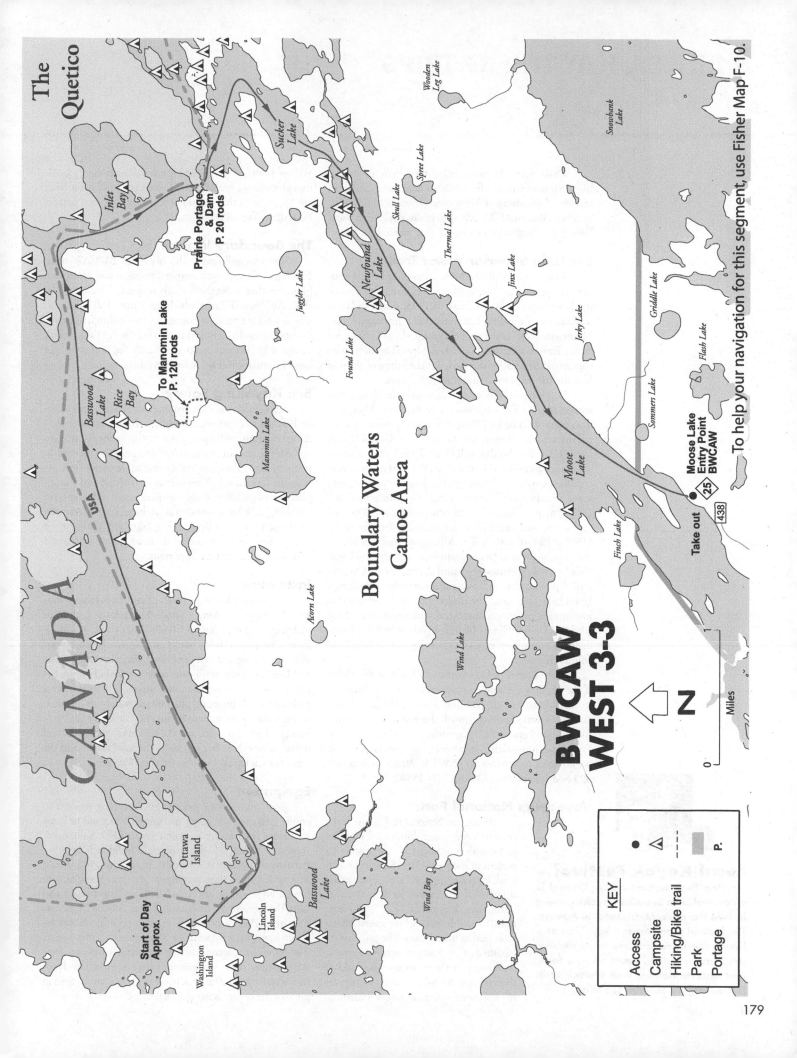

The Quetico

Inlet Bay

Prairie Portage & Dam
P. 20 rods

Sucker Lake

Wooden Leg Lake

Snowbank Lake

Spree Lake

Skull Lake

Thermal Lake

Jaggler Lake

Newfound Lake

Jinx Lake

Griddle Lake

To Manomin Lake
P. 120 rods

Found Lake

Jerky Lake

Flash Lake

Basswood Lake

Rice Bay

Manomin Lake

Sommers Lake

CANADA

USA

Boundary Waters
Canoe Area

Moose Lake

Moose Lake Entry Point BWCAW

25

438

Take out

Acorn Lake

Finch Lake

Wind Lake

Start of Day Approx.

Ottawa Island

Lincoln Island

Basswood Lake

Wind Bay

Washington Island

BWCAW WEST 3-3

N

Miles

0   1

To help your navigation for this segment, use Fisher Map F-10.

KEY

●	Access
△	Campsite
- - -	Hiking/Bike trail
�	Park
P.	Portage

III. SEA KAYAKING TRIPS

While many kayakers enjoy their craft in smaller lakes, Minnesotans are fortunate to have the exciting sea kayaking destinations of Voyageurs National Park and Lake Superior. Also, two BWCAW trips in this guide, East 3 and West 3, are designed for sea kayakers as well as canoeists.

The Lake Superior Water Trail

A group of paddlers who love kayaking on Lake Superior's spectacular North Shore conceived the idea of the Lake Superior Water Trail; in 1993, state legislation made the trail a reality. The water trail is managed by the Minnesota DNR and a support group, the Lake Superior Water Trail Association (LSWTA), formed by those who conceived the idea for the trail, but the future of the trail is in the hands of the Minnesota Legislature.

As this guidebook was going to press in 2004, a new section of the LSWT opened, extending from Duluth to Two Harbors. The DNR predicts that the fourth and final informational map, for the area from Grand Marais to the Canadian border, will be available by the summer of 2005, extending the trail to its full 150 miles. There are also plans to add more public landing points along some already established stretches. Three informational LSWT maps, which show existing public access points, rest areas, and campsites, are available free from the DNR (888-646-6367). The Minnesota trail will link to the Wisconsin trail (www.inlandsea.org), the Michigan trail (www.keweenaw.org), and eventually an Ontario trail, a process that will result in a route that circumnavigates Lake Superior. The philosophy of this trail is that low-impact recreation combined with protection of the lake and its shoreline will link kayakers and local residents in a common goal of preserving both natural and cultural resources.

The Minnesota Legislature will listen to this vision if the trail has a strong constituency: municipalities; resorts; and most of all, paddlers who use the trail. If you also love kayaking on the north shore and want the trail to thrive and grow, please consider joining the LSWTA. For more information or to join the association, visit www.lswta.org or write to LSWTA, Waters of Superior, 395 South Lake Ave., Duluth MN 55802.

Voyageurs National Park

Voyageurs National Park is one of the country's few water-dominated national parks, with four huge lakes comprising 40 percent of the park's 218,054 acres and 26 small lakes adding to the water mass. In the middle of this water park is the Kabetogama Peninsula, a 75,000-acre roadless wilderness where several hiking trails lead to inland lakes. The park was established in 1975, in part to commemorate the history of the voyageurs who paddled these lakes in birch-bark canoes and in part to preserve a spectacular tract of wilderness.

Walleye fishing is one of the big attractions in the park. Although there is a fair amount of motorboat traffic, the lakes are big enough that the noise and fumes do not detract from the wilderness experience.

The Boundary Waters

Kayakers will find in this book two BWCAW trips, East 3 and West 3, with minimal portages and maximum big water that make them nicely suited to kayaking. The BWCAW West 3-1 trip, which starts from Fall Lake, also allows wheels on all the portages. One outfitter, Superior Coastal Sports in Grand Marais, rents the PakYak, a kayak designed by Vetter Kayaks specifically for portaging; get more information at www.vetterkayaks.com.

Sea Kayaking Safety

Sea kayaking is a challenging, often dangerous activity best left to experienced paddlers. To learn proper paddling techniques for open water as well as the hazards involved, you should attend classes and immerse yourself in instructional videotapes and books; some useful ones are listed in appendix 3. With proper instruction and the application of paddling skills, experience, and judgment, sea kayaking can be a wonderful and exciting adventure. Without these, paddlers on big lakes are risking their lives. A few points, however, do need to be emphasized because they are so very important.

Instruction

If you don't know the basics of safe sea kayaking, start your learning by taking a good class, joining a club, or paddling with experienced friends. Later you can add information gained from books and videos. Practice your skills, including wet exits and deep water entries, on safe and familiar waters until your skills are second nature before venturing out on lakes like Superior. If you've never paddled on this huge and often treacherous body of water, taking a class from someone who knows the lake well may be a good place to start. For the names of companies and organizations that offer regularly scheduled classes and the names of sea kayaking clubs, see appendix 4.

Equipment

Your number-one priority for equipping yourself to ensure a safe sea kayaking experience is a wet suit or a dry suit and a snug-fitting but comfortable PFD. Your kayak should be equipped with watertight bulkheads or other flotation that makes it seaworthy. In addition, you should fit it with a spray skirt, a compass (that you know how to use), a bilge pump, and a paddle float. You should also carry the appropriate navigational map, either a McKenzie map or a USGS topographic map, or both. Each trip description provides information about the exact map to use. The route maps accompanying the trip descriptions show the paddling route and general locations of various landmarks and other useful sites, but they should not be used in place of the others as navigational maps.

Local Kayak Festival

The Two Harbors Kayak Festival is an annual Lake Superior kayaking event in Two Harbors, Minnesota, in August. The festival promotes sea kayaking as a family sport and features races, demonstrations, seminars, youth classes, food, and entertainment; visit www.kayak festival.org for more information.

Weather

Always check the local marine forecast before launching. Buying a marine radio is an investment in your survival and your peace of mind. Sea kayaking is an inherently dangerous sport, especially on Lake Superior, known for its capricious and violent weather changes. The weather can quickly turn from sunny and warm to gale-force winds and 10-foot waves—no time to be out on the lake in a kayak. Anytime paddling conditions look too difficult for your abilities, your judgment should tell you to stay onshore.

A common reason that kayakers and boaters in other small craft run into trouble on the Great Lakes is that they don't check or heed the local marine forecast. This is especially important when making a crossing, like the Susie Islands trip, or when traveling a stretch of shoreline where landings may be difficult or impossible; check your map carefully so that you always know what the shoreline is like ahead of and behind you and where the next access is. Tell someone onshore where you plan to paddle and when you expect to return.

The lakes of Voyageurs National Park also have lots of fetch (open water over which wind builds waves) on some of their wide-open expanses. High winds can kick up big waves in a hurry on these big lakes, putting kayakers at risk.

Cold

If you need to be convinced that Lake Superior's cold can kill, just go for a swim in the lake without a wet suit. Even with a wet suit or a dry suit, the amount of time a paddler can survive in the cold water (often around 50 degrees) is short. Considering that capsizing offshore could mean significant time spent in icy water, during which time your body heat is steadily draining away, the absolute necessity of knowing deep-water self-rescue and assisted-rescue techniques is clear. The less time you spend in the water, the less chance you have of hypothermia. The lakes of Voyageurs National Park are not as cold or as large as Superior, but immersion in any northern lake needs to be limited. If you do not wear a wet suit on the lakes of Voyageurs, carry a change of clothes in a dry bag.

Don't Paddle Alone

If you do capsize, being with a partner or a group is better than being alone in case of difficulties during the rescue. Know how to rescue yourself and others. When paddling with others, stay together at all times.

The beach at Fall River is a great picnic spot.

LAKE SUPERIOR WATER TRAIL 1
Gooseberry River to Little Two Harbors (6 miles)

From the water, this part of Lake Superior's north shore has some wonderfully dramatic scenery: rugged headland cliffs stained orange and gray-green with lichens rise high above the lake, and cobble beaches curve along the shore. Split Rock Lighthouse is impressive from land but truly awesome from the lake. To see this famous lighthouse and look for the wreck of the *Madeira* at Gold Rock Point, you can paddle a mile past the Little Two Harbors takeout and then back again.

Part of the Lake Superior Water Trail (LSWT), this is a route for sea kayakers experienced in paddling the open waters of Lake Superior. Five rest areas along the route provide emergency exit points, but kayakers on this temperamental lake must be prepared for sudden squalls at any time. Always check the local marine forecast before launching and avoid paddling when a northeast wind is blowing. This trip begins at Gooseberry Falls State Park, but you can paddle the trip in either direction. Use LSWT Map 2, free from the DNR, for information. **Use McKenzie map 105 for Gooseberry-Split Rock or USGS 1:100 K topographic map for Two Harbors** for navigation.

Camp by car at Gooseberry Falls State Park, 218-834-3855, or at Split Rock Lighthouse State Park, 218-226-6377. Both parks are extremely popular in the summer; reservations are strongly recommended (866-857-2757; www.stayatmnparks.com). Kayak campsites can also be reserved for a fee through the reservations system: one at Crazy Bay and one at Split Rock Creek. Additional kayak campsites are free on a first-come, first-served basis: one at the mouth of the Gooseberry River, four at Thompson Beach, and one at Crazy Bay.

Kayak rentals can be arranged at Superior Coastal Sports (800-720-2809; www.superiorcoastal.com) or Bear Track Outfitting (800-795-8068; www.bear-track.com), both in Grand Marais; or at the Ski Hut (218-724-8525), in Duluth. The Ski Hut requires written proof of a kayak safety course.

The 6-mile **shuttle route** from Gooseberry to Little Two Harbors is north on Highway 61. At Split Rock Lighthouse State Park, follow the sign for the Pebble Beach picnic area to the parking lot. Superior Shuttle, a **shuttle service** for the Superior Hiking Trail (218-834-5511; www.superiorshuttle.com), stops at both state parks. If you use the service, take out at Split Rock River instead of Little Two Harbors. The segment of the Gitchi-Gami State Bicycle Trail between Gooseberry and Split Rock Lighthouse State Parks is partially complete but not practical for a bike shuttle yet. More information is available at www.ggta.org/index.php.

A vehicle permit is required to enter the park. If you'll be parking overnight, tell the rangers, who will show you where to park. For a day trip, use the parking lot by Gooseberry's Lakeview Shelter. Carry down the stairs from the parking lot and **put in** next to the kayak campsite on the Gooseberry River. If the mouth of the river is blocked by logs, carry over the gravel bar. It's only 1.4 miles to Thompson Beach; after you round a point, the good landing is on a gravel beach.

From Thompson Beach, it's less than a mile to the Twin Points access, where a concrete boat ramp, a dock, and a picnic area adjoin the Iona's Beach State Natural Area's beautiful pebble beach. Past the two points, the curve of the shore leading to Split Rock Cabins is lined with high rhyolite cliffs that slope down to this private resort. Avoid the rocks where gulls perch; they're surrounded by barely submerged rocks, and gulls can be aggressive.

Around the point from the resort, at the mouth of the Split Rock River, is the Split Rock River access and picnic area, where the Superior shuttle stops. Down the shore loom the Split Rock Point cliffs. These massive sheer dark cliffs are stained orange with lichens, and gnarled white cedars grow from the rock face. Past the cliffs, where the shoreline dips back into Crazy Bay, you'll find two kayak campsites (one shared with backpackers) and see the tilted headland of Corundum Point. Follow the shoreline cliffs around Corundum Point to the next kayak campsite, located at the mouth of Split Rock Creek.

To reach the Split Rock State Park's Little Two Harbors access, paddle around the outside of the small island—connected to shore by a chain of rocks—to the pebble beach. A 100-yard trail leads to the parking lot. For some great views of the lighthouse, continue another mile past the lighthouse headland to the lichen-stained red cliffs of Gold Rock Point and another picnic area. If the water is calm, you may be able to see pieces of the wreck of the Madeira (the 1905 shipwreck that prompted the construction of the light) in the 10- to 20-foot-deep water around the point. Paddle back to the beach at Little Two Harbors for the **takeout**.

A kayaker approaches Split Rock Lighthouse on a foggy morning.

To help your navigation for this segment, use USGS 1:100,000 Topographic Map for Two Harbors.

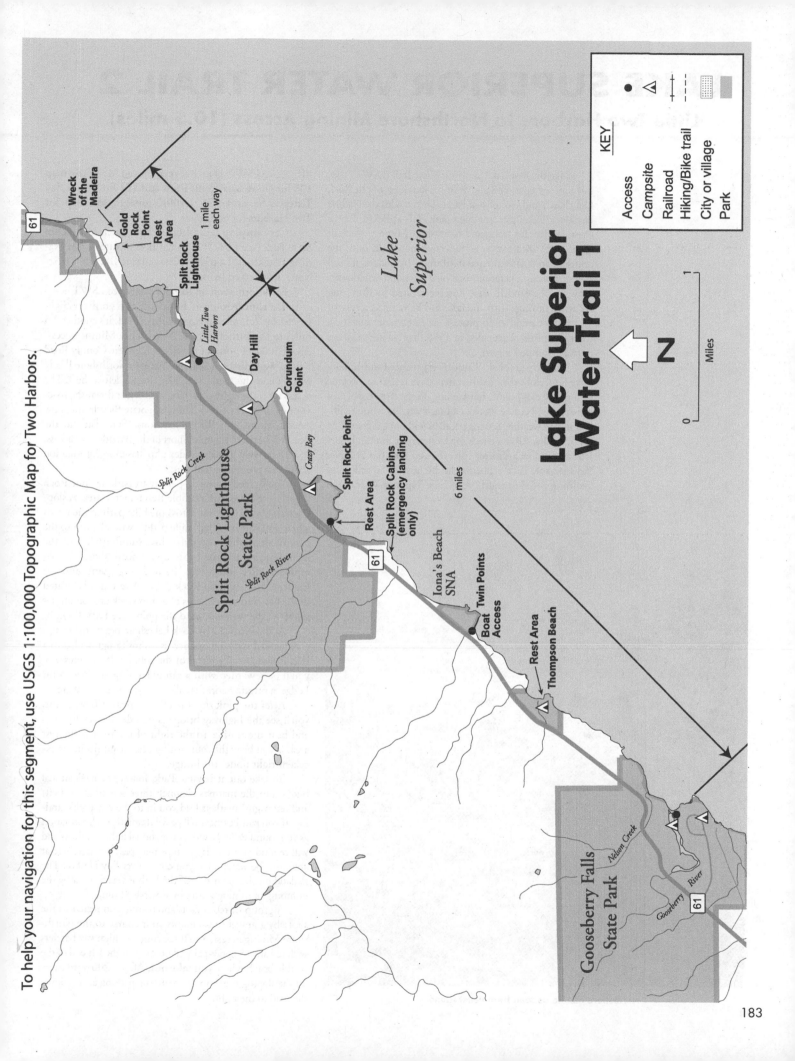

Lake Superior Water Trail 1

N

Miles
0   1

KEY

- ● Access
- △ Campsite
- ┼ Railroad
- ┆ Hiking/Bike trail
- ▦ City or village
- ▨ Park

Lake Superior

Wreck of the Madeira

61

Gold Rock Point

Rest Area

Split Rock Lighthouse

1 mile each way

Little Two Harbors

Day Hill

Corundum Point

Crazy Bay

Split Rock Creek

Split Rock Point

Rest Area

Split Rock Cabins (emergency landing only)

Split Rock Lighthouse State Park

Split Rock River

61

Iona's Beach SNA

6 miles

Twin Points Access

Boat

Rest Area

Thompson Beach

Gooseberry Falls State Park

Nelson Creek

Gooseberry River

61

LAKE SUPERIOR WATER TRAIL 2
Little Two Harbors to Northshore Mining Access (10.5 miles)

Like the first Lake Superior Water Trail (LSWT) trip, this journey takes you and your sea kayak past Split Rock Lighthouse and Gold Rock Point. Then it adds the Nadine Blacklock Lakeshore; the high pink cliffs at Beaver Bay; a chance to fish for trout; and Northshore Mining, which in its previous incarnation as Reserve Mining was once the center of an environmental maelstrom. Nowadays, it's still a busy mining operation, but pine trees and wildflowers grow on the landfill that Reserve created by dumping taconite tailings into the lake for 25 years at a rate of 47 tons per minute. To protect the lake's water quality, a federal appeals court ruled in 1980 that taconite tailings must be dumped inland.

This trip is for sea kayakers experienced in paddling Lake Superior's dangerous waters. Five rest areas provide emergency exit points, but landing on the large cobbles of the exposed Nadine Blacklock beach would be quite difficult in bad weather, leaving paddlers without a safe landing for 3.5 miles. Always check the local marine forecast before launching. For a shorter trip, you can take out at Silver Bay's Bayside Park, reducing the distance to 7.6 miles and avoiding the ship traffic. Use Lake Superior Water Trail Map 2 (see LSWT 1) for information and **McKenzie map 105 for Gooseberry Split Rock and 104 for Beaver Bay Tettegouche or USGS 1:100K topographic map for Two Harbors** for navigation.

Car **camping** is available at Split Rock Lighthouse State Park (see LSWT 1). A kayak campsite on the Nadine Blacklock Lakeshore is available free on a first-come, first-served basis.

For information on **kayak rentals**, see LSWT 1.

The **shuttle route** to the first access is north on Highway 61 for 7.5 miles to Bayside Park Road. It's another 2.5 miles to the turnoff for the Northshore Mining access. About 500 feet north of the stoplight where County Road 5 turns west, turn east at a sign that says Northshore Ready Mix. Follow this road to the lake, turning left at the T. The access is on the right; a parking area is just down the road. For bike shuttlers, the Gitchi-Gami State Bicycle Trail now extends from Split Rock Lighthouse State Park to the Beaver River, just 1.5 miles short of the Bayside Park access. A website, www.ggta.org/index.php, has more information about this promising trail.

You'll need a vehicle permit to park at Split Rock Lighthouse State Park's Pebble Beach picnic area. A sloping trail leads 100 yards across the bike path to the beach where you **put in**. A half mile paddle will take you to the base of the lighthouse cliff; this stunning view of the lighthouse is a favorite photo op for north shore photographers. After you round the towering point, another headland rises at Gold Rock Point. A rest area is located in the bay, and the remains of a shipwreck are sometimes visible in the waters around the point (see LSWT 1).

At the Nadine Blacklock Lakeshore beach, the campsite, marked with a water access campsite sign nailed to a tree, is near the north end of the cobbles. If you press on, you'll be rewarded with a sandy landing at Cove Point Lodge, a private resort that allows kayakers to rest there.

After the pink rhyolite cliffs at Beaver Bay's point, you'll see the highway bridge across the Beaver River—and hear the traffic. To the right of the river is the rest area. If you brought your fishing gear, trout fishing is excellent right under the bridge.

To take out at Bayside Park, follow the navigational buoys into the marina's channel: three sets of green (left) and red (right) markers lead you in to the city park's landing. If you paddle on, you'll pass a dramatic rock formation as you round Pellet Island. Navigational lights on the island will remind you that large ships may pass through here at any time; be watchful as you cross Silver Bay Harbor. The flatland on the other side of the harbor was formed by the dumping of mining wastes by Reserve Mining.

A group of red rock islands—one connected to the shore by a gravel spit—marks your course to the Northshore Mining access. You'll see concrete highway barriers with red arrows spray-painted on them at the left end of the cobble beach where you **take out**. After a 200-yard carry up the sloping beach to the road, the parking area is down the road to the right.

Northshore Mining as seen from Pellet Island.

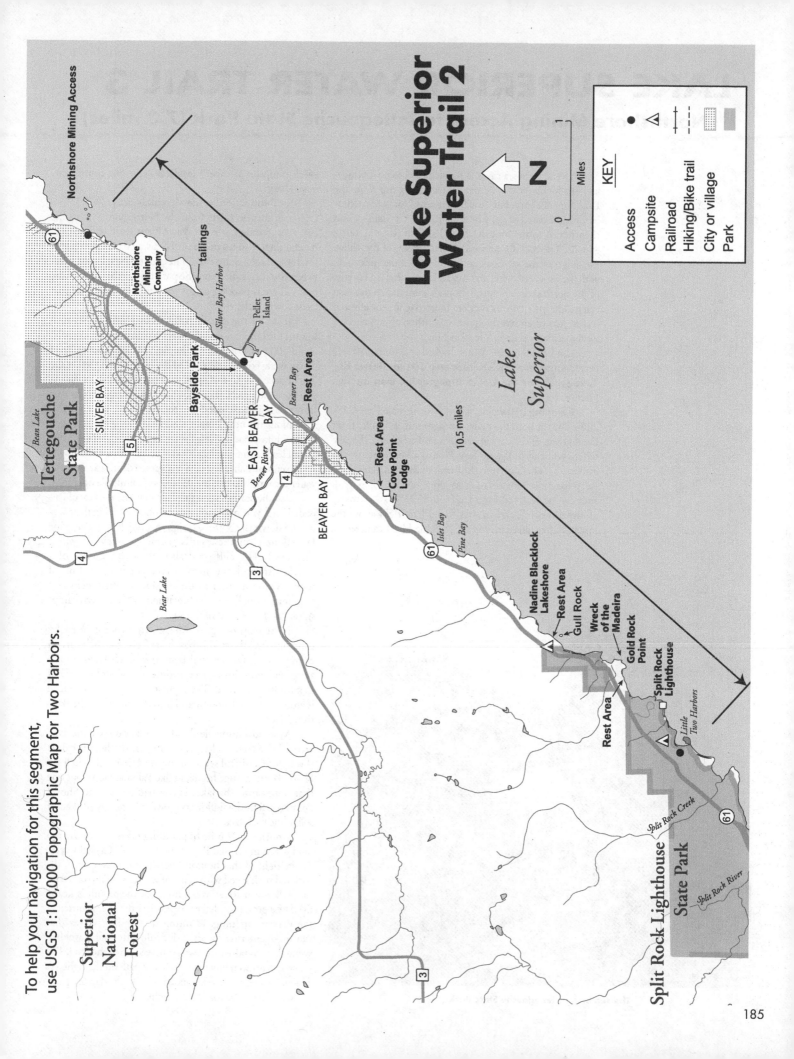

To help your navigation for this segment,
use USGS 1:100,000 Topographic Map for Two Harbors.

Lake Superior
Water Trail 2

N

Miles

0   1

KEY

● Access
△ Campsite
┼ Railroad
--- Hiking/Bike trail
City or village
Park

Superior
National
Forest

Tettegouche
State Park

Bean Lake

Northshore Mining Access

SILVER BAY

Northshore Mining Company

tailings

Silver Bay Harbor

Pellet Island

Bayside Park

Bear Lake

EAST BEAVER BAY

Beaver River

Beaver Bay

Rest Area

BEAVER BAY

Lake
Superior

10.5 miles

Rest Area
Cove Point Lodge

Islet Bay
Pine Bay

Nadine Blacklock Lakeshore

Rest Area
Gull Rock

Wreck of the Madeira

Gold Rock Point

Split Rock Lighthouse

Rest Area

Little Two Harbors

Two Harbors

Split Rock Lighthouse
State Park

Split Rock Creek

Split Rock River

185

LAKE SUPERIOR WATER TRAIL 3
Northshore Mining Access to Tettegouche State Park (7.3 miles)

Several large sea caves, a sea arch, and some spectacular cliffs highlight this exciting sea kayaking trip along the Lake Superior shoreline. You'll start near Northshore Mining, paddle past Tettegouche State Park to Crystal Bay, and then return to the mouth of the Baptism River at Tettegouche. The rock formations are the big star of this show: the magic of the sea caves and the detail of the rock itself, with the variety of color, texture, and shape that is a big part of the north shore's beauty. Choose a calm day so that you can paddle into the sea caves; sea caves magnify the effect of waves. July often has the quietest weather; always check a local marine forecast before launching.

Use Lake Superior Water Trail Map 2 (see LSWT 1) for information and **McKenzie map 104 for Beaver Bay Tettegouche or the USGS topographic map** for Two Harbors for navigation.

Camping is available at Tettegouche State Park (218-226-6365) at both the main campground, 1.5 miles from the takeout, and a cart-in campground adjoining the lake where you can pull your kayak onto a beach below the campsites. (The trail from the beach to the campsites is too steep for most mortals to carry up a kayak.) These park sites can be reserved for a fee (866-857-2757; www.stayatmnparks.com); cart-in sites K and J are right above the beach. A free alternative is the Palisade Head campsite, a kayak campsite at mile 3 available on a first-come, first-served basis.

For information on **kayak rentals**, see LSWT 1.

The **shuttle route** from the Northshore Mining access runs .5 mile north on Water Plant Road to Highway 61 and then 3 miles north on Highway 61 to the turnoff for Tettegouche State Park. The trail to the takeout is between the park office and the park bridge that crosses the river. There is parking across the road from the trail that leads down to the river.

To reach the **put-in** point from Highway 61, turn toward the lake at a sign that says Northshore Ready Mix, about 500 feet north of the stoplight where County Road 5 goes west. Follow this road to the lake, turning left at the T. The access is on the right, 200 yards from the road. As you leave the beach, watch for barely submerged rocks that lie between a small island and the point.

Along the next 2 miles of shore are several lovely, open bays with fascinating rock formations. Then you'll see Palisade Head, a massive headland topped with a radio tower. At the end of Palisade Head is a group of sea caves. If the water is calm, you can paddle through multiple openings.

Past the sea caves, on the cliffs that line the face of Palisade Head, you may spot rock climbers working their way up and down the 350-foot-high sheer rock face. Peregrine falcons nest on these cliffs (climbing is closed where they nest). The cliffs end abruptly at the mouth of a stream. Around the next curve, you'll see a line of rocks. Swing around to the outside of these rocks and then into a small bay; the beach and Palisade Head campsite are at the left end of the bay.

Next stop is a gravel beach right before a rocky promontory. Above this beach are Tettegouche's cart-in campsites. A narrow trail from the beach leads up the steep bank and through a campsite to a wider hiking trail that leads to the road. The regular access for Tettegouche is around the rocky point and into the mouth of the Baptism River.

More adventures lie ahead, so paddle on past the river, around the first rocky point, and (if the lake is calm) through a beautiful sea arch. Beyond that arch you'll see Shovel Point, a huge headland like Palisade Head, but one that slopes into the lake. If you paddle close to Shovel Point, you'll find wildflowers growing from tiny pockets of soil in the rock face.

Another half mile of paddling takes you to the red sand beach in Crystal Bay at the mouth of Crystal Creek. To the right of that beautiful beach, sea caves open in the dark red rock laced with veins of white. When you return to the Baptism River, you'll find that the mouth is nearly filled by a gravel bar. Lake waves batter the river's current at the narrow opening, resulting in standing waves that can make entering the river difficult. After the gravel bar, swing right to **take out**. Two paths lead up to the road. The stairway has too many turns; take the path on the right. It's a long, long carry up 65 wooden steps to the day-use parking areas down the road to the right.

The sea arch at Tettegouche State Park.

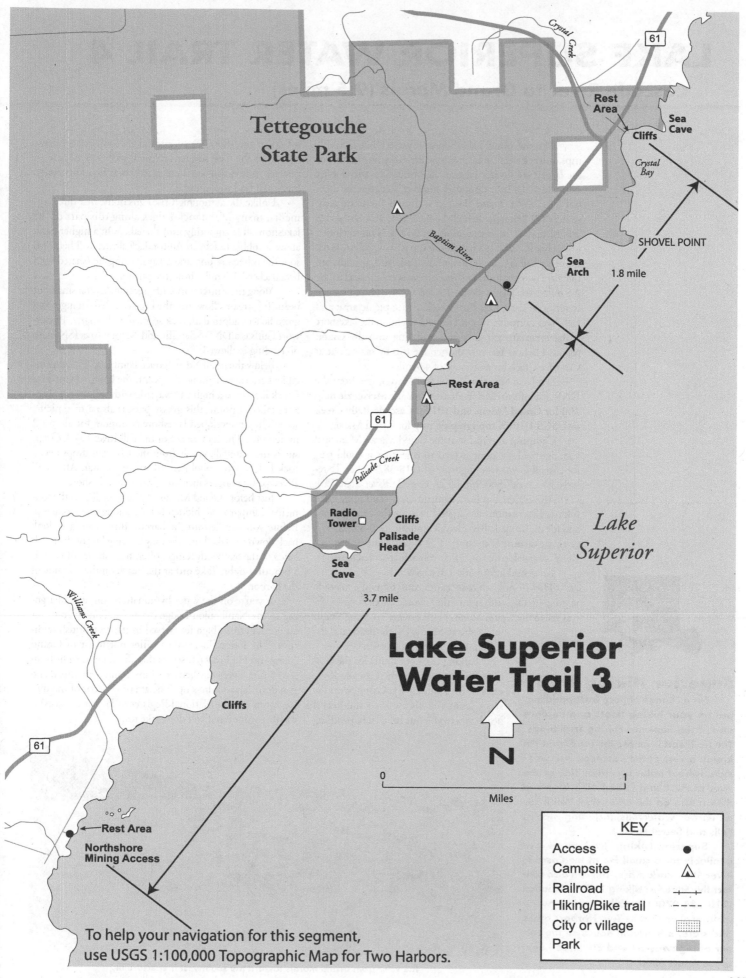

Tettegouche
State Park

Crystal Creek

61

Rest
Area

Sea
Cave

Cliffs

Crystal
Bay

Baptism River

Sea
Arch

SHOVEL POINT

1.8 mile

Rest Area

61

Palisade Creek

Lake
Superior

Radio
Tower

Cliffs

Palisade
Head

Sea
Cave

3.7 mile

Lake Superior Water Trail 3

↑
N

0 ——————————————————— 1

Miles

Williams Creek

Cliffs

61

Rest Area

Northshore
Mining Access

To help your navigation for this segment,
use USGS 1:100,000 Topographic Map for Two Harbors.

KEY

Access	●
Campsite	△
Railroad	—+—
Hiking/Bike trail	- - - -
City or village	▦
Park	▓

LAKE SUPERIOR WATER TRAIL 4
Cascade River to Grand Marais (9.5 miles)

Like the other Lake Superior Water Trail (LSWT) trips, this is a scenic journey along the rocky north shore of the largest freshwater lake in the world. The trip doesn't start where the last one ended, however. Between the take-out for LSWT 3 and the put-in for this trip are long stretches of privately owned shoreline with very few access points; that 41-mile section of the LSWT is not included in this book. Although half of this trip is along private land, the other half is Cascade River State Park land. In addition, there are two rest areas and one access, evenly spaced in the 9.5 miles. You'll pass the Butterwort Cliffs, part of Cascade River State Park; Cut Face Creek, a nice picnic area; and Fall River campsite, where a waterfall right on the lakeshore is the main attraction, before paddling into the Grand Marais Harbor. You can shorten the trip by taking out at Cut Face Creek for a distance of 4.6 miles.

Use Lake Superior Water Trail Map 3, free from the DNR, for information. For navigation, use **McKenzie map 100 for Grand Marais and 101 for Cascade-Bally Creek or USGS 1:100K topographic map** for Grand Marais.

Camping is available at the Grand Marais Municipal Campground—a campground so large that it could pass for a small town—on Highway 61 (218-387-1712). To reserve a site, call 800-998-0959. Cascade River State Park (218-387-3053) also has a campground—and some great hiking. Reservations are a good idea for the campground and for the Cascade River kayak campsite (866-857-2757); www.stayatmnparks.com). The kayak campsite at Fall River is available free on a first-come, first-served basis.

For **rental** information, see LSWT 1.

The 10-mile **shuttle route** runs from the wayside parking on the south side of the Cascade River along Highway 61 to the Grand Marais Harbor, where you angle right off Highway 61 to get to the beach and the adjoining parking lot and toilets.

Parking (six-hour limit) for the Cascade River access is at the Cascade River wayside on Highway 61. Carry down the steps from the highway to the gravel beach where you **put in**. Before paddling off down the shore, be sure to take a look at the scenic mouth of the Cascade River. You'll pass a picnic area a quarter mile down the shore; a stop may be unnecessary, but you'll find toilets there.

Unlike the abrupt high-rise cliffs of the first three segments, many of the rock ledges along this part of the lakeshore slide smoothly into the lake. On a higher bank above a cobble beach, an Adirondack shelter will help you spot the otherwise unmarked kayak campsite (shared with backpackers) 1.5 miles from the put-in.

Along the Butterwort Cliffs section, several small but beautiful streams flow into the big lake. Red, orange, and green lichens adorn dark rock seamed with quartz. Butterwort Cliffs is a DNR Scientific and Natural Area (SNA), so no landing is allowed.

Below the headland at Terrace Point, you'll see tiny incipient sea caves. Around the point, the beach at Cut Face Creek is next to a highway wayside with toilets. An alternate takeout point, this grassy park is also a nice picnic spot. The undeveloped lakeshore continues for almost 2 more miles. The centerpiece of the Fall River kayak campsite is the waterfall, visible from the lake as it drops over a rock ledge into a pool behind the gravel bar. After Fall River, private houses increasingly dot the lakeshore.

Just before Grand Marais Harbor, you'll pass the municipal campground, hidden behind a long rocky outcrop. Before you paddle into the harbor, turn around to look back down the lakeshore; the long curving line of the headlands of the Sawtooth Range, often hazy shades of blue, is a beautiful sight. **Take out** at the beach on the east side of the harbor.

If you're off the water by midafternoon, consider going to the Naniboujou Lodge (www.naniboujou.com) for an unusual treat: high tea, served in the best British tradition. The lodge, located 14 miles northeast of Grand Marais on Highway 61, serves this afternoon delight from 3 to 5 p.m. every day between June 1 and September, and you don't have to dress up. The amazing décor of the dining room (on the National Register of Historic Places) is worth a visit even if you don't take tea.

Superior Hiking Trail

For a change of pace from paddling, put on your hiking boots and explore one of the Superior Hiking Trail loops. The trailhead is across the road from the kayak access at the Cascade River wayside. Hike 4 miles up either side of the river to the County Road 45 bridge and then return on the other side. You'll see numerous waterfalls, including Hidden Falls and Secret Falls.

Superior Hiking Trail maps are available for a small fee at the Cascade River State Park office. You can also contact the Superior Hiking Trail Association (218-834-2700; suphike@mr.net; www.shta.org) or visit its Two Harbors office and store, a Victorian house on the corner of Highway 61 and 8th Street, next to the Agate Shop.

The view from Grand Marais toward the southwest is spectacular.

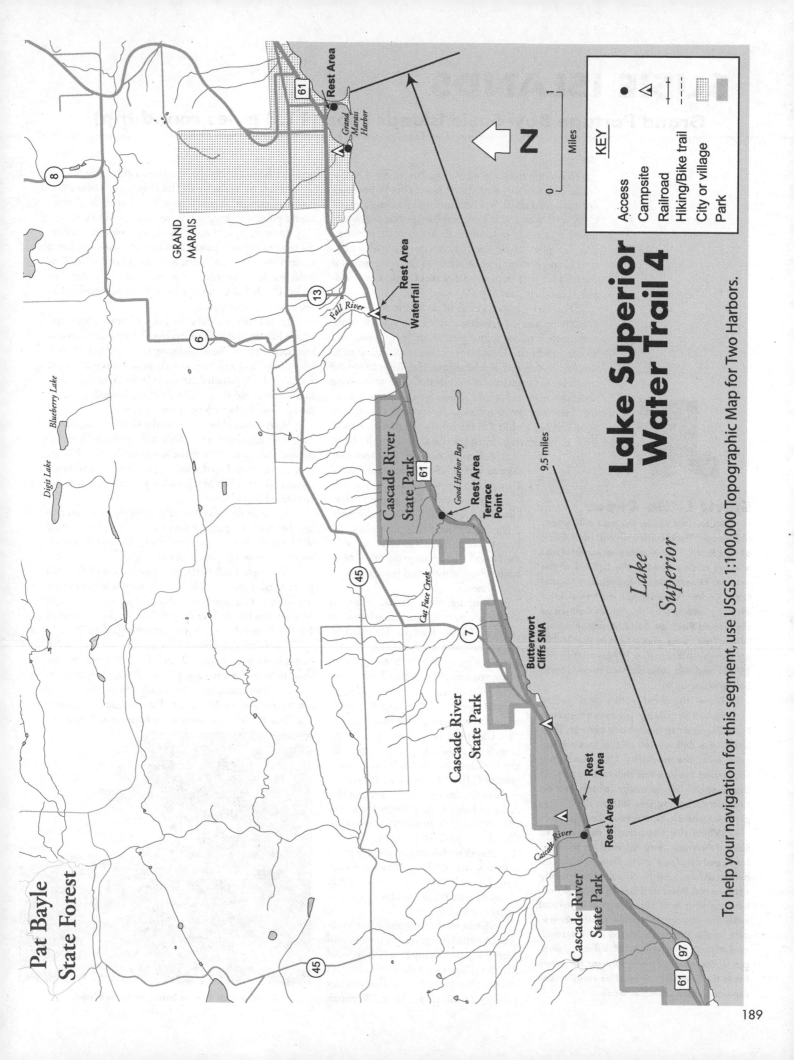

Lake Superior
Water Trail 4

Pat Bayle
State Forest

GRAND
MARAIS

Cascade River
State Park

Cascade River
State Park

Cascade River
State Park

*Lake
Superior*

Blueberry Lake

Digit Lake

Rest Area

Grand Marais Harbor

Fall River

Rest Area
Waterfall

Cut Face Creek

Good Harbor Bay
Rest Area
Terrace Point

Butterwort
Cliffs SNA

Rest
Area

Cascade River
Rest Area

9.5 miles

To help your navigation for this segment, use USGS 1:100,000 Topographic Map for Two Harbors.

KEY

● Access	△ Campsite
Railroad	Hiking/Bike trail
City or village	Park

N

Miles

0   1

SUSIE ISLANDS
Grand Portage Bay–Susie Islands Loop (11.3 miles round-trip)

Kayaking from Grand Portage Bay to the Susie Islands, a cluster of uninhabited islands off Minnesota's northernmost shore, is a beautiful and challenging trip. Combined with a visit to Grand Portage National Monument, it's also a mini-lesson on the history of the voyageurs and the Ojibwe of this region. Hikers can also walk the historic Grand Portage Trail: information and route maps for the 8.5-mile portage to the site of Fort Charlotte are available at the main gate.

Kayakers who paddle the whole loop must be experienced in paddling the open waters of Lake Superior, confident of their rescue techniques, properly equipped, and able to handle the 12-mile trip. Those who don't want to do the crossing can paddle around Hat Point to see the Spirit Little Cedar Tree, a round-trip of 3.5 miles along shoreline. Always check the marine forecast before launching; Lake Superior is notorious for its sudden dangerous squalls. If you paddle this trip in July, the weather is more likely to be favorable. In addition to the map in this book, use **McKenzie map 98—Grand Portage or USGS 7.5-minute maps** (Grand Portage and Pigeon Point quadrangles).

If you've ever taken the ferry from Grand Portage to Isle Royale, you've probably noticed these islands. Susie Island, the Frances Lee Jacques Preserve, is owned by the Nature Conservancy; the other 12 islands belong to the Grand Portage Band of the Ojibwe.

Camping is not allowed on any of the islands, but brief and limited landings on Susie Island itself are possible with written permission from the Nature Conservancy's office in Duluth (218-727-6119) before you leave. The Ojibwe Tribal Council asks that you contact its Trust Lands and Natural Resources Office (218-475-2415) before landing on the other islands.

Camping is available next to the launch site at the Voyageur Marina. Contact the Grand Portage Marina and Campground (218-475-2476) for a reservation as there are not many sites. You can also camp at Judge C. R. Magney State Park (218-387-3039) 20 miles southwest of Grand Portage on Highway 61.

Kayak rentals are available at Superior Coastal Sports (800-720-2809; www.superiorcoastal.com; fun@superiorcoastal.com) in Grand Marais, 35 miles southwest of Grand Portage on Highway 61.

Put in by the ferry pier at the Voyageur Marina, 1.5 miles east of the National Monument on County Road 17. To avoid the $3 parking fee for the marina lot, you can park free in the National Monument parking lot and launch by the Wenonah

ferry pier; however, you'll paddle an extra mile across the bay.

As you reach the tip of Hat Point, you'll hear a bell buoy on your right that marks a six-foot-deep shoal. Rounding the point, watch out for waves reflecting off the rocks.

To see the Spirit Little Cedar Tree, as voyageurs always did before a crossing, paddle about a third of the way down the east shore of Hat Point, just past a boathouse. This small, gnarled white cedar grows right out of the shoreline rocks. The Tribal Council asks that you not land unless you're with a tribal guide.

From Hat Point, head for the gap between Susie and Lucille Islands, visible on the horizon 2.5 miles away. As you cross the mouth of Wauswaugoning Bay, avoid Long Island, where huge flocks of herring gulls nest. Gulls will dive at paddlers who approach their nests. At the tip of Susie, pass to the right of the sheer cliff and follow the southeast shore for a counterclockwise loop around the island.

Sheer basalt cliffs rise from the shores of the island. Etched with strong fracture lines and covered with multicolored scaly lichens from the waterline up, the cliffs are topped with weathered white cedars, birches, and black spruces. Tiny pockets of soil tucked into cracks in the rock faces nourish wild flowers.

At the southwest end of Susie you'll find a narrow passage between two parts of the island where a kayak could slide over the barely submerged rocks. Unless the water is very quiet, however, your boat will scrape.

Although much of the shoreline is sheer cliffs, you'll pass several sloping cobble beaches suitable for rest stops; one of these faces east. From this beach, looking between Magnet and Lucille Islands, you'll see the low mound of Isle Royale and the tall, thin line of a navigational light.

The mainland shore of Pigeon Point, where a house is visible in the trees, lies just .25 mile from the northernmost shore of Susie. The land along Pigeon Point is private property, but in an emergency, a road ends near the shore about a half mile from a cobble beach that faces south. Return to Hat Point by the same crossing and **take out** at the marina.

Spirit Little Cedar

An ancient cedar, perhaps 500 years old, grows from a rock on the east shore of Hat Point. This weathered sentinel has always been sacred to the Ojibwe of the region. Manito Geezhigaynce, or Spirit Little Cedar Tree, stands on tribal land and is protected by the Tribal Council of the Grand Portage Band. Another name, Witch Tree, was given to it in the 1920s by Dewey Albinson, a WPA artist in the 1930s and 40s who painted many North Shore scenes.

Three hundred years ago, when voyageurs regularly journeyed across Lake Superior in birch-bark canoes, they heard the Ojibwe tell of this tree's influence over the powerful lake, and they too asked the spirit of this tree to protect them, sprinkling offerings of tobacco on the waters by the tree before their long, perilous paddle east across the big lake.

When the voyageurs returned to Grand Portage, they stopped on Susie Island, put on clean shirts, tied on their colorful sashes, and paddled triumphantly around Hat Point into Grand Portage harbor, singing and signaling their arrival with the voyageur paddle salute. Everyone in the stockade heard their arrival, and after a long winter of isolation, people in the stockade were eager for news from the outside world. The rowdy rendezvous often lasted a week.

A pebble barrier beach on Susie Island.

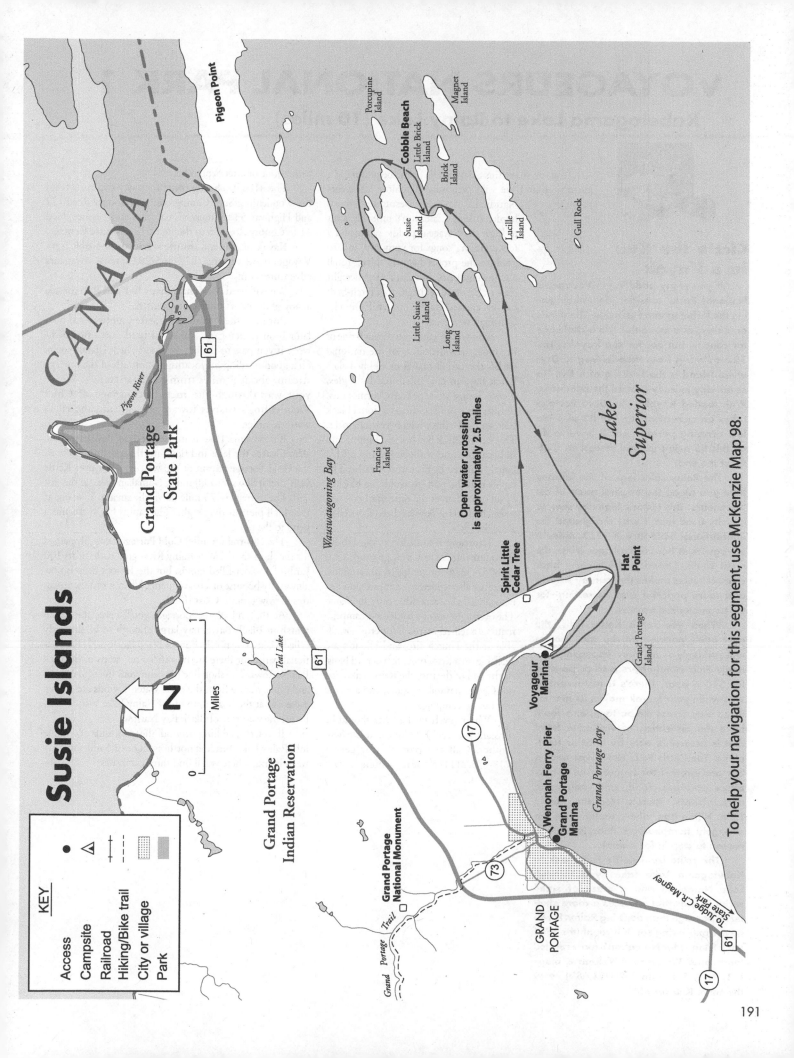

Susie Islands

KEY

●	Access
△	Campsite
┼┼┼	Railroad
– – –	Hiking/Bike trail
▒	City or village
▓	Park

N

Miles

0   1

CANADA

Pigeon Point

Pigeon River

Grand Portage
State Park

61

Teal Lake

61

Grand Portage
Indian Reservation

Grand Portage
National Monument

GRAND
PORTAGE

73

Grand Portage Trail

To Judge C.R. Magney
State Park

61

17

Wenonah Ferry Pier
Grand Portage Marina

Voyageur Marina

17

Grand Portage Bay

Grand Portage Island

Hat Point

Spirit Little
Cedar Tree

**Open water crossing
is approximately 2.5 miles**

Wauswaugoning Bay

Francis
Island

*Lake
Superior*

Long
Island

Little Susie
Island

Susie
Island

Lucille Island

⊘ Gull Rock

Porcupine
Island

Cobble Beach

Little Brick
Island

Brick
Island

Magnet
Island

To help your navigation for this segment, use McKenzie Map 98.

VOYAGEURS NATIONAL PARK 1

Kabetogama Lake to Rainy Lake (10 miles)

Circle the Kab in a Kayak

If you enjoy paddling in Voyageurs National Park, consider circumnavigating the Kabetogama Peninsula. The winds on Rainy Lake make this trip a challenge for canoes, but not for sea kayaks. The 12.5-mile trip from Woodenfrog to Dryweed Island is the first leg of a five- to seven-day journey around the peninsula. With loaded kayaks, the Gold Portage takes on new meaning, but it's also the last carrying portage you'll have to do on this 85-mile trip, and there's no shuttle at the end.

The Rainy Lake legs of the journey take you along the original route of the Voyageurs. This historic highway was so heavily used that it was designated the international boundary in 1783. Modern voyageurs in houseboats now cruise the main route. Choosing the quieter back channel routes makes the journey safer—and more peaceful and interesting—for the nonmotorized traveler.

When you reach Kettle Falls, the only other portage on the trip, motors will suddenly seem more appealing. The Kettle Falls Hotel offers a truck portage for $10 a boat. There's a restaurant to visit while your kayak makes its mechanized way across the portage, and you'll have the distinction of visiting a hotel that is accessible only by boat or floatplane. The Kettle Falls Hotel was once a bar and brothel for loggers, but it now offers portages, food, and lodging to park visitors. There's also the hotel's Tiltin' Hilton Bar, where walking on the strangely humpbacked floor is enough reason to stop in for a drink.

The route from Kettle Falls back to Kabetogama Lake takes you through Lake Namakan and a maze of small rocky islands that provides a more sheltered passage than does big Rainy. If you have time, swing south through the Wolf Pack Islands for Namakan's most rugged landscape. Waterproof McKenzie maps K-1, N-1, R-1, and R-2(1:31,680) cover the entire Kab circuit.

You can make this a day paddle or the beginning of a journey around the wild peninsula of remote Voyageurs National Park on Minnesota's northern border. In either case, you'll probably want to learn the Voyageur paddle salute and a few paddling songs for your trip, just to get into the proper historic spirit. You'll also portage once, but carry a lightweight sea kayak instead of the 26-foot birch-bark canoes carried by the colorful French-Canadian voyageurs.

This voyage takes you through one of the more secluded areas of the national park—the cattail marsh of Rainy Lake's Black Bay, an area inhabited by eagles, herons, loons, white pelicans, cormorants, beavers, dragonflies, the occasional black bear, and some three-billion-year-old rocks. This end of Black Bay has good spring and fall crappie and walleye fishing and is largely ignored by motorboat traffic. The rapids that the portage avoids are blocked by a beaver dam at the time this book was researched, so the flow has been reduced to a trickle.

Camping is available at the DNR's Woodenfrog State Campground. Call 218-757-3274 for campsite reservations. There are also wilderness campsites on Kabetogama Lake, accessible only by water. The overnight use of a wilderness campsite requires a self-registered free permit, available at the launch site, and all sites are available on a first-come, first-served basis. At the end of the trip, the Rainy Lake Visitor Center has toilets, water, and a picnic area but no camping.

Water levels in the lakes should be constant between early June and late September. Call the park visitor center (218-875-2111) if you're planning to visit before June or after September.

The 41-mile **shuttle route** for a day trip runs from the Woodenfrog State Campground via County Road 122 and Highway 53 to International Falls, and County Road 11 to County Road 96 to the Rainy Lake Visitor Center.

Kayak rentals and **shuttle service** are available from Voyageurs Adventures (877-465-2925; www.voyageurs adventures.com).

You will need **McKenzie maps K-1** and **R-1**, for sale at any of the park's three visitor centers.

Put in at the Woodenfrog State Campground boat launch on Kabetogama Lake and head north by northwest. If you pass to the left of Wood Duck Island, you're on a good heading for locating the mouth of the portage stream, about 3 miles from the boat launch. Weave your way through the rocky archipelago of Chief Woodenfrog's Islands toward this stream, the lake's western outlet.

Kabetogama Lake is in the Hudson Bay watershed. Water leaves the lake and flows northward through both the Gold Portage stream at the west end and over Kettle Falls after it flows into adjoining Namakan Lake, at the east end. The portage is .75 mile down the stream. Take out at the small pier on river right. The rapids begin around a bend to the right.

The **160-rod (.5 mile) Gold Portage**, probably named for the short-lived 1890s Rainy River gold rush, skirts 100 yards of boulder-filled rapids, but the 10-foot drop is now almost dry because of a beaver dam. When it isn't dammed, this narrow rapid is Class II–III.

At the end of the portage, you'll enter the cattail marsh in Black Bay, a bay large enough to be properly called a lake. The north shore of Black Bay is part of the national park, but there are no official rest stops until Black Bay Narrows. The shoreline has numerous inlets to explore and offers respite from the open water if winds are strong. **Take out** at the boat ramp of the Rainy Lake Visitor Center on the west side of Black Bay Narrows.

If you're paddling around the peninsula, continue into Rainy Lake, heading northeast about 2.5 miles to Dryweed Island, where you'll find three campsites.

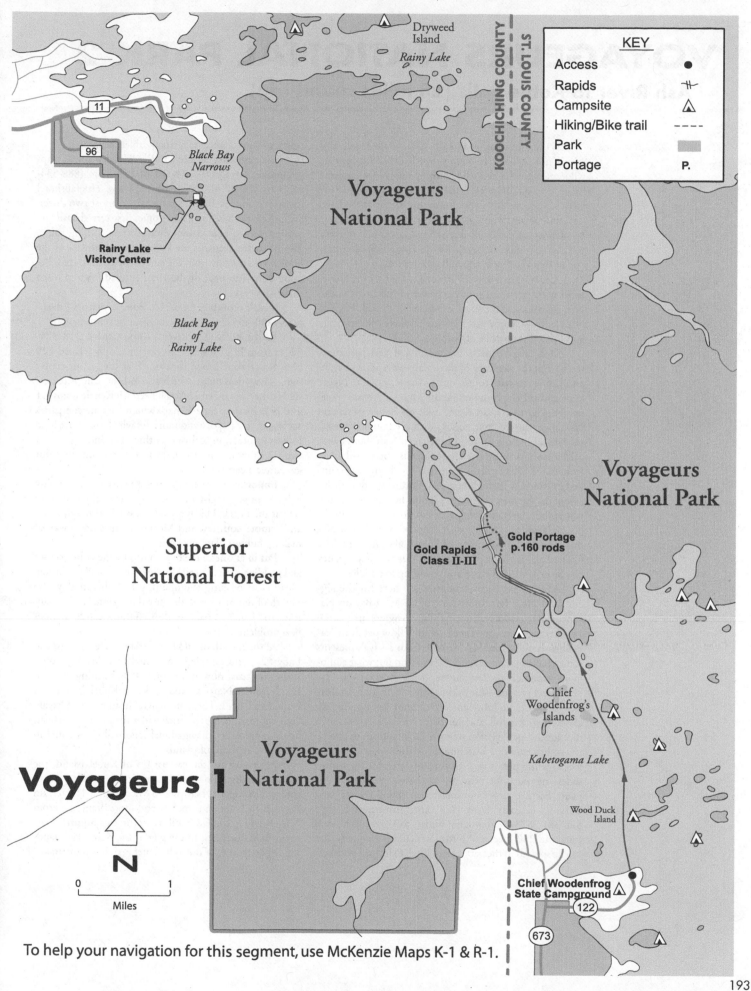

Dryweed
Island

Rainy Lake

11

96

*Black Bay
Narrows*

**Rainy Lake
Visitor Center**

**Voyageurs
National Park**

KOOCHICHING COUNTY

ST. LOUIS COUNTY

KEY

Access	●
Rapids	
Campsite	△
Hiking/Bike trail	- - -
Park	
Portage	P.

*Black Bay
of
Rainy Lake*

Superior
National Forest

**Gold Rapids
Class II-III**

**Gold Portage
p.160 rods**

**Voyageurs
National Park**

*Chief
Woodenfrog's
Islands*

Kabetogama Lake

Voyageurs 1

⬆
N

0   1
Miles

**Voyageurs
National Park**

*Wood Duck
Island*

**Chief Woodenfrog
State Campground**

122

673

To help your navigation for this segment, use McKenzie Maps K-1 & R-1.

VOYAGEURS NATIONAL PARK 2
Ash River to Kettle Falls (28 miles round-trip)

With a destination like the Kettle Falls Hotel, this trip is not just any kayaking expedition. This historic wilderness hotel is accessible only by boat or by seaplane, so a return paddle is essential, expanding the adventure to two days. Paddlers who don't want to stay at the hotel can camp at a nearby Voyageurs National Park campsite. Numerous campsites all along the route make it possible to take two days to reach Kettle Falls; this of course means that the whole trip will take four days.

Although sea kayaks are best suited to the sometimes wide-open and windy expanses of Kabetogama and Namakan Lakes, canoeists experienced in paddling big water will also enjoy this trip. Sea kayakers will especially appreciate the absence of portages.

One safety issue is the motorboat and houseboat traffic, but the intricacy of these waterways allows kayaks and canoes to take routes out of the way of the bigger craft and off the route marked by buoys. As you travel east and north toward Kettle Falls on Kabetogama and Namakan, the red "nun" buoys with even numbers mark the left side of the route and the green "can" buoys with odd numbers mark the right side; as you travel away from Kettle Falls, this is reversed. The buoys are numbered, which is useful when you want to verify your location on the map. A compass (know how to use it!) and waterproof navigation maps are essential for this trip.

Islands and backwaters beg to be explored, Namakan Lake flows into Sand Point Lake and then into Crane Lake without portages, and this two-day journey can be expanded as far as you're willing to paddle.

Many of the powerboaters are here for the legendary walleye fishing in these lakes. Mica Bay on Namakan has good walleye fishing. Anglers also catch smallmouth bass, northerns, and yellow perch in Kabetogama and Namakan. Fishing from a kayak presents some challenges, so practice first to find out what equipment, especially the landing net, works best for you.

Berry picking—for wild strawberries in June, raspberries in June and July, blueberries from July to August, chokecherries in July, and juneberries in late July—makes a nice lunchtime diversion if you're lucky enough to choose the right rest stop. Watching for wildlife—bald eagles, loons, white pelicans, river otters (watch for their mud slides), moose, bears, beavers—can also be good entertainment. For five years now, the annual Spring Birders Rendezvous in early June—for more information, call 888-381-2873—has brought birders to Voyageurs to look for about 240 species of birds, particularly warblers, that can be spotted in the park and to listen to learned ornithol-ogists, so your chances of seeing warblers seem high.

For **camping** at the DNR's Woodenfrog Campground, see Voyageurs 1. The Kettle Falls Hotel (888-534-6835, or 218-875-2070 off-season; www.kettlefallshotel.com) has rooms and cabin rentals. Almost two dozen campsites, available on a first-come, first-served basis, are located within reasonable reach of the paddling route. Two of these campsites are located just northwest of the hotel across the bay from the end of the portage trail. Because campsites near the hotel are limited, plan to reach these sites early.

Kayak rentals are available from Voyageurs Adventures (800-465-2925; www.voyageursadventures.com).

To reach the Ash River Visitor Center, 218-374-3221, from Highway 53, go east on County Road 129 (Ash River Trail), then turn north at the visitor center sign. Navigation maps, which also indicate campsites, are sold at the visitor center. You'll need **McKenzie maps K1 and N1**. Pick up a park map, which lists the campsites according to category and indicates which sites have food lockers (protection against bear thievery), and register for overnight camping. Registration is free but does not guarantee a campsite.

Important: Be sure to bring the necessary camping equipment and register at the center, even if you plan to stay at the hotel. This is a wilderness trip through a vast and remote country, and Mother Nature has a way of making human plans go awry.

Put in at one of the boat ramps by the visitor center and paddle north .25 mile to the tip of a small peninsula. Head east, passing the opening to Sullivan Bay, the mouth of the Ash River. Because this channel is the main route to Namakan Lake, motorized traffic can sometimes be a problem.

At the mouth of Old Dutch Bay where you pass can buoy #27, you paddle into Namakan Lake. The route turns northeast now at nun buoy #26, running through Blind Indian Narrows and between Kubel Island and Namakan Island. These are general headings; in a kayak, your choice of routes is much wider than in a powerboat. Your compass and navigational map will be essential in this intricate maze of islands.

After passing the eastern tip of Kubel Island, the route generally follows the international boundary north through Voyageurs Narrows to Mica Island. The terrain through this stretch is rockier and more dramatic. From Mica Island, paddle 2.5 miles east through Squirrel Narrows, then northeast to the pier at the Kettle Falls landing, where you **take out**. The hotel is right up the road.

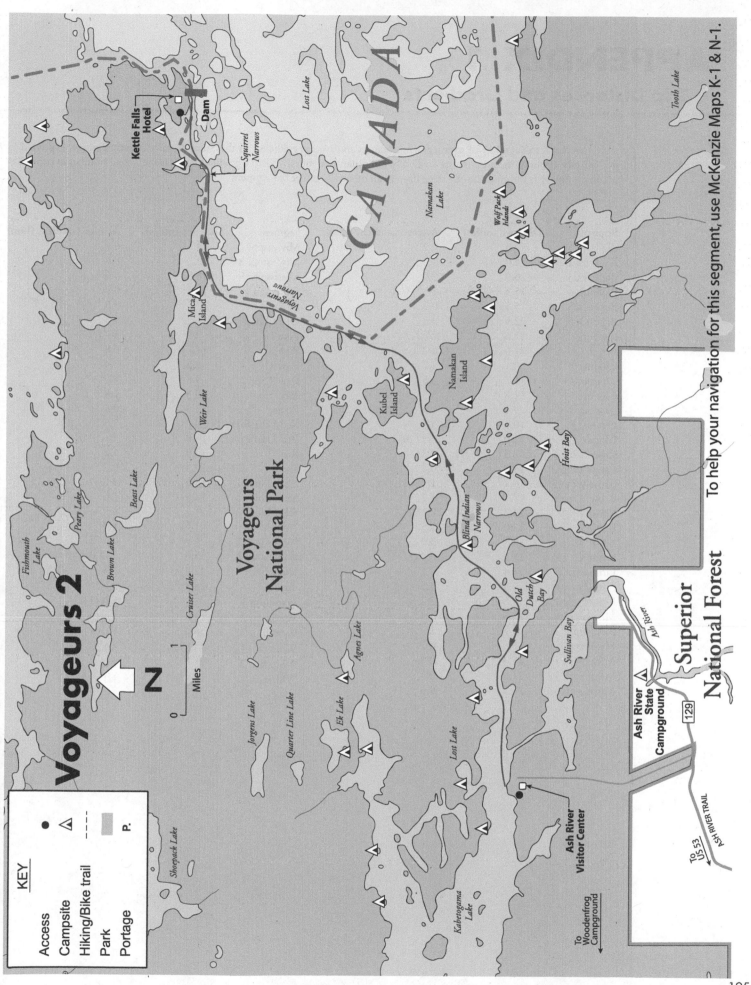

Voyageurs 2

N

Miles
0 1

KEY

- ● Access
- △ Campsite
- – · – Hiking/Bike trail
- ▨ Park
- P. Portage

CANADA

Tooth Lake

Lost Lake

Namakan Lake

Wolf Pack Islands

Squirrel Narrows

Voyageurs Narrows

Kettle Falls Hotel

Dam

Mica Island

Namakan Island

Kubel Island

Hoist Bay

Weir Lake

Fishmouth Lake

Peary Lake

Brown Lake

Beast Lake

Cruiser Lake

Shoepack Lake

Jorgens Lake

Quarter Line Lake

Elk Lake

Agnes Lake

Blind Indian Narrows

Old Dutch Bay

Sullivan Bay

Lost Lake

Kabetogama Lake

Voyageurs National Park

Ash River Visitor Center

Ash River State Campground

Ash River

129

Superior National Forest

To Woodenfrog Campground

TO US 53

ASH RIVER TRAIL

To help your navigation for this segment, use McKenzie Maps K-1 & N-1.

APPENDIX 1
Trip Distances and Gradients

This chart is a summary of river segment distances and average gradients for the entire distance of each segment, expressed in feet per mile (fpm, or the drop in feet divided by the distance in miles). When a gradient figure has a second number in parentheses, that number is the gradient of a steep drop in an otherwise rather flat segment.

Segment	Distance (miles)	Average Gradient (fpm)	Segment	Distance (miles)	Average Gradient (fpm)
Big Fork 1	19.3	0.9	Mississippi 7	24.5	0.4
Big Fork 2	14.0	1.3	Mississippi 8	12.2	0.8
Big Fork 3	16.0	2.0	Mississippi 9	18.8	0.6
Big Fork 4	15.5	1.9	Otter Tail 1	12.4	0.9
Big Fork 5	15.5	0.6	Otter Tail 2	7.6	0.5
Big Fork 6	22.9	0.8	Otter Tail 3	13.2	4.5
Big Fork 7	17.6	2.0	Pike 1	9.2	3.2 (16)
Boy	11.0	0.7	Pike 2	11.7	0.8
Cloquet 1	10.1	2.7	Pine 1	8.6	2.4
Cloquet 2	11.7	3.8	Pine 2	9.8	5.1
Cloquet 3	12.8	3.5	Pine 3	20.3	1.8
Cloquet 4	9.1	1.0	Prairie	13.3	0.4
Cloquet 5	10.0	3.7	Red Lake River 1	23.0	5.5
Cloquet 6	11.0	6.9 (20)	Red Lake River 2	14.8	4.1
Crow Wing 1	4.3	2.3	Rice	12.9	1.2
Crow Wing 2	13.8	0.6	Shell	10.3	0.5
Crow Wing 3	14.1	1.1	Saint Louis 1	13.0	2.6
Crow Wing 4	17.7	4.7	Saint Louis 2	18.5	1.4
Kettle 1	10.3	7.1	Saint Louis 3	21.7	0.5
Kettle 2	18.0	1.5	Saint Louis 4	21.8	1.0
Kettle 3	8.7	3.9	Saint Louis 5	3.9	8.7 (31)
Kettle 4	18.1	6.4 (11)	Saint Louis 6	5.0	-1.2 (upstream)
Little Fork 1	11.4	2.4	Sturgeon	12.3	2.3
Little Fork 2	9.5	3.5	Turtle	18.3	0.4
Little Fork 3	15.6	2.2	Vermilion 1	5.2	5.0 (23)
Mississippi 1	16.5	5.0	Vermilion 2	12.0	8.1 (80)
Mississippi 2	8.7	1.7	Vermilion 3	20.0	1.0
Mississippi 3	13.8	0.7	Whiteface 1	15.0	3.1
Mississippi 4	18.3	0.5	Whiteface 2	21.5	2.0
Mississippi 5	21.0	0.5	Whiteface 3	19.5	1.1
Mississippi 6	29.5	0.6			

A beginning paddler is NOT someone who has never paddled before. This book assumes that a beginner has basic river and lake paddling skills. Those new to paddling should always start with a class or accompanied by an experienced paddler. Many of the trips in this book do not require expert skills. Under optimal conditions (proper equipment, low to medium water levels, warm air and water temperatures), beginners can take many intermediate-level trips IF they paddle with experienced canoeists and kayakers. Even beginner-level trips will be dangerous in some situations (fallen trees, low bridges, bad weather, etc.). NO BEGINNER SHOULD PADDLE ANY RIVER AT HIGH WATER. Many rivers could be classified as either beginner or intermediate. In these cases, I chose the intermediate rating for the trip.

I. River Trips

Beginner
Big Fork River 5, 6, 7
Boy River
Cloquet River 4
Crow Wing River 1, 2, 3, 4
Glendalough Lakes
Kettle River 2
Mississippi River 1, 2, 3, 4, 5, 6, 7, 8, 9
Otter Tail River 1, 2
Pike River 2
Pine River 1
Prairie River
Rice River
Shell River
Saint Louis River 1, 2, 3, 4, 6
Turtle River
Vermilion River 1, 2, 3 (if all rapids are portaged)
Whiteface River 3

Intermediate/Experienced
Big Fork River 1, 2, 3, 4
Cloquet River 5, 6
Kettle River 1, 3
Little Fork River 1, 2, 3
Otter Tail River 3
Pike River 1
Pine River 2, 3
Red Lake River 1, 2
Vermilion River 2 (if all rapids are run)
Whiteface River 1, 2

Expert/Advanced
Cloquet River 1, 2, 3
Kettle River 4
Saint Louis River 5
Sturgeon River
Vermilion River 1, 3 (if all rapids are run)

II. Boundary Waters Trips

Beginner
BWCAW East 1 (day trip) Bearskin Lake
  to Rose Lake Loop
BWCAW East 3 (2 days) Seagull River/Red Rock
  Lake/Gull Lake Loop
BWCAW West 1 (day trip) South Hegman
  Lake-Trease Lake Loop

Experienced/Physically Fit
BWCAW East 2 (4 Days) Gull Lake/Saganaga
  Lake/Knife Lake/Ogishkemuncie Lake/
  Seagull River Loop
BWCAW West 2 (6 days) Mudro Lake/Border
  Lakes/Moose River North
BWCAW West 3 (3 days) Fall Lake/Basswood
  Lake/Moose Lake

III. Sea Kayaking Trips

Intermediate/Experienced
Lake Superior Water Trail 1, 2, 3, 4
Voyageurs 1, 2
BWCAW East 3 (2 Days) Seagull River/Red Rock
  Lake/Gull Lake Loop
BWCAW West 3 (3 Days) Fall Lake/Basswood
  Lake/Moose Lake

Advanced
Lake Superior's Susie Islands

APPENDIX 3
Resource Materials for Paddlers

IMPROVING PADDLING SKILLS
Books

American Canoe Association. *Introduction to Paddling: Canoeing Basics for Lakes and Rivers.* Birmingham, AL: Menasha Ridge Press, 1996.

Bechdel, Les, and Slim Ray. *River Rescue: A Manual for Whitewater Safety.* Boston: Appalachian Mountain Club Books, 1997.

Dowd, John. *Sea Kayaking: A Manual for Long-Distance Touring.* Seattle: University of Washington Press, 1988.

Hutchinson, Derek C. *The Complete Book of Sea Kayaking.* Old Saybrook, CT: Globe Pequot Press, 1994.

Jacobson, Cliff. *Canoeing.* 2nd ed. Old Saybrook, CT: Globe Pequot Press, 1999.

Landry, Paul, and Matty McNair. *The Outward Bound Canoeing Handbook.* New York: The Lyons Press, 1992.

Lessels, Bruce. *AMC Whitewater Handbook.* Boston: Appalachian Mountain Club Books, 1994.

McGuffin, Gary, and Joanie McGuffin. *Paddle Your Own Canoe.* Erin, Ontario, Canada: Boston Mills Press, 1999.

Videos

Essential Boat Control. 48 min., 1996. Waterworks, P.O. Box 190, Topton, NC 28781.

Heads Up! River Rescue for River Runners. 29 min., 1993. American Canoe Association, 7432 Alban Station Boulevard, Suite B226, Springfield, VA 22150.

Whitewater Self Defense. Video, 65 min., 1999. Performance Video and Instruction, 550 Riverbend, Durango, CO 81301.

Canoe and Kayak Camping

Bell, Patricia J. *Roughing It Elegantly.* 2nd ed. Eden Prairie, MN: Cat's-paw Press, 1995.

Daniel, Linda. *Kayak Cookery.* Birmingham, AL: Menasha Ridge Press, 1988.

Jacobson, Cliff. *Canoeing and Camping: Beyond the Basics.* 2nd ed. Guilford, CT: Globe Pequot Press, 2000.

Pearson, Claudia. *NOLS Cookery.* Mechanicsburg, PA: Stackpole Books, 1997.

Boundary Waters

Beymer, Robert. *Boundary Waters Canoe Area. Vol. 1, Western Region.* Berkeley, CA: Wilderness Press, 2000.

Beymer, Robert. *Boundary Waters Canoe Area. Vol. 2, The Eastern Region.* Berkeley, CA: Wilderness Press, 2000.

Furtman, Michael. *Magic on the Rocks: Canoe Country Pictographs.* Duluth, MN: Birch Portage Press, 2000.

Nute, Grace Lee. *The Voyageur.* 1931. Reprint, St. Paul: Minnesota Historical Society, 1955.

Olson, Sigurd F. *The Singing Wilderness.* 1956. Reprint, Minneapolis: University of Minnesota Press, 1997.

Olson, Sigurd F. *Spirit of the North: The Quotable Sigurd F. Olson.* Edited by David Backes. Minneapolis: University of Minnesota Press, 2004.

Minnesota Rivers and River History

Nicollet, Joseph N. *The Journals of Joseph N. Nicollet.* Translated from the French by Andre Fertey and edited by Martha Coleman Bray. St. Paul: Minesota Historical Society Press, 1970.

Lund, Duane R. *Our Historic Upper Mississippi.* Brainerd, MN: Nordell Graphic Communications, 1991.

Waters, Thomas F. *The Streams and Rivers of Minnesota.* Minneapolis: University of Minnesota Press, 1977.

APPENDIX 4
Paddling Instruction, Clubs, and Organizations

Instruction

Paddling classes are the best way for novices to learn good basic skills and for beginners and intermediate paddlers to improve their skills.

Bear Paw Outdoor Adventure Resort, White Lake, WI 54491 (715-882-3502; www.bearpawinn.com). Offers the full range of kayak instruction, with classes on the Wolf River in the Nicolet National Forest.

Canoe U Weekend (612-985-1111, ext.2; www.canoe-kayak.org). Run by the Minnesota Canoe Association, this is an annual camping and instruction weekend in May with formal instruction in paddling and cruising skills, solo and tandem whitewater canoe, and whitewater kayak by American Canoe Association–certified instructors.

Nicolet College Outdoor Adventure Series, Rhinelander, WI (715-356-6753; 800-585-9304; www.nicolet.tec.wi.us). The curriculum includes a wide range of canoeing and kayaking instruction, useful seminars, and fantastic trips. Call for a catalog or check online.

Kayak and Canoe Institute, Duluth, MN (218-726-7128; www.umdrsop.org). Run by the University of Minnesota–Duluth, classes at four ability levels and private instruction are offered in coastal kayaking, whitewater kayaking, whitewater rescue, tandem river tripping, whitewater open canoe, and instructor training. Offers guided sea kayaking trips on Lake Superior. Sponsors the Saint Louis River Whitewater Rendezvous and the Two Harbors Kayak Festival.

Superior Coastal Sports, Grand Marais, MN (800-720-2809; www.superiorcoastal.com). This outfitter offers group and private instruction in all the aspects of coastal kayaking, with courses for beginners as well as more advanced kayakers, including an Eskimo rolling course.

Superior Kayak and Outdoor Adventure Club (SKOAC), P.O. Box 581792, Minneapolis, MN 55458 (www.skoac.org). An organization of sea kayakers that holds ACA-certified skills workshops and has a good up-to-date kayaking event calendar with links on its Website.

Organizations and Clubs

Paddling with others is not only fun, you will be safer and can learn a lot from experienced paddlers.

Minnesota Canoe Association, Inc. (MCA), P.O. Box 13567, Dinkytown Station, Minneapolis, MN 55414 (www.canoe-kayak.org). An umbrella organization that publishes a newsletter (Hut!); promotes paddling, paddling safety, and the environmental health of rivers and lakes; and is an affiliate of the American Canoe Association. Great activities and a good list of online links.

Here is a list of MCA affiliates:

Headwaters Canoe Club (HCC) (www.canoe-kayak.org/pages/hwaters.html). For more information, see Mississippi River 3.

Inland Sea Kayakers (www.isk.canoe-kayak.org; isk@canoe-kayak.org). A volunteer organization dedicated to paddling and paddling safety that holds monthly meetings in the Metro area, sponsors a wide range of on-the-water instruction, and sets up trips to Voyageurs and various locations on Lake Superior. Families and single members are welcome.

Rapids Riders Club (www.rapidsriders.net). A volunteer organization of whitewater enthusiasts that originated the Canoe U Weekend, conducts skill and safety seminars, and has an active internet forum to schedule informal paddles.

River Ramblers (www.canoe-kayak.org/riverramblers/Ramblers04.html). A volunteer organization that holds an annual meeting and has a standard schedule of great annual paddling trips of all kinds, with an emphasis on leisurely outdoor fun. Nonmembers are welcome to join the trips.

Twin Ports Canoe Club (twinports@canoe-kayak.org). An outdoor group composed of members from Duluth; Superior, WI; and the Iron Range. In addition to canoeing, kayaking, sailing and biking trips in the summer, the group holds skating and skiing outings in the winter.

Minnesota Rovers Outing Club, P.O. Box 14133, Minneapolis, MN 55414 (www.mnrovers.org). A volunteer group devoted to all kinds of active outings, including paddling; holds weekly meetings in the Metro area.

The Rivers Council of Minnesota, 100 Second Avenue South, Suite 101, Sauk Rapids, MN 56379 (320-259-6800; www.riversmn.org). Not a paddling group, but a nonprofit organization dedicated to the health of Minnesota rivers, an issue dear to the hearts of Minnesota paddlers.

Sierra Club North Star Chapter, 2327 East Franklin Avenue, Suite 1, Minneapolis, MN 55406 (612-659-9124; north.star.chapter@sierraclub.org; www.northstar.sierraclub.org). Organizes several canoe outings during each summer. Check the calendar on the organization's Web site.

Two Harbors Kayak Festival (www.kayakfestival.org). An annual Lake Superior kayaking event held on the lake in Two Harbors in August. The festival promotes kayaking as a family sport and features races, demonstrations, seminars, youth classes, food, and entertainment.

APPENDIX 5
Useful Web Sites

Water Levels
www.dnr.state.mn.us/river_levels/index.html
www.mvp-wc.usace.army.mil/dcp
http://nwis.waterdata.usgs.gov/mn/nwis/current/?type=flow
www.americanwhitewater.org/rivers/state/MN
www.americanwhitewater.org/gauges/state/MN
www.shorelandtraditions.com/levels.htm

Weather
www.nws.noaa.gov
www.crh.noaa.gov/dlh/marine.htm

Rainfall
iwin.nws.noaa.gov/iwin/mn/climate.html

Minnesota DNR
888-646-6367 (888-MINNDNR)
www.dnr.state.mn.us/canoeing/routes.html
www.dnr.state.mn.us/water_access/counties.html
www.crk.umn.edu/nature-northwest/redlakewebsite/CanoeRouteindex.htm

BWCAW
bwcaw.org
www.rook.org/earl/bwca/lists/glossary
www.ely.org/canoetrips
www.gunflint-trail.com
www.piragis.com

Lake Superior Water Trail
www.lswta.org/main.html
www.dnr.state.mn.us/kayaking/lswt/index.html

Voyageurs National Park
www.nps.gov/voya
www.voyageurs.national-park.com

Paddling Instruction and Clubs
www.acanet.org
www.umdrsop.org
www.rapidsriders.net
www.isk.canoe-kayak.org
www.skoak.org
www.usacanoekayak.com
www.inlandsea.org
www.rivernetwork.org